Regu, qui Holmiæ est.
meridiem.

auftrale. 6·Dom: Comitis Aæelii Wachtmeister. 7·Ædes N·Tungel. J·v·L·Aveelen delin·et ſc·Holmiæ 1700·

Bill Nan
with love Pen

The Gardens
of Europe

Penelope Hobhouse
Jan 30th 1991.

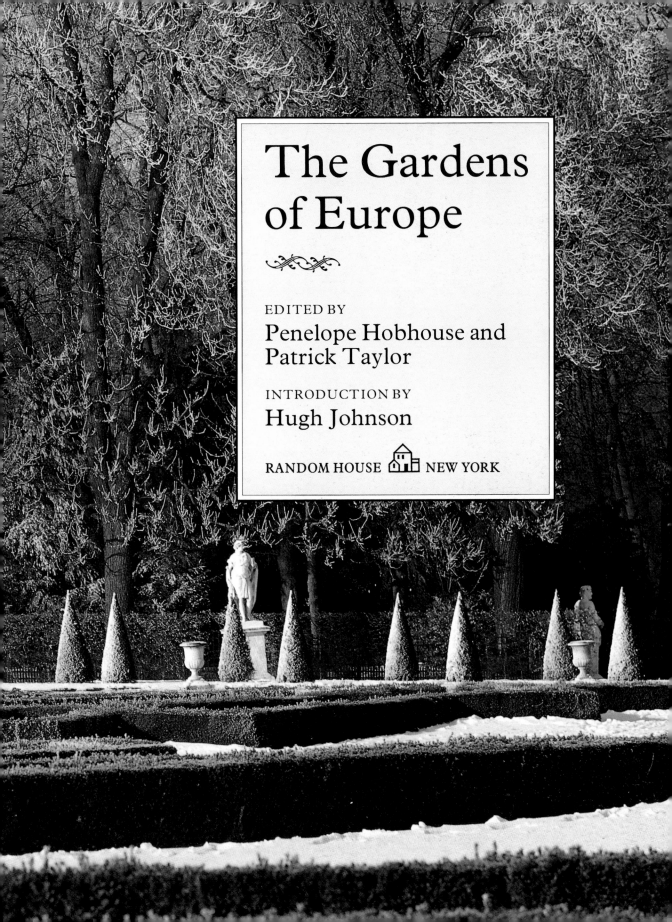

The Gardens
of Europe

EDITED BY
Penelope Hobhouse and
Patrick Taylor

INTRODUCTION BY
Hugh Johnson

RANDOM HOUSE 🏠 NEW YORK

Library of Congress Cataloguing-in-Publication Data
Hobhouse, Penelope
  The Gardens of Europe
  by Penelope Hobhouse and Patrick Taylor
  p.   c.m.
  ISBN 0-679-40041-9
  1. Gardens -- Europe.   I. Taylor, Patrick.   II. Title
  SB466. E9H63   1990
  712'.094-dc20   90-43323

Manufactured in Italy

Phototypeset by Keyspools Limited,
Golborne, Lancs.
Printed in Italy.

98765432

First US Edition

Illustrations Sources and Acknowledgements
Agence Top (Robert César), title page, pp. 78, 87, 91, 94, 95, 98, 102, 107; Archives Nationales, Paris, p. 71; Artorhek (Schach-Galerie), p. 111; Bibliothéque du Museé de Paris, p. 86; Bibliothéque Nationale, Paris, p. 88; Bildagenfur Mauritius, p. 274; Biofoto, pp. 231, 234; British Museum (by courtesy of the Trustees), p. 153; J. Allan Cash, pp. 251 (below), 311, 359, 363; ET Archive, pp. 25, 47, 59 (above right), 275, 336 (above); Professor Fati, pp. 331, 333; The Garden Picture Library, pp. 82, 83, 123, 126, 127, 134, 150-1, 166, 183, 186, 242-3, 251 (above), 262, 343 (Gary Rogers); Susan Griggs, pp. 222-3; Peter Hayden, pp. 55, 58, 118, 147, 239, 270, 278-9, 323, 326, 339, 340, 341, 342, 346, 347; R. Hendrik, p. 307; Marijke Heuff, pp. 210, 214, 219, 227; Penelope Hobhouse, pp. 354-5; Impact Photos (Pamla Toler), pp. 290, 291, 294, 295; Orsi Karoly, pp. 318, 319; A. S. Kersting, pp. 161, 164, 172; Knudsens fotosenter, p. 235; Koleva, p. 283; Kunsthistorisches Museum, Vienna, p. 250; Andrew Lawson, pp. 171, 175, 178, 179, 187, 374-5; Brian Lynch, p. 195; Paul Miles, pp. 67, 119, 170, 194; Tony Mott, pp. 28, 29, 31, 52 (right), 53, 59 (above left, below), 65, 247, 248, 261, 267, 302; The National Trust, p. 157; Nicole Newmark, p. 255; Hugh Palmer, pp. 162, 163, 167; Alex Ramsay, pp. 18-19, 37, 39, 42-3, 48 (left), 50, 51, 52 (left), 63; Nicholas Sapieha pp. 6-7, 142; Scala, p. 26; Edwin Smith, p. 48 (right); Harry Smith Horticultural Collection, p. 79; Patrick Taylor, pp. 131, 135, 138, 199; Ludwig Trauzettel, pp. 305, 308; Cynthia Woodward, p. 34.

Contents

Acknowledgements

This book has been a combined effort by a large team. The contributors from individual countries have given much helpful advice as well as their written descriptions. Margherita Azzi Visentini, Dott. Arch. Pier Fausto Bagatti Valsecchi and Ada Segre in Italy, Benoit Fondu in Belgium, Jelena de Belder and Lord John Scott need a special mention. Others such as Philip Mansel, Dr Heino Heine and Countess Ursula von Dohna have, in conversation, illuminated various points. Lydia Greeves who led the team at George Philip has been constantly encouraging. Without Patrick Taylor's enthusiasm all our spirits might have flagged with the sheer weight of information we had to handle. It is to him, and his wife Caroline who edited the text, that I owe my greatest debt of gratitude.

Penelope Hobhouse

Many people have been extremely generous with help and advice but the following have been especially helpful and I am very grateful to them: Baron Gösta Adelswärd, Walter Bauer, Patrick Bowe, Dr Heino Heine, Consuelo Martinez Correcher y Gil, Javier Meriátegui y Valdés and La Marquesa del Viso. Hugh Johnson very kindly agreed to write an introduction at double-quick pace and did so with his habitual charm and knowledge. Lydia Greeves of George Philip had the idea for this book and she has followed it through with unflagging cheerfulness and skill. Caroline Taylor, who edited the text, turned herself quickly into the *genius loci*. Anne-Marie Ehrlich searched diligently and found the marvellous pictures. Simon Bell designed the book most elegantly. Last, but far from least, it has been a very great pleasure to work with Penelope Hobhouse.

Patrick Taylor

END-PAPERS **An engraving of 1700 shows the King's Garden in Stockholm, laid out in an elaborate pattern with high hedges and parterres.**

HALF-TITLE ILLUSTRATION **Clipped box shapes lead down to the lower garden at the Villa Allegri.**

TITLE-PAGE ILLUSTRATION **Snow emphasizes yew topiary in the Parterre du Nord at Versailles.**

RIGHT **At Seteais, distant views of the Atlantic are visible from a parterre filled with box topiary shapes.**

Contributors to *The Gardens of Europe*

Jette Abel	Denmark
Baron Gösta Adelswärd	Sweden
Tony Baggs	Poland
Madame R. de Belder and associates	Yugoslavia
Patrick Bowe	Portugal, Spain, Ireland
Professor Magne Bruun	Norway
Michele Buffa	Sicily
Simone Maitrepierre de Chaptal	France
Dr Constantin Dragulescu	Romania
Florentine van Eeghen-Elias	Holland
Professor Vasile Fati	Romania
M. Benoit Fondu	Belgium
François and Olivier Goffinet	Belgium
Dr H. Günther	East Germany
Peter Hayden	Russia
Ing. Karel Hieke	Czechoslovakia
Penelope Hobhouse	England and Wales, France, Italy
Nelly Liambey	Greece
Margot Lutze	Austria, West Germany
Consuelo Martinez Correcher y Gil	Spain
Paul Miles	Italy
Tony Mott	Italy
Francesca Neonato	Italy
Nicole Newmark	Switzerland
Robin St Clair-Ford	Scotland
Lord John Scott	Turkey
Elza Stancheva	Bulgaria
Patrick Taylor	France, England and Wales, Scotland, Spain
Dott. Arch. Pier Fausto Bagatti Valsecchi	Italy
Signora Margherita Azzi Visentini	Italy
La Marquesa del Viso	Spain
Faik Yaltirik	Turkey
Professor Anna Zádor	Hungary
Bonica Zijlstin	Holland

Introduction by Hugh Johnson

It is a common fault among gardeners (and not only gardeners) to narrow their view of what is beautiful to what they feel at home with. In the British Isles the fault is compounded by the sin of pride; the easy assumption that no gardens can compare with ours in beauty. Enough has been written by visitors to these islands of the impact of our lawns, our light, our mellow walls, our luxuriant growth, our profusion of flowers, to make us feel complacent.

Nobody can deny that the British climate allows a wider range of plants to flourish than almost any other – or that the soft weather and long summer days provoke gardeners into more activity than in any other country. Spring in Britain is a slow process that merges into summer, lengthening the flowering season of plants that in their less temperate homes blaze and expire in May. Autumn winds down the year in similar slow-motion, keeping the garden full of beauty into the shortest days.

Complacency, though, has been founded more on ignorance than knowledge. Knowing our own gardens so well, being such confirmed borrowers of our immediate neighbours' ideas, we have scarcely made the effort to consider the evolution of our own gardening styles, much less to look at and learn from their historical sources and parallels in Europe and elsewhere.

British garden history as a popular study only came into being little more than a decade ago. Comparative European garden history, for which this book is a unique source of reference, is even now still struggling to be born.

That is not to say that the British have never visited Versailles, lingered by the fountains of the Generalife or lamented the dishevelment of the terraces of the Villa d'Este. These are Europe's horticultural set-pieces; pivotal moments in the history of taste preserved (more or less) as living museums. What most of us have never experienced, because we have never heard of them, never passed that way, or they have kept their gates shut to the world at large, are the thousands of European gardens that developed in parallel with the English tradition we know so well, intriguingly different in idiom, materials and manner, but clearly inspired by the same masters.

By visiting them we will learn that Europe's horticultural history shares one family tree. Ideas about garden design had international currency almost as soon as they were formulated. It is not national or regional boundaries that determine style so much as simple date. As the Renaissance surged through

Europe it was classical architectural gardens that everyone aspired to build. In the period of France's 17th-century ascendancy her grandiose style became the universal fashion. When England's power challenged France in the 18th century her revolutionary deformalizing of the garden instantly became the rage all over Europe.

Happily Europe, England apart, was spared the cool contractor who removed the evidence of almost all previous gardening in England. Had Brown's capabilities extended Europe-wide we would all be infinitely the poorer. As it is, we need to travel abroad to see the sort of gardens that once existed, and in large numbers, under English skies.

The story of gardening, like that of painting, is usually told in terms of its masterworks, its greatest practitioners and their influence on their contemporaries and successors. Unlike painting, though, gardening has a powerful vernacular sub-plot: the unselfconscious enterprise of everyman in growing whatever represents either use or beauty to him.

The parade of courts and courtiers passes by, anxious about its image, preoccupied with parterres. Meanwhile from the Egyptian or the Roman citizen with his onions, his bean-rows and his vine, to the monk with his few square metres of dedicated ground, to the all-purpose enclosures beside or behind every medieval dwelling, whether in country or town, in direct lineal descent to the layouts of Georgian cities or Victorian suburbs, the heritage of simple horticulture runs uninterrupted to the housing estates of today.

The great turning-point in horticultural history was when the two strands, that of gardening as art (or at least as fashion) and gardening as habit, necessity and private pleasure, began to merge. In the Middle Ages they had not necessarily been far apart. Indeed, in the *hortus conclusus*, the intimate enclosed orchard that offered, even to the great, their only privacy and peace among plants in the malodorous turmoil of medieval life, we can see an ancestor of many modern garden plans.

Show-gardening by the great began its spectacular career as their sense of security increased; as castles were succeeded by mansions. At first it took the form of massively enlarged and geometrically repeated versions of the old orchards, now outside the castle walls rather than inside them. As it developed in renaissance Italy it referred directly back to Imperial Rome; the last era when Europe had assumed the rule of law rather than armed chaos as the natural order of things.

The Italian architect's brief was comprehensive: house and garden were a unity; anything else would have been as illogical as having one tailor make a jacket and another the trousers. Column and architrave, staircase and balustrade were the grammar of the garden as they were of the house.

Certainly there was a role for specific gardening skills in keeping the bay-trees in their tubs in good health and the urns full of flowers. The growing, grafting and nurture of fruit trees was a principal preoccupation. But the limited repertoire of plants, at least of plants considered garden-worthy, was as much within the architect's scope as the choice of Doric or Tuscan for the banqueting-house or the stables.

Nor did matters greatly change with the gradual shift from Italian ideas, in which architectural stonework was the dominant medium, to French, in which architectural statements were hugely enlarged, eventually to encompass whole forests. This was the theme of Le Nôtre at Vaux-le-Vicomte and Versailles; he marshalled hunting-grounds into ante-rooms and colonnades and 'cabinets', all formed from regiments of trees, with statues as their furniture and fountains as their chandeliers.

Le Nôtre, it was true, called himself a gardener. He even claimed as his coat of arms three slugs surrounding a spade and crowned with cabbage leaves. But so might Henry Ford have taken as his badge a sparking plug or an exhaust pipe. The gardeners of the apron and the watering-can were still busy selecting more and more varieties of fruit, and becoming ever more adept at carpeting the ante-chambers with intricate scrolls and embroidery of hedges. So subordinated was horticulture to design that coloured earth or crushed tiles were considered more fitting to tint the parterres than flowers.

The English love of flowers began to assert itself in Tudor times. By Queen Elizabeth's reign, England's herbals had taken on their unique lyric quality, engendered by the sheer beauty of their subject (and of the English language at its moment of crystallization). But it was the Dutch who were the first flower fanatics. With no space for great parks in their small country, with no hills to offer views or even to power fountains, with immense wealth earned from trade but short physical horizons, the Dutch developed the still-life to sublimity – and with it florists' flowers. Floristry was not just the adoration of flowers, but the skill of breeding, enlarging and varying them ad infinitum.

In England towards the end of the 17th century, the fusion of architectural design after Italian and French models, and a passion for flowers developed with Dutch help, must have engendered gardens of striking beauty. Sir Walter Scott described a Scottish example that must have been typical of hundreds, if not thousands, up to the later years of the 18th century:

'The garden, which seemed to be kept with great accuracy, abounded in fruit-trees, and exhibited a profusion of flowers and evergreens, cut into grotesque forms. It was laid out in terraces, which descended rank by rank from the western wall to a large brook, which had a tranquil and smooth appearance, where it served as a boundary to the garden; but near the extremity, leapt in tumult over a strong dam ... and there forming a cascade, was overlooked by an octangular summer-house, with a gilded bear on top by way of vane.'

It is all too well known that the leaders of fashion did not approve. The elaborate creations of this kind we see in the engravings of Kip were accused, rightly or wrongly, of primness and affectation. Certainly gardening was falling into the hands of gardeners rather than architects. In England the first important firm of nurserymen-contractors dated from the 1680s. It was time for aesthetic principles, as understood by aristocrats, to reassert themselves. By degrees the bulldozing began that eventually swept all but a tiny handful of the old gardens away. And 'landskip' took their place.

The English landscape movement is the perfect expression of the feeling of English landowners for their land. It relates to families who spent a brief summer season in town, then retired to the country for the serious business of hunting and farming and intermarrying with their landed neighbours. Yet it became the rage throughout Europe.

Le Nôtre never idealized countryside; he aimed to dominate it. A vineyard or a cow in the picture would have been an unthinkable descent into realism. 'I cannot abide', he said, 'a limit to a view.'

The English, on the contrary, wanted their properties to be microcosms of nature; to embrace valleys and lakes and hills within their bounds. They raised temples to manly virtues and spiritual values in the same spirit; the idea was that a man's whole life should be epitomized in his estate. Fantasy was by no means excluded. In the heroic Augustan age it was even the fashion to plant woods in the formation of regiments or squadrons of ships in battle. Blenheim Palace memorialized its owner's most famous victory in oaks and elms. Later in the 18th century a Chinese pagoda or a Turkish tent became a modish piece of playfulness.

At the same time convenience was high on their list of priorities. The architects and designers they patronized were those whose morning-rooms faced east and who paid proper attention to drainage. If article one of their creed was the absurdity of planting trees in straight lines or clipping bushes into fantastic shapes, article two was the importance of gravel foundations. Capability Brown excelled in both respects. 'He was inferior to none' (wrote his successor) 'in what related to the comfort, convenience, taste and propriety of design in the several mansions ... which he planned.' 'English gardens', wrote Goethe, 'are not made to a plan, but to a feeling in the head.' But just because the plan was not ruled with straight lines did not mean that every effect was not calculated to the highest degree.

Into all this there entered the new idea of Taste. In 1784 James Barry defined it in his Lectures on Painting: 'The word Taste, as applied to objects of vision ... means ... that quick discerning faculty or power of the mind by which we accurately distinguish the good, bad and indifferent.'

By the time of Humphry Repton, Brown's successor in the 1780s, it was open season on the word. In Repton's great *Observations on the Theory and Practice of Landscape Gardening* of 1803 he opens with a preface on taste, which asserts that 'natural Taste, like natural Genius, may exist to a certain degree, but without study, observation and experience, they lead to error'. It concludes that 'Palladio, Vitruvius and Le Nôtre ... in the display of useless symmetry, often forgot the requisites of habitation. The leading feature of the good taste of modern times, is the just sense of GENERAL UTILITY.' Thus Repton, gracefully bowing out the classical age, bowed in the century of Utility and Queen Victoria. But no one ever wrote better on the principles of landscape design, nor was less dogmatic about their application. He insisted on 'Unity' and 'Proportion' – but within their constraints he gave full licence to the variety that all simple gardeners craved.

Brown had been a human dam, holding back a vast flood of new plants from every part of the newly-explored world. The only exotic tree he ever used in his landscapes was the cedar of Lebanon; all others were English natives. He made practically no provision for shrubs and flowers in his designs. Yet this was the age when new plants were the talk of society; when the botanic garden at Kew took shape, when Banks sailed with Cook for Australia, when South Africa and North and South America were being ransacked for plants, and when the inexpressible plant wealth of China, Japan and the Himalayas was just beginning to be revealed. The nursery-mens' lists of the time show that there was a burgeoning taste for plant novelties among more humble gardeners. It was the people of fashion who patronized Brown who were the last to be allowed them.

With Repton the sluice-gates were opened. With his successor, Loudon, every known plant was allotted its appointed garden place – and still new introductions flooded in. Now at last the gardener was level with the architect. This was the turning-point, when everyman's endeavours were to become simply those of the powerful on a smaller scale. The history of gardening since has been a long-drawn-out demonstration of how much more difficult it is to design with the infinite variety and complexity of plants than with the simple materials and familiar rules of architecture.

The ground-rules of gardening have not changed radically in the past 150 years. The one true innovation has been the woodland garden, designed as a lofty showcase for the rhododendrons, the delicate maples and other plants introduced chiefly from the Far East. Of course there have been many new ideas, more revivals of old ones, and countless lovely gardens created and destroyed. There have been famous feuds between advocates of the formal and the informal, who have left us excellent examples of both. Fashions for certain plants, ferns for example, have come and gone and come again. The mid Victorian craze for carpet-bedding has shown a mad resilience, while that for rustic-work mercifully has not.

The sheer technology of horticulture reached its labour-intensive height a century ago and has been in decline ever since. In the 20th century the craftsmanship that was the highest aspiration of the Victorian gardener has been replaced (at least as an aspiration) by artistry. Of all the succession of styles, of modes or moods, through which European gardens have passed, borrowing each other's ideas, in the past 500 years, the canons of such prophets as Miss Jekyll and Miss Sackville-West are perhaps the hardest to translate from one country's idiom to another – hardest, indeed, to follow in any language. But such great contemporary gardeners as Princess Sturdza in Normandy and Prince Wolkonsky in Brittany – a Norwegian and a Russian gardening in France – show what can be done.

The revelation of a new kind of beauty is one of the highest kinds of aesthetic excitement. It can leave an image with us that will stay as an inspiration for ever. Henry James described the emotions of his humble hero, Hyacinth Robinson, walking in the gardens of the country mansion rented by the Princess Casamassima, on a dewy dawn when pearly light caressed peacocks and battlements, roses and mossy walls. Surely he must have been remembering his own first experience of a great European garden in its glory.

No one can know the spirit, the true purpose, of the gardens of any country until they too have bathed their senses in them in solitude. The ethos of the garden tour, with the bus snorting at the gate impatient to carry us to the fourth garden of the day, can only leave us limp and uncomprehending.

This book is the key to secret doors across the whole of Europe. It leads us independently to gardens that will widen our horizons, refresh our perceptions, rekindle our creativity, and may, who knows, reshape our concept of beauty.

Editors' Introduction

The purpose of this book is to describe the most important gardens in Europe for the general reader, *and* to give a representative picture of the distinctive horticultural traditions of each of the countries included. All the gardens listed are accessible to the public – most are regularly open, some only by appointment. They have been chosen to give a balanced view of the range and type of gardens found. For example, there are more municipal gardens described in France, where they provide a distinctive style of gardening, than in Scotland, where they do not occupy a place of such importance. In England, where the very large number of good gardens is well covered in other books, we have been especially selective.

The criterion of 'importance' is hard to define. We take an important garden to be one that is exceptional by virtue of the design of its layout; the interest of its plants and their arrangement (considered both aesthetically and botanically); or its historical influence. It is a rare garden that combines all these characteristics. All gardens of major importance – for example Versailles, the Alhambra, the Villa Lante – have been included. Also included are many gardens of lesser importance which are none the less characteristic of their country and well worth the attention of the visitor. In this second category, however, we have had regretfully to be much more selective. We have included only a few botanic gardens and arboreta, with an emphasis on those that give an especially good view of the flora of a particular area.

For reasons of politics, fashion or blinkered prejudice, some European countries loom larger on the horticultural map than others. We regard it as one of our essential aims to try and reveal to the garden visitor the astonishing richness of gardening traditions in the less obvious countries. France, Italy and Great Britain are relatively well-mapped territory. But how many know the ravishing baroque garden of El Retiro that overlooks the airport at Málaga in Spain? Or Linnaeus's charming private garden at Hammarby in Sweden? Or the 18th-century splendours of Dobříš in central Bohemia?

One of the things we hope to show is the remarkable and attractive international character of gardening. A new idea in garden design spreads with astonishing speed. Le Nôtre's grand vistas influenced gardens all over Europe. Terraced gardens, in the style of the Italian Renaissance, were copied from Wales to Yugoslavia. By visiting gardens of a certain kind in different countries, we immensely increase our understanding of the essence of the art of gardening. The pursuit of good plants, too, is international. In the early 17th century, for example, John Tradescant the Elder, then head gardener at Hatfield House in England, swapped plants with Jean Robin, the royal gardener in Paris, and they both grew new introductions from America, hot off the boat (as it were), such as the American acacia (named *Robinia* after Monsieur Robin). The great botanical gardens of Europe, from Madrid in Spain to Batumi in Georgia, scorn political frontiers.

The historical development of garden styles has always been influenced by the current availability of plants, but the range of plants which can be successfully grown in any country or in any one garden depends on the prevailing climatic aspect. Introduced plants thrive when conditions approximate to those in their native habitat and for most plants there is a minimum temperature below which they cannot survive; susceptible plants' cells are irretrievably damaged by ice. In Europe, gardening possibilities are controlled by three main factors: the vast land mass of Asia to the east, which brings freezing winds and low temperatures across Russia and into central Europe and ensures extremes of winter cold followed by summer heat; the Sahara desert in North Africa, which brings warm airs from the south to the Mediterranean basin; and the Atlantic Ocean, which, at all latitudes in the western areas, keep winter temperatures up and ensures that summers are cool and damp. The Gulf Stream brings even milder winter conditions and wet summers to Ireland, western Britain, the west coast of Norway and northern Spain and Portugal; in these temperate regions a very wide range of plants from all over the world can be successfully grown.

Inland in western Europe, and depending on altitude, winter temperatures are lower; in central Europe and most of Russia and in northern Scandinavia minimum winter temperatures can average $-20°C$, severely limiting the range of plants possible. Growing periods for plants, measured by the number of days when the temperature exceeds $6°C$ and is less than $32°C$, are also considerations: in western Ireland there are 330 growing days, in central Europe 225 days and in parts of the USSR and the north of Sweden as few as 150 days. In the hottest Mediterranean regions plants grow only during the winter. There are, of course, other factors which control and influence planting possibilities, such as light, moisture, type of soil and nutrients. Some of these can be modified by the gardener seeking to extend his range. In the colder areas, for example, measures can be taken to reduce the adverse effects of 'wind chill'.

These are broad generalizations; in every region there exist favourable or unfavourable natural microclimates. In Alpine regions, snow coverage gives natural winter protection, especially to plants below ground; the Bosporus, has an almost Mediterranean climate, but experiences freezing winter winds which sweep down the narrow straits; yet in the southern Crimea, on the narrow Black Sea coastal strip, conditions are roughly similar to those in the valley of the Arno in Italy. On Lake Maggiore in northern Italy, the proximity of a large mass of water prevents freezing winters; this factor combined with high rainfall and hot summers provides exceptional growing conditions for fine trees and shrubs.

It is our hope that anyone contemplating a visit to an unfamiliar country will be able to use this book to plan their journey. In each country, gardens are listed alphabetically except where they are in or very near a town, in which case they appear under the name of the town. Each country also has an introduction giving a brief history of gardening and essential general information about its climate and flora. Current opening times are given and have been checked to the last possible moment – but, alas, these are subject to change. In some cases it has simply proved impossible to establish all the details. If a special journey is being made to visit some outstanding garden, it may be best to check beforehand that the garden will be open.

Many of the gardens in this book are private property and open only at the generous discretion of their owners. We are sure most readers are fully aware of this generosity – and will respect it. We have been allowed to include certain gardens which open only by prior appointment on the strict understanding that this condition is honoured. Unless a telephone number is given, 'by appointment' means by *written* permission. Many private gardens open by appointment have no scale of admission charges, but contributions to the upkeep of the garden, or to some charity, may be welcome. Many of the gardens described are attached to houses of distinction, but the visitor should not assume that the house also is open. All details refer to the garden only.

We have very occasionally commented on the bad maintenance of individual gardens. We hope to sharpen the awareness of the importance of gardens as works of art and it is appropriate that they should be looked after with the same devotion that we give to great paintings, sculptures or works of architecture.

Note: Two symbols are occasionally used immediately following the names of gardens:
★ denotes that the garden is an especially good one;
❀ denotes that the garden has a particularly good collection of plants.

PART ONE

The Gardens of Southern Europe

Italy

Italy is one of the hottest countries in Europe with an annual average of 1,825 hours of sunshine, but has huge variations in climate due more to topography than to latitude. The Italian peninsula extends far into the Mediterranean, bordered by the Ligurian and Tyrrhenian seas on the west and by the Adriatic to the east. Its northern boundary is determined by the Alps and its internal boundaries are formed by the great chain of the Apennines, which run from Genoa in the north-west to the Adriatic in the east and then turn south to form a backbone through central and southern Italy. The lower slopes of both Alps and Apennines are often thickly wooded with chestnut, oak, beech, pine and fir.

In the north, cold winds from the Alps sweep over the Lombardy plain in winter and damp, warm Mediterranean winds are intercepted by the Ligurian Apennines, so the mean winter temperature in Turin is lower than that of Copenhagen, while summer temperatures in Milan and Bologna are often higher than in Naples. Only plants able to withstand severe frosts can be grown, except in specially favoured spots or on the Italian Riviera, where olives, citrus, aloes, cactus and palm flourish.

In central Italy, striking differences in climate are related to proximity to the mountains. Thus the area west of the Apennines, from Tuscany down to Rome, has a mild winter climate and can grow mulberries, olives and vines. Central Tuscany is already affected by mountains, and the Abruzzi (apart from its Adriatic coastal strip) has the coldest climate of the whole of Italy. Potenza, further south, on the same latitude as Naples but in the mountains, has winter temperatures almost equal to those of the Abruzzi, and the lowest summer temperature of anywhere in Italy.

Southern Italy has a very different climate again, and in spite of a mountainous interior its coastal temperatures are as high as those of Greece or southern Spain.

Most of Italy's finest gardens lie today in the north or central parts of the country. Nothing remains of the gardens made between the decline of the

PREVIOUS PAGE **The layout of the Giardino Giusti in Verona dates from the end of the 15th century. A** *viale* **of cypresses leads the eye up a steep slope and towers above the baroque-style parterre, which replaced the earlier more geometric pattern.**

Roman Empire in the 5th century and the Renaissance, though royal gardens continued to be laid out in Sicily and on the mainland, especially at Naples, in the 13th and 14th centuries. Crescenzi and Boccaccio describe them; frescoes and miniatures depict them.

The renaissance gardens of the 15th and 16th centuries were inspired by classical Rome and its literature, and it is the Roman concept of the villa in the country (*villegiatura*) that is unique to Italy. Descriptions of Pliny the Younger's villas in Laurentium and Tuscany at the beginning of the 1st century AD were detailed and instructive; full enough to allow 15th-century writers on the architectural layout of villas and gardens to draw heavily on the text of his letters. And by the 16th century Hadrian's villa at Tivoli (q.v.) was being plundered for statues and ideas on layout. The ruins at Tivoli, the garden sites at Pompeii (q.v.), and accompanying scholarly reconstructions on paper, demonstrate many of the principles behind the design of the great gardens of the 15th and 16th centuries – gardens which have never been equalled in their perfection of proportion and expert manipulation of space.

The renaissance garden developed gradually. Early in the 15th century the idea of the villa in the country became popular among the nobility, first in Tuscany and later in other parts of the country. The villa was seen as a retreat for intellectual contemplation combined with the practical application of theories of agriculture. At first the garden was an enclosed *giardino segreto*; gradually this was enlarged to become an extension of the house and finally, in the baroque age, merged into the surrounding landscape. The fundamental characteristic of the later gardens was a new architectural concept, with geometric layouts based on symmetry and axiality, in which garden rooms, often on different levels, were linked to each other and to the villa itself. Although the first botanic teaching gardens were established at Padua and Pisa in 1545 (q.v.), and many new plant species were introduced from abroad at this period, garden plants were subservient to spatial and geometric requirements.

By the middle of the 16th century renaissance gardens were well established, and their influence had spread throughout western Europe. The confederation of the five principal powers in the 15th century – the kingdom of Naples, the duchy of Milan, the republics of Venice and Florence, and the papacy in Rome – had secured a period of peace and brilliant prosperity, and gardens are associated with noble families in the different areas: the Sforzas, the Medicis, the Montefeltros, the Estensis, the Viscontis, the Aragones. Bramante, in his design for the Belvedere Garden for Pope Julius II in 1503, further developed classical architectural concepts by emphasizing the importance of a central perspective and terraces linked by ramps and steps.

The Gardens of Italy

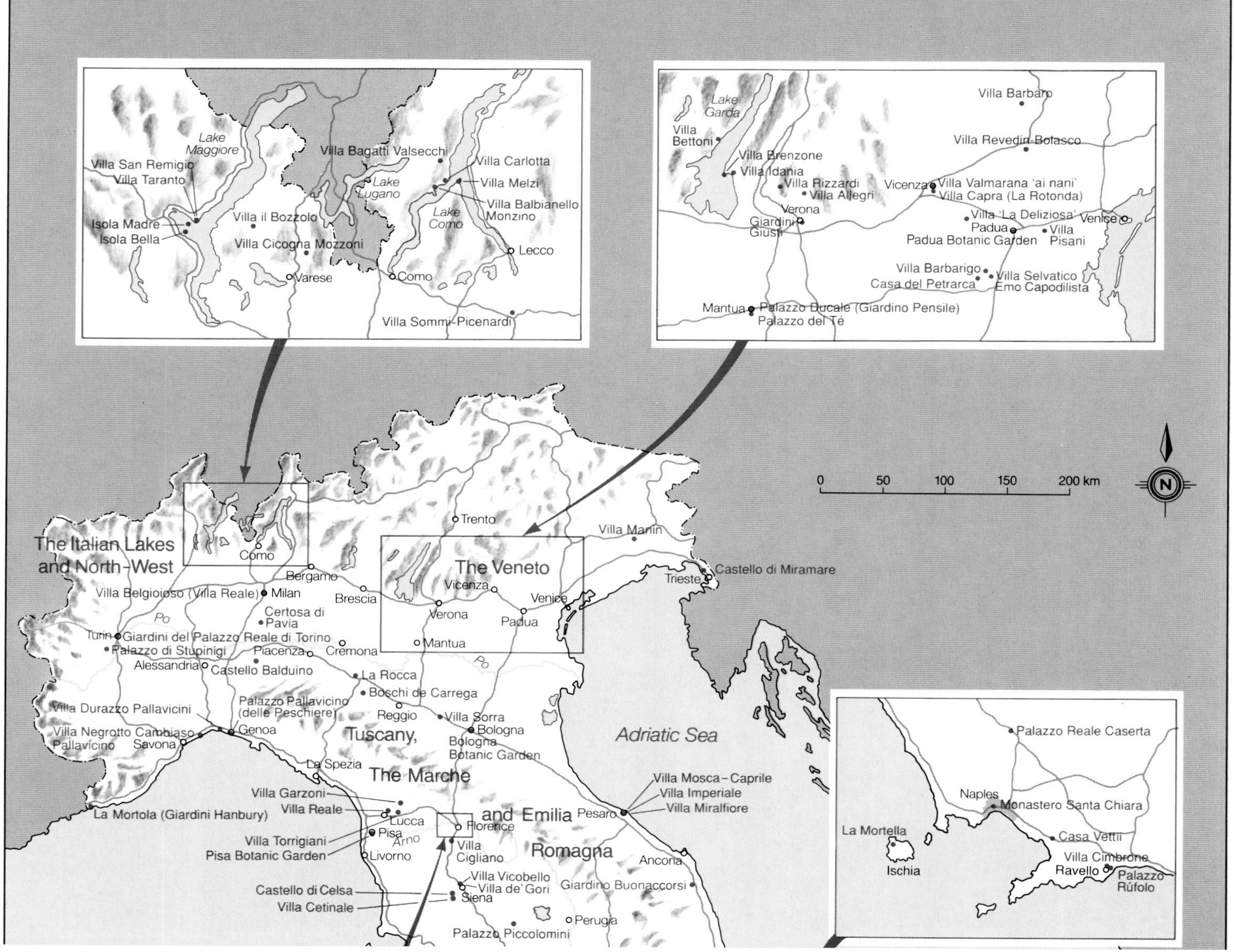

N

200 km
0 50 100 150 200

Top-left inset

Villa Barbaro
Villa Revedin-Bolasco
Villa Valmarana 'ai nani'
Villa Capra (La Rotonda)
Vicenza
Villa "La Deliziosa" Venice
Padua
Padua Botanic Garden Villa Pisani
Villa Barbarigo
Casa del Petrarca
Villa Selvatico
Villa Emo Capodilista
Villa Brenzone
Villa Idania
Villa Rizzardi
Villa Allegri
Verona
Giardini Giusti
Lake Garda
Villa Bettoni
Mantua Palazzo Ducale (Giardino Pensile)
Palazzo del Tè

Top-right inset

Palazzo Reale Caserta
Palazzo Rufolo
Villa Cimbrone
Ravello
Casa Vettii
Naples Monastero Santa Chiara
La Mortella
Ischia

Left inset

Villa Carlotta
Villa Melzi
Villa Balbianello
Monzino
Lecco
Villa Bagatti Valsecchi
Lake Como
Lake Lugano
Como
Villa Sommi-Picenardi
Lake Maggiore
Villa San Remigio
Villa Taranto
Isola Madre
Isola Bella
Villa il Bozzolo
Villa Cicogna Mozzoni
Varese

Main map

Castello di Miramare
Trieste
Villa Manin
Villa Mosca – Caprile
Villa Imperiale
Villa Miraflore
Ancona
Pesaro
Giardino Buonaccorsi
Peruga
Villa Vicobello
Villa de' Gori
Siena
Palazzo Piccolomini

Adriatic Sea

The Veneto
Venice
Padua
Vicenza
Verona
Mantua
Trento

Po

Tuscany, and Emilia
Romagna
The Marche

Villa Sorra
Bologna
Bologna Botanic Garden
Reggio
Boschi de Carrega
La Rocca
Piacenza
Cremona
Brescia
Bergamo
Milan
Certosa di Pavia
Palazzo Reale di Torino
Palazzo Pallavicino (delle Peschiere)
Genoa
La Spezia
Lucca
Pisa
Livorno
Florence
Villa Cigliano
Pisa Botanic Garden
Villa Torrigiani
Villa Garzoni
Villa Reale
Castello di Celsa
Villa Cetinale

The Italian Lakes and North-West
Como

Villa Belgiojoso (Villa Reale)
Turin Giardini del Palazzo Reale di Torino
Palazzo di Stupinigi
Alessandria Castello Balduino
Villa Durazzo Pallavicini
Villa Negrotto Cambiaso
Pallavicino Savona
La Mortola (Giardini Hanbury)

Po

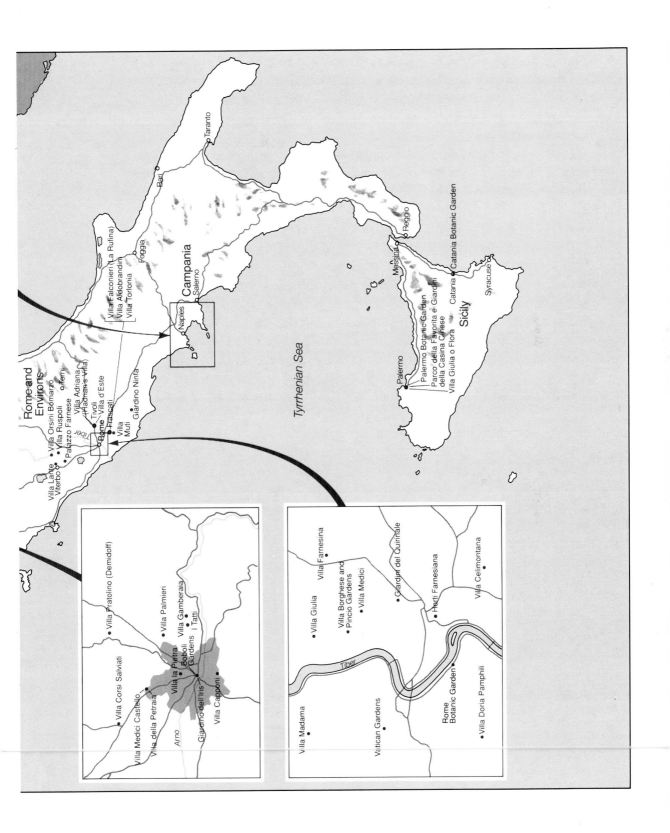

Rome and Environs

Villa Orsini Bomarzo
Viterbo
Villa Lante
Villa Ruspoli
Palazzo Farnese
Villa Adriana (Hadrian's Villa)
Tivoli
Villa d'Este
Frascati
Villa Aldobrandini
Villa Falconieri (La Rufina)
Villa Torlonia
Villa Muti
Villa
Tiber
Rome
Terni
Giardino Ninfa

Naples
Campania
Salerno
Foggia
Bari
Taranto

Tyrrhenian Sea

Palermo
Palermo Botanic Garden
Parco della Favorita e Giardini della Casina Cinese
Villa Giulia o Flora
Catania
Catania Botanic Garden
Sicily
Messina
Reggio
Syracuse

Villa Pratolino (Demidoff)
Villa Palmieri
Villa Gamberaia
I Tatti
Villa Corsi Salviati
Villa Medici Castello
Villa della Petraia
Villa La Pietra
Boboli Gardens
Giardino dell'Iris
Villa Capponi
Arno

Villa Farnesina
Villa Giulia
Villa Borghese and Pincio Gardens
Villa Medici
Giardini del Quirinale
Horti Farnesiana
Villa Celimontana
Villa Madama
Tiber
Vatican Gardens
Rome Botanic Garden
Villa Doria Pamphili

Bramante, Raphael and Baldassare Peruzzi (who also worked in Siena) were followed by other famous designers such as G. B. da Vignola and Pirro Ligorio. In Florence the Medicis employed Michelozzo Michelozzi in the 15th century and then Niccolò Tribolo, Bartolomeo Ammanati and Bernardo Buontalenti.

By the second half of the 16th century axial gardens had developed into a form of mannerist art in which intricate iconographical or allegorical features and complicated hydraulic and mechanical devices were employed to extend the garden into the realms of fancy. 'It is art's infinite capacity to outdo natural things, while still being seen to imitate them, that is striking.' Although gardens were still enclosed, sites were chosen which allowed vistas into the landscape beyond their boundaries. Later the baroque gardens explored a more theatrical approach. Often laid out on steep slopes, they included dramatic terraces and water cascades which distorted proportions and perspective, and visually extended the garden into the countryside – ideas which captured the imagination of the French. Tuscan gardens remained more domestic than those of Rome or Frascati, but everywhere dramatic changes of level and imaginative use of water characterized garden planning. Gardens in each region of Italy, dependent on climate and landscape, developed the baroque style in different ways, but by the middle of the 17th century the initiative in garden creativity had passed to France, where for the two previous centuries garden design had been dominated by Italian renaissance ideals. At Caserta near Naples, at Villa Crivelli (q.v.) in Lombardy (where little now remains except a *viale* of cypresses), and at Villa Pisani, Strà, on the Brenta Canal (q.v.), 18th-century gardens showed a strong French influence. Although exotic flowers and bulbs are known to have been grown in flowerbeds in the 16th and 17th centuries, by the 18th century the layouts, appreciated by travellers on their Grand Tours, were mainly seen as architectural conceptions with little emphasis on ornamental planting. Native evergreen oaks, cypresses and box were part of the overall layout and provided shade, while individual owners expressed their love of flowers and scent by growing roses, herbs and bulbs.

By the end of the 18th century some of these great garden layouts were swept away in favour of the current fashion for the *giardino inglese*, based on the English landscape park. In the early 19th century the neo-classical architect Giuseppe Japelli, working in the north of Italy, evolved his own

Volkamer's engraving (1714) of the Giardino Giusti
shows designs typical of Italian parterres during the
17th century.

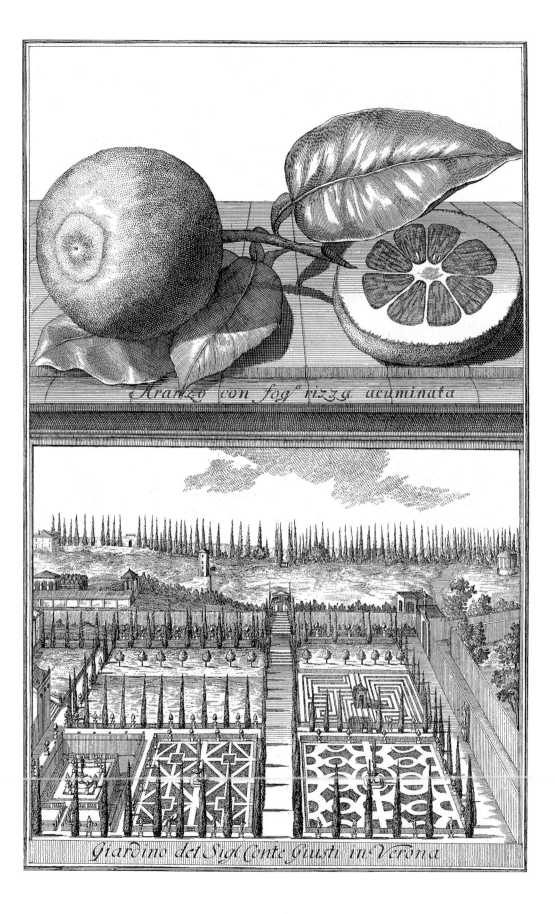

Aranzo con fog.ª rizza acuminata

Giardino del Sig.ᵃ Conte Giusti in Verona

Utens' painting (1598) of the newly completed Villa
Pratolino (Demidoff), the last in a series of fourteen
Medici villas which he portrayed, shows winding
cascades, grottoes and other water effects.

naturalistic style. At the end of the century fashions became more eclectic
and included both rustic and formal designs. Other great architectural
layouts were allowed to decay. Later, at the turn of the century, English,
American and other foreign owners (such as the Romanian Princess Ghyka at
Gamberaia, q.v.) and architects were instrumental in the restoration of some
of the early 15th- and 16th-century gardens, sometimes designing new
gardens around old renaissance villas in a style which can be called
'historicizing': a combination of early classical principles with more monumental stonework and boxwood parterres. Parallel with this emphasis on old
garden design was the development of plantsman's gardens. La Mortola at
Ventimiglia (q.v.) was started in 1867 by the Hanburys from England, who
took advantage of the unique microclimatic conditions of the Italian Riviera
to make an outstanding botanical collection of tender plants from all areas of
the world. At Villa Taranto (q.v.) on Lake Maggiore, where mild winters, hot
summers and a high rainfall provide exceptional growing conditions, a fine
woodland collection was established after 1931 by a Scotsman, Neil

McEacharn, on 17ha of sloping ground. The garden was laid out in both the English and Italian styles.

Although modern private Italian gardens are not always accessible for visits, many public parks and gardens have been landscaped by important designers. In 1984 Geoffrey Jellicoe was commissioned by the communes of Modena and Brescia to lay out public parks. There are interesting botanic gardens in many Italian university cities; those at Padua, Pisa and Bologna (q.v.) are particularly worth studying. There are also some fine collections of genera such as roses and irises. Fortunately, although many early gardens have disappeared or are poorly maintained, some of the greatest and most influential gardens in the history of western civilization are still extant and can be visited. Most of these are open on a regular basis and there is a keen awareness of the need to preserve historic sites.

The gardens of *Sicily* are today mainly of interest for the richness and variety of their flora rather than for exciting and historic architectural features. The mild climate makes it possible to grow many tender species from all over the world in the open air; it rains during the winter, from October to April (the growing period), but there is little cold weather and few frosts. The summers are very hot and dry, with mean temperatures over 25°C.

We know from contemporary descriptions and poetry that the Saracen emirs and later the Norman kings (who conquered the island in 1091) laid out their luxuriant hunting parks around Palermo 'like a necklace which ornaments the throat of a young girl'. The most important was the 'Genoard', a vast green space which surrounded the wonderful Moorish-style Norman palace of La Zisa. Yet all traces of these pleasure gardens have vanished; only the cloisters of San Giovanni degli Eremiti in Palermo and those of the cathedral of Monreale survive to recall the Moorish influence. Gardens from the following centuries have also disappeared. Even the extravagantly designed gardens of the early 18th-century country villas at Bagheria, 10km east of Palermo, have almost succumbed to neglect, although at Villa Palagonia (open to the public) and Villa Valguarnera (written permission necessary) traces of crumbling sculptures and stonework survive beneath the undergrowth.

There are, nevertheless, some fine gardens and parks, mainly laid out in a romantic English style, which date from the end of the 18th into the 19th century. Moreover, a love of plants and the favourable climate has led to the development of fine botanical collections of exotics and Mediterranean trees and shrubs such as evergreen oaks, arbutus and mastics (*Pistacio lentiscus*), with maquis undergrowth providing a more everyday background to the rarer plant specimens. In the more formal gardens there are hedges of box and oleander as well as the tender spiny *Duranta plumieri* from Mexico, while palm trees and cycads line two *allées* in the Palermo Botanic Garden (q.v.). Tropical specimen trees include the coral tree (*Erythrina crista-galli*) from Brazil, the banyan (*Ficus benghalensis*) from India and Africa, with spectacular foliage and hanging aerial roots to support branches, and from Australia the Moreton Bay fig (*Ficus macrophylla*) and the flame tree (*Sterculia acerifolia*). Citrus fruit trees, the loquat and naturalized prickly pears (forms of *Opuntia*) abound. Luxuriant palms and groves of rustling bamboos thrive in the mild climate to give a jungle effect.

The Italian Lakes and North-West

Castello Balduino

Montalto Pavese, S of Pavia; 10km S of Castéggio via S10
or A21
Owner: Conte Balduino
Opening times: By appointment, Montalto Pavese
27040, Pavia

Few gardens in Italy have topiary to compare with
the crisp geometric shapes at Castello Balduino;
mostly of box and yew, and hand-clipped, the topiary
parterres are best viewed from the terraces which
follow the bastions of the original 13th-century
castle. The castle and gardens were bought in 1909
by the Balduino family who brought in Giovanni
Chevalley to restore the gardens to the 1735 design of
Giovanni Antonio Veneroni. There is little in the
way of fountains or garden sculpture, but a narrow
walk with lemon trees in pots provides shade.

Villa Il Bozzolo ★

Casalzuigno, 20km NW of Varese, NE of S394 to Laveno,
in the Cuvia valley
Owner: Signora Bozzolo
Opening times: By appointment via the Tourist Office in
Varese

The 17th-century villa lies in the beautiful Cuvia
valley near the eastern shore of Lake Maggiore. Both
villa and gardens are neglected, but enough of the
garden remains to indicate its magnificent character.
Designed on a slope at the side of the villa, it is
dominated by a central vista leading up ornamental
balustraded steps to an octagonal grass-filled space at
the half-way point, and beyond to the hilltop above.
A fountain flanked by steps lies at the base of the
slope.

LEFT **Massed box topiary in the 18th-century garden
of Castello Balduino.**

RIGHT **The hillside cascade, flanked by soaring cypresses, above the Villa Cicogna.**

Villa Cicogna ★

Bisuchio, 8km N of Varese on S344
Owner: Conte Cicogna-Mozzoni (under auspices of FAI)
Opening times: Apr to Oct, Sun 9–12
Admission charge: Yes

The early 16th-century villa, still beautifully maintained, lies on the site of an earlier hunting lodge. In
Tuscan style, it is built into the side of a hillside so
that the garden terraces are on several levels. From
one, reached from the main rooms of the villa,
Lake Lugano can be glimpsed in the distance. The
eye travels up a water cascade with flanking steps to a
belvedere glorietta at the top of the slope; behind this
lies the old hunting park, now landscaped in English
style with winding paths. Below the southern facade
of the villa, in a sunken garden, a subterranean grotto
room drips with cool water and formal pools are
surrounded by rustic stone balustrading.

Lake Como: Villa Bagatti Valsecchi

Cardano de Grandola, W of Menaggio (on W shore of
lake), on the Lugano road
Owner: Arch. Pier Fausto Bagatti Valsecchi
Opening times: By appointment, Cardano de Grandola
22017, Lago di Como

Situated on the edge of a deep valley above Lake
Como, the gardens were landscaped in this century
by the father of the present owner on the slopes above

the 18th-century villa. The layout evokes the spirit of 19th-century romanticism, a mixture of the 'wild' and the domestic. From the courtyard of the villa a flight of steps leads upwards to a wrought-iron gate and pillars, beyond which more garden levels with linking stairways reveal spectacular views of the mountains and the lake far below. Lawns, sheltered by tall cypresses silhouetted against the mountain peaks, open out on to flatter areas where rustic balustrading makes a background for tamer planting of colourful perennials and annuals. Rock plants cling to the steeper cliffs below the villa. A cascade of spray from a mountain torrent far below seems part of 'untamed' nature; in fact the channel for the stream was blasted through the rock face to create this studied effect.

Lake Como: Villa Balbianello Monzino

On a promontory on the W shore of the lake, near Lenno. Hire a boat from Como or Lenno
Owner: Conte Monzino
Opening times: By appointment, Lenno 22016, Lago di Como

Built in 1790, the villa is a charming *casino* with picturesque landing gates on the shore. It overlooks the site of Pliny's villa 'Comedy', now submerged. The terraced garden, each level edged with balustrading, reflects the idealized style of the *giardino inglese*, with sweeps of curving beds and winding paths. Tall, perfectly groomed ilex trees and pollarded planes frame and shelter the villa from lake storms. The romantic beauty of the situation creates a memorable impression, one which is easily enjoyed from the lake in passing.

Lake Como: Villa Carlotta ★ ❀

On the W shore, 30km N of Como, on S340 between Tremezzo and Cadenabbia; or by boat from Bellagio or Como
Owner: Italian State
Opening times: Daily, Apr to Sept 9–18; Mar, Oct 9–11.30, 14–16.30
Admission charge: Yes

The villa was built in 1745 for Marshal Giorgio Clerici, later taking its name from Carlotta, Duchess of Saxe-Meiningen, who made the romantic garden

on the lake shore after 1843. The formal 18th-century garden descends in steep terraces to the lake; today clipped hedges frame colourful flowerbeds. Exotic species have been planted in the 'wilder' garden; avenues of azaleas here are famous for their spring displays. For the botanist, interest extends from scented climbers such as *Stauntonia hexaphylla* to giant redwoods and Japanese cryptomerias. Tender tree ferns (*Dicksonia antarctica*) thrive in a shady ravine.

Lake Como: Villa Melzi ❀

On Lake Como, within walking distance of Bellagio
Owner: Duca Gallarati Scotti
Opening times: Daily, Mar to Oct 10–12, 15–18
Admission charge: Yes

The early 19th-century neo-classical villa was designed by Giocondo Albertolli for Francesco Melzi d'Eril, Duke of Lodi, the vice-president of the Republic during Napoleon's occupation. The park is laid out in a landscape style with fine trees and shrubs; azaleas, rhododendrons and camellias are at their best in April and May, but interesting tender species, such as Montezuma pines with silvery needles, camphor trees and redwoods are beautiful all through the year. Near the house are formal flowerbeds with colourful annuals. A Japanese-style water garden, its pools edged with acers (a fine collection), iris and bamboo, is crossed by a bridge festooned with wisteria.

Villa Durazzo Pallavicini

Viale Pallavicini, Genova-Pegli, 10km W of Genoa on S1
Owner: Commune of Genoa
Opening times: Daily 9–sunset
Admission charge: No

The wonderfully romantic 11ha park, on the mountainside above Genoa, is part garden and part woodland. The scene-designer and architect Michele Canzio designed both palace and gardens in 1846. There is a small lake, with a Chinese bridge and

pagoda, a temple of Diana, an Egyptian obelisk, a temple of Flora and a beautiful neo-classical coffee house. What looks like a triumphal arch is in fact a country house. Everything is in a sad state of neglect but the gardens still contain exotic plant specimens which thrive in the favoured climate.

Lake Garda: Villa Bettoni

Bogliaco, on W shore of Lake Garda, just S of Gargnano
Owner: Sig. Bettoni
Opening times: By appointment, Bogliaco, Gargnano 25084, Brescia

The long facade of the 18th-century Villa Bettoni stands close to the edge of Lake Garda. The garden, on terraces behind the villa, was designed by Amerigo Pierallini. An impressive display of staircase ramps, statues (by Locatelli) and grottoes gradually ascend the hillside, from where there are splendid views of the villa and lake. The lower part of the garden can be seen from the main lakeside road which separates villa and garden. A balustraded bridge connects the two.

Lake Garda: Villa Brenzone (Villa Guarienti) ★

Punta San Vigilio, on E shore of lake, just N of Garda
Owner: Conte Guglielmo Guarienti di Brenzone
Opening times: By appointment, Punta San Vigilio, Garda 37016, Verona, or tel. 045 7255164

The promontory of the Punta San Vigilio is occupied by the early 16th-century villa and its contemporary garden layout. The villa was built in this picturesque setting for the humanist philosopher Agostino Brenzone by the great Veronese architect Santini Sanmichele. The garden, one of the few from this period to survive in northern Italy, is in a series of rooms with separate themes, illustrated by statues and Latin inscriptions. The sculpture includes mythological divinities, a semi-circle of classical Roman busts set in a cypress grove, a tomb of Catullus and a head of Petrarch, all illustrating the philosophy of Brenzone and his reverence for the past. Exotic plants flourishing in the mild lakeside climate extend the original 16th-century vegetation of box, bay, myrtle and cypress.

Lake Garda: Villa Idania ❀

E side of lake, near Garda
Owner: Contessa Ida Borletti
Opening times: By appointment, Garda 37016, Verona or tel. 045 7255131

This modern English-style garden was made by Alex Edwards for the owner in the 1950s, with advice from Henry Cocker. It lies on steep slopes on the eastern side of Lake Garda. Taking advantage of the mild Mediterranean climate, many interesting species have been planted. Two level meadows are united by a rock garden and by wide grass-covered steps. Features include a pool with lotus flowers, a rose garden, stylized modern statues and an orchard of fruit trees. The garden is framed by cypresses and olive trees.

Genoa: Palazzo Pallavicino (delle Peschiere) ★

15 Salità San Bartolomeo degli Armeni
Owner: Marchese Pallavicino/Soc. Italnavi
Opening times: Office hours

The villa was designed for Tobia Pallavicino by Galeazzo Alessi in *c.*1560. The terraced garden, although incomplete, retains its secluded and almost secret position overlooking the city. On the terrace level with the villa is a pool with a statue by Giacomo Valsoldo and below is a grotto decorated with coloured pebble mosaic.

Lake Maggiore: Isola Bella ★ ❀

One of the Borromean islands; reached by boat from Stresa, Baveno or Pallanza
Owner: Principe Borromeo-Arese
Opening times: Daily, Apr to Oct 9–12, 14.30–17.30
Admission charge: Yes

The palace and magnificent terraced gardens were laid out on the bare rock of the island. Angelo Crivelli's plans, begun in 1630, were completed by Carlo Fontana and Milanese architects for Count Vitaliano Borromeo later in the 17th century. Carved in the shape of a great galleon, with a crowning balustrade of statues standing out against the sky like the poop of a ship, the garden is a vast extravaganza with rococo theatre, pavilions, statuary by Valmara and decorative wrought-iron flowers in tall vases. An engraving by Marc Antonio dal Ré (1726) shows palace and garden with clear-cut architectural features in evidence, but only thirteen years later the French historian Charles de Brosses describes the terraces rich with 'oranges, jasmine and pomegranates'. Today, bright-flowered annuals grow in the flowerbeds and rare and tender wall shrubs and climbers clothe the balustrades and tumble down terrace walls in romantic profusion.

Lake Maggiore: Isola Madre

One of the Borromean islands; reached by boat from Stresa, Baveno or Pallanza
Owner: Principe Borromeo-Arese
Opening times: Daily, Apr to Oct 9–12, 14.30–17.30
Admission charge: Yes

On the site of an unfinished renaissance villa, the gardens of Isola Madre are arranged on steep south- and west-facing terraces above the lake, where lemons, oranges, myrtles and exotics thrive in the mild climate. In the centre and northern section the English-style landscape wood contains many rare and beautiful trees. There is a fine *Cupressus cashmeriana*, as well as camphor (*Cinnamomum camphora*) and pepper trees (*Schinus molle*). White peacocks stroll on the open lawns.

Lake Maggiore: Villa San Remigio

On a hill above Pallanza (S34 on the W shore of Lake Maggiore) and Villa Taranto
Owner: Regione di Piemonte
Opening times: Weekdays 9–12.30
Admission charge: Yes

In a magnificent situation high above Lake Maggiore, the late 19th-century villa was built on the site of a chapel by an Irishman, Mr Brown. A garden, with statues and balustrading in formal Italian style, was laid out on the steep slopes. Behind the villa, steps lined with hedges of box descend to a pool framed in rustic stonework and a baroque-style pavilion.

Lake Maggiore: Villa Taranto ✲
On the W shore of the lake at Pallanza: S34 or, more
romantically, by boat from Stresa
Owner: Ente Villa Taranto
Opening times: Daily, Apr to Oct 8.30 – sunset
Admission charge: Yes

The gardens contain an important botanical collection. It was originally planted in the 1930s by Neil McEacharn, a Scotsman, who made full use of the exceptional site with its mild winters, high rainfall (up to 160cm) and hot summers to assemble a wide range of plants from all corners of the world. Tender shrubs such as gardenias thrive beside hardy rhododendrons and magnolias. Woodland slopes and valleys, formal parterres, water gardens and greenhouses extending over 17ha contain many plants of interest. American and Asiatic magnolias, davidias, dogwoods and the rare *Emmenopterys henryi* (which has flowered here) all grow to large size and are underplanted with azaleas and drifts of hostas.

Mantua: Palazzo Ducale (Giardino Pensile)
Piazza Sordello
Owner: Italian State
Opening times: Daily 9–14, except Mon; hols 9–13
Admission charge: Yes (free on Sun)

The hanging gardens of the late 13th-century fortress-like palace of the Gonzaga family were designed in 1579 by Francesco Traballese and are now the only remaining courtyard garden in Italy dating from the 16th century. On a level with the *piano nobile*, the garden is surrounded on three sides by a portico with ceilings painted with charming images of climbing plants. Gravel paths lead between box-patterned flowerbeds.

Mantua: Palazzo del Té
Viale Té
Owner: Italian State
Opening times: Daily, Apr to Sept 9–12.30, 15–18.30, except Mon; hols 9–13
Admission charge: Yes

The summer residence of the Gonzaga family was designed and richly decorated by Giulio Romano from 1525–35. A colonnade, the Loggia of David, leads from the palace and courtyard to a bridge over a fishpond and thence to the main garden, which has grassed parterre divisions edged in box. On either side of this were once two secret gardens. The one to the north-east still contains a grotto with decorations by Romano and Francesco Primaticcio. The portico at the far end of the garden was designed by Paolo Pozzo in 1783.

Milan: Villa Belgioioso (Villa Reale) ★
Via Palestro
Owner: Commune of Milan
Opening times: Daily, sunrise–sunset
Admission charge: No

The neo-classical villa, which now houses the Gallery of Modern Art, was designed by Leopold Pollack in 1790–3. There are statues on the parapet by Parini and Appiani. The garden, also by Pollack but completed by Villoresi, is in romantic landscape style with a serpentine lake; it was described by the Italian garden designer Ercole Silva in 1801 in his treatise on *The Art of English Gardens*.

La Mortola (Giardini Hanbury) ★ ✲
On the Mediterranean, 4km W of Ventimiglia on S1
Owner: University of Genoa
Opening times: Daily except Mon, summer 9–18; winter 10–16
Admission charge: Yes

The gardens of La Mortola (named after the thickets of wild myrtle on the rocky shore), now more than a hundred years old, were planted by an Englishman, Sir Thomas Hanbury, after 1867. The magnificent and favoured site, the slopes already covered with oak, bay, robinia and fig trees and with steep cliffs descending to the sea, was landscaped by the German botanist Ludovico Winter. The garden was planned as a botanic collection of outstanding interest; tender exotics from South Africa, Australia, New Zealand and South America were planted and flourished. Today their seedlings struggle in impenetrable groves. Eucalyptus, acacia and palm trees tower

At La Mortola (Giardini Hanbury), exotic plants from all over the world thrive and seed on the steep slopes above the Mediterranean.

above banks of fruiting bananas. A path from the upper gateway (on the main road) leads down to the shore, passing succulents and cycads, dasylirions and puyas of exotic aspect. On the lower terraces citrus orchards, including large grapefruit trees, protect flowerbeds of blue-flowered *Scilla peruviana*. A track crosses the Roman Aurelian Way to the villa and seashore below; there, planting has a more English aspect with pergolas clustered with roses. Although some areas are closed and the rest in need of renovation and replanting, the gardens are still spectacular and grow a unique assemblage of rare and tender plants.

Villa Negrotto Cambiaso Pallavicino ★
Centre of Arenzano, 20km W of Genoa on S1
Owner: Commune of Arenzano
Opening times: Daily 9–sunset
Admission charge: No

Alessandro Pallavicino built a villa in 1825 on a hill overlooking the sea in which he incorporated a medieval tower; his park was constructed to the designs of the architect Cremona. Towards the end of the century the park was altered to conform with the romantic tastes of the period, the tower was moved to a higher position and a three-windowed portico was built in its place. In 1907 a monumental greenhouse was added. Today, rows of pines and palms stretch towards the sea. Terraces with fountains are still partly paved, archways are clad with roses, and there are fine specimen monkey puzzles and redwoods and a collection of cycas.

Certosa di Pavia
Off S35 between Pavia (8km) and Milan (25km)
Owner: Carthusian Monastery
Opening times: Daily, Jan to Apr, Sept to Dec 9–11.30, 14.30–16.30, except Mon; May to Aug 9–11.30, 14.30–18, except Mon
Admission charge: Weekdays, yes; Sun, no

The Carthusian monastery was founded in 1396 by

Gian Galeazzo Visconti as a family mausoleum; most of the building dates from the 15th and 16th centuries. It is situated on the edge of the park which once extended from the Castello Visconteo in Pavia. The Little Cloister, with terracotta decorations, is planted with flowers surrounding a baroque fountain. Each of the 24 monks' cells on three sides of the Great Cloister has its own enclosed garden.

Villa Sommi-Picenardi ★
Olgiate Mólgora, 30km SW of Lecco via S36 and S342
Owner: Sommi-Picenardi family
Opening times: By appointment, Olgiate Mólgora 22056, Como

The original 17th-century garden, on a steep slope behind the villa and contemporary with it, was restored during the 19th century, but the basic layout of balustraded terraces, fountains and statues, designed to be viewed from the rooms of the villa like a stage set, remains intact. The coloured mosaic decoration of the central stairway and grotto reflects the taste of 17th-century Rome rather than that of the north. The garden in front of the villa is landscaped with fine specimen trees.

Palazzo di Stupinigi ★
10km S of Turin on S23
Owner: Ordine Mauriziano
Opening times: Daily 10–12.30, 14–17.30, except Mon and Fri
Admission charge: Yes

Vittorio Amadeo II commissioned the Stupinigi Palace (1729–35) for entertaining hunting parties. The architect was the Sicilian Filippo Juvarra; it has frescoes, rococo and chinoiserie decoration, and charming hunting scenes. The original French garden layout has been much simplified. The main part was designed from 1740 by Bernard in the style of Le Nôtre, with a grand *allée* leading to a circular *bosco*. Today, there is a large open park which leads to the *bosco*; within this small wooded area there is a small landscape garden with a lake.

Turin: Giardini del Palazzo Reale di Torino ★
Piazza Castello
Owner: Italian State
Opening times: Daily 9–18
Admission charge: No

The spectacular geometric parterres of the royal palace, a series of grass flowerbeds in formal French style, were designed by André Le Nôtre in 1697. Partly bounded by the ancient city walls, the parterres lie behind the royal palace and are reached through the courtyard. A terrace on the other side of the palace looks over a circular water basin decorated with statues by Simone Martinez. The surrounding park, with fine specimen plane trees, 19th-century plantings of purple-leaved beech and further statues, is also worth visiting.

The Veneto

Villa Allegri ★
Cuzzano, 11km N of Verona on Grezzana road
Owner: Sig. Ottavio Arvedi
Opening times: By appointment, Cuzzano in Valpantena, Verona
Admission charge: No

With a *parterre de broderie* and sculptures in box wood, this garden laid out along terraces on the eastern slope of the hill, crowned by the 17th-century villa, recalls the pattern displayed in the engravings of this garden by Montalegre published by Volkamer in 1714. The garden is perfectly preserved.

Villa Barbarigo ★

Valsanzibio, 18km S of Padua, 6km W of Battáglia Terme
on A13 or S16
Owner: Conte Fabio Pizzoni Ardemani
Opening times: Daily, Mar to Nov 10–12, 14–17.30,
except Mon (excluding the terrace near the villa)
Admission charge: Yes

Set among the foothills of the Euganean hills, this
unique garden, mainly designed in the second half of
the 17th century, is justly famous for its pavilions,
fountains, water tricks and fine baroque vases and
statues. Other notable features such as avenues of
clipped evergreens, a maze and a rabbit island all
contribute to make exploration a delight. The garden
consists primarily of two axes. The first, a hedged
alley backed by tall cypresses outlined against the
sky, stretches from the facade of the villa along the
flat bed of the valley. The second, a cross axis, is a
water canal, which descends to the gate into the
garden. Here the visitor first gets a glittering view of
the natural green amphitheatre of the Euganean hills,
seen rising above pools, cascades and fountains

**At the Villa Pisani, Strà, the elegant stables are
reflected in the long canal behind the villa.**

which fill the air with sound and movement. Recently
scholars have speculated on the often ambiguous
symbolism of the renaissance and baroque Italian
garden, which had to function both on a practical as
well as a philosophical level. It was a place for
botanical and medical research, a display theatre for
mechanical and hydraulic contraptions, and also a
retreat for quiet meditation and repose. At Valsanzibio, where the garden was laid out by the owner
himself, Procurator Antonio Barbarigo, the theme of
water became identified with *natura generans*, and the
garden an allegorical conception of paradise beyond
and above the snares of fate and death, a primeval
Eden regained on earth.

Villa Barbaro (formerly Volpi)

Maser, 26km NW of Treviso via S348 and 248 to Ásolo
Owner: Contessa Diamante Dalle Ore Luling Buschetti
Opening times: Tues, Sat, Sun; Jun to Sept 15–18; Oct
to May 15–17
Admission charge: Yes

In front of the 16th-century villa designed by Palladio for his patron, Daniele Barbaro, the garden is
designed symmetrically and has the remains of
parterres. There is a lively 17th-century *nymphaeum*

behind the house, with a grotto inhabited by a river god and a semi-circular pool enriched by stucco decoration (attributed to Alessandro Vittoria, but probably the work of Marcantonio Barbaro).

Villa 'La Deliziosa' (formerly Conti, Lampertico)

Montegaldella, 17km SE of Vicenza off S247
Owner: Tillio Campagnolo-Vicenza
Opening times: Thurs, Sat 9–12
Admission charge: Yes

The villa was begun in 1622 but was not completed until the 18th century. The garden is famous for its 18th-century statuary, some of which is signed by Orazio Marinali.

Villa Manin ★

Passariano Friuli, Codroipo, 27km SW of Udine off N13
Owner: Provincial Administration of Friuli-Venezia Giulia
Opening times: Summer, Thurs–Sat 15–18, Sun 9.30–12.30, 15–18
Admission charge: Yes

Napoleon, who stayed with Ludovico Manin when he signed the Treaty of Campoformido in 1797, felt that this milky white palace floating in the vast plain of Friuli like a mirage was too rich and sumptuous to remain a private residence. Built in the late 17th and early 18th centuries for the Manin family, who were originally from Fiesole outside Florence but had been substantial landowners here since the 14th century, this is one of the grandest villas in the north of Italy, a miniature Versailles. In 1863 the original 18th-century garden, with statues by Giuseppe Torretto, was transformed by Quaglia into a romantic park. It still contains two artificial mounts, representing Etna and Parnassus, with accompanying allegorical sculpture, which date from the earlier layout. More recently the garden has become known for its exotic trees, among which are specimens of *Pinus strobus* and *P. wallichiana*, tulip trees and ginkgos. After years of neglect, the palace has been restored with help from the Ente Ville Venete and has become the cultural centre of the region.

Castello di Miramare

Miramare, 7km NW of Trieste on the Adriatic via S14
Owner: Italian State
Opening times: Daily, summer 9–13, 14–17; winter 9.30–16; Sun 9.30–13.30
Admission charge: No

Built in 1856–60 for the ill-fated Archduke Maximilian of Austria (*see* Tervuren in Belgium), the terraced garden extends along the shore of the Adriatic to the north of the castle. A wisteria pergola leads from near the castle to the 22ha outer park. Dense woods of ilex and pine shelter this magnificent property.

Padua: Botanic Garden of the University of Padua ★ ❀

Via Orto Botanico, Padua
Owner: University of Padua
Opening times: Daily, summer 9–17; winter 9–13; hols in summer 10–13
Admission charge: Yes

Founded in 1545 as an apothecary garden for the medical school at the university, the botanic garden is today still enclosed by its 16th-century circular wall. Laid out in four quarters with axial paths meeting in the centre and stone-edged flowerbeds of triangular shape, the design is typical of the renaissance period. The gateways, statues and busts along the wall were added in the 18th century. Venetian contacts abroad helped the garden to flourish and many exotic plants were first grown at Padua (including the common lilac (1565) and the potato (1590)). Goethe's famous palm is a reminder of the poet's visit in 1786. As a result of his study of plants at Padua, Goethe anticipated the theory of evolution.

Casa del Petrarca

Arquà Petrarca, 20km S of Padua via S16 or A13, and 7km NW of Monsélice
Owner: Italian State
Opening times: Daily, except Mon and hols, mid Mar to mid Oct 9–12.30, 14–19.30; mid Oct to mid Mar 9.30–12.30, 13.30–16.30
Admission charge: Yes

Petrarch lived at Arquà from 1370 until his death in 1374. Here the great Italian poet and humanist wrote and gardened according to philosophical principles. The house dates from Petrarch's time, although the loggia is 16th-century. There is a small garden behind the house, with box hedging and a view over the surrounding Euganean hills. The villa is a place of pilgrimage and the visitors' book records Byron's visit in 1817.

The original baroque parterres, patterned in box, survive at the Villa Allegri at Cuzzano.

Villa Pisani ★

Strà, on the Brenta canal, 8km E of Padua on S11
Owner: Italian State
Opening times: Daily 9–14, except Mon and public hols
Admission charge: Yes

The villa, on the Brenta canal near Padua, was rebuilt after 1720 for the brothers Alvise and Almoro Pisani. Girolamo Frigimelica's ambitious project included the garden between the main villa (by Francesco Maria Preti some years later) on the canal bank and the elegant stables behind, although the long reflect-

ing pool was only excavated in the early 20th century. According to Felibien des Aveaux, the garden layout is thought to have been inspired by Pliny the Younger's Laurentian villa. Frigimelica also built other garden features: the portals leading into the garden, a rococo orangery, a coffee house and a labyrinth (*see* La Gaude, France) with a look-out in the centre turret; many of these survive. Although not well kept, the garden is full of atmosphere.

Villa Revedin-Bolasco

Borgo-Treviso 46 (Il Paradiso); in E suburb of
Castelfranco Veneto on S53 Treviso road
Owner: University of Padua
Opening times: Tues–Sat and 1st Sun in month 15–18
Admission charge: Yes

Once the residence of the noble Cornaro family, the villa was redesigned by Vincenzo Scamozzi at the beginning of the 17th century for Giorgio Cornaro, with an ornate garden of pools and statues. This was enlarged during the 18th century; at least a hundred statues, mostly from the workshop of Marinali, decorated a rectangular *viale*. Declining fortunes left the villa in ruins and it passed first to the Revedins and then to the Bolascos, who totally altered its appearance, using Meduna for the house and Antonio Caregaro Negrin for the garden. Negrin designed the Moorish greenhouse and other garden pavilions, utilizing some of the old statues, such as the two steeds which are placed by the lake and others which surround a 'riding school' area. The walls of a modern hospital encroach on the garden layout.

Villa Rizzardi ★

18km NW of Verona near Negrar
Owner: Contessa Cristina Rizzardi
Opening times: Apply to custodian (not midday); groups by appointment, Pojega di Negrar, Verona or tel.
045 7210288
Admission charge: No

This exceptional garden, laid out on a slope behind the villa, has many features of interest and beauty. An alley of pleached hornbeam leads to the green theatre with seats in clipped box. Another of cypress leads to a hillside belvedere. A temple is ornamented with shells and petrified stalactites. Drawings for the garden, preserved in the Biblioteca Civica di Verona, are by the Veronese Luigi Trezza and are dated 1783–91.

Villa Selvatico Emo Capodilista

Sant'Elena di Battáglia, 14km SW of Padua via A13 or
S16; just S of Battáglia Terme
Owner: Società Estensi SAS
Opening times: By appointment, Sant'Elena di Battáglia
35041, Padova

Built on the initiative of Bartolomeo Selvatico at the end of the 16th century, this hillside villa was 'improved' in the baroque style in the succeeding century. Tomio Forzan designed the monumental stairway to join the hanging terrace, rich with lemon trees and fountains, to the road from Padua. In 1816 the new owner, Agostino Meneghini, seeking to renew interest in the thermal spas of the Euganean area, employed Giuseppe Japelli to turn the surrounding slopes into an English-style garden. Japelli sought to evoke the journeys of Virgil through Hades, but the garden is now so overgrown it is difficult to trace this 19th-century interpretation.

Verona: Giardino Giusti ★

Via Giardino Giusti on the E bank of the river
Owner: Conte Niccolò Giusti del Giardino
Opening times: Daily, sunrise–sunset, except Mon
Admission charge: Yes.

This city garden, dating from the 1570s, lies on a steep hillside above the left bank of the River Adige. From the belvedere, a grotesque mask at its summit, there are views to the Alps and south across the Po valley to Mantua. Thomas Coryat visited in 1608 and described the *viale* of cypresses, a grotto decorated with shells and mirrors and a pavilion for refreshment on the hilltop. John Evelyn, Joseph Addison, Charles de Brosses and Goethe (who picked a posy of flowering capers and cypress leaves here) have all left written testimonies to the garden's charms. Today, tall trees still line a path to the base of the wooded hill, where caves and grottoes are visible. Parterres and a maze (where Charles de Brosses was lost) have recently been restored.

Vicenza: Villa Capra (La Rotonda)

On the S outskirts of the town
Owner: Conte Ludovico di Valmarana
Opening times: Daily 10–12, 15–18
Admission charge: Yes

Palladio's famous Villa Capra with its four identical facades sits on a small hill overlooking the surrounding countryside. Built *c.*1566, its garden of balustraded terraces anticipates by nearly two centuries William Kent's claim that a garden should be seen as an integral part of its natural surroundings. La Rotonda served as a model for 18th-century buildings in England, such as Chiswick House, London, and Mereworth Castle, Kent.

Vicenza: Villa Valmarana 'ai nani'

Via San Bastian in the S suburbs
Opening times: Daily 15–17; summer, Thurs and Sat 10–12, 15.30–18
Admission charge: Yes

The 18th-century villa is noted for the lively country frescoes by both Giambattista Tiepolo and his son Giandomenico who decorated the villa and the guest house (*la foresteria*) respectively in the 18th century. It is named after the grotesque stone statues of dwarfs (*nani*) which adorn the encircling wall. The simple garden layout, projecting over the valley below, contains fountains, statues and a fine Russian olive (*Elaeagnus angustifolia*), with glistening silver leaves and fragrant flowers.

Tuscany, The Marche and Emilia Romagna

Bologna: Botanic Garden of the University of Bologna

42 Via Irnerio, under the walls of NE Bologna
Owner: University of Bologna
Opening times: Public hols 10–13
Admission charge: Yes

Called the Giardino della Viola, the garden was only moved to its present site at the beginning of the last century. The first botanic garden was founded in 1568, although a small teaching garden of 'simples' had already been planted by Luca Ghini, the great botanist and doctor, forty years earlier. Shady trees and other often rare plants make the garden an oasis of peace in the busy city. Liquidambars, swamp cypresses, plane trees, a huge American walnut, willows and poplars are the basis of a collection which also includes areas for Mediterranean and Apennine plants. Succulents are grown in a greenhouse.

Giardino Buonaccorsi ★

Signposted from Potenza Picena, 30km S of Ancona, 8km from coast
Owner: Società Agripicena
Opening times: Daily 8–12; groups by appointment, Via Giardino 9, Potenza Picena 62018, Macerata, tel. 0733 688189
Admission charge: No

There are few important historic gardens in the Marche, but thanks to concerned owners and its isolated position the Buonaccorsi garden is a significant and well-preserved example of an early 18th-century garden. It abounds in interesting details from mosaic stonework to statues, and still looks as it appears in the mid 18th-century painting reproduced in Georgina Masson's *Italian Gardens*.

Five terraces look out towards the sea; on the upper terrace parterres are divided by raised stone edging forming diamond and star shapes. In a grotto niche there are baroque figures of a friar and the devil. Sculptural representations of *Commedia dell'Arte* characters are ranged along the balustrade between the first and second terraces, and a statue of Flora in another niche on a lower level forms part of the garden boundary wall. Citrus fruits are espaliered on the walls.

Boschi de Carrega

Sala Baganza de Collecchio, 10km SW of Parma via S62
Owner: Regione Emilia Romagna
Opening times: Tel. 0521 650519

Lying at the edge of the plain south of Parma, in the foothills of the Apennines, these woods of beech, hornbeam, holm oak, chestnut and pine, with exotics such as cedar, redwood, swamp cypress and red pine (*Pinus resinosa*), are of great beauty and interest. There are five small lakes hidden in the forest. The original planting, the central core of a hunting estate, and a pavilion, the Villa Casino dei Boschi (built by Petitot), date from the end of the 18th century and were designed for the Bourbon Duchess Maria Amalia. Extensive beech woods and another *casino*, del Ferlaro, in neo-classical style, were added in 1828. A grotto with bathing pool can also be seen.

Castello di Celsa

Celsa, SW of Siena; 10km N of Sovicille on S73
Owner: Principessa Aldobrandini
Opening times: By appointment, Sovicille S3018, Siena

Romantically situated in the ilex woods west of Siena, this 19th-century gothic revival villa replaced a 16th-century villa and an even earlier fortress. Although Baldassare Peruzzi's 16th-century circular chapel remains, the garden reflects 19th-century restoration, and the gravel and box parterre representing the Aldobrandini arms was laid out more recently. To the east of the *castello* a path between undulating clipped cypress hedges leads through a

The view over the 17th-century Villa Cetinale shows the *viale* of cypresses, the gardens, and the park or Thebaid of Cardinal Chigi.

meadow of wild flowers to a recently restored 17th-century fishpond decorated with rustic stonework. Beyond the pool open rides radiate through the dense ilex wood.

lemon trees in pots; the original raised beds, the *tori*, today planted with modern annuals, are typical of a renaissance garden.

Villa Cetinale ★
Cetinale, 13km SW of Siena, between Ancaiano and Celsa, via S73
Owner: Viscount Lambton
Opening times: By appointment, Sovicille S3018, Siena
Admission charge: No

Built in 1680 for Cardinal Flavio Chigi, nephew of Pope Alexander VII, the villa was designed by Carlo Fontana, a pupil of Bernini. Set on the edge of dense woodland, the villa and its garden are joined by a simple axis stretching north and south. To the north, across a lane, a gateway leads into a park, the Thebaid or penitentiary of Cardinal Chigi, with a vista to a giant figure of Hercules. From the south facade a wide grass alley, lined with pencil cypresses and framed by 19th-century statues by Bernardo Mazzuoli, leads to a semi-circular terrace at the base of a wooded hill. Steep steps rise to a hermitage on the summit. Now owned by Lord Lambton, the 17th-century garden has been carefully restored. Under the walls of the villa mixed borders of roses and flowers give a more English atmosphere.

Villa Cigliano
20km SW of Florence; 3km N of San Casciano on A2
Owner: Marchese Antinori
Opening times: By appointment, San Casciano in Val di Pesa 50026, Firenze

The 15th-century villa, built in typical Tuscan renaissance style, sits on a ridge looking over the Val di Pesa. The original walled garden lies behind the house and courtyard. In 1691 Niccolò Francesco Antinori remodelled the walls, adding the scrolled baroque decoration and urns, and adorned the *limonaia* with ornamental pebble panelling. A statue of Neptune of the same period overlooks a pool. In the 19th century attempts were made to turn the formal walled garden into a *giardino inglese* by introducing winding paths to destroy the symmetry. Nevertheless, the atmosphere remains Italian, with

Villa Corsi Salviati ★
Via Gramsci, Sesto Fiorentino; in suburbs 9km NW of Florence
Owner: Conte Guicciardini-Corsi-Salviati
Opening times: May to Oct, Tues, Fri 15–sunset; groups by appointment via Agriturist, Piazza San Firenze 3, Firenze 50100
Admission charge: No

The villa lies on a flat plain, now part of Florence's industrial suburb of Sesto. Frescoes by Bernardino Poccetti in the house show the simple country villa and garden which Simone Corsi bought in 1502. By 1644 the garden had been extended and divided into four separate areas, and in 1738 Marchese Antonio Corsi completed the remodelling in baroque style. A 1740 engraving by Zocchi shows the new layout.

The two-storey house was crowned with a balustrade studded with urns and statues; the boundaries between the garden rooms were swept away; an earlier fishpond was converted into a rectangular canal and flanked by elegant urns and statues; a rabbit island and pool were formalized with fountains; woodland to the east was extended to include the old kitchen garden, and a box maze concealed at its centre. In the 19th century this woodland became a romantic landscape garden with lake and mock castle, and by the middle of the century the villa had become famous for its large hothouses and its tropical plants, and also for the hybridization of a double ranunculus, *Roselline di Firenze*.

In 1907 Marchese Giulio Guicciardini-Corsi-Salviati restored much of the garden to its appearance at the end of the 17th century. Today, the formal areas are cared for, but the lake and eastern parts of the garden are sadly neglected.

Florence: Boboli Gardens ★
Behind the Pitti Palace
Owner: Italian State
Opening times: Daily 9–sunset; closed public hols
Admission charge: No

The earliest part of the Boboli gardens stretches behind the Pitti Palace in a vast amphitheatre. According to Vasari in his *Lives of Artists*, Niccolò Tribolo began the garden in 1549 for Cosimo de' Medici's first wife, Eleanor of Toledo, delineating the outline of the horseshoe valley by walks symmetrically cut through plantations. In the 17th century the formal stone amphitheatre was built, and the gardens became a centre for pageants and displays. Near the palace, Bernardo Buontalenti designed a grotto, richly decorated with minerals and sculptures, and with frescoes by Bernardo Poccetti (permission to view is necessary).

A long alley, the Viottolone, leads down to the charming balustraded *isolotto*, a little island reached by two bridges, where the focal point is the 16th-century Oceanus sculpture by Giambologna. During the summer the *isolotto* is decorated with citrus plants in pots.

In 1644 the diarist John Evelyn was amazed by the Boboli gardens: 'Here is everything to make such a paradise delightful ... in the garden I saw a rose grafted on an orange tree.' Today, the gardens are a popular retreat for tourists, who can look down on the city from the highest point, marked by a colossal statue of Abundance by Giambologna.

Florence: Villa Capponi ★

3 Via Pian de' Giullari, on the hill at Arcetri, S bank of the Arno
Owner: Sig. Benedetti
Opening times: By appointment, Via Pian de' Giullari 3, Firenze 50100, or via Agriturist, Piazza San Firenze 3, Firenze 50100

Bought by Gino Capponi in 1572, the villa lies hidden behind a high wall on the hill at Arcetri, looking over the valley of the Arno. The garden, one of the most beautiful in Florence, retains the plan and spirit of the early Renaissance. However, English and American owners of the last hundred years have enriched the planting and now scented flowers and colour give a more cosmopolitan atmosphere. The first terrace behind the house is laid out with a lawn; to the south-east stone pillars, surmounted with griffins, frame a walled garden with vast lemon trees; vases and geometric box-edged beds are filled with forget-me-nots in spring. Roses and wisteria cling to the walls. To the north-west another garden room,

the *giardino segreto*, is reached down steep steps; here, sheltered from winds by a high crenellated wall, more box-edged beds are planted with white flowers.

Florence: Giardino dell'Iris

Piazza Michelangelo, on the hill below San Miniato al Monte
Owner: Società Italiana dell'Iris
Opening times: Mid May to early Jun
Admission charge: No

Over a thousand varieties of iris are grown here, many bred from the original *Iris florentina*, the orris root, found in the valley of the Arno.

Florence: Villa La Pietra ★

120 Via Bolognese, 1.5km N of the city
Owner: La Pietra Corporation
Opening times: Apr to Jun via Agriturist, Piazza San Firenze 3, Firenze 50100
Admission charge: Yes

In 1462 Francesco Sassetti designed a country villa on a grand scale, where surrounding gardens, orchards and vineyards were closely linked with the dwelling. Architectural features of the period survive, although Cardinal Capponi altered the villa in the 16th century, and all traces of the early garden layout were swept away during the 19th century in favour of a *giardino inglese*. The present gardens to the south-east, laid out in the early part of this century by Arthur Acton, father of Sir Harold, are a reconstruction of a renaissance design. The arrangement is simple: a series of broad terraces descending from the villa are linked by steps and paths. Dark hedges, immaculately clipped, enclose garden rooms, and statues are framed by bay and box. In a green theatre Venetian figures by Francesca Bonazza highlight the tones of the vegetation. Grass alleys, one terminated by a figure of Hercules, are cool in summer, and a curving colonnade closes the view at the bottom of the garden. On one side of the terraces a vista has been cut in the boscage to reveal the hills beyond Florence, which lies in the valley below.

A 17th-century walled garden to the north of the main block remains as a lemon garden, with a *limonaia* decorated in *rocaille* work.

Villa Gamberaia ★

Via del Rossellino, 2km on the far side of Settignano, 8km NE of Florence

Owner: Dott. Marcello Marchi

Opening times: Weekdays, summer 8–12, 14–18; winter 8–12, 13–17; or when owner is away, via Agriturist, Piazza San Firenze 3, Firenze 50100

Admission charge: Yes

The villa, badly damaged in World War II, has been restored to its 16th-century appearance. Around it is one of the most beautiful and immaculately kept gardens in Italy. A long bowling alley and a grotto garden with *rocaille* decoration date from the early 18th century when the property was acquired by the Capponi family. The rest of the garden was laid out by the Serbian Princess Jeanne Ghyka and her American friend Miss Blood at the end of the 19th century, but the series of garden rooms has a strong renaissance pattern. Reflecting water panels on the south terrace are framed with box and elaborate pebble paths. A semi-circle of arcaded cypresses reveals glimpses of the distant hills round Vallombrosa; to the west, balustrading, decorated with statues of dogs, frames views of Florence. Roses, peonies and annuals provide colour and scent.

Villa Garzoni ★

Collodi, 17km NE of Lucca off S435

Owner: Contessa Grazini Gardi

Opening times: Daily, May to Oct 8–sunset; Nov to Apr 8–13, 14.30–16.30; Nov to Mar 9–12

Admission charge: Yes

Commissioned by Romano Garzoni early in the 17th century, the Villa Garzoni was built over the foundations of a medieval fortress belonging to the city of Lucca. The famous gardens were constructed during the second half of the century and, although municipalized and sometimes shoddy, they are still in essence a grand example of baroque garden art. Far removed in spirit from the secluded, geometric Tuscan garden rooms of the 15th and 16th centuries, these gardens with their graceful curves and cascading water are designed to astonish and impress – great public gardens on a par with the Villa d'Este at Tivoli (q.v.) and the architectural fantasies of the 16th-

In the original 17th-century lemon garden at La Pietra, outside Florence, rocaille work decorates the walls.

century gardens in Rome.

The gardens lie slightly to the side of the villa, with their main axis on a steep central staircase surmounted by a series of water cascades. The splendid double-ramped steps connecting the lower terraces look over a sloping parterre enclosed in a hemisphere of clipped yew. On either side thick woodland presses close to the main axis, stone balustrading, steps and statues merging into the natural groves of cypress, bay and box which clothe the hillside.

From the grand entrance at the bottom of the hill, framed by stone pillars, the visitor mounts slowly to the dramatic water cascades above, where a statue of Fame blows a trumpet and reclining figures of the cities of Lucca and Florence flank the summit. Lower down the slope an open-air theatre with statues lining the back of the stage is merely a conceit, too small for practical use. In the centre of the dark boscage a labyrinth leads to a concealed grotto.

William Beckford visited Garzoni in 1819: 'Leaving our horses at the great gate of this magic enclosure, we passed through the spray of fountains and mounting an endless flight of steps, entered an alley of oranges, and gathered ripe fruit from the trees. While we were thus employed, the sun broke from the clouds, and lighted up the green of the vegetation; at the same time spangling the waters, which pour copiously down a succession of rocky terraces, and sprinkle the impending citron trees with perpetual dew' (from *Travels in Italy*).

Villa de' Gori

N of Siena on the road to Vicobello near the Monastero Osservanza

Owner: Signor Gianneschi

Opening times: By appointment, Via di Ventena, Siena 53100

The villa and garden date from the 1620s. Two tunnels of pleached ilex lead across the garden from the terrace. One, to the west, reaches a theatre with wings originally of clipped cypress but now replaced in bay; the auditorium is backed by a corridor of ilex. The south tunnel opens out to form a circular hedge which conceals a bird snare of lime.

ABOVE **At Garzoni, the garden axis lies to the side of the rococo-style villa: an exuberant 17th-century baroque staircase (LEFT) descends to a sloping parterre.**

Villa Medici Castello ★

S of Sesto Fiorentino, 6km NW of Florence
Owner: Italian State
Opening times: Daily, except Mon, summer 9–18.30; winter 9–16.30
Admission charge: Yes

Cosimo, the first Grand Duke of the Medicis, spent much of his childhood at the 15th-century villa of Castello. In 1538 he ordered Niccolò Tribolo to lay out the gardens, and Buontalenti completed the work after Tribolo's death in 1550. Allegorical features recorded the importance of the Medicis. The layout of this garden, and that of the famous Grotto of the Unicorn, are considered to be the most influential of all Italian garden designs.

With the main axis focused on the villa, the ground was originally divided into large rectangular terraced areas, with steps connecting one level to another and groves of trees surrounding statues and fountains. Castello was a garden rich in mythology and allegory, often taken – as in the Grotto of the Unicorn – from Ovid's *Metamorphosis*. Although much has been altered and statues moved or taken away (Giambologna's Venus is now at Petraia, q.v.), the general layout still remains. Great vases on the corners of box-edged flowerbeds contain ancient lemon trees. The grotto is in good condition and Ammanati's colossal statue of the Apennines still sits in the dark pool on the upper terrace. Many of the features seen today can be identified in G. Van Utens' lunette of 1598 in the Topographical Museum in Florence ('Firenze com'era') and there are other contemporary and later engravings. Above all, there are eye-witness accounts. Vasari visited in 1580 and gives a full description of the garden in his life of Tribolo. So did Michel de Montaigne, who wrote dismissively of the austere house but enthusiastically about the garden.

Villa Palmieri

Fiesole, 6km NE of Florence
Owner: Benelli family
Opening times: By appointment, Fiesole 50014, Firenze

In his introduction to the *Third Day of the Decameron* (*c.*1350), Boccaccio evokes the gardens of the Villa Palmieri, giving one of the earliest and most vivid descriptions of a medieval garden: 'In the middest of the garden was a square plot, after the resemblance of a meadow, flourishing with high grasse, hearbes, and plants, beside a diversities of flowres, even as if by the art of Painting they had beene there depicted.' Most of the garden seen today was laid out by the Earl of Crawford and Balcarres as a *giardino segreto* during the 1870s, when Queen Victoria used to visit Palmieri. Recently some box parterres have been reinstated. The lemon garden adjoining the south front dates only from the late 17th century.

Pésaro: Villa Imperiale ★

Colle S. Bartolò
Owner: Conte Guglielmo Castelbarco
Opening times: By appointment, summer only, one visit a week via Azienda di Soggiorno, Via Rossini 41, Pésaro 61100, tel. 0721 69341
Admission charge: Yes

Eleanora Gonzaga created the existing 16th-century villa from a Sforza castle for her military husband Francesco, Duke of Urbino, 'in compensation for sun and dust'. The lovely interior *trompe l'oeil* decoration depicts garden-like settings: caryatids spring from laurel trees; trellised jasmine combines with leafy garlands.

From the central courtyard – originally a garden room with espaliered fruit trees – spiral staircases lead up to terraces above the house: the first a lemon garden but now planted with flowers; the top terrace a large walled garden, now containing box-edged parterres but formerly planted with myrtles, bays, vines and espaliered citrus plants.

Pésaro: Villa Miralfiore

Via Miralfiore
Owner: Conte Castelbarco Albani
Opening times: By appointment, Via Miralfiore, Pésaro 61100

Well-maintained box-edged parterres of 16th-century design are laid out around the villa. A neo-classical colonnade separates the parterres from the *bosco*.

Pésaro: Villa Mosca-Caprile

Colle S. Bartolò, S16 to Rimini
Owner: Istituto Tecnico Agrario, Provincia di Pésaro
Opening times: Daily, July, Aug 15–19
Admission charge: Yes

The villa was built *c.*1640, and the garden extended in 1780. Villa Caprile's elaborate system of water tricks operated by valves in the pathways made it a popular place of amusement. A tilting tread in a stairway sprays water over the unwary visitor.

Underneath the staircase which leads from the villa to the first of the series of terraces is a delightful grotto with painted automatons. The charming parterres are edged in box and decorated with pots planted with lemons and flowers.

Villa della Petraia

Castello, S of Sesto Fiorentino, 6km NW of Florence
Owner: Italian State
Opening times: Daily, except Mon; Mar, Apr, Sept, Oct
9–17.30; May to Aug 9–18.30; Nov to Feb 9–16.30
Admission charge: Yes

One of the Medici villas, the original castle was acquired by Cardinal Ferdinando de' Medici, who commissioned Buontalenti to alter it from 1575. Niccolò Tribolo designed the terraced gardens, which have fine views over the Arno valley towards Florence. Like Castello (q.v.) nearby, and fourteen other Medici properties, La Petraia is depicted in a Giusto Utens' lunette of 1598 in the Topographical Museum ('Firenze com'era') in Florence. The lowest

Giambologna's allegorical figure of 'Winter' lurks in an ilex grove at Villa Medici Castello.

terrace has two symmetrical parterres with notable circular arbours incorporated in the design. These offered shade, and are renaissance features rarely found in any of the surviving gardens of the time. The second terrace has a long fish tank, and on the top terrace is Tribolo's lovely marble fountain of Venus, moved here from Castello.

Palazzo Piccolomini

Pienza, 50km SE of Siena, E of S2
Owner: Commune of Pienza
Opening times: Daily 10–12.30, 15–18, except Mon
Admission charge: Yes

Pienza, lying on a hilltop overlooking the Val d'Orcia to the south, was the birthplace of Aeneas Silvius Piccolomini, Pope Pius II. The Pope, scholar, humanist and author, employed Bernardo Rossellino from 1459–63 to build both a new renaissance village and the Palazzo Piccolomini with its spectacular views. From the shadowy inner courtyard of the palace it is possible to look straight across the small sunlit garden terrace outside, and then through clipped openings in a screen of box to the vast space over the valley beyond. The hanging garden provides an atmosphere of seclusion, the *giardino segreto* of the Renaissance; it has hardly altered in layout since the 15th century. Stone-edged raised beds enclose three sides; four central restored beds, laid out as a geometric parterre, are surrounded with double hedges of box.

Pisa: Botanic Garden of the University of Pisa

Via Luca Ghini, S of the Piazza del Duomo
Owner: University of Pisa
Opening times: Mon to Fri 8–12, 15–17
Admission charge: No

Founded in 1545, the Pisa botanic gardens are, by a margin of months, the oldest in Italy. The garden was moved twice before 1591 when Ferdinand I, Grand Duke of Tuscany, acquired the present site. In the 19th century more ground to the north was added.

The first director, appointed by Grand Duke Cosimo I in 1544, was the renowned botanist and teacher Luca Ghini. His successor, Andrea Cesal-

pino, became famous for his taxonomic system which influenced Tournefort, Ray and Linnaeus. Georges Santi, director from 1782–1814, was author of the first Tuscan Flora and his successor, Gaetano Savi, wrote the *Flora Pisani*, an interest reflected today in a bed reserved for local flora. Some trees, such as a large horse chestnut, were planted in the late 1500s. A magnificent cedar of Lebanon, fine ginkgos and tender camphor trees all thrive in the mild climate. Groves of rustling bamboo shelter many tender shrubs.

Villa Pratolino (Demidoff)

Pratolino, 12km N of Florence on S65
Owner: Italian State
Opening times: May to Sept, Fri, Sat and public hols 9–19
Admission charge: No

Today the Parco Demidoff (originally one of the Medici villas) is a richly wooded landscape which has narrowly missed suburban development. It was turned into an English landscape garden in 1819 to avoid the cost of upkeep. However, many of the 16th-

The Pope's palace at Pienza, the Palazzo Piccolomini, commands views over the hanging garden, now restored in renaissance style, and Monte Amiata in the distance.

century fountains and architectural details of the original (and unusually irregular) plan by Buontalenti can still be located, though the scale of the gardens and the extent of their decay has precluded any comprehensive restoration. Nevertheless, Pratolino's fascination remains, thanks to detailed and entertaining accounts given by visitors in the 16th and 17th centuries. Michel de Montaigne reported in 1580: 'They are erecting the body of a giant which is three cubits wide at the opening of an eye.' This, the colossal Appennino figure by Giambologna, is one of the few marvels to have survived. Montaigne also described the numerous trick fountains under the (now demolished) villa: 'There is not only music and harmony produced by the movement of water, but also the movement of a number of statues and doors of different actions.' Only the entrance to these grottoes survives, with another sculpture, of the river god Mugnone, by Giambologna.

Villa Reale (Pecci Blunt) ★

Marlia, 10km NE of Lucca, off S435 for Montecatini
Terme

Owner: Conte Pecci Blunt

Opening times: Daily, except Mon; *guided tours* summer
10, 11, 16, 17, 18; winter 10, 11, 14, 15, 16; Aug and Sept
Tues, Thurs, Sat only

Admission charge: Yes

The gardens at Marlia were laid out for the Orsetti
family in the second half of the 17th century as a
series of interlocking rooms hidden in woodland.
The villa and gardens were sold in 1806 to Napoleon's sister Elisa Bacciocchi, Princess of Lucca
and Piombino until 1814. She started to redesign the
garden in the then fashionable style of the *giardino
inglese*, but fortunately kept the basic structure of the
formal gardens. She also left the view open to the
south of the villa, but planted groves of trees and
shrubberies around the edges of the lawn.

**The garden facade and loggia of the Palazzo Piccolo-
mini at Pienza, built by Rossellino in the 15th
century for Pope Pius II.**

Today the two distinct garden styles still exist at
Marlia. Trees have grown to frame the views of
Monte Pisano to the south, and lawn still sweeps up
to the main facade of the villa. To the east ilex and
yew hedges enclose garden compartments which are
truly baroque in style. A wide pool is surrounded by a
sweeping balustrade where ornamental pots filled
with colourful flowers are reflected in the shimmer-
ing water. A vast *nymphaeum* to the north is attributed to the 17th/18th-century architect Filippo
Juvarra. A niche of tufa and different coloured stones
is the setting for a statue of Leda and the swan. A
lemon garden stretches to the south and leads to a
further small formal garden where low hedges of
silvery santolina enclose beds of coloured gravels. A
vista to the east reveals a fountain and pool, beyond
which a green theatre, complete with terracotta
figures of Columbine, Harlequin and Pulcinella from
the *Commedia dell' Arte*, has wings of clipped yew and
footlights in box. Here, in the early 1800s, the
princess listened to Racine's *Phèdre*.

At the bottom of the garden, an ornate 16th-
century pavilion built round a central *cortile*, the
Bishop's Villa, was incorporated into the property
during Elisa Bacciocchi's time. Here too is a grotto,
dedicated to Pan and decorated with rich pebblework
arabesques and scrolls. This is the oldest *nymphaeum*
in the Lucca district and was constructed 1570–80,
just in time for a visit from Michel de Montaigne.
The famous French essayist saw many of the Luc-
chese villas during 1580–81 when he was taking the
waters near Bagni di Lucca.

**Giambologna's famous figure of the Apennines,
sculpted towards the end of the 16th century, can still
be seen at the Villa Pratolino (Demidoff).**

La Rocca

Soragna, 30km NW of Parma; 6km N of S9 or A1 at Fidenza
Owner: Meli-Lupi family
Opening times: Daily, summer 9–12, 15–19; winter 9–12, 14–17
Admission charge: Yes

The Farnese family transformed a medieval fortress into a villa in the early 18th century. The romantic wooded park with fine trees, a lake and wild flowers was opened up by the Cremona architect Luigi Voghera for Prince Casimir Meli-Lupi in the middle of the 19th century. Statues of classical gods lurk in the vegetation and the villa is reflected in the still waters of a lake.

The courtyard of the 16th-century Bishop's Villa in the grounds of the Villa Reale at Marlia. This building and a grotto were visited by Montaigne in the 1580s.

Siena: Villa Vicobello ★

12, Via Vicobello, just outside the city walls N of Siena
Owner: Marchesa Chigi-Bonelli
Opening times: By appointment, Via Vicobello 12, Siena 53100
Admission charge: No

Lying on the summit of a narrow ridge from which the ground falls away steeply on either side is the villa designed for the Chigi family, reputedly by Baldassare Peruzzi. The Chigis, bankers of Siena and Rome, were as important in 15th- and 16th-century Siena as the Medicis were in Florence at the same period. Their crest (six money bags) appears clipped in box on the lawn and as architectural features. A walled lemon garden lies to the south of the villa, sheltered on the north by lemon houses and with a decorative terminal niche on an axis with the entrance gate and box-edged flowerbeds. To the west of the house, which sits on a broad expanse of open lawn, the ground descends by terraces linked by

A fountain pool at the Villa Reale.

steep steps. Today a huge ginkgo dominates the lowest terrace; a clock in santolina is set at ten to two. Acers, azaleas and Mexican orchids demonstrate a continuing gardening interest.

Villa Sorra ★

Castelfranco, 13km SE of Modena, via S9
Owner: Commune of Castelfranco
Opening times: May to Oct, Sat pm and Sun
Admission charge: No

The 18th-century villa, in the fertile valley of the River Po, lies at the centre of a system of tree-lined *allées*, some several kilometres long, which converge from the surrounding farmland; a French-style *cavallerizza* (riding school) is also connected to nearby villages by three avenues of poplars. A supreme example of the integration of garden with farmland and of formal with informal landscape styles, the whole 'park' can be viewed from the terraces and stairways below the villa.

After 1827 the garden behind the villa was landscaped in romantic style. Still containing the remnants of an earlier French-style parterre, the new park layout by Giovanni de' Brignoli is today one of Italy's most important 19th-century gardens. Bordered by a canal that flows into a lake and thence emerges as a stream, it contains various romantic features (now in need of repair), including a neo-gothic tower and orangery, a cave, a Swiss chalet and various wooden bridges. Dense woodlands are traversed by winding pathways which reveal further views.

I Tatti

26 Via Vincigliata, Settignano, 8km NE of Florence
Owner: University of Harvard (Centre for Renaissance Studies)
Opening times: By appointment, Via Vincigliata 26, Settignano 50100, Firenze, Tues or Thurs pm

The villa, famous as the home of the art historian Bernard Berenson from 1905–59, dates from the 16th century and the original lemon garden from that period survives. The rest of the garden was created by Cecil Pinsent and Geoffrey Scott 1905–15.

Designed in the spirit of the Renaissance with a

The lemon garden at Villa Vicobello was laid out for the Chigis, bankers of Siena and Rome, in the early 16th century. The villa and terraced gardens are attributed to Baldasarre Peruzzi.

central axis, terraces with soaring cypresses and box hedging clipped in geometric shapes descend from the villa to the woods below.

Villa Torrigiani (Santini) ★

Camigliano, 14km NE of Lucca, off S435 to Montecatini Terme
Owner: Contessa Colonna Torrigiani
Opening times: Daily, Easter to Oct 9–12, 15–18, except Thurs
Admission charge: Yes

Sir Harold Acton, describing the villas near Lucca in his *Tuscan Villas*, writes: 'Even the most flamboyant, such as ... Villa Torrigiani at Camigliano, have a firm 16th-century bone structure under a baroque veneer. ... Most of the fine formal gardens, of which a few tantalizing plans survive, were swallowed up by the growing preference for landscape gardens in the so-called English style, but the general landscape is so carefully terraced and cultivated, the vegetation so exuberantly fertile, that one scarcely misses the vanished parterres and fountains.'

The Villa Torrigiani, originally the Villa Santini, lies in the foothills of the Apennines to the east of Lucca, facing south across the valley to Monte Pisano. The approach is a magnificent 750m avenue of mature cypresses (now diseased) aligned directly on grand entrance gates and the imposing baroque south front of the villa, backed by large ilex trees and the mountains to the north. By the ornamental gate piers the avenue broadens into a courtyard. The house itself is ornate – a mannerist exterior imposed on a simple 16th-century villa.

The glory of Torrigiani is the perfectly preserved small sunken garden which dates from the mid 17th century. This intimate *giardino segreto* is reached from its north side by double flights of balustraded stairs. The stairway covers and contains a cool grotto and subterranean passageway, the latter concealing the taps which control the elaborate water tricks (still in working order). At the south end of the garden is an octagonal *nymphaeum* with a curving tufa facade and adorned with intricate shell patterns and mosaic

pebblework. Marble statues personifying the winds
stand in niches. At every step the unwary can be
soaked, the sprays so arranged as to capture and
imprison a fleeing victim.

The 17th-century garden plan shows *parterres de*
broderie in the French style, laid out by the Santini
family both in front of and behind the villa. In the
19th century all traces of these were removed, but the
central *bassin* to the south remains. Now tall trees and
wild orchids in the grass have their own charm.

Rome and Environs

Palazzo Farnese (Caprarola) ★

Caprarola, 18km SE of Viterbo off the Via Cimina
Owner: Italian State
Opening times: Daily 9–16, except Mon
Admission charge: Yes

The original fortress of Caprarola was commissioned by Cardinal Alessandro Farnese (later Pope Paul III), and designed by Antonio da Sangallo and Baldassare Peruzzi. From 1550 G. B. da Vignola, scholar and artist, transformed it into a magnificent country palace for his nephew, Cardinal Alessandro Farnese II, making ingenious use of the pentagonal shape of the fortress.

The walled park-like garden was designed in two parts, separated by plantations of trees. Bridges across the fosse connect the palace to the rectangular parterre gardens aligned on the two southerly faces of the pentagon. The garden to the south-west of the villa has had its original quarterings replanted in box; on the south-east camellias flower in spring and wild orchids seed in grass. From here, a path goes uphill through huge ilexes, firs, pines, chestnuts and beeches to emerge suddenly in a grassy glade surrounded by larches and with a circular pool and fountain. A water stairway lined with dolphins, more fountains and cascades leads up to the loggia'd front of Vignola's 1560 *casino*. Behind it, reached by dolphin staircases, are balustraded terraces, charming pebble mosaics and statuary.

The present arrangement of the rest of the garden is early 17th century; rustic grottoes were added by Girolamo Rainaldi in 1620, as was the parterre lined with lively herms and caryatids.

Frascati: Villa Aldobrandini ★

Centre of village, 22km SE of Rome, on S215
Owner: Principe Aldobrandini
Opening times: Weekdays 9–13; tickets from Azienda di Soggiorno, Piazza Marconi 1, Frascati
Admission charge: No

In 1598 Pope Clement VII gave the Contugi family villa to his nephew, Cardinal Pietro Aldobrandini. The most impressive of all the Frascati villas, overlooking the main square, it was remodelled by Giacomo della Porta, Carlo Maderno and subsequently Domenico Fontana. On the steep slope behind the villa is a spectacular water theatre (designed by della Porta, Maderno and Orazio Olivieri), which amazed and entertained visitors in the 17th and 18th centuries. Five niches contain water effects and mythological figures, including an impressive Atlas holding the world. On either side of the villa are magnificent plane trees; there is also a modern parterre with hydrangeas and symbols from the Aldobrandini coat of arms depicted in box.

In 1670 John Evelyn found the villa 'one of the most delicious places I ever beheld for its situation, elegance, plentiful water, groves, ascents, and prospects'. According to Evelyn, there were 'hydraulic organs and all sorts of singing birds, moving and chirping by the force of water, with several other pageants and surprising inventions.' There was a monster (Polyphemus) who made a 'terrible roaring noise' with his horn, but 'above all, the representation of a storm is most natural, with such fury of rain, wind and thunder as one could imagine oneself in some extreme tempest.'

On the hillside above, the atmosphere of the garden changes dramatically. Beyond the charming garlanded Pillars of Hercules is an area thickly wooded with oak and chestnut. A series of dramatic cascades confirms the axial design of the garden and leads to the summit of the hill, with distant views of the Roman *campagna* and the villa below.

Frascati: Villa Falconieri (La Rufina)

22km SE of Rome, on S215
Owner: Centro Europeo Educazione
Opening times: By appointment, Frascati 00044, Roma

The villa was built for Cardinal Ruffino in the mid 16th century. The Falconieri family acquired it in the 1660s and enlarged it with designs by Borromini. The rich interior decoration includes a beautiful garden salon (*la Stanza della Primavera*) with *trompe l'oeil* foliage painted by G. F. Grimaldi. A small *giardino segreto* next to the palace probably dates from the 17th century; entrance piers with lions are attributed to Francesco Borromini. Opposite, another lion gateway leads to a little lake surrounded by lofty cypress trees. This was part of the Falconieri modifications made in the early 18th century.

Frascati: Villa Torlonia
Viale Vittorio Veneto, 22km SE of Rome on S215
Owner: Commune of Frascati
Opening times: At all times
Admission charge: No

Only fountains, the splendid water theatre with its 22 niches, and the lovely cascade above it remain of the 17th-century layout in what is now the public garden in the centre of Frascati. Designed for the Borghese family, the garden was largely created from 1623 by the architect Carlo Maderno. The ramps and staircases leading to the garden were added for the Conti family in the late 17th century.

Villa Lante ★
Bagnaia, 3km E of Viterbo
Owner: Italian State
Opening times: Daily 9–sunset, except Mon
Admission charge: Yes

The forested site in the Cimini hills belonged originally to the city of Viterbo. In 1566 a bishop of Viterbo, Cardinal Gambara, commissioned G. B. da Vignola to build him a villa here as a summer retreat. At the Villa Lante (named after subsequent owners) the garden and its relation to the surrounding countryside is all important; the twin *palazzine* that make up the villa are simple adjuncts to the garden design.

Vignola's garden falls into two parts: a wooded park and a formal garden where water provides the central focus. A stream emerging from a grotto at the top of the garden descends via a series of enchanting pools, fountains and stairways, and sometimes hidden underground, to the calm pool in the centre of the parterres below the villa.

The visitor enters through the park, to be faced immediately by Giambologna's striking Pegasus statue in its pool. An earlier bishop built a hunting box in the park, which still exists, and there are remains of fountains, pergolas and a labyrinth,

though the park is now in disrepair. Originally, it was possible to walk through it to the top of the formal garden and descend from level to level, but today Vignola's creation is first seen from the bottom. Here the parterre garden, and the pool with its charming *isolotto* and fountain, are best seen from the terrace above. The two *palazzine* framing the view were built at different times: the Palazzina Gambara in *c.*1578 (frescoes show the Villa Lante and Caprarola) and the Palazzina Montalto in 1612. Giacomo del Duca continued work on the villa after Vignola's death in 1573, and further alterations and additions to the garden were made after 1612, when Cardinal Montalto had taken over the villa.

Tall trees and box hedges close in on fountains, steps, sculpture, a long stone table with a water channel down the centre and a ravishing cascade fed from the mouth of a crayfish, or *gambero* (a play on the cardinal's name). Montaigne described it in 1580 as: 'one of the most richly ornamented places I ever saw. It is so well provided with fountains that it surpasses Pratolino and Tivoli.'

Villa Muti
On the road to Grottaferrata from Frascati
Owner: Società Immobiliare
Opening times: By appointment, Frascati 00044, Roma

Cardinal Arrigoni bought the villa in 1595, and the garden terrace on a level with the house dates from this period. The lower and upper terraces were added in the 17th century. The Muti family who owned the villa in the mid 17th century created the Italian-style garden with box hedges on the lower terrace, and in spite of anglicization in the 1860s the garden retains its original layout and remains an important example of 17th-century garden design. Woodland areas, a grand avenue and the parterre of arabesque patterns are all impressive.

OVERLEAF **The semi-circular 17th-century *nymphaeum* at the Villa Aldobrandini at Frascati. The water theatre, originally decorated by a statue in each niche, was designed by Carlo Maderno, Giacomo della Porta and Orazio Olivieri.**

PREVIOUS PAGE: ABOVE LEFT **Looking up the water cascades at the Villa Lante towards the grotto shaded by ancient plane trees.**

ABOVE RIGHT **Shallow steps at the Palazzo Farnese at Caprarola lead up to the *casino* built by Vignola and water cascades between carved stone dolphins.**

BELOW **The gardens at Ninfa were made among the ruins of a deserted village. Profuse English-style planting with climbers curtaining old walls creates a romantic atmosphere.**

Giardino Ninfa ★ ✲

17km NNE of Latina, 70km SE of Rome, on the road to Norma
Owner: Fondazione Roffredo Caetani
Opening times: Apr to Oct, 1st Sat in the month 9–12, 14.30–18 (guided tours)
Admission charge: Yes

The gardens are laid out in the ruins of the small town of Ninfa, named after a mythical nymph whose tears shed for a lost lover are said to have become the cool stream which runs through its centre. Sacked and burnt in 1382 and beset by malaria, Ninfa was abandoned by its inhabitants, who settled in the higher villages of Norma and Sermoneta. After the mosquito hazard was removed by the draining of the Pontine marshes in 1922, the Duchess of Sermoneta and her son Prince Caetani (Ninfa was acquired by the Caetani family in 1297) began to lay out a romantic garden among the ruins and by the river.

At least 10,000 plants were collected from all over the world and were established in the favourable microclimate and fertile soil watered by the sparkling River Ninfa. Planting has been continued ever since. Today magnolias, dogwoods and other exotics have reached maturity; roses and clematis twine on crumbling stonework and climb tall cypress trees. On the river banks giant gunnera and arum lilies give a tropical atmosphere, while drifts of flowers and bulbs have spread on the grassy slopes.

Villa Orsini (Sacro Bosco) ★

Bomarzo, 16km NE of Viterbo, N of S204
Owner: Sig. Giovanni Bettini
Opening times: Daily 8–17
Admission charge: Yes

The *castello* of Bomarzo overlooks the famous woodland sculpture garden in the valley below, where colossal human and animal grotesques, carved from solid rock and representing mythological creatures of many different centuries and traditions, lie hidden among the trees.

The garden has lent itself to many interpretations. Its creator was Vicino Orsini, who retired from military campaigning to Bomarzo in 1567. Orsini had literary friends who may have influenced the design, and G. B. da Vignola may have contributed. Certainly he designed the Temple of Eternity, as a memorial to the Duke of Orsini's wife Julia, at the top of the garden, with its mixture of classical, renaissance and Etruscan features.

Most of the garden is thickly wooded with constantly changing levels. The overall plan is completely irregular and, apart from some fountains, the emphasis is on the sculptural and architectural.

Rome: Villa Borghese and Pincio Gardens

N of city centre
Owner: Italian State
Opening times: 7–sunset
Admission charge: No

The gardens of the *Villa Borghese* are now a public park. The boundaries, with a circumference of 6km, have remained unchanged since the early 17th century when the villa was designed for entertaining and to house Cardinal Camilio Borghese's art collection and library. At the time, it presented a new concept of villa and garden design in a suburban situation where both house and surrounding gardens were of equal importance. Moreover, as a plaque of 1620 inviting access makes clear, the vast grounds have always been open to the public. Today, inside this huge area, gardens in different styles date from many periods.

The first gardens clustered round the villa were designed by Girolamo Rainaldi; in the early 17th century these were expanded by Domenico Savino, Giovanni Fontana designed the waterworks, and there are sculptures and fountains by Bernini. A *viale* bordered by box-hedged squares filled with trees connects the villa with the Porta Pinciano. Elaborate 17th-century domed aviaries by Luigi Vanvitelli still exist (but in bad repair) near the villa.

John Evelyn visited in 1644 and exclaimed at the

abundance of 'all sorts of delicious fruits and exotic simples ... adjoining to it a vivarium for ostriches, peacocks, swans, cranes, etc and diverse strange beasts, deers and hares'. Falda's views in *Ville e Giardini di Roma* (1683) show the gardens at this time. Jacob Moore, a Scottish designer, laid out part of the park in an English style at the end of the 18th century. In 1885 Prince Marcantonio Borghese decided to sell the park and villa; it was finally purchased by the city in 1902, but not before some of the balustrading had found its way to the gardens of Cliveden in England.

The *Pincio Gardens* were laid out (1809–14) by Giuseppe Valadier on a site noted for its gardens in ancient Rome. They include a series of avenues, a fascinating water clock, and the Fountain of Moses. According to Thackeray's daughter Annie Ritchie, who came here in the late 19th century, the splendid views over the city should be seen in the evening with 'a fashionable halo of sunset and pink parasols'.

Rome: Botanic Garden of Rome University ❀
Entrance 24 Via Corsini
Owner: Rome University
Opening times: Weekdays, hols 9–12
Admission charge: Yes

The botanic gardens, founded by the university in 1660, only moved to the present site towards the end of the 19th century. The earliest botanic gardens in Rome were established in the 13th century but these, which also moved their location from near the Vatican to other sites, were private gardens belonging to the popes. The gardens today are known for a fine collection of palms, including *Washingtonia* and *Phoenix* specimens, tender sun-loving dasylirions, and a woodland section on the steep slopes of the Janiculum, with many interesting trees such as *Araucaria bidwillii*, celtis and zelkovas. Glasshouses contain tropical plants and orchids. There is a modern garden of 'simples' laid out in raised beds.

Rome: Villa Celimontana (Mattei)
On Monte Celio
Owner: Commune of Rome
Opening times: Daily 8–sunset
Admission charge: No

Ciriaco Mattei's *casino* was built by Giacomo del Duca from 1581–6. The garden then consisted of a series of labyrinths, box-patterned beds and *boschetti*, once inhabited by animal statues. In the early 19th century the garden was transformed into a landscape-style park, and today the rich vegetation of conifers, palms and lime trees make it a welcome retreat from the city. Fragments of the 16th-century plan survive in the theatre and obelisk.

Rome: Villa Doria Pamphili
Via S. Pancrazio, SW of city centre; entrance beyond Porta San Pancrazio
Owner: Commune of Rome
Opening times: Daily, sunrise–sunset
Admission charge: No

Now a large public park on the south-west outskirts of the city beyond the Janiculum hill, the present villa was built in the 17th century for the powerful Donna Olympia Maidalchini by her admirer Camillo Pamphili. It is on the site of a garden (a graveyard of antique sculptures) belonging to Galba, a Roman governor in Andalusia. Alessandro Algardi was employed on both house and *giardino segreto* in 1644, and some fountains also date from this period. Thirty years later the last (female) Pamphili married a Doria and made further alterations to the garden. Pamphili lily and dove motifs and Doria eagles can still be seen in the box parterres which Corot painted in the mid 19th century. The *exedra* and a *nymphaeum* were also added in the 17th century. Part of the garden was landscaped in the 18th century, with cascades and fountains; the lake created at that time still looks as it did when De Camps painted it in 1839 (the painting hangs in the Wallace Collection in London). The rest of the vast garden was anglicized in the 19th century.

Rome: Horti Farnesiana
Approached through the Forum off the Via di San Gregorio, or from the Via del Fori Imperiali
Owner: Italian State
Opening times: Daily, except Tues, Jun to Sept 9–19; Oct to March 9–17
Admission charge: Yes

Situated on the Palatine Hill above the classical excavations, the gardens provide wonderful views over the Forum and the whole city of Rome. The original layout, with twin aviaries and triple terraces hanging over the Forum, was designed 1534–9 by G. B. da Vignola for Pope Paul III on the site of classical ruins from the time of the Emperors Tiberius and Domitian. The Pope was a knowledgeable botanist and a collection of rare plants was developed here; Tobia Aldini's *Exactissima descriptio rariorum quarundum plantarum, quae continentur Romae in Horto Farnesiano*, published in 1625, was an important landmark in our knowledge of plants known and grown in renaissance Rome. Today, although the rare plants have gone and little remains of the original layout, the site is still well worth a visit for the magnificent views over the city and for its historic associations. The aviaries above steep stairs descending to a dripping fountain in a niche below still survive, and the upper gardens are attractively laid out. Here pines, cypresses, evergreen oaks and palm trees shade areas hedged with box, a maze and a small water garden.

Rome: Villa Farnesina

Via della Lungara at the foot of the Janiculum hill, in Trastévere
Owner: Italian State
Opening times: Weekdays 9–13
Admission charge: Yes

The villa was built by Baldassare Peruzzi at the beginning of the 16th century as a suburban residence for the Sienese banker Agostino Chigi. In 1579 Cardinal Alessandro Farnese acquired it. Open-air banquets were given in a separate dining portico which at that time overlooked the Tiber, and the Pope visited by barge. The loggia of the villa is decorated with frescoes (some by Raphael); painted garlands show fruit and flowers which were grown in the 16th century. On the upper floor frescoes by Peruzzi show *trompe l'oeil* views of Rome. The garden was conceived in three parts and is still laid out with large box-hedged areas and a bay arbour. The section on the river is now occupied by the Lungotévere della Farnesina.

Rome: Villa Giulia (Villa di Papa Giulio) ★

On NW fringe of Villa Borghese park
Owner: Italian State
Opening times: Weekdays 9–14, except Mon; Sun and hols 9–13
Admission charge: Yes

The villa, built 1551–3 for Pope Julius III, originally stood in thick woods which swept down to the east bank of the Tiber. Although this setting has gone and only the formal courtyard and gardens at the back of the villa (now the beautifully laid out Etruscan Museum) still exist, the gardens are breathtakingly beautiful. G. B. da Vignola (G. Vasari and B. Ammanati also worked here) designed the semicircular loggia in the square courtyard at the back of the villa, from which curving balustraded steps lead down to a sunken *nymphaeum* and fountain. A sculptured wall, now with three rectangular openings in place of the original one, separates the two levels. At the bottom of the garden, cool rustic grottoes that once contained statues of divinities provided shady retreats from the summer heat. Today much of the rich marble and stucco decoration and statuary has gone, but the elegant proportions are unaltered. Gardens beyond and at the side of the courtyard are laid out as simple renaissance-style box-edged patterns. Bay trees, oleanders and roses grow as they would have in the 16th century, but modern plantings of Japanese lily-turf under the pine trees keep the garden fresh and green.

Rome: Villa Madama

Monte Mario, NW of city centre, near Olympic stadium
Owner: Italian State
Opening times: By appointment from the villa, tel. 06 36911
Admission charge: Yes

The Villa Madama, the first of the Roman suburban villas, was designed by Raphael from 1510 on the Monte Mario just north of the Vatican. It was

The Fountain of Neptune. Water is a dominant theme in the 16th-century gardens at the Villa d'Este at Tivoli.

completed by Antonio da Sangallo after Raphael's death, but partially destroyed in the Sack of Rome in 1527. Terraced gardens overlooking the Tiber and the city still contain the famous elephant statue designed by Giovanni da Udine and the doorway flanked by two colossal sculpted figures by Baccio Bandinelli.

Rome: Villa Medici ★

On the Pincian hill at the top of the Spanish Steps
Owner: French Academy
Opening times: Wed 9–11; about 4 guided tours (NB at time of writing, visits suspended for security reasons)
Admission charge: Yes

The villa, on an imposing site on the Pincian hill, was modified by Bartolomeo Ammanati for Cardinal Ferdinando de' Medici after 1576. The facade is richly decorated with bas-relief sculpture depicting myth-ological themes. The basic 16th-century garden layout survives, although now substantial ilex, bay and box hedges give it a more wooded appearance than it would originally have had. Sixteen beds north of the villa, their centres planted with fruit trees, no longer exist, but the area immediately in front of the facade has always been a low-growing parterre. The Mount (Parnassus), with cypress trees planted along a spiral walk to its summit, was built with earth moved from the Porta Pinciana. There are views to the city from the top. Velasquez painted at the villa in 1649–50, portraying the reclining figure of Ariadne in the loggia which overlooks the Villa Borghese. Henry James visited in January 1873 and described it as 'perhaps . . . the most enchanting place in Rome . . . with a long mossy staircase climbing up to the Belvedere, rising suddenly out of the leafy dusk.'

Rome: Giardini del Quirinale

City centre
Owner: Italian State
Opening times: By appointment from Direttore dei Giardini del Quirinale, tel. 06 4699 2526. (Strict security measures as the palace is the residence of the President of the Italian Republic)

The villa gardens were first laid out for Cardinal Ippolito d'Este (*see* Villa d'Este, Tivoli) before 1550 by Ottavio Mascherino. By 1574 the palace was occupied by Pope Gregory XIII and from that date until it became royal property in 1870 it was the summer city residence of the popes (22 of them died here in spite of the salubrious breezes). There are splendid views of Rome from the north-west and western boundaries of the garden. Labyrinths shaded by interlacing branches, and exotic fruits such as citrus and pomegranates covering the walls, were some of the features which made it one of Rome's most exciting gardens. Today, where in the 16th century there were low box-edged parterres, tall hedges of clipped ilex, yew, cypress and bay divide the garden into secret compartments overlooked by palm trees. An ancient ilex is said to have been planted in the cardinal's time. Pieces of statuary lie about and in the courtyard below the palazzo are the crumbling remains of a great water organ.

Rome: Vatican Gardens ★

Vatican City
Owner: Vatican State
Opening times: Tues, Thurs, Sat 10, Wed 14.30 (guided tours); tickets from Ufficio Pellegrini, Piazza San Pietro beside St Peter's
Admission charge: Yes

The Vatican is a city of gardens stretching up the hillside behind the dome of St Peter's. Although its present layout much resembles G. B. Falda's 17th-century engraving, most of the garden features are modern. These include well-maintained parterres, interesting specimen trees, a rock garden, dense shady woodland and, on the upper slopes, a charming garden where the evergreen scented climber, *Trachelospermum jasminoides*, is trained into arches above the pathways.

The beautiful *casino* of Pope Pius IV, the *Villa Pia*, is the most interesting historic feature in the gardens. Designed by Pirro Ligorio in the 1560s, after he had completed the Villa d'Este at Tivoli (q.v.), it was intended as a place of rest for the pope; the design for the oval courtyard decorated with sculptures and a fountain was inspired by the classical ruins of the Temple of Praeneste at Palestrina.

The famous *Belvedere Garden*, designed by Donato Bramante in the first years of the 16th century, no longer exists; the site of the Belvedere's courtyard, loggias (never in fact fully completed) and

ITALY

great terraces is today occupied by the Vatican museums and library. For its time, the garden layout was revolutionary; the central perspective axis and curving terraces linked by ramps and stairways marked a major departure from the earlier renaissance garden with its enclosed but separate garden rooms laid out round the house. Antique sculptures which once adorned these gardens, in particular the Apollo Belvedere and the Laocoön, are now in the Vatican Museum.

Villa Ruspoli

Vignanello, 17km SE of Viterbo
Owner: Principe Alessandro Ruspoli
Opening times: By appointment with Amministrazione Ruspoli, Vignanello 01039, Viterbo
Admission charge: No

Originally a fortified castle, Ruspoli was transformed into a domestic villa for the Orsini family in 1574. Box parterres, the finest remaining in Italy, were laid out both in geometric patterns and to trace the initials of Octavia Orsini and her sons, Sforza and Galeazzo, in the early 17th century. These level areas are sheltered by encircling ilex woods.

Tivoli: Villa Adriana (Hadrian's Villa) ★

30km E of Rome on S5
Owner: Italian State
Opening times: Daily 9–sunset, except Mon
Admission charge: Yes

The complex of buildings that made up Hadrian's Villa (AD 118–38) was once rich in architectural and sculptural decoration. Much has been removed – particularly during the Renaissance when artefacts were used for garden ornaments. However, although the garden areas have disappeared, it is still possible to see how water was used to enliven architecture, and to gain some idea of the Roman influence on renaissance style.

The first major feature is the Pecile, a massive porticoed public building surrounding a rectangular pool. Nearby are substantial remains of the Marine Theatre, a circular canal surrounding a tiny villa on an island. The villa had its own garden and could be completely cut off from the 'mainland' by swinging away wooden bridges which spanned the canal. The Canopus, further off, is a large canal once surrounded by a colonnade and sculpture. An apse-like portico at one end was probably a dining area, and a cooling veil of water cascaded across the open end of the building.

Tivoli: Villa d'Este ★

Centre of town, 30km E of Rome on S5
Owner: Italian State
Opening times: Daily 9–sunset, except Mon; *fountains from 10 and 14*
Admission charge: Yes

This garden, renowned for its use of water, which is brought through tunnelled aqueducts from the River Aniene, was created for Cardinal Ippolito d'Este after 1559 by the architect and archaeologist Pirro Ligorio. His original scheme laid out on the steep slope below the villa still survives. Although now romantically overgrown with tall pines, evergreen oaks, cedars and bay, the main central axis running down the slope, and a series of cross axes, all linked by stairways or more gently descending ramps, still reveal views of the magnificent fountains and other architectural features which were already in place when the essayist Michel de Montaigne visited in

The Rometta at the Villa d'Este, where the city of Rome and the cascades of Tivoli are represented in miniature. In the water (the 'River Tiber'), a stone boat and obelisk represent the Church of Rome.

1581. They were described in some detail by John Evelyn in 1645, who noted a 'noble aviary, the birds artificial, and singing till an owl appears, on which they suddenly change their note'. Almost a century later the French historian Charles de Brosses was impressed by the Ovata Fountain but thought the upkeep poor.

In planning the garden, Ligorio derived inspiration from classical ruins, but a principal theme compared the D'Este family's monumental task of harnessing water with the cleansing of the Augean stables by Hercules. A vast statue of the legendary Greek hero stood originally in a niche enclosed by curving staircases on the main axis, where it would have been immediately visible to people coming into the garden from the bottom, as was intended. From the statue, there was a choice of routes to the topmost terrace; one pathway led to the Grotto of Diana symbolizing platonic chaste love, another path led towards the Grotto of Venus and carnal love. Later, Diana was replaced by Bacchus, and the Dragon Fountain now marks the place where Hercules stood.

Today, visitors first see the garden, now impeccably kept, from the upper terrace; from here the valley seems to be full of sparkling spray and the senses are confused by the continual sound of falling water. Three tranquil fishponds at the base of a steep slope at the bottom of the garden seem a distant haven, only to be reached by the intrepid mountaineer. But in fact the descent is easy, with steps and ramps at oblique angles bisecting the main cross paths leading from fountains at one side of the garden to the more architectural features at the other. Past the Grotto of Venus and the Ovata Fountain, framed by ancient plane trees, one can walk the length of the Path of One Hundred Fountains to the remains of the miniature Rometta, constructed by Curzio Maccarone in 1568 to represent Rome and its seven hills and washed at its base by the river 'Tiber'. The Fountain of the Owl, on a lower level, has had its stucco relief figures and mosaics restored, but is now without its automated birds. A further descent, past the Dragon Fountain, reaches the lowest level and the Organ Fountain, the most famous of all the features of the Villa d'Este. Based on hydraulic theories first outlined in c.AD 100 by Hero of Alexandria, and designed by Bernini, it was completed, with its cascades, in 1661. In the flatter area towards the lower entrance gate, where orchards and covered *berceaux* once made formal patterns, soaring cypresses form a central rondel. Both Hubert Robert and Jean-Honoré Fragonard painted the garden while they were pupils at the French Academy in the Villa Medici on the Pincio in Rome (q.v.) in 1760. Perhaps their views, taken when the garden was in romantic decline, best capture its spirit.

Campania

Caserta: Palazzo Reale ★

Owner: Italian State
Opening times: Daily 9–1 hour before sunset, except Mon and public hols
Admission charge: Yes

Caserta was planned as the capital of the Kingdom of the Two Sicilies. The designs by Luigi Vanvitelli in 1752 for Charles III, the Spanish king, were for a palace and gardens to rival Versailles. Vanvitelli completed the plans after the king's death in 1773 for Ferdinand, Charles's son. He replaced a scheme for a belvedere and cascade with a more rustic waterfall falling over massive blocks of stone into the fountains of Diana and Actaeon (1769). In the gardens below the palace, green lawns surrounded by ilex and camphor trees have replaced the original *parterre de broderie*. Fountains and canals stretch for 3km to the foot of the vast 78m cascade, fed from Monte Taburno 50km away, which provides the water supply. The informal English garden, laid out for King Ferdinand's Austrian queen, Maria Caroline, is reached from the Aeolus fountain where Juno confronts Aeolus. It was laid out in the 1780s by John Andrew Graefer, who was recommended by the British botanist and explorer Joseph Banks through Sir William Hamilton, British minister to King

At the Villa La Mortella on the island of Ischia, tender exotics flourish in the mild climate.

Ferdinand's court. Graefer, probably a German but already working in England, was a follower of William Kent; the garden, with winding paths, classical temples and ruins, is being restored. A *Camellia japonica* planted in 1782 still survives.

Ischia: La Mortella ★

Above Forio; take Aliscato ferry from Mergellina to Ischia
Owner: Lady Walton
Opening times: By appointment, Forio 80075, Ischia, Napoli
Admission charge: Yes

Russell Page designed this modern valley garden for Sir William and Lady Walton in successive stages. During the 1950s, while the villa was being built into the cliff, retaining walls were constructed for the garden layout. It was originally intended as a dry garden, making use of the natural boulders of the terrain, but later the Waltons, with Russell Page's aid, added pools, rivulets and fountains which splash and sparkle in the sunlight. A large collection of trees includes not only Mediterranean natives but many tender plants which thrive in the warm climate. On the cliff above the villa there is a commemorative plaque to Sir William Walton, with a tribute to Russell Page.

Naples: Monastero Santa Chiara

Via Santa Chiara
Owner: Monastero Santa Chiara
Opening times: Daily
Admission charge: No

A pergola of *c*.1740 in the cloisters of the convent of Santa Chiara has pillars made of decorative majolica tiles depicting bunches of flowers and fruit.

Pompeii: Casa Vettii

Owner: Italian State
Opening times: Daily 9–1 hour before sunset
Admission charge: Yes

The House of the Vettii is the best known of the Pompeian houses. It belonged to two wealthy merchants, and has many of its wall paintings preserved. The restored peristyle garden is typical of small Roman courtyard gardens, though, as well as the jets in the middle, there were originally fountain statues against the columns of the portico, which directed water into marble basins in the water channels at the edge of the garden. Several gardens of this type, often with open summer dining porticoes, have been restored in Pompeii as a result of archaeological research and with help from Pompeian paintings. The fresco decorations of Livia's garden at Prima Porta in Rome (now in the Museo delle Terme, Rome) show the type of plants grown. These included shrubs such as myrtle, bay, oleander, box and viburnum; and trees such as pomegranate, quince,

date palm, and strawberry tree. Flowers included rose, poppy, daisy, iris, acanthus and hartstongue fern.

Other important gardens at Pompeii include the House of Loreius Tibertinus, the House of C. Trebius Valens, the House of the Gilded Amorini, the House of the Faun and the House of the Ship Europa.

Ravello: Villa Cimbrone

On foot from centre of Ravello, 25km W of Salerno
Owner: Willeumier family
Opening times: Daily 8.30–sunset
Admission charge:

The villa is a 19th-century Moorish/English hybrid, by William Beckett, Lord Grimthorpe, who owned the property until 1900. The garden, with superb views, was designed on a rock jutting out 106m above the Mediterranean. Trees, shrubs and flowers grow in profusion. An axial walk leads from the entrance to the belvedere on the cliffs with its overhanging balustrading and balcony. On either side of the central walk various garden themes include a stretch of lawn decorated with statues (copies from the Archaeological Museum in Naples), a sunken tea-house garden, a rose garden and a shady grove of umbrella pines and cypresses which descends down the steep slopes to the valley below.

Ravello: Palazzo Rúfolo

Piazza del Duomo, centre of Ravello, 25km W of Salerno
Owner: Italian State
Opening times: Daily 9.30–13, 14–16.30
Admission charge: Yes

The Palazzo Rúfolo, in a paradisal setting with superb views over the Amalfitano coast, is one of the oldest surviving palaces in Italy, dating from the 13th century. The architecture, which includes a court-yard cloister, shows a strong Moorish influence. On the upper terrace umbrella pines and cypresses shade a wellhead beside a tower. In bright sunlight on a lower level, classical geometric beds edged with box are filled with modern flowers. Tender plants which thrive in the mild climate are a feature on the lower terrace. Wagner wrote *Parsifal* here.

Sicily

Catania: Botanic Garden of Catania University ❀
Via A. Longo
Owner: Catania University
Opening times: Daily 9–13
Admission charge: No

Though the university of Catania is one of the most ancient in Europe – it was founded in 1434 – the botanic garden was only created in 1858, by the botanist Francesco Tornabene. The garden is divided into two main parts: the 'Orto Generale' containing mostly exotic plants; and the 'Orto Siculo', with species indigenous to Sicily and southern Europe.

Many plants of tropical and subtropical origin are cultivated in the *Orto Generale*. Genera represented include dasylirions, nolinas, yuccas, dracaenas; there are over forty different types of palms – *Washingtonia*, *Phoenix* and *Sabal*; and many other plants that thrive in the mild climate of Catania. There are agaves and succulents – cacti and euphorbias – grown both out-of-doors and in greenhouses.

The *Orto Siculo* has many different species from the Mediterranean area, including the holm oak, carob tree and white poplar; it also has rare indigenous plants, such as *Celtis aetnensis*, which grows only on the lava of Mount Etna.

Palermo: Botanic Garden of Palermo University
Via Lincoln
Owner: Palermo University
Opening times: Mon–Fri 9–12, 14–16, Sat 9–11; mid Jul to mid Oct 9–12

The botanic garden was founded as a teaching garden in 1795, and plants were arranged according to Linnaeus's classification. This formal area still survives with its cross *allées* of palms and cycads. To the east a water garden contains water lilies and lotus flowers. Exotic trees and shrubs, planted as random specimens, are of considerable botanical interest.

Palermo: Parco della Favorita e Giardini della Casina Cinese
Piazza Niscemi
Owner: Italian State
Opening times: Daily 8 or 9–14, except Thurs; hols 9–13
Admission charge: No

Now the property of the city of Palermo and a green oasis in the city centre, the park was founded by King Ferdinand III in 1799; it was named 'La Favorita' after the royal palace at Portici near Naples. Many of the original features, including statues and fountains, have vanished, but the garden still has faded charm and atmosphere. Large areas are planted with indigenous evergreen Mediterranean trees and shrubs but, in open sunlight, orange and lemon groves are fragrant in early spring. The Italian parterre garden, where specimen petticoat and Canary Island palms flourish above the flowerbeds, surrounds a curious Chinese-style palace.

Palermo: Villa Giulia o Flora
Via Lincoln
Owner: Commune of Palermo
Opening times: Daily 9–20
Admission charge: No.

This public garden, founded in 1778 by the Palermo city council, was laid out in a geometric pattern by the architect Niccolò Palma. Eight main avenues, lined by Judas trees, jacarandas, *Ficus benjamina*, plane trees, washingtonia palms and citrus fruits, bisect the square area, while more random planting of araucarias, other palms and Mediterreanean pine trees gives an informal air. Goethe visited the Villa Giulia in 1788 and delighted in the garden where 'strange trees, all unknown to me, spread their leaves in odd ramifications'.

France

Although many features of Roman gardens survive in France (for example, the *nymphaeum* at Nîmes), it would be fanciful to suggest that there has been any continuity of influence dating from Roman times. However, the intensive romanization of France emphasizes a decisive influence on the nature of French gardens: the climate. The Romans clearly found here a congenial climate similar to their own. The Mediterranean climate of the Midi and the mild temperate climate of central France have allowed a style of gardening, often using exotic plants, that a harsher environment would have forbidden. In Nice the minimum winter temperature very rarely drops below $-4°C$ and localized microclimates on the Côte d'Azur (for example at the Cap d'Antibes) may be free of frost. In the cold north-east, however, for example at Lille, frost will be experienced in eight months of the year, with severe temperatures below $-10°C$ in three months. Nice has one quarter of the rainfall of Lille and almost twice as much sunshine. The mountainous regions – the Alps, the Massif Central and the Pyrenees – introduce further diversity. These provide the perfect environment for collections of mountain plants, of which the alpine garden of Le Col du Lautaret, 2,100m high in the foothills of the Alps, is a remarkable example.

In the Middle Ages the great influence on gardening in France, as elsewhere in Europe, was the monastery garden, which was concerned chiefly with the provision of medicinal herbs and food. Pictures of late medieval gardens (for example, in the *Très riches heures du Duc de Berry* at Chantilly) show a probably idealized type of garden familiar from other medieval sources – trellis work, fountains, turf seats and espaliered trees enclosed in a rectangular space. There seems to be nothing here that distinguishes French gardening from what is going on in other European countries. But in the Middle Ages, because of the Angevin connection with the Kingdom of Naples, there was already a strong Italian influence on French gardens. This influence, in one form or another, was formative.

Under François I (1494–1547), many Italian artists (including both Leonardo da Vinci and Benvenuto Cellini) came to France and some of them worked on French gardens; at Fontainebleau (q.v.), for example, the recently restored 16th-century Italianate grotto was possibly designed by Sebastiano Serlio. The Italian influence was strengthened by the marriage of Catherine de Medici (daughter of the Duke of Urbino and his French wife) to Henri II,

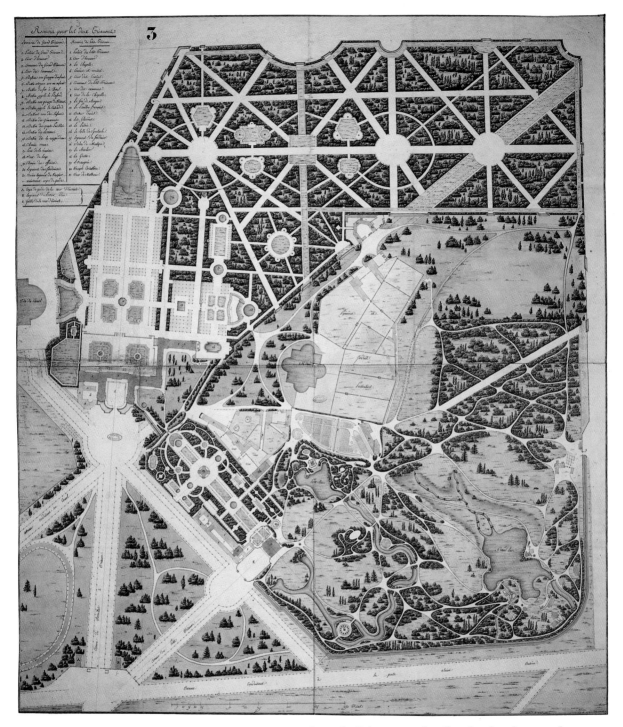

An early 19th-century drawing showing the grounds of the Trianons at Versailles. The original formal design is combined with the landscaping associated with Marie-Antoinette's *Hameau* which was laid out in 1783.

the son of François I. Catherine de Medici took a great interest in gardens and initiated many horticultural projects, among them the new Jardins des Tuileries (q.v.). The rediscovery in the Renaissance of the classical ideals of architecture outlined in the 1st century by Marcus Vitruvius Pollo (known as Vitruvius) exerted a powerful influence. The crucial principle of harmony of design between house and garden was seen particularly in the work of the architect Philibert de l'Orme (*c*.1510–70), who was instrumental in the introduction of Vitruvian ideas. He designed the Château d'Anet (q.v.) and its strongly architectural and symmetrical garden, framed with elaborate galleries, with house and garden on the same axis. The knot garden (*entrelac*) was part of this architectural vocabulary and inspired a great many books of designs in the 16th century, *L'agriculture et maison rustique* (1570) by Charles Estienne being a culminating example.

In the 17th century the influence of André Le Nôtre, in intimate contact with the great architects and artists of the day, created the classical age of the French formal garden. No gardens on this scale had been made before. They were the product of a harmonious collaboration between many remarkable men and the greatest surviving examples, at Vaux-le-Vicomte (q.v.) and Versailles (q.v.), still have a magical if intimidating power. The major characteristic of these gardens is a powerful axial emphasis, centred on the great rooms of the house, and very often extending deep into the country beyond the garden. About these axes are disposed fountains, parterres, *bosquets* (ornamental woodland glades) and sculptures. This new style of gardening, much more ostentatiously flamboyant than anything seen before, was entirely appropriate to the world of Louis XIV, *le roi soleil*. It swept all before it and was widely influential throughout Europe; it was perhaps the first truly international style of gardening.

Early in the 18th century English ideas of landscape design became influential, as in the garden created by Montesquieu at the Château de la Brède in 1731. Romantic ideas, the picturesque and chinoiserie (of which the Désert de Retz (q.v.), now being restored, is the epitome) began to erode the supremacy of the formal garden. In the end, the *jardin anglais*, often in a highly debased form, became a craze which continued well into the 19th century and destroyed many earlier gardens. The latter half of the 18th century saw the introduction of the idea of public gardens, often as part of urban planning (for example at Nancy). These were even more important in the 19th century, especially in Paris (for example the Parc Montsouris, q.v., and the Buttes-Chaumont, q.v.) and became connected with a distinctive style of French garden design. The practice of *mosaïculture*, a kind of hybrid of carpet- and flower-bedding, was developed in the second half of the century and is still seen, executed with great skill, in many municipal gardens. The 19th century also saw the founding of many arboreta and botanical gardens.

In the 20th century there has been considerable foreign influence on French gardening – especially from British designers and Britons living in France. The garden created by Lord Brougham on the Côte d'Azur from 1825 was followed by many others made by his fellow countrymen. A 20th-century example is that created by Lady Aberconway and the Norman family at the Château de la Garoupe (q.v.). The English garden designer Russell Page made several gardens on the Côte d'Azur and evolved an attractive, eclectic style well suited to the environment. Les Moutiers in Normandy, which Edwin Lutyens built for the Mallet family in 1898, has a garden strongly influenced by English ideas in the same tradition as those which produced Sissinghurst (q.v.). These ideas continued to be influential in the period after World War II, Kerdalo (q.v.), Le Vasterival (q.v.) and La Chèvre d'Or (q.v.) all having connections with the eclectic English tradition, and showing a strong emphasis on unusual plants.

Very recently there has been a great increase of popular interest in gardening. A large number of garden centres (the English expression is used) have opened, and some distinguished nursery gardens, which follow the great tradition of the Vilmorin family with their continuous history as plantsmen and nurserymen since the 17th century. All these influences and tendencies in a country with the cultural vigour and the climatic diversity of France are bound to produce a horticultural scene of exceptional interest.

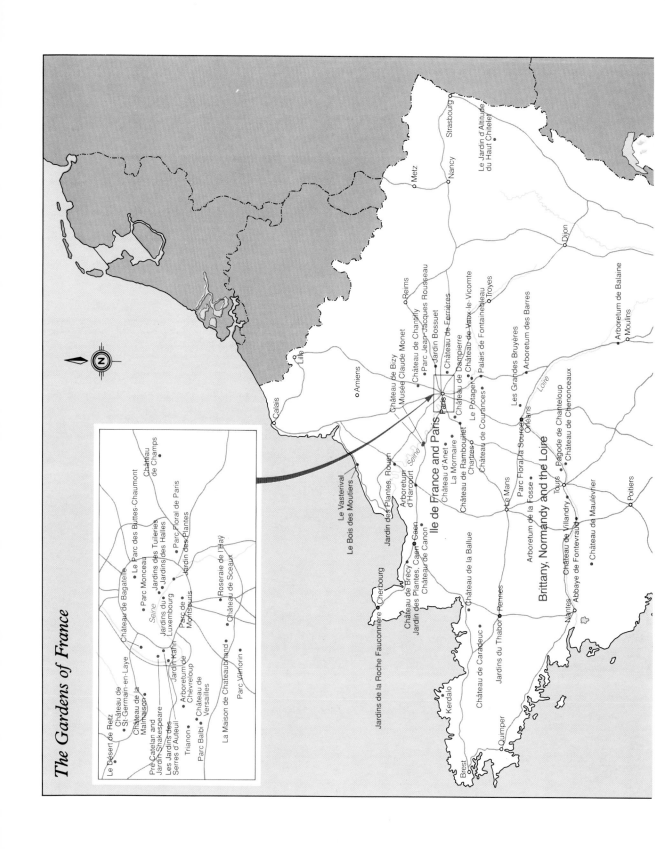

The Gardens of France

Le Désert de Retz
Château de St-Germain-en-Laye
Château de la Malmaison
Pré-Catelan and Jardin Shakespeare
Les Jardins des Serres d'Auteuil
Château de Bagatelle
Le Parc des Buttes-Chaumont
Parc Monceau
Jardins des Tuileries
Jardins des Halles
Parc Floral de Paris
Jardins du Luxembourg
Jardin des Plantes
Jardin Kahn
Arboretum de Chèvreloup
Trianon
Parc Balbi
Château de Versailles
Roseraie de l'Haÿ
La Maison de Chateaubriand
Château de Sceaux
Parc Vilmorin
Château de Champs

Ile de France and Paris

Brittany, Normandy and the Loire

Calais
Lille
Amiens
Strasbourg
Nancy
Metz
Le Jardin d'Altitude du Haut Chitelet
Dijon
Reims
Château de Bizy
Musée Claude Monet
Château de Chantilly
Parc Jean-Jacques Rousseau
Jardin Bossuet
Château de Ferrières
Château de Dampierre
Château de Vaux-le-Vicomte
Palais de Fontainebleau
Troyes
Arboretum de Balaine
Moulins
Les Grandes Bruyères
Arboretum des Barres
Château d'Anet
La Mormaire
Château de Rambouillet
Chartres
Château de Courances
Le Potager
Arboretum d'Harcourt
Le Mans
Parc Floral/La Source
Orléans
Pagode de Chanteloup
Château de Chenonceaux
Le Vasterival
Le Bois des Moutiers
Jardin des Plantes, Rouen
Seine
Loire
Tours
Poitiers
Château de Villandry
Château de Maulévrier
Arboretum de la Fosse
Cherbourg
Château de Brécy
Jardin des Plantes, Caen
Caen
Château de Canon
Château de la Ballue
Rennes
Château de la Roche Fauconnière
Jardins de la Roche Fauconnière
Kerdalo
Château de Caradeuc
Jardins du Thabor
Nantes
Abbaye de Fontevraud
Brest
Quimper

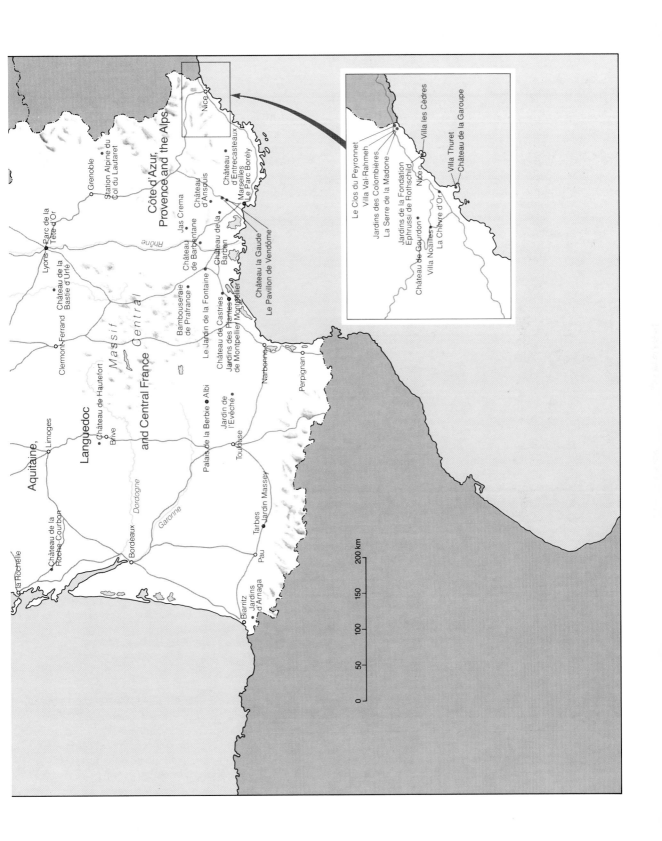

Côte d'Azur, Provence and the Alps

Aquitaine, Languedoc and Central France

Massif Central

Grenoble
Station Alpine du
Col du Lautaret
Parc de la
Tête d'Or
Lyons
Château de la
Bastie d'Urfé
Clermont-Ferrand
Château de Hautefort
Limoges
Brive
Château de la
Roche-Courbon
la Rochelle
Bordeaux
Dordogne
Garonne
Biarritz
Jardins
d'Arnaga
Tarbes
Jardin Massey
Pau
Toulouse
Palais de la Berbie ● Albi
Jardin de
l'Evêché
Narbonne
Perpignan
Château de Castries
Jardins des Plantes
de Montpellier Montpellier
Le Jardin de la Fontaine
Bambouseraie
de Prafrance
Château la Gaude
Le Pavillon de Vendôme
Château de la
Barben
Château
de Barbentane
Jas Crema
Rhône
Château
d'Ansouis
Château
d'Entrecasteaux
Marseilles
Le Parc Borély
Nice

Le Clos du Peyronnet
Villa Val-Rahmeh
Jardins des Colombières
La Serre de la Madone
Jardins de la Fondation
Ephrussi de Rothschild
Château de Gourdon
Villa Noailles
La Chèvre d'Or
Nice
Villa Thuret
Château de la Garoupe
Villa les Cèdres
Villa Thuret

0   50   100   150   200 km

Ile de France and Paris

Château d'Anet

Anet, 20km N of Dreux via D928
Owner: M. and Mme de Yturbe
Opening times: Daily, Apr to Oct 14.30–18.30, except
Tues; Sun and public hols also 10–11.30; Nov to Mar, Sat
2–5, Sun and public hols 10–11.30, 14–17
Admission charge: Yes

This famous château was built in the mid 16th
century for Diane de Poitiers by Philibert de l'Orme.
Nothing survives of the renowned and influential
renaissance garden and little of the Le Nôtre scheme
that followed it. There is magic still in what remains
of the château but little, alas, in the garden.

Jardin Bossuet

Meaux, 56km E of Paris on N3
Owner: Ville de Meaux
Opening times: Daily, summer 9–20; winter 9–17
Admission charge: No

This miniature garden hidden behind the episcopal
palace lies to the north of the cathedral of St Etienne.
It was designed by the great 17th-century Bishop of
Meaux, Jacques-Bénigne Bossuet. Shaped like a
bishop's mitre, pleached lime walks surround a lawn
edged with beds filled in summer with bedding
plants.

Château de Champs

Champs-sur-Marne, 20km E of Paris off N34
Owner: The State
Opening times: Daily 9.30–sunset, except Tues
Admission charge: Yes

The château, a restrained masterpiece, was built in
the early 18th century by the financier Poisson de
Beauvalais. The gardens sloping down to the River
Marne were originally designed formally by Le
Nôtre's nephew Claude Desgots, but replaced in the
19th century by a *jardin anglais*. However, the
original gardens were triumphantly restored in the
late 19th century by Achille Duchêne with lime
alleys, *parterres de broderie* and very fine statues.

Château de Chantilly

Chantilly, 50km N of Paris on N16
Owner: Institut de France
Opening times: Daily, except Tues, Apr to Sept 10–18;
Oct to Mar 10.30–17.30
Admission charge: Yes

The château was started in the 15th century by the
Montmorency family. In the 17th century it passed
to the Princes of Condé and in the 19th century to
King Louis Philippe's son, the Duc d'Aumale, who
built the present gigantic building.

Nothing is visible of Le Nôtre's great garden as one
climbs the giant steps that lead from the entrance to
the château. Austere but magnificent, it lies beyond
the building. Parterres of turf, and pools with water
jets flank a broad canal, across the far end of which
runs a gigantic dog-leg canal. This scheme, devoid of
any planting, remains almost exactly as it was in the
17th century. To the north-west lies a melancholy
19th-century *jardin anglais* with streams winding
through woods. To the east a smaller canal leads to a
picturesque 'hamlet'. Le Nôtre thought it one of
his best gardens and wrote to the Duke of Portland
in 1698: 'Remember all the gardens you have seen
in France – Versailles, Fontainebleau, Vaux-le-
Vicomte and the Tuileries – but above all, Chantilly.'

La Maison de Chateaubriand

87 rue de Chateaubriand, Châtenay-Malabry, 19.5km S of
Paris via N306 and D2
Owner: Département des Hauts-de-Seine
Opening times: Wed, Fri, Sat, Sun, Apr to Sept 10–12,
14–18; Oct to Mar 13.30–16.30; Mon, Tues, Thurs groups
by appointment, 87 rue de Chateaubriand, 92290
Châtenay-Malabry
Admission charge: Yes

Set in the romantically named Vallée-aux-Loups,
Chateaubriand's elegantly classical house is surrounded by magnificent woodland. He was a keen
gardener and trees planted by him at the beginning of
the 19th century are now in splendid maturity. House
and park have recently been impeccably restored. A
drive winds uphill to the house, south of which a

generous apron of grass is fringed with many fine trees. Some are of exceptional size, among them a black poplar, a cedar of Lebanon and a large-leaved lime.

Arboretum de Chèvreloup ❀

Le Chesnay, N of the Domaine de Versailles between N307 and N186
Owner: Muséum d'Histoire Naturelle
Opening times: Guided tours Sat at 10 or 14.30; or by appointment, 78150 Le Chesnay
Admission charge: Yes

Built on the site of Louis XV's deer park, this 200ha arboretum was started in 1927. It now contains a very large and comprehensive collection of both species and cultivars representing all the major groups of hardy trees. One tree survives from the mid 18th century, a splendid pagoda tree (*Sophora japonica*).

Château de Courances ★

Courances, 23km W of Fontainebleau via D409 and D972
Owner: Marquis de Ganay
Opening times: 1st Sun in Apr to Oct, Sat, Sun and public hols 14–18.30
Admission charge: Yes

The 17th-century château on the edge of the village has one of the most memorably beautiful entrances of any house. The short drive leading from a great iron gate is flanked by slender canals and a magnificent avenue of planes, said to have been planted in 1782. To the west of the house, box *parterres de broderie* (not open to the public but visible through railings) form the start of a vista that continues along a large pool and a broad alley of grass with mixed woodland on either side to culminate in a circular pool overlooked by a statue of Hercules. This axis is crossed by rides, alleys and a handsome stepped canal which is linked to another immense and sombre canal lined with black poplars like the columns of a cathedral nave. This series of green rooms – with the intrusion of no bright colours – is a stately harmony of trees, water and grass.

André Le Nôtre is said to have had a hand in the design. If he did, he was certainly in an uncharacteristically intimate frame of mind. The formal parts of the garden owe most of their present appearance to the work, just before World War I, of the neo-classical designer Achille Duchêne, who removed a romantic 19th-century park *à l'anglaise*. South of the house is a 20th-century 'Japanese' garden with a small lake, an island and a waterfall. The effect is charming, but not in the slightest way Japanese despite the presence of *Acer japonica*. The distinctive and unforgettable character of Courances comes from the grave beauty of its formal gardens, among the loveliest in France.

Château de Dampierre

Dampierre-en-Yvelines, 18km SW of Versailles via D91
Owner: Duc de Chevreuse
Opening times: *Gardens* daily, except Tues, Apr to mid Oct 14–18; *Parc Floral* 11–17
Admission charge: Yes

The secluded château, in the wooded valley of the Chevreuse, has two gardens. The first is the eloquent remains of André Le Nôtre's formal gardens, which provide a harmonious setting for the 17th-century house (designed by François Mansart). Here, a central vista from the château is decorated with parterres, pools, lime alleys and urns. The new *Parc Floral*, created since 1978, is quite separate from the formal garden, lying at the far end of a dog-leg canal linking the two. It is an 8ha woodland garden in which blocks of colour, from bulbs in the spring to herbaceous perennials and bedding plants in the summer, are disposed in old woodland. Some of this works well, especially the spring plantings of massed bulbs. In the summer it seems an uneasy compromise between the quieter English tradition of woodland gardening and the sometimes strident French tradition of municipal bedding.

Château de Ferrières

Ferrières, 33km E of Paris via A4
Owner: Les Chancelleries de l'Université de Paris
Opening times: Daily, except Mon and Tues, May to Sept 14–19; Oct to Apr 14–17.30
Admission charge: Yes

The château and its park are the work of the English architect and garden designer Sir Joseph Paxton, who was commissioned by Baron James de Rothschild. The house was finished in 1859.

A short drive leads from the entrance gates to the château. The garden lies beyond it, to the south, where the land slopes down to a handsome curvaceous lake. On each side, and beyond the lake, are beautiful groups of trees with many of a decidedly Victorian flavour – sequoias, copper beeches, blue Atlantic cedars, thujas and the uncommon Greek fir, *Abies cephalonica*. There are fine specimens of the silver lime and of the American red oak. Between these groups of trees serene parkland is glimpsed extending to the far distance. About the house there is a note of formality with clipped yew, stone balustrades and statues. This seems a small concession to French taste in a piece of authentic and very beautiful English parkland transported to the Ile de France.

Oval steps at the Château d'Anet date from Philibert de l'Orme's mid 16th-century design.

Palais de Fontainebleau

Fontainebleau, 65km S of Paris via A6
Owner: The State
Opening times: Daily 8–sunset (some parts of the garden open at 9)
Admission charge: No

Fontainebleau has been associated with the French royal family since at least the 12th century. Napoleon, aware of this ancient connection, called it 'the real home of kings'. Of brick and stone, it is a beguiling mixture of fantasy and sobriety. Many architects worked on it, including Philibert de l'Orme and J. A. du Cerceau.

The best way to start a visit to the garden is by entering the Cour du Cheval Blanc through the beautiful iron gates built under Napoleon. An avenue of bays and orange trees in Versailles boxes leads to the double serpentine staircase of the main entrance. Passing through a door in the south-east corner of

this courtyard you reach the great carp pond with its enchanting banqueting pavilion on an island. To one side is the Grand Parterre, the work of Le Nôtre. A square pool, with a tiered fountain, is surrounded by gravel walks and lawns with clipped cones of yew and edged in summer with bedding plants. Round the whole are stately walks shaded with pollarded limes. A terrace to the east gives a vantage point from which to view the canal, straight and unadorned, aimed at the horizon. It was built in 1609 by Henry IV, a remarkably early experiment in the grand style.

Returning towards the palace, passing south of the parterre, one comes to a round pool with a bronze statue of Romulus, jets of water playing about his head. Beyond this there is a large 19th-century *jardin anglais*, in which a stream ambles through attractive woodland. It contains fine but not exceptional trees – old planes, a handsome *Metasequoia glyptostroboides*

and some good swamp cypresses. The path returns to the south-west corner of the palace, where there is a rare and seductive grotto built in the 16th century, guarded by monumental stone figures supporting arches. The interior has recently been convincingly and attractively restored.

Roseraie de l'Haÿ ★ ❀
Rue Albert Watel, L'Haÿ les Roses, 5km S of Paris via A6 and D126
Owner: Département du Val de Marne
Opening times: Daily, Jun to Sept 10–18; Jun, Jul, Fri and Sat, evening visits until 23.30
Admission charge: Yes

This exquisite rose garden on a flat site on the edge of L'Haÿ was founded in 1892 – the first in the world. It now contains 3,200 varieties, of which 120 were known before 1800. Gravel paths lead through a formal arrangement of beds, arbours, trellis work and

The Roseraie de l'Haÿ, started in the late 19th century, is the largest collection of roses in France.

arches. The standard of upkeep is exceptionally high and the garden is one of the great horticultural delights of France.

Château de la Malmaison

Rueil-Malmaison, 15km W of Paris on N13
Owner: The State
Opening times: Daily 10–17.30, except Tues and public hols
Admission charge: Yes

The château, rebuilt after 1799, is the epitome of Empire style, but retains only a tiny fragment of its original garden. At La Malmaison, the Empress Josephine had a remarkable collection of plants and summoned Pierre-Joseph Redouté to paint them. In her garden today there is a modest collection of roses grown before 1800, some of them very beautiful. But that is tucked away in a corner and before you get there you run the gauntlet of the Hybrid Tea roses in the *cour d'honneur*. There is an attractive park *à l'anglaise*, the Bois-Préau.

Musée Claude Monet ★

Giverny, 4km E of Vernon on D5
Owner: Institut de France
Opening times: Daily, Apr to Oct 10–18, except Mon
Admission charge: Yes

The house and garden close to the Seine where Monet went to live and paint in his mature years have been magnificently restored and give a uniquely vivid impression of his sources of inspiration. The garden lies on gently sloping ground and is divided into two parts – the Clos Normand and the lily pool. The first is a series of long narrow beds running downhill and filled with poppies, lupins, delphiniums and peonies. Standard roses, roses trained over arches, and fruit trees give height. The borders are edged with irises, santolina or variegated ground elder. In summer the atmosphere is of abundant colour and luxuriant growth. Monet saw it as a kind of idealized farmyard in which turkeys pecked.

The lily pool is reached by a tunnel under a road. Here is an abrupt change of mood: grassy paths

amble through sheaves of day-lilies bordering the stream that feeds the pond. Arched bridges, painted an acid apple green, are festooned with wisteria, and the draped fronds of weeping willow frame the water-lilies – Monet's paintings brought unnervingly to life. The place is an unqualified delight and a brilliant act of horticultural reconstruction. Vita Sackville-West, the English gardener and writer, called it 'a rumpus of colour'.

Paris: Château de Bagatelle ★

Bois de Boulogne, intersection of Allée de Longchamp and Allée de la Reine Marguerite; Métro: Pont de Neuilly
Owner: Ville de Paris
Opening times: Daily, Oct to Mar 9–17; Apr to Sept 8.30–18
Admission charge: Yes

The miniature château and its garden, on the edge of the Bois de Boulogne, make one of the most seductive sights of Paris. The château was built in 1777 by the Comte d'Artois and enlarged by its English owner, the Marquis of Hertford, in the 19th century. It remained in English hands until Sir Henry Murray Scott sold it in 1905.

Beautiful blue and gilt wrought-iron gates lead into the garden. Paths wander through dense plantings of trees and shrubs, opening out near the château on to lawns with specimen trees – a fine Corsican pine, a decorative persimmon and many others. A lake with a grotto is overhung with an immense weeping beech. At the other, eastern, end of the garden there is an orangery overlooking parterres and an outstanding rose garden, in which rose trials are held and past medal-winners are kept in impeccable box-edged beds. On the slope above, an airy Chinese pagoda surveys the scene across sweeping lawns.

Paris: Le Parc des Buttes-Chaumont

Rue Botzaris; Métro: Buttes-Chaumont
Owner: Ville de Paris
Opening times: Daily, summer 7–20; winter 8–20
Admission charge: No

This 25ha public park, laid out by Jean-Charles-

Adolphe Alphand in 1864, has a wonderfully wild and romantic air. Among wooded hillocks two streams flow into an artificial lake spanned by a bridge, a waterfall plummets 30m and a temple crowns the highest point. From this airy and refreshing place, the city glimpsed through the trees seems far away.

Paris: Parc Floral de Paris

Route de la Pyramide; Métro: Château de Vincennes
Owner: Ville de Paris
Opening times: Daily 9.30–20
Admission charge: Yes

This 35ha public park was made in 1969 for an international flower show and is full of the atmosphere of that time. Few things date more quickly than what is thought to be modern. Groups of trees line curving paths among rather unnatural land shapes. A lake has a modernistic waterfall and beds are filled with large free-form blocks of single colours. There are collections of beeches, oaks, azaleas, Mediterranean and medicinal plants.

Paris: Jardins des Halles

Rue Berger; Métro: Halles
Owner: Ville de Paris
Opening times: At all times
Admission charge: No

On the site of the old market halls a public garden of great charm and ingenuity has been made in recent years. Alleys of lime and horse chestnut give leafy formality. There are beautifully made fountains, cascades, hedges of yew and elaeagnus and many benches. A children's play area is guarded by two huge rhinoceroses made of clipped ivy. Two pyramid-shaped glasshouses have interesting collections of tropical ferns, palms and other tender plants.

Paris: Jardin Kahn

Rue des Abondances, Boulogne-Billancourt; Métro: Pont de St Cloud
Owner: Département des Hauts-de-Seine
Opening times: Daily, Mar, Oct, Nov 9.30–12.30, 14–18; Apr, Sept 9.30–12.30, 14–19
Admission charge: Yes

The banker Albert Kahn started to make this garden at the turn of the century. In a richly wooded setting there are an elaborate Japanese garden; a *jardin anglais*; an exquisite ornamental fruit and rose garden; and an orangery. Soothing woodland walks among romantic rocks overlook a pool.

Paris: Jardins du Luxembourg

Rue de Vaugirard; Métro: Luxembourg
Owner: The State
Opening times: Daily, sunrise–sunset
Admission charge: No

The original palace was built in 1612 by Marie de Medici and modelled on the Palazzo Pitti, her Florentine home. The present house is largely 19th-century and since 1879 has been the seat of the Senate. The garden is, justly, one of the most popular public gardens in Paris and is kept to a very high standard. The English writer John Evelyn went there in 1644 and wrote: 'Certainly one of the sweetest places imaginable … perfectly beautyfull & magnificent.'

The south front of the palace overlooks a large octagonal fountain pool encircled with gravel walks and large pomegranates, oleanders and orange trees in Versailles boxes. To the south a firm axial vista is formed by an avenue of pleached horse chestnuts among which lurk handsome statues of queens of France. The vista is cut by the rue Auguste Comte and is continued on the other side of the street by the Avenue de l'Observatoire. To the east of the palace is the reconstructed Medici fountain overlooking an attractively sombre canal edged with giant garlands of ivy. Here and there, despite the public crush, there are still flashes of the atmosphere that Jean-Antoine Watteau painted with such vivacity as the background to his *fêtes champêtres*.

THE GARDENS OF SOUTHERN EUROPE

Paris: Parc Monceau

Boulevard de Courcelles; Métro: Monceau
Owner: Ville de Paris
Opening times: Daily, summer 8–sunset; winter 8–19
Admission charge: No

In 1774 the Duc d'Orléans commissioned Louis Carrogis Carmontelle to lay out a picturesque landscape garden on what was then a bare site on the outskirts of Paris. The royal architect Claude-Nicholas Ledoux added a neo-classical domed entrance lodge which survives today. In 1861 J.-C.-A. Alphand overlaid the earlier garden with a *jardin anglais*, but without destroying the character of the

RIGHT **Monet's lily garden at Giverny, with its arched Japanese bridge, inspired many of his paintings.**

BELOW **The Chinese pagoda at Bagatelle in the Bois de Boulogne was built in the late 18th century when the landscape garden was laid out.**

earlier period with its serpentine lake, ghostly ruins, statues, and cascades plunging over rocky crags. The atmosphere of all this makes a striking contrast with the sedate residential district that now surrounds it.

Paris: Parc de Montsouris

Boulevard Jourdan; Métro: Cité Universitaire
Owner: Ville de Paris
Opening times: Daily, summer 7–21; winter 8–sunset
Admission charge: No

A public park designed by Alphand in the 1860s. A steeply sloping site of 15.5ha has been artfully shaped and richly planted with fine trees. At the bottom of the slope a romantic lake is fed by a stream gushing over rocks. Among the many good trees there is an outstanding, very large *Zelkova carpinifolia*. A curious survival is the scaled-down version of the palace of the Bey of Tunis erected for the Exposition of 1867, which now makes a garden folly of grandiose presence. Less picturesque are the railway lines that cut across the garden.

Paris: Jardin des Plantes

57 rue Cuvier; Métro: Jussieu
Owner: Muséum Nationale d'Histoire Naturelle
Opening times: Daily 9–sunset
Admission charge: No

These botanic gardens were found in 1626 by Louis XIII, who instructed his physician to start a garden of medicinal herbs. It became a leading botanical research institute where Georges-Louis Leclerc Buffon, the natural historian, was director from 1739–88 and Jean-Baptiste de Monet Lamarck, the 19th-century pioneer of evolutionary theory, had a chair. The garden falls substantially into two parts – the botanic garden proper, in which systematic beds display plants in their correct botanical groups, and a public park. The first is divided into attractive horseshoe-shaped beds which are not, alas, kept to a very high standard. None the less, there are some beautiful and rare plants – an exceptional willow-leaved ash (*Fraxinus salicifolia*), the curiously knobbly *Zanthoxylum americanum* and many others. The park, much used by local inhabitants, is crossed by a fine avenue of planes running on either side of a spacious rectangle of gravel. Beyond the trees, beds with beautifully grown annuals are punctuated by handsome tender plants trained as standards – *Cyphomandra betacea* with plum-like fruit, *Lantana camara* and *Plumbago capensis*. One side of the beds is bordered by a row of giant pillars of different forms of variegated holly.

Paris: Pré Catelan and Jardin Shakespeare

Bois de Boulogne
Owner: Ville de Paris
Opening times: Daily; *park* sunrise–sunset; *Jardin Shakespeare* 15–15.30, 16.30–17
Admission charge: *Park* no; *Jardin Shakespeare* yes

The Pré Catelan is a well-kept public park in the Bois de Boulogne. Its chief interest is the open-air theatre dedicated to Shakespeare with a garden containing 150 plants mentioned in his plays and garden scenes evoking some of his plays. All this is done with charm and panache.

Paris: Les Jardins des Serres d'Auteuil (Fleuriste Municipal)

Avenue de la Porte d'Auteuil, Boulogne-Billancourt; Métro: Porte d'Auteuil
Owner: Ville de Paris
Opening times: Daily 10–18
Admission charge: Yes

This extraordinary garden with an interesting combination of horticultural activities in an unlikely situation was made in 1895 as a municipal nursery garden serving all the public gardens of Paris. Even today half a million plants are produced every year. It is also a very distinguished arboretum with beautifully kept lawns and walks. A huge and ornamental palm house is impeccably maintained. Among the trees there is an exceptionally large Chinese wingnut (*Pterocarya stenoptera*), a fine *Acer saccharinum laciniatum* and a very large *Ailanthus giraldii*. Despite the garden's proximity to the frenzied *boulevard périphérique*, it breathes an air of calm delight.

Paris: Jardins des Tuileries

Quai des Tuileries; Métro: Tuileries
Owner: Ville de Paris
Opening times: At all times
Admission charge: No

In 1567 Catherine de Medici commissioned Philibert de l'Orme to build her a new château not far from the Louvre. Elaborate renaissance gardens followed, but these were swept away under Louis XIV when André Le Nôtre, whose father had been head gardener at the Tuileries, designed a new garden. Of this the chief survival is the central axis aligned with the west courtyard of the Palais du Louvre and with the Avenue des Champs Elysées – a grandiose and effective blending of garden design and town planning. Squares of pleached horse chestnuts surround lawns with benches and many fine statues – including some by Aristide Maillol and Auguste Rodin. The Ministry of Culture now plans to restore many of the features of Le Nôtre's original design for a formal garden of alleys and parterres. Although rather unkempt in its present state, with its lovely river setting it still possesses the magic that the German poet Rainer Maria Rilke found in 1900: 'Today we had a wonderful autumn morning. We walked across the Tuileries. Everything to the east in front of the sun was dazzling. The illuminated parts were shrouded in mist like a grey curtain of light. Grey in their greyness, the statues warmed themselves in the sun.'

Château de Rambouillet

Rambouillet, 53km SW of Paris via N10
Owner: The State
Opening times: Daily, sunrise–sunset
Admission charge: No

The relatively small château was built on flat land on the edge of the town. Its present appearance dates from Napoleon's time. André Le Nôtre laid out the formal gardens to the south of the château, with three canals radiating from a semi-circular pool and penetrating woodland. Nearer the house are lawns and parterres planted with summer bedding and punctuated by yews clipped into sentry-box shapes. To the south-west of all this, through a *jardin anglais*, is a

charming folly – the *Chaumière de Coquillages* (shellwork cottage) built in the late 18th century. One of the rooms is encrusted with a profusion of exotic shells; another exquisitely painted with birds and flowers. Even more remarkable is the superb dairy built in 1788 for Marie-Antoinette and designed by Jacques-Jean Thévenin. It is in the form of a Greek temple, with a magnificent dome and a grotto containing a marble figure of the nymph Almathea and her goat, which suckled Jupiter himself.

Le Désert de Retz

6 allée Frédéric Passy, SW of Chambourcy, E of A13
Owner: Société Civile du Désert de Retz
Opening times: By appointment, 6 allée Frédéric Passy, 78240 Chambourcy

This extraordinary romantic landscape garden is a dreamlike survival from the late 18th-century passion for the picturesque. Lying on the edge of the ancient royal forest of Marly, it was made from 1774 onwards by an enigmatic Monsieur de Monville – a Gallic William Beckford, but more so. Here he made a landscape garden enriched with remarkable buildings – a giant ruined column (disguising a luxuriously furnished house), a pyramidal ice house, an intricate Chinese house, a temple to Pan, a grotto and so on. 'How grand the idea excited by the remains of such a column!', wrote the American president Thomas Jefferson on his visit in 1786. Snatched from the brink of irretrievable collapse, this fascinating place is undergoing meticulous restoration.

Parc Jean-Jacques Rousseau ★

Ermenonville, 47km NE of Paris, 14km SE of Senlis
Owner: Touring Club de France
Opening times: Daily 9–12, 15–17
Admission charge: Yes

This is a superb landscape garden in the tradition of the English Stourhead and Stowe (q.v.). It was made by the Marquis de Girardin from 1766 onwards. Girardin visited England and drew inspiration from the 18th-century poet and gardener William Shenstone, to whom there is a memorial in the garden. Another profound influence was the philosopher Jean-Jacques Rousseau, who became a friend of

Girardin. In laying out the garden he was helped by the architect J.-M. Morel. J. C. Loudon, the English garden writer, visited it shortly after it was made and pronounced it, 'to be laid out in chaste and picturesque style ... somewhat different and superior to contemporary English places'.

The park that survives today is only a part of a much larger scheme of about 900ha that included a wilderness and a model farm. What survives is an intensely romantic landscape garden surrounding a long narrow lake. From the shores of the lake paths wind up into the densely planted woods that clothe the steep slopes. Here are fine trees; on this protected site Scots pines, oaks, beeches, limes and horse chestnuts have grown to great size. From the slopes there are tantalizing glimpses of the château (not open) that lies beyond the northern extremity of the lake. Carefully positioned in the woods are ornamental buildings – a 'ruined' temple of philosophers (with pillars inscribed with the names of Girardin's mentors), a 'prehistoric' grotto, a pillar dedicated to reverie, and so on. At the extreme southern end of the lake on a small island is Rousseau's tomb, sheltered by a semi-circle of Lombardy poplars. Rousseau died and was buried here, but his body was disinterred during the Revolution and reburied in the Panthéon in Paris. The tomb is inscribed: 'Here lies the man of Nature and of Truth.'

The Parc Jean-Jacques Rousseau is well cared for by the Touring Club de France. A caravan park regrettably disfigures one of the approaches. But, turning your back on that, you can easily lose yourself in this wild and atmospheric 18th-century landscape of authentic character.

Château de St-Germain-en-Laye

St-Germain-en-Laye, 29km NW of Paris
Owner: Domaine Nationale
Opening times: Daily 9–sunset
Admission charge: No

The royal château dates from the 12th century and many hands worked on the gardens (including Philibert de l'Orme and J. A. du Cerceau). After 1670 the gardens were laid out by Le Nôtre. All that remains of his design today is the truncated but fine Petite and Grande Terrasse, 2.5km long, the Grande Terrasse backed by magnificent limes said to have been planted in 1745. From both there are superb views

A mid 19th-century lithograph by Charles Rivière shows the Jardin des Plantes in Paris laid out very much as it is today – double avenues of plane trees flank elaborate parterres.

towards Paris. Le Nôtre's scheme for the terraces is still visible, but the parterres and other formal elements are badly neglected. A 19th-century *jardin anglais* – with 'turfy avenue and light-checkered glades', as the American writer Henry James noted – has a fine collection of trees, including an exceptionally large sycamore, an immense acacia, a fern-leaved beech and other good specimens.

Château de Sceaux

Sceaux, 11km S of Paris via N20
Owner: Département des Hauts-de-Seine
Opening times: Daily, sunrise–sunset
Admission charge: No

The château and garden were built for Louis XIV's finance minister Jean-Baptiste Colbert. The present château, now municipal offices, is 19th-century, but the garden is an authentic if somewhat forlorn work of Le Nôtre. In front of the house the land falls away dramatically. Here Le Nôtre made a spectacular cascade, of which a much less elaborate 19th-century version exists today. At the bottom is a great octagonal pool and the vista is continued up the hill beyond. There are an outstanding late 17th-century orangery and fine 18th-century pavilions.

Château de Vaux-le-Vicomte ★

Maincy, 5km E of Melun via N36 and D215
Owner: Comte Patrice de Vogüé
Opening times: Daily, Apr to Oct 10–18; Feb, Mar, Nov, Sat, Sun 14–17
Admission charge: Yes

The château and its great garden were made 1656–61 by Nicolas Fouquet, finance minister to Louis XIV. The architect was Louis Le Vau and the garden was the first great work of André Le Nôtre. The ensemble of house and garden is one of the most spectacularly beautiful in France. The construction of the garden, overseen by Fouquet himself in consultation with Le Nôtre, was an extraordinary logistical feat; at one time 18,000 men were working on it. The house, despite its top-heavy awkwardness, seems to float in the moat that surrounds it like some exotic ship. On the garden side the pedimented frontispiece, surmounted by a dome, commands a view down an enormous central vista with, on the distant horizon, a gigantic gilt figure of Hercules gazing across the

At Vaux-le-Vicomte, the main vista from the house is flanked by classical *parterres de broderie*. On the horizon is a giant figure of Hercules.

garden towards the house. About this axis are disposed a glittering array of formal conceits – parterres, obelisks and mounds of clipped yew, statues, urns, pools and jets of water, A huge canal, with a grotto in the retaining wall above it, cuts across the main axis and ends in a cascade. Beyond the canal the land rises, with a broad grassy walk between limes leading to the figure of Hercules. Looking back towards the house the garden takes on a character of lightness and delicacy, with the house airily reflected in the mirror-like pools.

Vaux is not a garden that reveals itself on a brief visit. Its ingredients are so complex, Le Nôtre's shifting views so intricately composed, that several visits would still leave much unexplored. Nevertheless, despite its colossal scale, it is a garden of irresistible charm.

Guyot's etching of 1785 shows the lake in the Désert of the landscape garden at Ermenonville, the Parc Jean-Jacques Rousseau.

Versailles: Parc Balbi

Rue du Maréchal Joffre, S of the Château de Versailles
Owner: Ecole Nationale Supérieure d'Horticulture
Opening times: Daily, except Mon, Apr to Sept 13–18; Oct to Mar 13–17
Admission charge: Yes

This is the former *potager du roi*, the royal kitchen garden, designed for Louis XIV by Jean-Baptiste de la Quintinye between 1678 and 1683. It is now in the care of the national college of horticulture and a wide range of fruit and vegetables is still grown in the great square beds of the original layout. The beautifully espaliered fruit trees produce dazzling displays of blossom in spring and fruit in autumn.

Versailles: Trianon (Grand Trianon and Petit Trianon) ★

22km W of Paris off A13
Owner: Musées Nationaux
Opening times: Daily sunrise–sunset
Admission charge: No

The two Trianon châteaux are part of the Versailles estate, continuous with the grounds of the Château de Versailles. Faced in alarmingly pink marble, the *Grand Trianon* was designed by Jules Hardouin-Mansart in 1687 for Louis XIV to entertain Madame de Maintenon. Immediately to the west of the house on a raised terrace are parterres with summer bedding plants. To the south there is a handsome view of the Petit Canal stretching into the distance flanked by groves of horse chestnut. Beyond the parterres is an area of woodland criss-crossed by alleys and with a fine formal waterfall designed by Hardouin-Mansart. From the north-east corner of the château a bridge leads past a formal garden with the charming Pavillon Français (formerly the royal menagerie, designed by Ange-Jacques Gabriel and completed in 1749) to the Petit Trianon.

The *Petit Trianon*, an exquisite small château designed by Gabriel in 1768, has gardens of exceptional interest. Immediately to the north of the house is a remarkable old pagoda tree (*Sophora japonica*) surviving from the original plantings under Louis XV. Beyond this a romantic landscaped garden has meandering paths, streams, rustic bridges and a lake overlooked by a very fine belvedere with a wonderfully painted interior. From here paths lead through woodland with many good trees (among them an outstanding tulip tree and giant plane) to the Grand Lac with the model rural village of Le Hameau. Grouped around the lake are miniature farm buildings with thatched roofs, balconies and half timbering – a dairy, a mill, a dovecote and so on.

Versailles: Château de Versailles ★

22km W of Paris, off A13
Owner: Musées Nationaux
Opening times: Daily sunrise–sunset
Admission charge: No

The history of the gardens at Versailles is long and complicated. In essence they are the creation of Le Nôtre, who worked on them from 1661 for well over twenty years. Louis XIV, for whom they were built, took an intense interest and wrote a guidebook to them. By the late 18th century the original plantings were showing their age, and in 1775 Louis XVI replanted the entire garden. In the early 19th century Louis XVIII replaced a huge pool with the charming *jardin anglais* that we see today. There have been many other changes, but the essential character seems to remain, for the most part, true to Le Nôtre's intentions, although many modern plants, unknown to Le Nôtre, have been introduced, including ageratum, begonia hybrids, large-flowered tagetes and many others.

The site, flat and featureless, must have seemed completely without possibilities. Le Nôtre built up the ground to the west of the château and thus allowed the vista that we see today, which slopes down to a canal and fountain and rises gently towards the horizon. In some circumstances the gardens at Versailles can seem intensely oppressive, the product of aggressive megalomania – the English writer Horace Walpole referred to them as 'littered with statues and fountains . . . the gardens of a great child'. The very idea of the garden with its east-west axis stretching from the king's chambers beyond the very horizon, the sun's axis parallel to the Sun King's as though he was the origin of all things, is a chilling thought. At other times, perhaps at dawn on a misty autumnal morning with the sun filtering gently through the trees, glinting on water and statues, it can seem bewitchingly beautiful. As soon as you turn away from that daunting axis ('such symmetry is not for solitude,' wrote the English poet Lord Byron) and wander in the *bosquets* that lie on either side, you find yourself in a more private world. Versailles is not only formal gardening on an intimidatingly grand scale. In the *Bosquet de la Reine*, for example, a 17th-century bronze of Aphrodite bathes in light filtered through a grove of tulip trees – an informal woodland setting for a very formal statue. The scale is intimate and the spirit of classical antiquity perfectly caught. As you wander – and it is pre-eminently a garden for wandering in – you are constantly charmed by one aspect or another: the ravishing quality of the statuary and urns (by many of the greatest masters of the day), a brilliant jet of water against sombre foliage, the patchwork of plants outside the orangery.

Parc Vilmorin ⊛

2 rue d'Estienne-d'Orves, Verrières-le-Buisson
15km SW of Paris via N306
Owner: M. de Vilmorin
Opening times: By appointment, 2 rue d'Estienne-d'Orves, 91370 Verrières-le-Buisson

In 1815 the great collection of plants assembled in the 18th century by Pierre Andrieux was brought here by Philippe-André de Vilmorin. There is an arboretum of over 2,500 species and cultivars and a collection of alpine plants. Some of the remarkable trees bred in the arboretum at Verrières testify to the pioneering arboricultural work of the Vilmorin family – for example the walnut *Juglans × intermedia* var. *vilmoreana* and a hybrid of the Spanish fir, *Abies × vilmorinii*.

Brittany, Normandy and the Loire

Château de la Ballue

Bazouges-le-Pérouse, 39km E of Dinan via D794 and D796
Owner: Mme Claude Arthaud
Opening times: Jul to Aug 10–12, 14.30–17.30

The distinguished early 17th-century granite château commands sweeping views over an idyllically rural landscape. The gardens are the creation of the present owner, Madame Claude Arthaud. On the south side of the house she has made a Louis XIII garden with parterres of yew and box. This leads into a lively formal garden full of jokes and surprises – a maze, a green theatre, unexpected water jets springing from the turf – and with avenues and walks giving dramatic perspectives.

Château de Bizy

SW of the centre of Vernon on D181
Owner: Duc d'Albuféra
Opening times: Daily, Apr to Nov 10–12, 14–18.30, except Fri; rest of year by appointment, 27200 Vernon
Admission charge: Yes

Shady lime walks and pleached alleys fringe the fine early 18th-century château. Everywhere there is excellent statuary and stonework. The magnificent cascades, canals and other waterworks were designed by Le Nôtre's nephew Claude Desgots but, alas, they are deprived of water and thus of meaning.

In the 17th-century walled garden at the Château de Brécy, terraces rise up from box *parterres de broderie* at the back of the house.

Le Bois des Moutiers ★

Varengeville-sur-Mer
Owner: Mallet family
Opening times: Mid Mar to mid Nov, Tues–Fri 10–12, 14–18, Sat, Sun and Mon 14–19
Admission charge: Yes

The house, designed by the English architect Edwin Lutyens in 1898, fits into the wooded Normandy scenery remarkably harmoniously. The garden, in part influenced by the English designer Gertrude Jekyll, is full of charm. By the house a white garden, held in check by disciplined box hedges, is full – too full some would say – of white valerian, 'Iceberg' roses, white irises, *Thalictrum aquilegifolium* 'Album' and other ghostly plants. Nearby a pair of lavish mixed borders show Jekyllian influence. The formal elements of the garden gradually give way to handsome woodland, planted with many rhododendrons, flowing down the steep valley that leads to the sea. None of this is as well looked after as it should be.

Château de Brécy ★

Brécy-Saint-Gabriel, 10km E of Bayeux off D12
Owner: Mme de Lacretelle
Opening times: Daily, Apr to Nov 14–18, except Wed; otherwise by appointment, 14480 Brécy-Saint-Gabriel, 14.30–17
Admission charge: Yes

The Château de Brécy is the perfect introduction to the French formal garden, intimate in scale and exquisite in detail. Set in a wooded hamlet, the château resembles a Norman farmhouse, but the

great pedimented entrance comes from a different world. The house and its garden were built in the first half of the 17th century and it is possible that the grand entrance and the exquisite formal garden were designed by François Mansart, who built the nearby Château de Balleroy. The garden, which is quite small and entirely walled, lies immediately behind the house and consists of five contrasted terraces, becoming simpler as they rise away from the house. Fine stonework, elegant parterres, pools, box-topiary, well-kept lawns and handsome gate-piers are the restrained but eloquent ingredients of this charming garden. On the final terrace, a wrought-iron gate pierces the wall and reveals the unspoilt Normandy countryside, with clumps of woodland framing a distant gap on the axis of the garden.

Caen: Jardin des Plantes
5 Place Blot, NW of city centre
Owner: Ville de Caen
Opening times: Daily, variable hours
Admission charge: No

This beautifully-kept public garden has a handsome sloping site and some fine trees – a fern-leaved beech, an Indian bean tree and the uncommon ironwood *Ostrya virginiana*. There is an elegant orangery and excellent greenhouses with an immense range of tender plants.

Château de Canon ★
Mézidon-Canon, 25km E of Caen via N13
Owner: M. F. de Mézerac
Opening times: Easter to Jun, Sat, Sun, public hols 14–19; Jul to Sept, daily 14–19, except Tues
Admission charge: Yes

This exceptional garden is the creation of a remarkable man – Jean-Baptiste-Jacques Elie de Beaumont. He was a successful barrister in 18th-century Paris, a friend of the philosopher Voltaire and of the English writer Horace Walpole, who influenced his gardening ideas. The elegant classical late 17th-century château overlooks an unadorned rectangular pool flanked with pollarded limes and, at the end, a row of Italian busts which gaze back towards the house. The vista is continued through

woodland beyond by an avenue of beeches.

A broad path cutting through the woods crosses the main vista, with a classical temple (*La Pleureuse* – in memory of Elie de Beaumont's wife) at one end and a brilliant scarlet chinoiserie kiosk overhanging a stream at the other. From here there are Elysian views of fields and woodland. To one side is a unique and charming survival – the *chartreuses* – or linked walled gardens where fruit and herbaceous plants are grown. Arched doorways link several *chartreuses*, over which presides a white marble figure of Pomona. To an exceptional degree the garden preserves its original atmosphere – the rural retreat of a civilized man.

Château de Caradeuc
Tinténiac, 22km S of Dinan via D2, W of Bécherel on D20
Owner: M. de Kernier
Opening times: Daily 9–sunset
Admission charge: Yes

An elaborate formal garden of the same period surrounds the distinguished early 18th-century house. To the south, flanking the entrance, are ornate parterres with beds of red and yellow roses, pyramids of yew and mounds of clipped laurustinus. North of the château the land is scooped away dramatically to reveal fine views over the Rance valley. A broad gravel terrace forms the centre of a cross axis with, at its east end, a fine giant Carrara marble statue of Louis XVI. To the west several crossing axes are punctuated with very good statuary and ornamental stonework. The garden has excellent bones but the flesh is weary.

Pagode de Chanteloup
3km S of Amboise off D431
Owner: Groupement Forestier de la Pagode de Chanteloup
Opening times: Daily, Apr to mid Sept 8–19; mid Sept to mid Nov 8–18; mid Nov to Mar 9–17
Admission charge: Yes

An enchanting chinoiserie pagoda built by the Duc de Choiseul in 1775 is all that remains of his great formal garden, although the outlines are still visible, like a ghost from the past, from the upper storeys.

Château de Chenonceaux

Chenonceaux, 35km E of Tours on N76
Owner: M. Menier
Opening times: Daily, Feb to Nov 9–sunset; Dec to Jan 9–12, 14–16
Admission charge: Yes

The 16th-century château, partly built by Philibert de l'Orme, juts out into the River Cher. A former royal property, it was inhabited in turn by Diane de Poitiers and Catherine de Medici, whose names are given to the two parterres that constitute the chief part of the garden today. Despite the great fame of the château it retains an air of serene intimacy that is emphasized by the gardens.

In the *Jardin de Diane* to the east, a broad raised walk looks down on to impeccably raked gravel paths (forbidden to visitors) and *parterres de broderie* formed of clipped santolina with domes of yew and box. On the other side of the château the *Jardin de Catherine*, another parterre, has standard roses hedged by clipped lavender encircling a pool with a jet of water. Beyond, ancient woodland of oak and chestnut is intersected with broad rides.

Cherbourg: Jardins de la Roche Fauconnière ✷

Owner: Dr Charles Favier
Opening times: By appointment, 50100 Cherbourg

A private botanical garden, the creation of the Favier family since 1870, this is one of the best collections of plants in France, containing well over 3,000 species and cultivars. There are superb trees (especially those from the southern hemisphere such as nothofagus and eucalyptus), outstanding and rare shrubs (with a notable collection of New Zealand species such as olearias and hebes), and many other treasures rarely seen outside their native countries.

Abbaye de Fontevraud

Fontevraud, 15km SE of Saumur via D947
Owner: The State
Opening times: Daily, except Tues, Apr to Sept 9–12, 14–18.30; Oct to Mar 9.30–12, 14–18
Admission charge: Yes

The great abbey was founded in 1099 and is the burial place of four medieval English kings and queens. Handsomely restored, it now serves as an exhibition centre. A recently completed medieval garden is divided into a flower garden, a garden of medicinal plants, an orchard and a vegetable garden. All the plants used are known to have been in cultivation before 1200. Although still a little sparse, it gives a fascinating impression of a garden of this period in an authentic and beautiful setting.

Arboretum de la Fosse ✷

Montoire-sur-Loire, 20km W of Vendôme via D917
Owner: M. P. Gérard
Opening times: By appointment, 41800 Montoire-sur-Loire

The Gérard family have lived here since the mid 18th century and have a long history of involvement with horticulture. One of the present owner's ancestors advised the Empress Josephine at Malmaison. This 20ha woodland garden is on acid soil and contains a very fine collection of ornamental trees and shrubs (especially those from North America), including many not commonly seen – umbellularias, stewartias, many dogwoods and wingnuts.

Les Grandes Bruyères ✷

Ingrannes, 25km NE of Orléans via N60 and D921
Owner: Comte et Comtesse B. de la Rochefoucauld
Opening times: By appointment, Ingrannes, 45450 Fay-aux-Loges
Admission charge: No

This 30ha garden and arboretum has some outstanding collections of plants. As its name suggests (*bruyère* = heather), it is especially rich in heathers and other ericaceous plants. Of the genus *Erica* there are 600 species and varieties attractively grown and arranged to provide an effective seasonal succession of colours. There is, in addition, a substantial woodland garden with excellent specimens of several different species of birch, magnolias, dogwoods, oaks and zelkovas. The tender pink-flowered *Albizia julibrissin* from China does well among many other rarities. A growing collection of old-fashioned roses is a further attraction in this excellent plantsman's garden.

ABOVE **In the woodland garden of Le Vasterival, rich plantings of herbaceous and woody plants are set in sweeping beds.**

RIGHT **Tender ceanothus and the rose 'La Follette' flourish in the protecton of a wall at Kerdalo.**

Arboretum d'Harcourt

6.5km SE of Brionne on D137
Owner: Académie d'Agriculture de France
Opening times: Daily 14–19
Admission charge: Yes

An arboretum of 6ha containing about 250 species, including many conifers, surrounds a spectacular but dilapidated moated and fortified castle.

Kerdalo ★ ⊛

2km E of Tréguier on D786
Owner: Prince Wolkonsky
Opening times: By appointment, 22220 Trédarzec

Kerdalo has been created by Prince Wolkonsky since he came to live here in 1964. In a protected and usually frost-free valley, on rich acid soil, he has made a garden of rare character and charm. It is, indeed, one of the most outstanding gardens made in Europe since World War II. Prince Wolkonsky is an artist and this is seen everywhere in his garden – in subtle colour harmonies, striking plant shapes and the masterly use of different levels. Above the house, a very ornamental 17th-century manor, informal grassy terraces, abundantly planted with trees and shrubs, rise up the hill. To the west are substantial belts of sheltering trees, with many holm oaks to protect the garden from the fierce westerly gales that are its only climatic hazard. The house and its flanking walls give protection for many tender plants – the lobster claw plant (*Clianthus puniceus*), *Vallea stipularis* from the Andes, and many others.

In front of the house decorative steps fringed with *Erigeron karvinskianus* lead down from a level lawn to an informal parterre, in which all hard edges are blurred by the richness of the planting – philadelphus, santolinas, cotinus, artemisias, sages and euphorbias. A fine variegated dogwood, *Cornus controversa* 'Variegata', rises handsomely above all this. To the left a rectangular lily pool with a Chinese pagoda is flanked by rhododendrons. To the right the garden continues down the valley, spreading on both sides, punctuated by cascades and follies. These, including a recent charming grotto, were made by the Prince himself. The stream was dammed by Prince Wolkonsky to form small lakes and many moisture-loving plants flourish here – the bog arum, skunk cabbage, many ferns, including the tender tree fern *Dicksonia antarctica*, ligularias and drifts of Asiatic primulas. Although there are very many rare plants, they are not treated as botanical exhibits but fit in harmoniously with the beauty of their setting.

Château de Maulévrier

Maulévrier, 13km SE of Cholet via D20
Owner: Commune de Maulévrier
Opening times: Daily 9–19, except Mon
Admission charge: Yes

This extraordinary garden was made 1899–1917 by Alexandre Marcel, an architect in love with the East. Richly wooded, it is full of exotic garden monuments – Japanese pavilions, snow lanterns, statues and a Khmer temple. Apart from this rather frenzied Orientalism, there is a studiously romantic lake with cascades and fine trees. In all this there is an attractive exuberance and the garden was beautifully restored 1984–7.

Rennes: Jardins du Thabor

Rue de Paris, E of city centre
Owner: Ville de Rennes
Opening times: Daily 8–sunset
Admission charge: No

This especially handsome public garden is laid out on the site of the gardens of the Abbey of St Mélaine. It is 11ha in extent and lies on attractively sloping ground. There are good specimen trees (including a magnificent cork oak), a pagoda dovecote, a sombre grotto and elegant palm houses.

Rouen: Jardin des Plantes

114 Avenue des Martyrs-de-la-Résistance, SW of city centre
Owner: Ville de Rouen
Opening times: Daily 8–sunset
Admission charge: No

These public gardens are kept to a high standard with some excellent collections of garden plants (irises, day-lilies, Hybrid Tea roses). Well-kept greenhouses contain a very wide range of tender plants.

Parc Floral La Source
8km SE of Orléans off N20
Owner: Ville d'Orléans
Opening times: Daily, Apr to Oct 9–18; Nov to Mar 14–17
Admission charge: Yes

This municipal garden on the grand scale was started in 1964 and now covers 30ha. There are very large reference collections of irises, roses and dahlias, fine specimen conifers and other well-grown ornamental trees. Unfortunately, there are also bedding schemes of shrill colours and a jumble of horticultural styles.

Le Vasterival ★ ⊛
1km W of Varengeville-sur-Mer on D75
Owner: Princess Sturdza
Opening times: By appointment, 76119 Varengeville-sur-Mer

The garden at Le Vasterival has been made by Princess Sturdza since 1958. It lies 1km from the sea on an undulating site surrounded by natural woodland of oak, ash, beech and pine. The soil is acid clay and it is a tribute to the Princess's planting skills that all the plants are bursting with vitality. The garden covers 7ha and it is maintained to perfectionist standards. The ground is very carefully prepared for planting, each new plant is placed in deep, rich, moisture-retentive compost, and all is heavily mulched with quantities of leaf-mould. The design of the garden is informal; paths wander through richly planted woods and open out into glades from which broad, impeccably-kept grass walks lead temptingly in all directions.

Although this is one of the finest plant collections in France, the collector's mania nowhere takes precedence over the beauty of the planting. A patch of colour nearby echoes the identical colour in another plant far away across dense foliage. A vast yellow border, flamboyant but disciplined, dazzles the eye. There are major collections of rhododendrons, hydrangeas, maples, birch, viburnums and camellias. Indeed, the garden is a connoisseur's collection of the very best woody plants grown in ideal conditions. Furthermore, Princess Sturdza has chosen her plants so that something wonderful is happening on every single day of the year. Few gardens elicit superlatives as easily as Le Vasterival. It sets standards that all gardeners should aim at but few will attain.

Château de Villandry ★
Villandry, 15km W of Tours on D7
Owner: M. and Mme R. Carvallo
Opening times: Daily 9–sunset
Admission charge: Yes

The Château de Villandry, a moated renaissance house of 1536, lies on flat land by the banks of the River Cher immediately before it flows into the Loire. The house passed through many hands and suffered many changes before it was bought in 1906 by the grandfather of the present owner, Dr Joachim Carvallo, a Spaniard who had come to France to study medicine. He meticulously restored the château and made the garden that exists today, influenced by the book *Les plus excellents bâtiments de France* by J. A. du Cerceau (*c*.1515–*c*.84), an irreplaceably valuable source of information about renaissance gardens and houses.

The garden, like an immense patchwork quilt, lies on three levels to the south and west of the house. At the lowest level is the ornamental kitchen garden, the *potager*, divided into nine equal squares, each of a different design outlined by low box hedges. Within these beds is planted an exquisite array of fruit and vegetables surrounded by ornamental annuals. The plantings are changed twice a year and are never exactly the same from year to year. In the spring there may be radishes, peas, oak-leaf lettuce, strawberries, sorrel, artichokes, chives and savory. These may be framed by rows of pansies of different colours, double white daisies and forget-me-nots. In the summer there will be ornamental cabbages of many kinds, gourds, leeks, tomatoes and many other vegetables carefully chosen for the beauty of their leaf and fruit. These will be edged with annual flowers – blue sage, verbenas and rudbeckias. All this is done with great panache – the liveliness of the plant shapes and colours contrasting with the rigour of the design.

Steps lead under a long arbour covered in grape vines to the second level. Here is a great parterre, the Garden of Music, in which clipped box hedges and shapes surround massed plantings of herbaceous perennials and low shrubs (irises, asters, lavender, santolina and rosemary). Tall shapes of clipped yew

like 'dumb-waiters' and elegant single jets of water provide lively vertical notes in a chiefly horizontal plan. At the same level, on the other side of a canal, is the Garden of Love, another parterre with box hedges and punctuation marks of clipped yew. Plantings in the beds are changed twice a year: in the spring pansies, stocks, tulips and forget-me-nots; in the summer dwarf dahlias in different colours.

On the third and final level there is a complete contrast – like a refreshing lemon sorbet after a delicious, but rich, meal. Here, a calm pool is surrounded by lawns and smaller pools with single jets of water. The whole is enclosed with a walk of pleached limes from which visitors look down on the exquisite garden tapestry that lies below. Set to one side to the west of the parterres are a handsome maze and a growing collection of 'simples' – medicinal herbs.

In the great ornamental *potager* at Villandry, decorative contrasts of leaf-colour and shape are exquisitely arranged.

Although this is a garden of great complexity it is never overwhelming. Despite the grave formality of its design, there is about it much vivacity and variety. In all respects it is maintained to a dazzlingly high standard.

Aquitaine, Languedoc and Central France

Albi: Palais de la Berbie

Place de la Cathédrale de Sainte Cécile, N of town centre
Owner: Ville d'Albi
Opening times: Daily 9.30–19
Admission charge: No

The garden of the episcopal palace, on a spectacular site overlooking the River Tarn, was laid out in formal parterres in the 18th century. These have now been impeccably restored, with elaborate scrollwork of dwarf box and summer bedding plants.

Jardins d'Arnaga

Cambo-les-Bains, 20km SE of Biarritz via D932
Owner: M. Triaud
Opening times: Daily, May to Sept 10–12, 14.30–18.30; Palm Sun to Apr, and early Oct 14.30–18
Admission charge: Yes

This is an engaging curiosity – a dapper French formal-style garden made at the turn of the century by the writer Edmond Rostand. His Basque villa below a tree-covered bluff looks over formal pools, yew topiary, fountains and elegant pavilions to the swift-flowing River Nive.

Arboretum de Balaine ❀

Villeneuve-sur-Allier, 16km NW of Moulins via N7 and then D433 towards Nonay
Owner: M. et Mme Maillard
Opening times: Daily, Apr to mid Nov, except Tues, Fri
Admission charge: Yes

One of the finest arboreta in France, Balaine was founded in 1804 by Aglaé Adanson, the daughter of the distinguished botanist Michel Adanson who worked at the Petit Trianon under Marie-Antoinette. Now covering an area of 20ha, it is especially rich in American trees, many of which were planted by its founder. Here are exceptionally large tulip trees, hickories, American oaks and swamp cypresses. The garden is attractively laid out: serpentine paths wind among shrubs and smaller trees and there are many streams and ornamental bridges.

Arboretum des Barres ❀

Nogent-sur-Vernisson, 19km S of Montargis on N7
Owner: Ecole Forestière
Opening times: Daily 9–12, 14–18, except Sun and hols
Admission charge: Yes

This fine arboretum was started by Philippe-André de Vilmorin, of that great dynasty of nurserymen and gardeners, in 1821. Today it extends to almost 300ha and is a treasure house of woody plants. Apart from very large collections of ornamental trees and shrubs there is an extraordinary *fructicetum*, a collection of over 1,500 species and cultivars of fruit trees, bushes and vines.

Château de la Bastie d'Urfé

Saint-Etienne-le-Molard, 14km N of Montbrison via D5 and D42
Owner: Private
Opening times: Daily 9–11.30, 14.30–18
Admission charge: Yes

The château was built in the mid 16th century by Claude d'Urfé, Ambassador to Rome in the reign of Francis I. It was he who built the unique and remarkably well-preserved grotto which survives today – the oldest in France. Arches, pilasters, figures, swags and geometric patterns are exquisitely fashioned of *rocaille*. In its heyday there were also elaborate water-works, but these have long since disappeared. Figures representing the seasons formerly stood in elaborate niches – one of the statues survives in a fine classical rotunda in the château grounds.

Château de Castries

Castries, 13km NE of Montpellier via N113 and N110
Owner: Duc de Castries
Opening times: Daily, Apr to Dec 10–12, 14.30–18, except Mon (open hol Mons)
Admission charge: Yes

The château, started in 1565 by ancestors of the present owner, dominates the centre of the village. Water for the garden is brought by an aqueduct 7km long, made in the 1660s by the great engineer Pierre Paul de Riquet, the architect of the Canal du Midi. The water emerges in a dripping grotto which feeds two circular pools with fountains at each end of a terrace lying before the house. On the other side of the terrace, below a balustrade, a further pool is revealed with an axial *allée* cut through woodland beyond it. To the left of the terrace there is a *parterre de broderie* with tall cones of clipped box and orna-mental double ramps at either end. All this, on a fairly modest scale, is an early design by André Le Nôtre dating from 1666.

Jardin de l'Evêché

Place de la République, in the centre of Castres, 42km S of Albi via N112
Owner: Commune de Castres
Opening times: Daily 9–12, 14–18 (closes 17 in winter)
Admission charge: No

Here is a remarkable sight – a garden by André Le Nôtre surviving in the very heart of a small town. It is the garden of the former bishop's palace, now the Musée Goya. It lies on the banks of the River Agout, below the south facade of the palace which was designed in the late 17th century by Jules Hardouin-Mansart. The garden was designed in 1676 and at its heart is a fine *parterre de broderie*, flamboyant scrolls of box clipped, unusually, to resemble high-relief carving, surrounded by cones and drums of clipped yew and flanked by pleached screens of hornbeam. At the centre of the garden is a generous circular pool.

Château de Hautefort ★

Hautefort, 42km E of Périgueux via N89 and D704
Owner: Mme Durosoy
Opening times: Daily, Palm Sunday to All Saints Day 9–12, 14–19, except Tues
Admission charge: Yes

The château is built on a spectacular elevated site on the edge of the village. In the Middle Ages it was in the ownership of the de Born family. Bertrand de Born, the most famous of the 12th-century troubadour-poets (mentioned by Dante in the *Divine Comedy*), lived here. The present buildings, how-ever, date almost entirely from the 17th century. In 1929 the estate was bought by Baron Henry de Bastard whose widow still lives here and has con-tinued the vast programme of restoration inaugur-ated by her husband.

The approach to the castle is from the west, by a spacious courtyard. The northern side of this court-yard is bounded by an immense tunnel of thuja, beautifully trained and clipped, with 'windows' and 'doors'. The garden lies to the south of the castle, hugging its ramparts. Made entirely in the 20th century by the Bastard family, it consists chiefly of romanticized versions of 17th-century-style parterres. Meticulously clipped box hedges and topiary of box, yew and thuja surround rows of bedding plants – begonias, verbenas and pelargoniums. The topiary, strongly architectural in character, echoes the forms of the house. A charming *parterre de broderie* in santolina spells out the interlaced initials (H and S) of the Baron and Baroness de Bastard. Behind these beds the sheer wall of the castle forms a dramatic backdrop. It is covered with several neatly wired and trained *Magnolia grandiflora* which rise to a great height and whose flowers in summer fill the garden with their citrus scent. At the foot of the ramparts, among the trunks of the magnolias, waves of the white form of *Agapanthus campanulatus* soften the stone of the massive walls.

For the exquisite beauty of its site, and the lively harmony of its 20th-century planting, Hautefort is one of the most perfect small gardens in France.

Lyons: Parc de la Tête d'Or ※

Avenue Verguin, NE of city centre
Owner: Ville de Lyon
Opening times: Daily, Apr to Sept 6–23; Oct to Mar 6–20
Admission charge: No

This is one of the finest and largest botanic gardens in France, convincingly disguised as an attractive public park. It covers an area of over 100ha in the centre of Lyons and was laid out by the Bühler brothers in the middle of the 19th century. Here are literally thousands of species and cultivars of hardy plants and a vast collection of exotics in glasshouses. The range is bewildering – like the dream stock of some celestial nurseryman. It is the most valuable garden in France in which to get a clear idea of the variety of garden plants which may be grown in southern gardens.

Montpellier: Jardin des Plantes ※

Boulevard Henri IV, NW of city centre
Owner: Ville de Montpellier
Opening times: Daily 8–12, 14–18, except Sat pm, Sun and public hols
Admission charge: Yes

This is the earliest botanic garden in France, founded by Henry IV in 1593. Although now in a rather urban setting, it is surrounded by massive stone walls and provides a leafy retreat from the traffic thundering outside. In the 19th century part of the garden was made into a *jardin anglais* with well-watered lawns, specimen trees, winding sandy paths and a pool containing the sacred lotus, *Nelumbo nucifera*, whose umbrella leaves and pink flowers rise from the water. Very extensive glasshouses shelter tropical plants and 'systematic' beds show plants arranged in their correct botanical order. There is a fine orangery and many plants are well displayed in containers. There is an especially good display of oleanders in several different colours.

Château de la Roche-Courbon

Saint-Porchaire, 17km NW of Saintes via N137
Owner: M. Guillebaud
Opening times: Daily, summer 9–12, 14–19; winter 9–12, 14–17.30
Admission charge: Yes

The château, a medieval house with massive towers, was rebuilt in the 17th century. At the same time a fine formal garden was made and is shown in detail in a surviving contemporary painting. This was used for the remarkable restoration undertaken between 1925 and 1935 by the neo-classical garden designer Ferdinand Duprat. The garden spreads south of the house with parterres and clipped cones of yew near the château and an axial vista continued by a scalloped pool which leads to a monumental fountain grotto flanked by giant steps. Some of the ideas are those of Le Nôtre, but the atmosphere of the garden is distinctly personal – a free reinterpretation of the great age of French gardening.

Tarbes: Jardin Massey

Promenade du Maubourget, N of city centre
Owner: Ville de Tarbes
Opening times: Daily 8–18
Admission charge: No

Placide Massey, born at Tarbes in 1777, became director of the gardens at Versailles but retired to his birthplace to make this charming garden, which was completed in 1853. It is laid out in the style of an

At the Château de Hautefort, reconstructed 17th-century parterres are spread below the ramparts of the castle.

Built on old olive terraces, the garden of La Chèvre d'Or combines formality and plantsmanship.

informal landscape with twisting sandy paths and spacious lawns displaying a fine collection of specimen trees and shrubs. In the summer there is a lavish display of bedding plants. A bandstand, an elegant glasshouse and various other buildings and monuments add architectural charm.

Côte d'Azur, Provence and the Alps

Aix-en-Provence: Le Pavillon de Vendôme
32 rue Célony, NW of town centre
Owner: Ville d'Aix-en-Provence
Opening times: Daily 10–12, 14–17, except Tues
Admission charge: Yes

The Pavillon Vendôme, most elegant of '17th-century follies, was built in 1665 for Louis de Mercoeur, Duc de Vendôme, by the architect Antoine Matisse. The layout of the garden is contemporary with the house and its original cruciform plan was followed when it was reconstructed in 1953. The facade of the house is decorated with fine sculptures with rural motifs – ears of corn, bunches of grapes, ripening fruit and swags of flowers. To the south the ornamental garden has at its centre a basket-shaped urn planted with canna lilies surrounded by flowering shrubs. A gate leads through to the formal garden with sandy paths radiating from a central pool and water jet. One of the paths forms a central alley, with the house at one end and a decorative fountain at the other, its length bordered with box topiary clipped into spirals and mushrooms. The whole is enclosed in the leafy shade of an alley of plane trees to the east and by figs, limes, maples and acacias on the other side.

Château d'Ansouis
Ansouis, 21km N of Aix-en-Provence via D556 to Pertuis and D56
Owner: Duc de Sabran-Pontevès
Opening times: Daily, Jan to Dec 14.30–18, except Tues; groups by appointment, 84240 Ansouis
Admission charge: Yes

Château d'Ansouis lies in a commanding position at the feet of the Lubéron hills, guarding the Aygues valley. Building started in the 12th century and the château is, remarkably, still in the possession of the family that built it. The garden, austere and dramatic, is fitted into the vertiginous terraces that lie below the château. An alley of pleached horse chestnut gives way to simple parterres of square-cut hedges and spheres of box. The spaces within the parterres have no flowering plants, only neatly raked gravel. From these terraces the land falls away dramatically and there are fine views over the landscape, with the snow-covered Alps frequently visible.

Château de la Barben

La Barben, 26km NW of Aix-en-Provence via N7 and D572
Owner: M. Pons
Opening times: Daily 10–12, 14–18, except Tues in winter
Admission charge: Yes

The castle, very much a medieval fortress with battlements and machicolations, rises spectacularly from a wooded bluff overlooking the River Touloubre. Formerly the property of the monks of St Victor in Marseilles, it passed to the de Forbin family in the 15th century and remained in that family until the present owner, Monsieur Pons, bought it in 1963. The garden lies to the south of the house, set out on a long terrace on the precipitous slopes going down to the river. At the centre of the terrace is a long parterre, perhaps the source of the legend that the garden was designed by Le Nôtre. It is edged in box, with the ghostly vestiges of *broderie* and a circular pool in the middle. Alas, it is heavily overshadowed by tall conifers which give soothing shade but have caused parts of the box parterre to wither. At the eastern extremity of the terrace is a pool and a simple grotto.

Château de Barbentane

Barbentane, 9km SW of Avignon via N570 and D35
Owner: Marquis de Barbantane
Opening times: Daily, end Mar to Oct 10–12, 14–18, except Wed; daily, Jul to Aug
Admission charge: Yes

The château was built in the 17th century, in beautiful golden Beaucaire stone, by the Marquis de Barbantane. A handsome wrought-iron gate leads into the garden to the south, ornamented with a rectangular pool surrounded with roses and with balustrades decorated with statues and baskets carved in stone edging the lawns. The double entrance staircase is emphasized with myrtle, and terracotta pots of geraniums ornament the south facade. All this is enclosed by a rich planting of bays, medlars and strawberry trees. To the right of the front, statues of Hercules and Pomona lead down to the north terraces; here are statues, Judas trees and, lower down, spectacular 200-year-old oriental planes, which twist their ancient branches up to the very windows of the château.

La Chèvre d'Or ★ ❀

Biot, 8km NW of Antibes via N7 and D4
Owner: Mme Pierre Champin
Opening times: By appointment, 06410 Biot

La Chèvre d'Or was one of the first gardens on the Riviera to be planted for all-year-round interest rather than for enjoyment only in the fashionable winter months. Both the Vicomte de Noailles (*see* Villa Noailles) and Mr Basil Leng gave advice when the garden was planned after World War II. The existing terraces of olive trees were incorporated in a formal design of Italian inspiration. It is the strict architectural layout combined with superb planting which makes La Chèvre d'Or one of the most beautiful gardens in France.

In the first years, stone pines, maritime pines and cypresses were planted to make a framework. From a central path flanked with orange trees, the main axis continues with an avenue of cypresses. On one terrace clipped olives tower above a lower hedge of box, and in another garden orange trees in ornamental pots are surrounded by patterned box. Canopies of wisteria flowering at eye-level are encircled with bushes of blue ceanothus and beds of blue-spiked *Echium candicans*. In a small cobbled courtyard plants of *Cestrum nocturnum* fill the evening air with fragrance and the leaves of scented geraniums are brushed in passing.

Château d'Entrecasteaux

Entrecasteaux, 25km SW of Draguignan via D562 and
D50
Owner: Mrs McGarvie-Munn
Opening times: Daily, Apr to Sept 10–20; Oct to Mar
10–18
Admission charge: No

The impassive château perched high on a rock in the
centre of this remote and ancient village dominates
the scene. At its feet lies a formal walled garden of
much charm. A parterre of box hedges has a circular
pool at the centre. Tradition attributes this to Le
Nôtre, who is supposed to have made designs without visiting the site on behalf of his friend the
Marquise de Sévigné, mother-in-law of the owner of
the château at the time, Monsieur de Grignan. Above
the parterre rise handsome Judas trees and the
decorative shiny-leaved nettle tree.

Château de la Garoupe ❀

Cap d'Antibes, S of Antibes
Owner: Mr and Mrs Anthony Norman
Opening times: By appointment, 06160 Juan-les-Pins

La Garoupe was laid out and planted by Lady
Aberconway, from Bodnant in Wales (q.v.), in 1907.
She and her husband acquired the property, the
whole of the Cap d'Antibes bounded on three sides
by sea, in 1905 and built the large white Italianate
château. The front gardens to the south were in
keeping; a parterre of Edwardian proportions was
reached by broad marble steps; more steps led to
lower terraces and the sea beyond.

Today her grandson, Mr Anthony Norman, has
redesigned the vast parterre in a geometric pattern of
massed lavender, rosemary and santolina, all clipped
to one level. In the centre, pyramids of box surround
elegant Italian stone urns. On the lower level, tall
pencil-thin cypresses line the terrace walk and
rugged Aleppo pines grow by the sea-shore. On
either side groups of yuccas and American agave are
planted in the dry rocky soil where pink-flowered
Amaryllis belladonna also flourish. Other side gardens are colourful in summer with sun-loving annuals such as *Lantana camara*, clarkia and petunia.
Further out and almost encroaching on the garden

proper are native *garrigue* plants (indicative of the
presence of arid limy soil), which make a low scrub.
Myrtus communis, *Phillyrea angustifolia*, *Coronilla
glauca* with *Cistus monspeliensis* and *C. albidus* and
French lavender are encouraged to seed. Naturalized
between them are scented spring-flowering freesias
and paper-white narcissi which flower in December.

To the north of the house the style of gardening is
less formal. Fruit trees, including groves of olives and
oranges and an ancient almond 3m in girth, give some
shade. Japanese cherries, flowering crabs and Judas
trees, rosy-lilac in spring before the leaves unfurl, are
underplanted with roses and spiraea. An avenue of
olives, flanked with wide borders of German iris and
Cyclamen persicum, leads to an arboretum. La Garoupe combines a well-defined design with planting of
exceptional interest.

Château la Gaude ★

Les Pinichats, 5km N of Aix-en-Provence
Owner: La Baronne de Vitrolles
Opening times: Daily 9–sunset
Admission charge: Yes

Little is known of the original history of the château,
but the gardens were laid out in the 18th century. A
moated box parterre, designed by Charles Albert
Pisani in about 1750 in the form of a circular
labyrinth, is a copy of that at Villa Pisani (q.v.) at Strà
near Padua in Italy. It has recently been restored and
is immaculately maintained. Steps descend through
two broad terraces below the labyrinth and finally
lead to an expanse of smooth lawn where clipped yew
specimens surround a basin of water with a fountain.
Both the fountain and statues of stone dogs are by
Chastelle, the 18th-century sculptor from Aix-en-
Provence.

Château de Gourdon

Gourdon, 14km NE of Grasse via D2085 and D3
Owner: Comtesse de Zalewska
Opening times: Daily, Jul to mid Sept 11–13, 14–18; mid
Sept to Jun 10–12, 14–18, except Tues
Admission charge: Yes

This extraordinary site, 450m high on the edge of the
precipitous valley of the River Loup, has been

crowned by a fortress since the Saracens occupied the area in the 9th century. The present château, sturdily built round an inner courtyard, dates chiefly from the 17th century. It was acquired by an American, Miss Norris, in 1918 and she restored it. The gardens, clinging to the edge of the cliff, were laid out in 1972 by the garden designer Tobie Loup de Viane with a formal garden combining herbs and old roses, a parterre of box hedges clipped into rounded tops and a solemn but effective rectangle of box cones, with a standard box at each corner clipped into a sphere. Roses and seeded valerian festoon the high walls, from which there are remarkable views.

Le Jardin d'Altitude du Haut Chitelet ❁

Col de la Schlucht, 37km W of Colmar via D417
Owner: Jardins Botaniques de la Ville et de l'Université de Nancy
Opening times: Daily, Jun to mid Oct, sunrise–sunset
Admission charge: No

Started in 1966, this unique garden is a collection of high-altitude plants from all over the world. It is situated on a spectacular site at a height of over 1,200m in the Vosges mountains. The plants are grouped in 'geographical' beds which contain over 2,300 different species. It is enthralling to see so many alpine plants, many of great rarity, flourishing in such perfect conditions.

Jas Crema

Le Barroux, 12km N of Carpentras on D938
Owner: Baronne de Waldner
Opening times: By appointment, 84330 Caromb

Jas Crema is an old *bastide* lying on a south-facing slope opposite the hill town of Le Barroux. From the house and garden there is a view of the snow-capped mountain of Mont Ventoux across the plain of Carpentras. The climate in this part of Haute-Provence is severe; cold winters followed by months of fierce sun make water and some shade indispensable. Bought by Baronne de Waldner in 1979, the garden is entirely her creation and bears her personal stamp. Although strongly architectural, with borders running along the terraces or cutting across them at right angles, the garden is richly and imaginatively

planted. A distinctive feature is the use of unusual plants trained into animal shapes. A main avenue, bordered with oleanders, bisects the terraces, on which small hedged enclosures have different themes. A greenhouse, designed by Madame de Waldner and her architect Alexander Fabre, houses a fine collection of 500 species of passion flower, only a few of them hardy enough to be grown outdoors. Below the house, a field of lavender, in a geometric pattern with paths radiating from a central focal point, makes a link with the tradition of lavender cultivation in Provence.

Station Alpine du Col du Lautaret ❁

28km NW of Briançon via N91
Owner: University of Grenoble
Opening times: Daily, 20 Jun to 20 Sept 8–12, 14–18, except Fri
Admission charge: Yes

Set 2,100m up on an alpine col, this is one of the highest gardens in Europe. It was started in 1894 by Professor Lachman of the University of Grenoble and has now become one of the finest collections of high altitude plants in the world. Over 5,000 varieties are attractively displayed in small beds linked by winding sandy paths. Here are collections of indigenous plants from the European Alps, the Himalayas, the Atlas Mountains and most of the botanically important mountainous regions of the world. This is not a garden in which to admire fine design, but it is a place where one may relish an extraordinary collection of plants growing vigorously in ideal conditions.

Marseilles: Le Parc Borély

62 Avenue Clot-Bey, S of city centre
Owner: Ville de Marseille
Opening times: *Park* at all times; *botanical garden* daily 8–17.30, except Sat, Sun and public hols
Admission charge: Yes

The house was built from 1767 onwards in grand neo-classical style by the shipowner Louis Borély. Ornate wrought-iron gates open on to a formal garden with, on one side, two alleys of plane trees. A circular pool is flanked by two parterres of turf enclosing pools with jets of water. Colour is provided by four giant baskets usually planted with canna lilies in bright colours. A balustraded terrace, with a rectangular pool, separates the house from the garden. Beyond the formal garden is a 19th-century landscape garden designed by Jean-Pierre Barillet-Deschamps where a grotto of glistening *rocaille* lies in the shelter of a fine swamp cypress. Nearby is a very rare tree from China, *Torreya grandis*. Paths amble towards a lake with an elegant pavilion on an island. In addition to all this is a substantial botanic garden made in 1915 with a comprehensive collection of indigenous French plants, a large collection of orchids, and several groups of plants arranged according to their qualities – oleaginous, aromatic, toxic and so on.

Menton: Jardin des Colombières

Boulevard de Garavan
Owner: Mme E. Ladan-Bockairy
Opening times: Daily, Jan to Sept 9–12, 15–sunset
Admission charge: Yes

The house, on south-facing slopes above Menton, is now a hotel. The garden was created in the early 20th century by the artist Ferdinand Bac. His plan was to make small private spaces about the house and, as the garden extended up the precipitous hillside, to make it increasingly wild. He introduced fine garden buildings and monuments – an arcaded bridge, a *nymphaeum*, a mausoleum and a pool and garden dedicated to Homer. These are carefully placed, either to frame or become part of some view or to command a vista over the glittering bay of Menton below. Rows of pencil cypresses march up the slopes and maritime pines dotted about give welcome shade.

Menton: Le Clos du Peyronnet ❀

Avenue Aristide-Briand, E outskirts of Menton-Garavan
Owner: Mr William Waterfield
Opening times: By appointment, Avenue Aristide-Briand, 06500 Menton-Garavan

This garden, laid out on south-facing terraces, belonged to Mr and Mrs Derick Waterfield who came here in 1915. They left it to their son, Humphrey Waterfield, the landscape gardener, who died in

1971. It is now the property of his nephew. Rich and varied plantings are seen against the background of some of the old olives and cypresses that were growing on the terraces when the Waterfields came here. In this favoured microclimate many rare and tender plants flourish – the evergreen winter-flowering *Buddleja asiatica*, very many different sages, the brilliant South American marmalade bush (*Streptosolen jamesonii*) and countless other unusual plants. Water is an important ingredient; there is a circular lily pond and a series of stepped pools that descend the hillside giving reflections of sky and foliage. Although there are pergolas, stone arches and other architectural elements, the overwhelming feeling is one of tropical abundance.

Menton: Villa Val-Rahmeh Botanic Garden ❀

Avenue St Jacques, E outskirts of Menton-Garavan
Owner: Muséum d'Histoire Naturelle in Paris
Opening times: Daily, except Tues, Oct to Apr 10–12, 14–16; May to Sept 10–12, 15–19
Admission charge: Yes

A line of Canary Island palms (*Phoenix canariensis*), a feature of many Mediterranean coastal town boulevards, flanks the drive leading to the villa. The garden was originally planted by Lord Radcliffe at the beginning of this century; it was later maintained by Miss Campbell. It lies on a steep slope where terraces and high retaining walls provide sheltered sites for many plants, rarely seen even in this favoured locality. Rainfall is over 75cm, light intensity is high and frost is exceedingly rare. Specimens of the more commonplace pepper tree, from South America, with delicate ferny foliage and cherry-red fruit in season, cast light shade, and daturas, potato bushes (including the spectacular *Solanum rantonnetii*, with massed purple flowers), avocado pears, citrus fruits, mimosas, tender yuccas and floriferous lantana seem perfectly at home here. The villa walls are clothed with the tender *Phaedranthus buccinatorius*, with tubular flowers of pale orange, and the smaller leaved red-flowered *Quamoclit coccinea*. Be-

The peony garden at the Villa Noailles includes a spiral water-column copied from an Italian renaissance model.

low the house the lotus used to thrive in a central pool, but it and other exotics suffered from severe winters in 1985–7. Climbers such as bougainvillea, tecoma and thunbergia cling to the terrace and house walls above. A catalogue is available of the plants grown in the gardens and every plant is labelled.

Nîmes: Le Jardin de la Fontaine
Quai de la Fontaine
Owner: Ville de Nîmes
Opening times: At all times
Admission charge: No

Le Jardin de la Fontaine is a cascade of verdure, terraces and gushing water on the slopes of Mont Cavalier. The spring which feeds this garden is of great antiquity, ante-dating the Romans who built a spectacular temple of Diana and other buildings. The garden today owes its form to the military engineer Mareschal, who in the 18th century preserved the classical remains and built a handsome new setting for the spring.

Passing through the superb entrance gates and crossing the first canal, the visitor discovers parterres with summer bedding and pollarded horse chestnuts. Further on, canals curve round a great pool fed by the subterranean spring. To one side is a fine 18th-century statue of a nymph by Dominique Raché, surrounded by stone balustrades and carved urns. To the right steps lead to the foundations of the Roman theatre where a spring gushes from 19th-century ornamental shell-work incorporating the palm tree and crocodile – symbols of Nîmes since the 16th century. In this shady place are many summer bedding plants and ornamental trees – Judas trees, medlars and the Indian bean tree. Paths wind uphill through informal planting and the energetic walker is rewarded with marvellous views of the town.

Villa Noailles ❁
Avenue Guy-de-Maupassant, W of Grasse
Owner: M. de la Haye-Jousselin
Opening times: By appointment, Avenue Guy-de-Maupassant, 06130 Grasse

The gardens lie on south-facing terraces on a steep hillside just west of Grasse; they were laid out by the Vicomte de Noailles in the years after World War II. An adequate water supply from hillside springs and protection from north winds makes it possible to grow a very wide range of plants. The layout, dictated by the original pattern of olive terraces which stretch westward beyond the villa, is compartmental. A series of hedged horizontal 'rooms' connected by paths and steep steps have been planted in different themes. Some of these gardens are secret enclosures; others are deliberate stage settings framing wide views to the valley. In one enclosure near the house, made with mounded box hedges, tree peonies are undercarpeted with a lattice-work of pink oxalis. Another room alongside is edged with ornate topiary alternately cut to frame statues and to open vistas to the hills beyond the garden. A pergola on which pink- and white-flowered Judas bushes are trained stretches to the west along the top terrace. In the entrance court fountains set in the walls fill the air with the sound of splashing water, while further cascades gush down the hillside and are caught in stone-edged pools. This formal layout provides a perfect setting for native Mediterranean plants with aromatic leaves and flowers as well as rare exotics. In the flat meadow at the bottom of the slope planting is more naturalistic. Here, between ancient olive trees, 40-year-old magnolias, poplars and davidias thrive in the moist soil and enjoy the summer heat. The gardens reflect the late Vicomte de Noailles' sense of history and his great love of plants.

Bambouseraie de Prafrance ❁
Anduze, 13km SW of Alès via N110 and D910
Owner: M. Yves Crouzet
Opening times: Daily, Easter to Oct 9.30–12, 14–19; Jul, Aug 9.30–19
Admission charge: Yes

This garden was started in 1855 by Eugène Mazel, a spice merchant with business connections in the East. He became interested in bamboos, then little known in Europe, and built up the remarkable collection of over 100 species and varieties that exists today, thriving in the rich soil and warm Mediterranean climate of the Cévennes. Water is provided by 5km of irrigation canals. The entrance to the garden sets the scene – an extraordinary 400m avenue of the giant bamboo *Phyllostachys mitis*, which has grown to a height of 20m. In addition to the bamboos there are many conifers, magnolias, ginkgos, a lotus garden (where the sacred lotus *Nelumbo nucifera* flourishes), a Japanese garden and a handsome avenue of the palm *Trachycarpus excelsus*. Bamboo features extensively in the garden buildings – in door handles, railings and pipes, and woven into matting.

Jardins de la Fondation Ephrussi de Rothschild ✳

Villa Ile de France, Avenue D. Semeria, St-Jean-Cap-Ferrat, 5km E of Nice
Owner: Institut de France
Opening times: Daily, Dec to Oct 9–12, 14–18, except Mon; for groups tel. 93 01 33 09
Admission charge: Yes

At the beginning of this century Baroness Ephrussi de Rothschild laid out the villa gardens in a series of compartments representing different architectural and planting styles. A Spanish garden has a grotto of pink marble and a dolphin fountain; the Italian garden, with a double staircase and wrought-iron balustrading, is shaded by large Judas trees and the evergreen camphor tree. A Japanese area has traditional stone ornaments and foliage plants. The largest section, laid out below the south facade of the villa, is French in style with clipped pyramids of bay giving vertical accents above massed planting of silver-leaved gazanias. There are many interesting tender plants which thrive in the favourable climate. Hedges of *Teucrium fruticans*, *Pittosporum tobira* and the drought-resistant American holly (*Ilex vomitoria*), used as an edging plant instead of the more traditional dwarf box, create a formal framework between scented bushes of the florists' broom (*Cytisus maderensis*), cestrums and raphiolepis.

Villa Thuret ✳

Chemin G. Raymond, Cap d'Antibes, S of Antibes
Owner: Institut Nationale de Recherche Agronomique
Opening times: Daily 8–12, 14–18, except Sat, Sun and hols
Admission charge: No

The botanist Gustave Adolphe Thuret started this garden in 1856. The site is unexcitingly flat and the view of the sea is now obscured by dense planting. It is primarily a botanical research station with a special interest in the acclimatization of exotic plants to the Mediterranean climate. Here is a very large collection of Australasian plants (especially myrtles, eucalyptus and mimosas), palms, and many subtropical rarities not often seen in Europe.

Note

At the time of writing there were various gardens for which it was impossible to give details because of uncertainty of access – either because of change of ownership or because of restoration work. The following gardens in France have been omitted for these reasons. In each case they are outstanding examples and the reader is advised to try and discover the latest position as regards access to them. But it should *not* be assumed that owners welcome visitors and application must be made in writing before attempting a visit:

Villa les Cèdres, St-Jean-Cap-Ferrat (Côte d'Azur. NW of town centre.) A very large collection of tender plants established in this century, one of the finest botanical collections in France.

La Mormaire, Grosrouvre, Montfort-l'Amaury (Ile de France. 23km W of Versailles off the N12.) Dramatic and beautifully conceived formal garden of clipped hedges and topiary made by an English gardener, Gordon Turner, in the 20th century.

Le Potager, Fleury-en-Bière (Ile de France. 13km SW of Melun by the N372.) Informal plantsman's garden landscaped since 1950 by the Danish landscape architect Mogens Toede.

La Serre de la Madone, Menton (Côte d'Azur.) This famous garden was made by Lawrence Johnston in the inter-war years after he had made his English garden at Hidcote (q.v.). Terraces form different compartments in which water and rich planting combine in disciplined luxuriance.

SPAIN AND PORTUGAL

From the horticultural point of view Spain and Portugal, surprisingly, have much in common with Great Britain. Both have great variations in climate which allow the cultivation of a very wide range of plants and both initiated plant-hunting expeditions which introduced countless new plants to Europe. But the extremes of climate are much greater in the Iberian peninsula which, after Switzerland, is the most mountainous region of Europe. In the high tableland of Spain there is a range of temperature as wide as any found in Central Europe. At Leon, for example, the mean January temperature is 2.7°C (with minimum temperatures plunging many degrees below zero); in Seville, in the deep south, it is 10.5°C with a minimum temperature of 2.7°C. Mean July temperatures are 24°C and 28°C respectively. In the tableland the average annual rainfall is in the region of 48cm – almost exactly the same as that for Seville; whereas in Santiago, in the northern maritime zone, it is 166cm. Lisbon has a climate similar to that of Seville but, because of its position on the Atlantic coast, it is more temperate and with an appreciably higher rainfall – an annual average of 70cm. This diversity of climate, and immensely wide range of sites, goes hand in hand with a very large and fascinating endemic flora, the most extensive in Europe.

Gardens of the Iberian peninsula were, to their great benefit, exposed to decisive foreign influence. Spain and Portugal were heavily romanized. Pliny the Elder spent some time in Spain and left a valuable account of what he saw, including much detail of the flora. The characteristic Spanish or Portuguese garden with covered walks, courtyards and arcades has much in common with what is known of the Roman villa gardens. Excavations at Mérida, Conimbriga and Italica (the birthplace of the Emperors Hadrian and Trajan) have shown how magnificent the Roman villas in Spain and Portugal were. At the Finca de la Concepción (q.v.) near Málaga, the existing Roman remains, fallen columns sprawling among the subtropical foliage, contribute much to the atmosphere of the garden.

After the collapse of the Roman Empire and the subsequent rule of the Visigoths from the early 5th century, when the great Roman estates were laid waste, virtually nothing is known of the horticultural history of the Iberian peninsula. The arrival of the Islamic invaders, Moors from North Africa, in the early 8th century was a crucial event in its cultural history. Later Islamic colonists came from Damascus and this remarkable civilization was at its

A water-colour by L. H. Fischer shows the Patio de l'Acequia in the Generalife in the late 19th century (1885).

height during the caliphate of Córdoba in the 10th and 11th centuries. The Caliph Abdur al Rahman III founded the university at Córdoba where classical learning was rediscovered 400 years before the Renaissance in Italy, and where there was a flourishing school of botany. The Caliph also built the exquisite city-palace of Medina Azahara (q.v.), just outside Córdoba, which is being meticulously restored and where a 20th-century visitor may have a vivid impression of what an aristocratic Islamic garden of the early 11th century was like. Particularly in the south, there are countless examples of the Islamic influence on Spanish and Portuguese gardening: the widespread decorative use of brilliantly coloured tiles, *azulejos* (usually blue but often in other colours, including green, the colour of the Prophet's head-dress); the ingenious and frequently ornamental irrigation systems – such as may still be seen in the Patio de los Naranjos (q.v.) at Córdoba (which may be the most ancient continuously gardened site in Europe) and in many other Spanish and Portuguese gardens; and the many courtyard gardens, especially the delightful *carmenes* of Granada, described by James Dickie in *The Islamic Garden* as the typically Islamic 'emphasis on the intimate and the within'. Under Christian rule, the Islamic tradition of the intimate patio garden continued on grander town estates, such as the 16th-century Casa de Pilatos (q.v.) and Palacio de las Dueñas (q.v.) in Seville and the Palacio de Viana (q.v.) in Córdoba. This period also produced the distinctive *mudejar* architecture, a decorative style associated with Islamic work under Christian rule.

Following the decline of the Islamic empire, Spain was unified under Ferdinand and Isabella in the late 15th century, and a stable and separate kingdom of Portugal emerged under the House of Avis. The next major influence on garden development was the Italian Renaissance. In Portugal in the early 16th century Afonso de Albuquerque made a garden at the Quinta da Bacalhôa (q.v.) which was influenced by what he had seen in Italy. The first Habsburg king of Spain, Charles V, and his son Philip II, laid out a renaissance garden at Aranjuez (q.v.); in the early 17th century Philip IV made the Buen Retiro (q.v.) in similar style. Under the first Bourbon king of Spain, Philip V (1683–1746), the grandson of Louis XIV, there was great French influence on garden design; avenues and *allées* were planted using limes and hornbeams, trees new to Spain; French gardeners such as the Esteban (Stéphane) Boutelous, father and son, came to Spain; and fashionable parterres were introduced at Aranjuez (q.v.). For Philip V's new palace of La Granja (q.v.), formal water gardens were laid out of a complexity to rival Versailles (q.v.) or the Villa d'Este at Tivoli (q.v.).

The 18th-century English landscape garden also influenced Spain and Portugal. In Portugal, the English aesthete William Beckford made a landscape garden at Monserrate (q.v.) in the 1790s and the park at the Castelo da Pena (q.v.) was laid out in the mid 19th century, with wooded slopes, serpentine paths and a rustic cottage, both gardens being inspired by the northern European romantic tradition. In Spain romanticism was allied with neo-classicism and produced such distinctively Spanish gardens as El Retiro (q.v.) and La Concepción (q.v.) in Málaga, El Laberinto de Horta (q.v.) in Barcelona and the Royal Botanic Garden (q.v.) in Madrid. The next distinctive garden style to emerge was, perhaps, that of the extraordinary modernistic city park of Gaudí's Parque Güell (q.v.) in Barcelona, which was started in 1900. The French architect J. C. N. Forestier, who came to Spain at the invitation of King Alfonso XIII in 1918, designed several outstandingly attractive gardens ranging in size from the tiny garden for the Casa del Rey Moro (q.v.) in Ronda to the Montjuïc gardens in Barcelona (q.v.).

Today, although tourism flourishes in Spain and Portugal, garden visiting, with the exception of the world-famous sites such as the Alhambra (q.v.) or the Palácio de Fronteira (q.v.), is a neglected pleasure. There are many outstandingly good gardens where, even in the height of the holiday season, one may well be the only visitor. The Spanish and Portuguese gardening traditions are certainly among the most interesting, and most unjustly neglected, in European horticulture.

Spain

Northern Spain: Galicia, Cantabria and Catalonia

Barcelona: Parque de la Ciudadela

Passeig de Picasso, NE of city centre
Owner: Municipio de Barcelona
Opening times: Daily 10–sunset
Admission charge: No

This public park was laid out on the ruins of the old citadel in 1868 to the design of J. Fontsere y Mestres, but later altered (in one part by the French garden designer J. C. N. Forestier, who in 1919 designed the Plaza de Armas). It contains a variety of fine specimen trees, including cedars, limes, magnolias, paulownias and tree yuccas. There are formal and informal sections, much sculpture of quality by Catalan artists, a great cascade and lake.

Barcelona: Parque Güell

Carrer d'Olot, off Travessera de Dalt, NW of city centre
Owner: Municipio de Barcelona
Opening times: Daily 10–sunset
Admission charge: No

Originally intended as a garden city of sixty houses, this hillside park, begun in 1900, is the work of the original Catalan architect, Antonio Gaudí, commissioned by his patron and friend, Eusebio Güell.

Although there are palm, pine and carob trees, the principal interest is in the buildings, most of which are covered in fantastic polychromatic tile-work. Many are supported on arcades of stone columns like fossilized palm trees, inspired, perhaps, by the follies in the Parque de Samá at Cambrils (q.v.) designed by Gaudí's master, J. Fontsere y Mestres.

Barcelona: El Laberinto de Horta

La Vall d'Hebron, 5km NW of city centre off B20
Owner: Municipio de Barcelona
Opening times: Daily 10–sunset
Admission charge: No

Situated on a hill overlooking the city and bay, El Laberinto is a most magnificent example of a late 18th-century formal terraced garden in the neo-classical style, with an elegant summer house, pool, temples, a grotto, sculpture, balustraded staircases and a maze.

Barcelona: Parque de Montjuïc

Plaza d'España, SE city centre
Owner: Municipio de Barcelona
Opening times: *Main park* at all times (*see below*)

Between 1915 and 1929 a wooded hillside in the city was transformed into a public park to the designs of the French garden designer J. C. N. Forestier, who was brought to Spain by King Alfonso XIII, and subsequently to Barcelona by the artist José Maria Sert. Forestier's garden, recently restored, has elegant terraces, watercourses, pergolas and clipped cypresses in a neo-Muslim style.

In addition there are further self-contained gardens distributed about the hillside. The *Mirador del Alcalde* (open daily) has mosaic floors, succulent plants, tropical trees and a beautiful view of the port. The *Jardin de Mosen Jacinto Verdaguer* (open daily), laid out in 1970, is dedicated to Catalan poets. It has many bulbous plants from America and South

The Gardens of Spain and Portugal

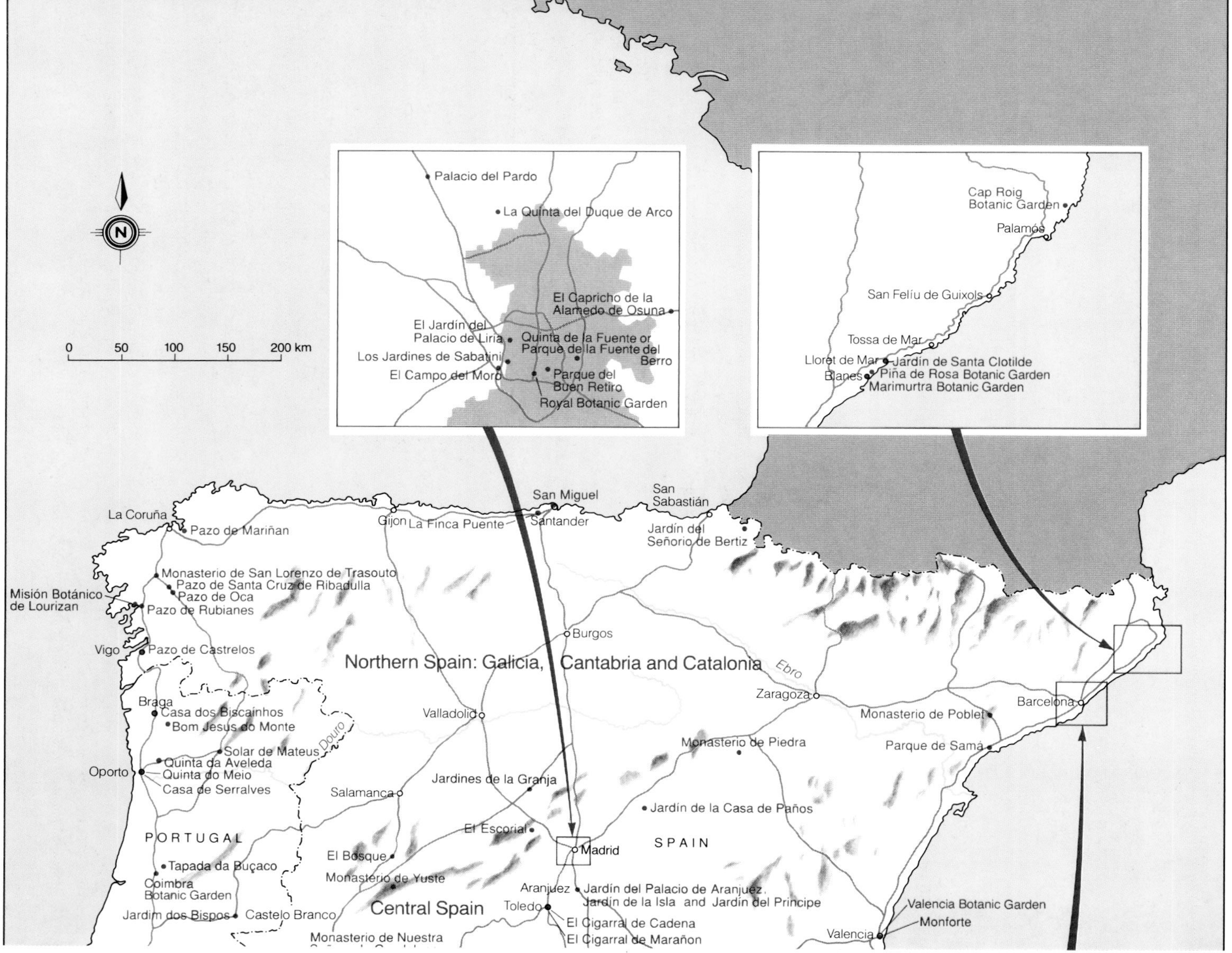
N
0
50
100
150
200 km
Palacio del Pardo
La Quinta del Duque de Arco
El Capricho de la Alamedo de Osuna
El Jardín del Palacio de Liria
Quinta de la Fuente or Parque de la Fuente del Berro
Los Jardines de Sabatini
El Campo del Moro
Parque del Buen Retiro
Royal Botanic Garden
Cap Roig Botanic Garden
Palamós
San Felíu de Guixols
Tossa de Mar
Lloret de Mar
Jardín de Santa Clotilde
Blanes
Piña de Rosa Botanic Garden
Marimurtra Botanic Garden
La Coruña
Pazo de Mariñan
Gijon
La Finca Puente
San Miguel
Santander
San Sebastián
Jardín del Señorio de Bertiz
Monasterio de San Lorenzo de Trasouto
Pazo de Santa Cruz de Ribadulla
Pazo de Oca
Misión Botánico de Lourizan
Pazo de Rubianes
Burgos
Vigo
Pazo de Castrelos
Northern Spain: Galicia, Cantabria and Catalonia
Ebro
Braga
Casa dos Biscainhos
Bom Jesus do Monte
Valladolid
Zaragoza
Barcelona
Monasterio de Poblet
Douro
Solar de Mateus
Monasterio de Piedra
Parque de Samá
Oporto
Quinta da Aveleda
Quinta do Meio
Casa de Serralves
Jardines de la Granja
Salamanca
Jardín de la Casa de Paños
PORTUGAL
El Escorial
SPAIN
Madrid
El Bosque
Tapada da Buçaco
Monasterio de Yuste
Coimbra Botanic Garden
Aranjuez
Jardín del Palacio de Aranjuez, Jardín de la Isla and Jardín del Principe
Central Spain
Toledo
Valencia Botanic Garden
Monforte
Jardim dos Bispos
Castelo Branco
El Cigarral de Cadena
Monasterio de Nuestra
El Cigarral de Marañon
Valencia

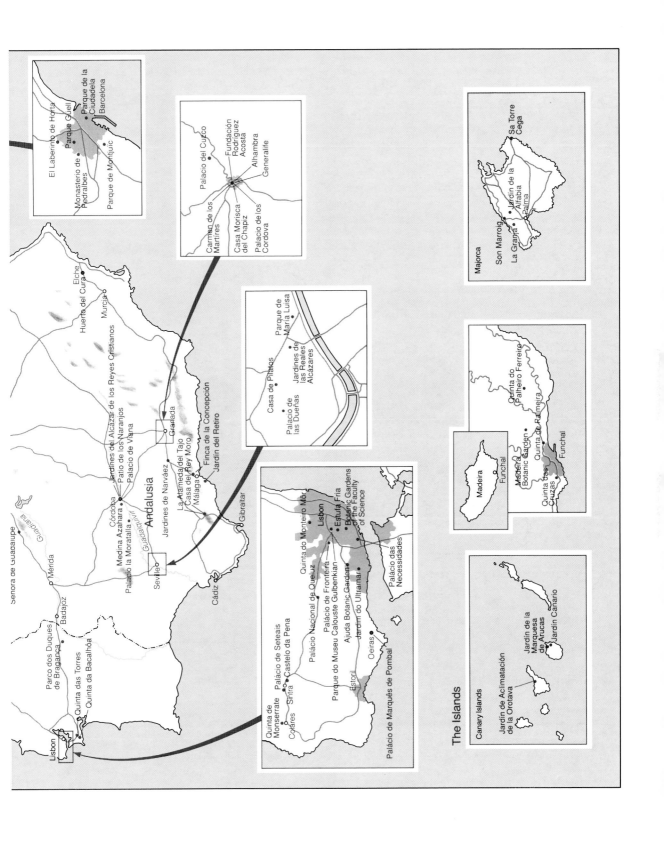

Barcelona (inset)
- El Laberinto de Horta
- Parque Güell
- Monasterio de Pedralbes
- Parque de Montjuïc
- Parque de la Ciudadela
- Barcelona

Granada (inset)
- Palacio del Cuzco
- Carmen de los Mártires
- Casa Morisca del Chapiz
- Palacio de los Córdova
- Fundación Rodríguez Acosta
- Alhambra
- Generalife

Majorca
- Son Marroig
- La Granja
- Jardín de la Alfabia
- Sa Torre Cega
- Palma

Seville (inset)
- Casa de Pilatos
- Palacio de las Dueñas
- Parque de María Luisa
- Jardines de las Reales Alcázares

Andalusia
- Elche
- Huerto del Cura
- Murcia
- Jardines del Alcázar de los Reyes Cristianos
- Patio de los Naranjos
- Palacio de Viana
- Córdoba
- Granada
- Jardines de Narváez
- La Alameda/del Tajo
- Casa del Rey Moro
- Málaga
- Finca de la Concepción
- Jardín del Retiro
- Medina Azahara
- Palacio la Moratalla
- Guadalquivir
- Sevilla
- Cádiz
- Gibraltar
- Señora de Guadalupe
- Guadiana
- Mérida
- Badajoz
- Parco dos Duques de Bragança
- Quinta das Torres
- Quinta da Bacalhõa

Madeira
- Quinta do Palheiro Ferreiro
- Quinta de Palmeira
- Madeira Botanic Garden
- Quinta das Cruzas
- Funchal

Lisbon (inset)
- Quinta de Monserrate
- Colares
- Palácio de Seteais
- Castelo da Pena
- Sintra
- Palácio Nacional de Queluz
- Quinta do Monteiro Mor
- Palácio de Fronteira
- Parque do Museu Calouste Gulbenkian
- Estufa Fria
- Botanic Gardens of the Faculty of Science
- Ajuda Botanic Garden
- Jardim do Ultramar
- Lisbon
- Estoril
- Oeiras
- Palácio das Necessidades
- Palácio de Marquês de Pombal
- Lisbon

The Islands

Canary Islands
- Jardín de Aclimatación de la Orotava
- Jardín de la Marquesa de Arucas
- Jardín Canario

Africa. The *Jardín del Poeta Joan Maragall (open by appointment)* is a formal garden with sculptures, parterres and fountains surrounding the Palacete de Albéñiz. The *Jardín de Mosen Costa y Llobera (open by appointment)* is a rock garden designed by Juan Panella on a south-facing slope; it contains an extensive collection of cacti and other succulents, including many very old specimens. The *Jardín Botánico (open daily 10–13, except Sun, Mon)* was founded on the site of an old quarry and its south-facing slope has been made into a rock garden with many species from the Balearic Islands, North Africa and the southern Mediterranean, while in cooler areas, shaded by deciduous trees, are many indigenous plants from northern Europe.

Barcelona: Monasterio de Pedralbes
Avenue de Pedralbes off Avenide de la Diagonal
Owner: Real Monasterio de Santa Maria de Pedralbes
Opening times: Tues–Sat 10–13, 16–18, Sun 9–16.30
Admission charge: No

The 16th-century cloister garden of a 14th-century convent of the Poor Clares on a hillside above Barcelona preserves the traditional cross plan, with herbs, fragrant shrubs, bulbs, fruit trees and cypress irrigated in Arabic manner from the central fountain. In one corner, 18th-century tiled benches form an outdoor room around a second fountain. The kitchen garden seen from the hospital windows is also neatly cultivated and under traditional irrigation.

Jardín del Señorio de Bertiz
Bertizarana, 40km N of Pamplona on the N121
Owner: Diputación Foral
Opening times: Daily, June to Sept 9–13, 14–20; Oct to May 9–13, 16–18
Admission charge: No

An extensive park with holm oaks, Spanish chestnuts and Italian cypresses is separated from the garden proper by a grille. Here are many conifers – monkey puzzles, cedars (*Cedrus atlantica* and *C. libani*) and *Sequoiadendron giganteum* – interspersed with flowering shrubs, among which are camellias and azaleas. The River Bibasoa, overlooked by a decorative gazebo, flows through the garden and is an essential part of it. A romantic bridge leads across an ornamental lake to an island with a pergola. With its *art nouveau* architecture and its foaming cascade, this landscape garden is an atmospheric piece of 19th-century romanticism.

Pazo de Castrelos
Castrelos, 2km SW of Vigo off C550
Owner: Concelio de Vigo
Opening times: Daily sunrise–sunset
Admission charge: No

A large, wooded park with a house (now a museum) dating from the 17th century. Behind the house is an extensive formal box garden, flanked by a rose walk and a terrace wall against which a series of stone escutcheons has been assembled. Avenues of magnolias and plane trees traverse a romantic garden in which grow a tulip tree, a *Magnolia grandiflora* and a *Camellia japonica* cultivar, respectively reputed to be the oldest in Europe, the biggest in Galicia and the oldest in Galicia.

Misión Botánico de Lourizan ❀
4km W of Pontevedra on C550
Owner: Junta de Galicia
Opening times: By appointment, Apartado de Corrers, 36080 Pontevedra
Admission charge: No

This late 19th-century house and estate in a sheltered valley above Pontevedra Bay has been a forestry research station since 1943. A small arboretum, with tall tree ferns and camellias (some 25m high) luxuriating in the temperate climate, survives from the original planting. Along the outlying drives, North American and European conifers and a large range of Australasian trees are being grown in forestry trials, as are disease-resistant forms of Spanish chestnut.

Marimurtra Botanic Garden ❀
Blanes, 45km S of Gerona, E of A11
Owner: Fundación Carlos Faust
Opening times: Daily 10–sunset, except Jan 1, 6, Dec 25
Admission charge: Yes

A 2ha estate on a beautiful stretch of the Costa Brava was purchased piecemeal from 1924–52 by Karl Faust, a German businessman resident in Barcelona. On 0.25ha of rock perched on a cliff over the sea he made the botanic garden in which over 3,500 species are now cultivated, including a wide range of Mediterranean plants and succulents as well as exotic flora from Australia, South Africa and South America.

Pazo de Mariñan

4km N of Betanzos off LC163, 16km SE of Coruña
Owner: Diputación Provincial de Coruña
Opening times: By appointment, Mariñas de Betanzos, Sada, Coruña
Admission charge: No

Terraced gardens are reached from the house by means of a double staircase with fringes and fountains carved in Galician granite. A large box parterre extending towards the sea is edged by woodland with some of the first *Eucalyptus globulus* to be introduced to Galicia.

Pazo de Oca ★

San Esteban de Oca, 25km SE of Santiago de Compostela, off N525
Owner: Duquesa de Medinaceli
Opening times: Daily, summer 10–13.30, 16–19.30
Admission charge: Yes

A magnificent manor house of 1746, joined by a gallery to a later baroque church, has a patio-like garden around an 18th-century fountain of an unusual trefoil shape.

Oca's glory, however, is the inner garden watered by a stream coming to rest in two large, formal pools. These are divided by a bridge in the baroque style of neighbouring Santiago and a stone boat manned by sailors in 18th-century dress 'floats' in the lower pool. The surrounding walks are shadowed by box trees and the mild, moist climate ensures a green pall of mosses and lichens over all the stonework, engendering a dream-like atmosphere increased when the garden is shrouded in mist.

In the late 19th century the garden was given horticultural interest with the advice of Francisco Vie, the French-born head gardener at the Royal Palace, Madrid, so that now fine camellias, including a magnificent *Camellia reticulata*, photinias, magnolias and *Cryptomeria japonica* overhang the principal walks. The garden has been restored and is maintained sympathetically by its present owner.

Monasterio de Piedra

Nuévalos, off the N11 SW of Zaragoza, 11km SE of Alhama de Aragón
Owner: Monasterio de Piedra SA
Opening times: Daily 9–21
Admission charge: Yes

The Cistercians built a monastery on this rocky site in the 12th century and what remains of it is now a hotel. In the 19th century the gardens were made into a wild and imaginative park by the landscape architect J. F. Muntadas. La Piedra derives its name from the natural outcrops of stone which were incorporated into the design and used to fashion the fantastic grottoes and cascades (one of them 52m high) of this romantic garden. Precipitous paths and vertiginous steps lead through woodland which is criss-crossed with rushing streams.

Piña de Rosa Botanic Garden ✳

Blanes – Santa Cristina, 45km S of Gerona, E of A11
Owner: Dr Ing Fernando Riviere de Caralt
Opening times: Daily, summer 9–18; winter 10–16
Admission charge: Yes

One of the most important succulent, tropical and desert plant collections in the world, founded by Dr Riviere in 1951 on a cliff overlooking the sea. More than 7,000 species are arranged systematically in rock-edged beds. The collection of opuntias (600 species of 18 genera) is considered by many to be the most important in the world, that of the agaves, aloes, yuccas and mesembryanthemums among the best in Europe.

Monasterio de Poblet

2km SW of Espluga de Francoli on A240, 90km W of Barcelona via motorway E90
Owner: Patrimonio Nacional
Opening times: Daily 10–12.30, 15–18, except Dec 25
Admission charge: Yes

A 12th-century Cistercian monastery, later abandoned but under restoration since 1940, is surrounded by nut groves and a great walled enclosure. In the gardens and cloisters the monks maintain a judicious selection of culinary and medicinal herbs, roses, mixed shrub borders and fine specimens of cedar and cypress.

RIGHT **Cypresses line a precipitous path in the Marimurtra Botanic Garden at Blanes leading to a cupola overlooking the Mediterranean.**

CENTRE **In the 18th-century garden of Pazo de Oca, a statue stands on the prow of a stone 'boat' floating in a pool.**

BELOW **A parterre of box and palm trees in the terraced garden of Pazo de Mariñan.**

Cap Roig Botanic Garden

1km S of Calella de Palafrugell, 45km SE of Gerona via
N255
Owner: Generalidad de Cataluña
Opening times: Daily, summer 9–21; winter 9–18
Admission charge: Yes

In 1924, Col. and Madame de Woevodsky bought the
then bare peninsula of Cap Roig. Over the next 45
years they planted its 40 ha with pines, built a castle
and laid out the garden, all of which they gave to
Spain in 1971. The achievement of the garden lies in
the skilful weaving of exquisitely-designed terraces
and much exotic planting (including fine collections
of mesembryanthemums and acacia species) into the
native woodland framework.

Pazo de Rubianes

4km E of Villagarcia de Arousa on Pontevedra road
Owner: Marquesa de Aranda
Opening times: By appointment, Villagarcia de Arousa,
Pontevedra
Admission charge: Yes

The facade of the granite house dating from the 11th
century is almost obscured by a pair of magnificent
Magnolia grandiflora. In the garden most of the great
trees are about 100 years old and include a fine
Norfolk Island pine, *Cryptomeria japonica*, a camphor tree and an exceptionally large group of *Eucalyptus globulus*, one of which is probably the largest
in Europe. An English-style park, camellia walks and
ramped parterre date from the early years of this
century.

Parque de Samá

Cambrils, 1km S of exit 37 on motorway E15, 17km W of
Tarragona
Owner: Marqués de Marianco
Opening times: Mon–Fri 10–18, except public hols
Admission charge: Yes

A 14ha park designed in romantic style in 1881 by the
architect J. Fontsere y Mestres for the Marqués de
Marianco. A 5km aqueduct feeds a 1ha lake with

three linked islands, one in the form of an artificial
hill with a pavilion on top and a cave underneath. The
house is approached by an avenue of oriental planes
(originally with a parrot on a perch between each
tree) through mandarin groves. In one corner of the
park there is a prospect tower set high on an artificial
hill, its slopes punctuated by caves. There is a well-
grown collection of trees, including many rare
species of palm and yucca. Abandoned aviaries and
animal houses throughout the park are all that remain
of a private zoo.

La Finca Puente San Miguel

3km from Torrelavega, 30km SW of Santander
Owner: Señor Don Emilio Botin
Opening times: May to mid Sept, 1st, 3rd Wed in month
9.30, 11.30 (guided tours)
Admission charge: No

Here is a garden on a miniature scale – like a precious
piece of highly-wrought jewellery. Classical ideas are
fused with the Islamic and Spanish styles of gardening in a garden of subtle changes of level and box-
edged compartments. Entirely surrounding the garden is a large and romantic 18th-century landscape
park in which branches of unpruned trees sweep
down to the ground. There is one of the largest
Magnolia grandiflora in Europe, over 200 years old
and with a canopy now covering an area of 700sq m;
an exceptionally fine coastal redwood (*Sequoia sempervirens*); a *Platanus × hispanica* and many other
good specimens which flourish in the humid climate.

Jardín de Santa Clotilde

At Playa Boadella S of Lloret de Mar, 45km S of Gerona, E
of A11
Owner: Marqués de Roviralta
Opening times: By appointment, Lloret de Mar, Gerona
Admission charge: No

Fine statuary and judicious planting distinguish the
garden designed in 1929 by N. M. Rubio, a pupil of
the French architect J. C. N. Forestier. The entrance
is marked by four large cylinders of clipped cypress
and the terrace gardens are crossed by elegant ramps
and stairs, one of which, the Siren's Staircase,
appears green from below because of the ivy trained
across the risers.

Santiago de Compostela: Monasterio de San Lorenzo de Trasouto

Calle Pozo de Bar in a NW suburb on the Noya road
Owner: Duque de Soma
Opening times: Daily, summer 11–13, 16–20; winter 11–13, 16–18
Admission charge: Yes

Dating from the 13th century, but reconstructed in the 17th, this Franciscan monastery has a cloister garden with fantastic topiary representing, among other things, the grid on which St Lawrence was burned, the cross of Santiago, the cross of Caladers and four shoes.

Pazo de Santa Cruz de Ribadulla

Ribadulla, 18km S of Santiago de Compostela off C241
Owner: Don Juan Armada Diez de Rivera
Opening times: By appointment, Ribadulla, Coruña
Admission charge: Yes

The house, dating from 1583, is surrounded by a 400-year-old avenue of olive trees, ancient box hedges and a large *Phytolacca dioica*, the 'Bella Sombra' of the Argentine.

A romantic garden of exotic trees and shrubs was planted 1880–99 by the Marqués de Santa Cruz de Ribadulla. It includes over 200 camellia cultivars from Belgium and Portugal, tree ferns in a river valley, and many specimen trees, among them a very large *Magnolia grandiflora*.

Central Spain

Aranjuez: Jardín del Palacio de Aranjuez, Jardín de la Isla, and Jardín del Principe ★

57km S of Madrid via N IV
Owner: Crown
Opening times: *Jardín del Palacio de Aranjuez* and *Jardín de la Isla* daily 9.30–sunset; *Jardín del Principe* daily 10–12.30, 15–18.30 (17.30 in winter), except Tues
Admission charge: No

The Italian traveller Baretti, describing the royal gardens at Aranjuez in his *Tour* of 1776, wrote: 'a poet would say that Venus and Love had here consulted with Catullus and Petrarch to construct a country-residence worthy of Psyche, of Lesbia, of Laura – or of some Infanta of Spain.' The late medieval palace which Philip II made a royal property in 1561 was completely rebuilt in the 18th century. The gardens, still full of interest, fall into three separate parts.

Jardín del Palacio de Aranjuez. A stone arcade and a side door lead into the palace gardens, where a small parterre dates from the time of Philip II. Many original features of the garden were discovered in recent excavations and are in the process of restoration. Dating from a much later period is a large parterre designed by Esteban Boutelou the Elder in 1746. Railings with ornamental urns run along one side and there are views of the river on the other. A fountain with a figure of Hercules is surrounded by *Magnolia grandiflora* and flanked by two splendid strawberry trees (*Arbutus unedo*).

Jardín de la Isla. This garden has one of the most beautiful sites of any Spanish garden – on a man-made island in the River Tagus. It is reached from the palace parterre over a fine stone bridge which leads to avenues dotted with fountains that run the length and breadth of the island, eventually leading to a beautiful fountain with a figure of Neptune. Running parallel to the river is a handsome avenue of century-old planes. All the avenues and courts of this renaissance garden, originally laid out in the 18th century by Esteban Boutelou, father and son, are bordered with hedges or trees. Among them are many finely-made stone seats.

Jardín del Principe. Dating from the reign of

Ferdinand VI (1746–59), this woodland garden by the Tagus was intended as a place of relaxation for the royal family. The great stone pier with its two sentry boxes and steps down to the river date from this period, when excursions on the river were one of the chief amusements. Later Charles IV and his architect Juan de Villanueva built the present stone walls (capped with decorative urns on the river side) and the four magnificent entrance gates. Broad avenues with double rows of trees criss-cross the garden. It follows the style of late 18th-century landscape gardens, with enormous fountains decorated with mythological figures, a small lake with a temple and a pagoda, and a mount with an observatory and pavilions. There is also a ravishing Trianon-like *Casa del Labrador* (labourer's cottage), with a parterre, and a *Casa de Marinos* (sailors' house), which houses a collection of royal pleasure boats.

La Quinta del Duque de Arco

3km from the Carretera del Pardo (11km N of Madrid) on C601
Owner: Crown
Opening times: Daily 10–13.15, 16–18.30, except Tues
Admission charge: No

The 18th-century house and its neo-classical gardens were given to Philip V in 1745 by the Duchess of Arco. The garden is laid out on two terraces, each with a pool and fountain in the centre, and surrounded by walls with niches for statues and ornamental urns. Lofty conifers mark the axis of the upper parterre and a retaining wall with a cascade in the middle supports the lower one, with steps flanking the water on either side. The whole garden has recently been handsomely restored.

El Bosque

Béjar, 72km S of Salamanca by N630
Owner: Oliva Abreu brothers
Opening times: Fri 14–18
Admission charge: No

A lake with an island survives from the original 16th-century garden. To this have been added many later features – including a 19th-century summer-house of curious neo-Moorish style. On one side is a stone fountain with a semi-circular bench – one of several in the garden. A stone staircase leads down to a lower garden with a gazebo. Here are *Sequoiadendrum giganteum*, elms (*Ulmus communis*) and planes (*Platanus × acerifolia*). There is an ancient ornamental fountain with jets like Italian renaissance *zampilli* – concealed jets of water to surprise the unwary.

Elche: Huerto del Cura

Porta de la Morera, E of city centre
Owner: Señora Maria Serrano de Orts
Opening times: Daily 9–21, except Mon
Admission charge: Yes

Elche is famous for its great grove of palms, El Palmeral. Palms (*Phoenix dactylifera*) were brought here by the Phoenicians, and the Palmeral, like a huge oasis on the edge of the city, possesses almost sacred status: it has been forbidden to fell the trees from ancient times.

The Huerto del Cura, lying on the edge of the western edge of the Palmeral, was originally a date orchard. Today the great trees (among them the Imperial Palm, at least 150 years old) cast deep and welcome shade on winding paths. Cultivated plants typical of a Mediterranean orchard – pomegranates, oranges and lemons – are intermixed with many exotic flowering plants – strelitzias, *Monstera deliciosa*, arum lilies and an important collection of cacti. On the other side of a road is another interesting garden in the ownership of the same family.

El Escorial: Jardín del Monasterio de El Escorial, Casita del Principe and Casino del Infante (Casita de Arriba)

45km NW of Madrid via A6 motorway or N505
Owner: Crown
Opening times: *Escorial gardens* at all times; *Casita del Principe* and *Casino del Infante (Casita de Arriba)* daily 10–13.30, 15.30–18, except Mon and public hols
Admission charge: Yes

Jardín del Monasterio de El Escorial. The Escorial monastery, massively built of granite on the slopes of a hill, is the most impressive work commissioned by Philip II and was completed in 1584. The late 18th-

In the royal gardens of Aranjuez, made in the 16th and 18th centuries, columns are a repeated motif.

century neo-classical hanging gardens (which in Philip II's time were richly planted) nestle against the south and east facades, protected from the wind and supported on a 6m wall and a vast range of 77 arches. A dozen flights of stairs, arranged in pairs, lead to an orchard and a pond. A parterre of sober beauty is divided into box-edged enclosures with a square fountain in the centre of each. Returning to the east facade, an iron gate opens into the Jardín del Prior, where the parterre was reserved for the use of the reigning monarch; three double flights of steps lead up to his private orchard and a little wood. The Jardín del Prior may be visited only with special permission.

Casita del Principe (SE of monastery on road to station). In 1772 Charles III commissioned the architect Juan de Villanueva to build the Casita del Principe (the Prince's pavilion) for his son, Prince of Asturias. It was intended as a hunting lodge and its 45ha estate is surrounded by a stone wall. The garden proper, made in the late 18th century, is 2ha in extent and is entered by one of three gates which open on to double avenues of pines, chestnut, limes, elms and false acacias. It is designed in a neo-classical style and has three clearly defined areas. The first, embellished with a round fountain, lies in front of the lodge and has an avenue adorned with six beautiful stone seats running parallel to it. On the other side of the house, the second and central area has clipped box hedges and many conifers. At the end, a third area, raised on a slope, has a large irrigation pool with a ramp on either side. The many 19th-century conifers are now disproportionately large for the garden, which is otherwise beautifully designed.

Casino del Infante or *Casita de Arriba* (3km SW of the monastery on the Ávila road). The *casino* is a summer retreat designed in the late 18th century for the Infante Don Gabriel, son of Charles III. The formal garden has exquisite parterres. To the south a terraced parterre, surrounded by a granite wall over which tumble old-fashioned roses, is planted with double box hedges. At either end of this terrace are more parterres, with box hedges and fountains. The central garden is embellished with a very fine carved stone fountain and a table and benches. From the terraces there is a splendid view of the monastery of El Escorial. Conifers, planted in the late 19th century, are now too tall and regrettably overshadow the parterres.

Jardines de la Granja ★

La Granja de San Ildefonso, 11km SE of Segovia on N601
Owner: Crown
Opening times: Tues–Sat 10–13.30, 15–17.30, Sun and public hols 10–14. *Fountains* play May 1, May 30, Aug 25 at 17.30
Admission charge: No

The palace was built in 1721 by Philip V, grandson of Louis XIV and first Bourbon king of Spain. It became his favourite residence. The baroque French-style gardens – a Hispanic Versailles on a more intimate scale – have a spectacular mountain setting in the foothills of the Sierra de Guadarrama. The English traveller Lady Holland visited La Granja in 1811 and wrote: 'The gardens are reckoned among the finest in Europe; they are in the old French style of high clipped hedges, *salons de verdures*, alleys, etc; that is the style I prefer beyond any other.'

The most surprising features are the extraordinary fountains and, despite the precipitous ground, the formal layout. The drop is great enough for water falling from an enormous pool at the highest part of the garden above the palace to the north to set off a series of fountains below, one after another. Entering the garden to the right of the palace the visitor comes to the *La Fama* parterre of clipped box and yew with many sculptures and urns. Here is the most spectacular of the fountains, rising to a height of 47m and said to be visible from Segovia. At the end of this parterre is the *Baños de Diana* with a huge baroque fountain and multi-layered cascade. This was the last and most expensive of the fountains, completed just before the king died: 'You have entertained me for three minutes, but you cost me three million (*reales*),' he said. An avenue leads to the *Ranas* – the fountain of Frogs – then to the fountain of *Las Tazas* (cups), to the left of which is the great cascade falling towards the palace. A path from the cascade leads to a point from which eight avenues radiate, each terminating in a fountain. To the north lies a further parterre with the fountains of Neptune and Andromeda. From this point springs a stream which flows back towards the palace and borders the parterre called *La Selva* (the jungle) at the north-east corner of the palace. At the bottom of this sloping parterre is a bridge leading to the kitchen garden and greenhouses which are not open to the public.

This Spanish vision of Versailles, in its wild and mountainous setting, is one of the most extraordinary gardens in Spain.

Monasterio de Nuestra Señora de Guadalupe

Guadalupe, 130km NE of Mérida via E90/NV and N401
Owner: Patrimonio Nacional, Arzobispado de Toledo and Comunidad de Franciscones
Opening times: Daily 9.30–13, 15.30–18.30
Admission charge: Yes

The golden buildings of the monastery, of several different periods from the 14th century, rise prominently over the village. The main court, built in handsome *mudejar* style with two-tiered cloisters, is planted with orange trees recalling its original use as an orchard. The cruciform paths are lined with clipped box and lead to a spectacular cathedral-like pavilion built in the early 15th century in elaborate *mudejar* style with pointed windows and gothic tracery. In the north-west corner is a fountain-pavilion where the monks used to wash before meals. The atmosphere is intimate and peaceful, perfumed with the scent of the fruit and flowers of the orange trees.

Madrid: Royal Botanic Garden ⊛

Plaza de Murillo, S of the Prado
Owner: Consejo Superior de Investigaciones Científicas
Opening times: Daily 10–sunset
Admission charge: Yes

These gardens were designed by the architect Juan de Villanueva after they were moved to their present site in 1781. They received the huge collection of 10,000 plants brought back in 1794 by Alessandro Malaspina after his five-year voyage to the New World. The layout, dating from 1789, divides the garden into three terraces with a central axis leading from the king's gate to Villanueva's pavilion, a former greenhouse. A recent restoration has refurbished the two lower terraces which are divided into squares, each with a diminutive granite fountain at the centre. The upper terrace, laid out in 1859, has a wrought-iron pergola covered in vines.

Madrid: El Campo del Moro

Calle Virgen del Puerto, W of the old town
Owner: Crown
Opening times: Daily 10–18; closed for receptions at the palace
Admission charge: No

The mid 18th-century royal palace, jointly designed by the Italian architect J. B. Sachetti and the Spaniard Ventura Rodriguez, which is now used by King Juan Carlos for state receptions, stands on the site of a Muslim fortress. The park on the west side of the palace was made in 1844 when the ground was levelled, and in 1845 the great Fountain of the Tritons was brought from Aranjuez (q.v.). The present appearance, with a central vista with ramps on either side leading from the palace to the fountain, dates from 1890. Informal woodland, penetrated by winding paths, contains a great variety of trees and shrubs, including magnolias, maples, Judas trees and oriental planes.

Madrid: Quinta de la Fuente or Parque de la Fuente del Berro

End of the Calle de Jorge Juan; access from the Calle de Enrique d'Almonte; well to E of city centre
Owner: City of Madrid
Opening times: At all times
Admission charge: No

This romantic landscape garden, on a steep slope, was bought by Philip IV in 1631; water from its spring, transported by mule, supplied the royal household for centuries. A brick gateway leads into a square dominated by a round pool and fountain adorned with a decorative urn in the centre, and surrounded by clipped privet. From here paths wander about the garden, which has a decorative duck-pond, a dovecote, a waterfall and several monuments (including one to the Russian poet Alexander Pushkin). Unfortunately, the busy ring road that goes round the north-east corner of the park has destroyed its quiet intimacy and upset the microclimate, causing the loss of rare and precious plants.

Madrid: El Jardín del Palacio de Liria

20 Calle Princesa, NW of the old town
Owner: Duquesa de Alba
Opening times: By appointment (max 12 people), Fundación Casa de Alba, 20 Calle Princesa, Madrid, tel. 91 247 53 02
Admission charge: No

The palace, designed by the architect Ventura Rodriguez, was completed in 1780. The garden has two areas of clearly different styles. The entrance leads into an informal woodland garden with trees and shrubs. Behind the palace, against the north facade,

Louis Meunier's 1650 engraving of the Hermitage at Buen Retiro in Madrid.

there is a formal garden designed in the early 20th century by J.C.N. Forestier, with a central pool surrounded by a box *parterre de broderie* and large clipped yews. A flight of steps leads to a fine terrace with a wisteria-covered pergola. On the west, behind a hedge, lies a row of dogs' graves.

Madrid: El Capricho de la Alameda de Osuna ★

Plaza de la Fuente; Paseo de la Alameda, E of city centre off motorway N11 Avenida de América; Underground: Canillejas

Owner: City of Madrid
Opening times: Sat, Sun 10–sunset
Admission charge: No

Created in the late 18th century by the Duchess of Osuna, this romantic garden reflects her personal tastes and those of her time. Lady Holland, an English traveller living in Madrid in 1803, wrote:

'The garden is rather crowded with a profusion of different ornaments . . . the mansion is excellent and well-furnished.' Today the garden consists of three chief parts. Between the entrance and the neo-classical palace there is a formal garden on level ground, with a parterre, a fountain and an elaborate *exedra* with a bronze figure of the duchess surrounded by sphinxes. To the south, in a lower area, there is an informal woodland garden where formerly there were orchards, a maze and shady walks. To the north lies a landscape garden with an abundance of decorative and whimsical features – a temple of Bacchus, a figure of Saturn devouring his son and an ornamental beehive which formerly had windows through which one could study the bees at work. A stream flows into a lake with an island bearing the tomb of the 3rd Duke of Osuna (1574–1624). From the lake another

Yew columns rise above the box parterre in the Sabatini gardens to the north of Madrid's royal palace.

At the Quinta de la Fuente in Madrid, an ornamental pool is surrounded by clipped privet.

stream flows towards the Dance Pavilion surrounded by a carpet of bulbs. A twisting path leads to the hermitage and a small rustic house, the Casa de la Vieja ('very pretty', wrote Lady Holland). Judas trees and lilacs line the paths. This remarkably interesting garden, much harmed by the ravages of time, is now undergoing restoration.

Madrid: **Parque del Buen Retiro** *or* **del Retiro**

Calle de Alcalá; Alfonso XII; Plaza de la Independencia; Avenida Menendez Pelayo, E of the old town
Owner: City of Madrid
Opening times: At all times
Admission charge: No

Originally attached to a monastery and then in the reign of Philip IV in the 17th century becoming a royal estate, El Buen Retiro is now an immensely popular public park. It is surrounded by fine iron railings and entered by one of nine large gates. The maze-like layout is a distinctive feature, with sandy

paths edged with narrow irrigation channels (a *riego a manta* of Islamic origin). Other paths, edged with privet, wind through rich plantings of trees and shrubs. Some of the garden has recently been replanted with lawns and conifers. In this informal setting are many attractive features – a baroque parterre dominated by a splendid swamp cypress, an octagonal pond and a garden of modern roses.

Madrid: **Los Jardines de Sabatini**

Cuesta de San Vicente and Plaza de Oriente, NW of the old town
Owner: City of Madrid
Opening times: At all times
Admission charge: No

These 20th-century gardens, by the north facade of the royal palace, were created in 1936 on the site of the old stables. A spacious terrace has a formal layout of clipped box hedges with a square pool and fountain surrounded by four Spanish firs (*Abies pinsapo* – native to the hills near Ronda). There are four subsidiary parterres with granite pools. Equestrian statues flank generous steps which lead to a circular pool and an equestrian statue of Charles III.

Jardín de la Casa de Paños

Paseo de la Fábrica, Brihuega, 76km NE of Madrid via
E90/NII
Owner: Hermanos Gonzalez
Opening times: Mon–Fri 9–13.30, 15.30–19; Sat 9–12
Admission charge: No

Until the middle of the 19th century, this was an
important cloth factory (*paño* = cloth) and it has
buildings constructed in the late 18th century. The
factory was surrounded by terraced gardens overlooking the lovely valley of the Tajuña river. These
gardens, once beautifully harmonious, are now
rather neglected, but are still worth seeing for the
magnificent site and the remains of the formal garden
– arcades of cypresses and a parterre of box planted in
squares.

Palacio del Pardo

El Pardo, 11km N of Madrid on C601
Owner: Crown
Opening times: Mon–Sat 10–13, 15.30–18; Sun, public
hols 10–18
Admission charge: No

The palace, which dates from the 16th century but
has been remodelled several times subsequently, was
a favourite game reserve of the royal family. In Philip
II's time, the waterless moat surrounding it was filled
with flowers, and had exotic birds in aviaries under
two of its four bridges. Today fruit trees, especially
cherries, are planted here. A romantic but neglected
landscape garden dating from 1828 was restructured
when the palace became the official residence of the
head of state under General Franco. There is now a
drive flanked by parterres with a semi-circular parterre in front of the palace.

Toledo: El Cigarral de Cadena

44 Callejón de la Bastida, W of city centre across the river
Owner: Señora Vda de Aguirre
Opening times: By appointment, 25 Calle Gral Martinez
Campos, Madrid, tel. 91 448 19 68
Admission charge: No

The typical 17th-century country house enclosed by
high stone walls belonged to the Jesuits, who used it
as a place of recreation. It retains the characteristic
features of the traditional houses around Toledo.
The way up to the house, which has a fine view of the
city in the distance, is marked by whitewashed
parapets. The orchard-like garden lies below on a
steep slope with many olive and almond trees. A
rosemary-edged path leads past a decorative round
seat and continues to the foot of the garden where
grapevines and roses encircle a granite fountain.

Toledo: El Cigarral de Marañon (or Menores)

68 Carretera de Piedrabuena, W of city centre across the
river
Owner: Señor Gregorio de Marañon y Bertrán de Lis
Opening times: By appointment, tel. 925 22 01 44
Admission charge: No

El Cigarral de Menores was a convent founded in
1612, whose terraced gardens were already famous in
the 17th century. In 1922 the property was acquired
and restored by the distinguished physician and
writer, Dr Gregorio Marañon. The house and garden
are exceptionally well maintained and command a
beautiful view of Toledo. The path leading to the
house is flanked with cypresses and, beyond these,
the olive groves so typical of estates of this kind.
Below the house sandy paths bordered by lilac or
lavender lead down the hill past cascading fountains
and little pools. At the summit of the garden, in a
grove of cypresses, is a contemporary sculpture by
Eduardo Chillida, to commemorate the centenary of
Dr Marañon's birth.

Valencia: Botanic Garden

Calle Beato Gaspar de Bono off Calle Cuart, NW city
centre
Owner: University of Valencia
Opening times: Daily 10–sunset
Admission charge: Yes

Founded in the 16th century, these outstanding
botanic gardens were established on the present site
by the River Turia in 1902. There is a large and
varied collection of trees, including such exotics as

the beautiful American live oak (*Quercus virginiana*) and the Brazilian floss silk tree, *Chorisia speciosa*. The garden is irrigated by ditches in the Muslim tradition.

suffuse the air with their sweet scent and a long pergola, shady and mysterious, runs along a wall. Beyond, a romantic garden has a mount and a grotto overhung with large trees – the perfect ending.

Valencia: Monforte

Calle Artes Graficas, E of city centre
Owner: Ayuntamiento de Valencia
Opening times: Weekdays 10.30–20; public hols closed 14.30–15.30
Admission charge: No

Once on the outskirts of the town, this atmospheric 19th-century garden is now engulfed by urban development. It is a distinctively Spanish mixture of neo-classical and romantic styles. Clipped box, myrtle and cypress are punctuated with white marble statues of classical deities, orange and lemon trees

Monasterio de Yuste

Cuacos, 125km NE of Cáceres via E803/N630 and C501
Owner: Patrimonio Nacional
Opening times: Daily 9.30–13, 15.30–18.30
Admission charge: Yes

The abdicated Emperor Charles V came in 1556 to this hidden valley, La Vera, to spend his last years. The modest palace with its small garden, now shaded by eucalyptus and orange trees and surrounded by woodland of oak and Spanish chestnut, has a pool surviving from ancient times.

Andalusia

Finca de la Concepción

7km N of Málaga, W of N321
Owner: Private
Opening times: Daily 9.30–12.30, 14.30–18.00, except Sun

Although overlooking a busy main road, the garden, laid out on a steep hill, has the aspect of a tropical jungle. From the iron gates an avenue of planes winds uphill towards the handsome 18th-century house. The air is heavy with the scent of *Pittosporum tobira* and dense foliage crowds in on either side. Enormous rubber trees (*Ficus elastica*), the bold leaves of *Sparmannia africana*, soaring pillars of the date palm *Phoenix dactylifera* and an exceptionally large Norfolk Island pine (*Araucaria heterophylla*) rise above strelitzias and clivias. Half-concealed in this dense planting are fine Roman remains and the striking

survivals of a substantial formal garden – half-hidden runnels of water, a large pergola entwined with wisteria, a pool with black swans and a waterfall erupting from a froth of *Monstera deliciosa*. It is said to be the site of a Roman garden. Today it is a shady retreat in which heady scents and many unfamiliar plants combine in a dream-like tropical vision.

Córdoba: Patio de los Naranjos

On the N side of the Mezquita
Owner: Mezquita
Opening times: Daily, Apr to Sept 10.30–13.30, 16–19; Oct to Mar 10.30–13.30, 15.30–17.30
Admission charge: No

This walled garden of orange trees, first laid out in the late 8th century and extended in the late 10th century, must be one of the most ancient continuously gardened sites in the world. Symmetrically arranged rows of orange trees with an intricate system of irrigation runnels make a charming contrast to the exotic grandeur of the great mosque that overshadows them.

Córdoba: Jardines del Alcázar de los Reyes Cristianos

W of the Alcázar

Owner: Ayuntamiento de Córdoba

Opening times: Daily, Jun to Sept 9.30–13.30, 17–20 (*floodlit openings* 22–24); Oct to May 9.30–13.30, 16–19

Admission charge: Yes

The old part of the garden is reached through a great tower in the north wall of the *alcázar*. Above a pair of rectangular carp-pools is a small enclosure with box hedges shaded by a gigantic eucalyptus. Below the pools an Italianate arrangement of box-edged beds has roses and orange trees. To the west is a 20th-century garden with the character of a lively public park. Avenues of giant cypresses, clipped and wired into columns, divide the space, and there is a series of formal beds with geometric shapes of juniper, box, euonymus or grey-leaved atriplex. They are bordered by a very decorative walk of orange trees clipped into mop-heads, beyond which lies a long rectangular pool with jets of water and rather ugly green lights.

Córdoba: Palacio de Viana ★

Plaza de Don Gome

Owner: Caja Provincial de Ahorros de Córdoba

Opening times: Daily, except Wed, Jun to Sept 9–14; Oct to May 10–13, 16–18; Sun, public hols 10–14

Admission charge: Yes

The entrance to the Palacio de Viana is an ornate stone pedimented gateway surmounted by the arms of the Viana family. The house is chiefly 16th-century and the garden is an astonishing maze of interconnected patios, thirteen of them in all, each with its own flavour. It is an enchanting set of variations on the theme of the miniature enclosed garden with elegant arcades, splashing fountains,

formal parterres, cool pebbled floors, and a profusion of pots – ingredients repeated in different combinations. At any time of day some patios will be in brilliant sunshine, others in soothing shade. Orange and lemon trees, arum lilies, bougainvillea, date palms, the orange flowered *Clivia miniata*, oleanders, sweet jasmine, agaves and the rubber tree (*Ficus elastica*) are used repeatedly in different settings. From spring until winter the patios are suffused with scent. Palacio de Viana is one of the most richly memorable of all southern Spanish gardens.

Palacio del Cuzco

Viznar, 7km NE of Granada off N342

Owner: Don Jose F. Figares y Mendez and Doña Esperanza de Damas y R. Acosta

Opening times: By appointment, Viznar, Granada, Provincia de Granada

Admission charge: No

A late 18th-century mansion, built by the Bishop of Granada, stands next to the church in Viznar. It has a beguiling formal garden of clipped box parterres with fountains, dominated by two 100-year-old *Magnolia grandiflora* and cypresses. The arcades of the house are painted with charming scenes from *Don Quixote* and the garden walls with architectural *trompe l'oeil*. It is a superb site with views over the hillside.

Granada: Fundación Rodríguez Acosta

Callejón Niño del Rollo

Owner: Fundación Rodríguez Acosta

Opening times: By appointment, Callejón Niño del Rollo, Granada, Provincia de Granada

Admission charge: No

This garden clinging to the vertiginous slopes of the Alhambra hill was built by the painter Rodríguez Acosta in 1920. It is a virtuoso arrangement of abrupt terraces, sudden descents, dramatic perspectives and calm pools. Giant walls and arcades of clipped cypress provide the background for sculptures of different periods.

In the Palacio de Viana, a figure of a water-bearer lurks within a *glorieta* of clipped cypress.

Granada: Alhambra ★

Owner: Patrimonio Nacional
Opening times: Daily 9.30–20
Admission charge: Yes

The Alhambra has one of the most spectacular sites in the world. East of the centre of Granada, it rises abruptly on its tree-covered slope, a silhouette of ancient buildings and tall cypresses. It commands exceptional views – down towards the old city, the Albaicín, and to the south to the great mountain range of the Sierra Nevada, which is indeed usually fringed with sparkling, silvery snow. Alhambra means 'red castle', and the buildings are of a seductive tawny-pink stone. The earliest, the old citadel or Alcazaba at the western extremity of the Alhambra, dates from the 9th century, but the finest buildings, those of the Alcázar, were built in the 14th century under the Nasrid dynasty. After the Christian 're-conquest' in 1492, Charles V added the vast and ponderous palace in the early 16th century.

The two finest patios in the Alcázar are the *Patio de los Leones* and the *Patio de los Arrayanes* (myrtles). The Patio de los Arrayanes is a long rectangular court with a slender pool (8m × 44m) running down the centre. On each side of the pool is a wide, low hedge of clipped myrtle, introductions of the late 19th century; no one knows how the garden was originally planted. The Patio de los Leones is surrounded with ornate arcades of carved stucco. In the centre a fountain is borne on the backs of twelve stone lions spouting water. Four narrow runnels quarter the patio, flowing from inside the open rooms to the fountain. The only plants are four shaped orange bushes. Whatever the historical correctness of these patios there is no doubt that the present arrangement, austere yet refined, is extraordinarily effective. Other patios within the palace walls have none of the distinction of these two.

East of the Alcázar lie the *Partal* gardens. These are of the 20th century, a patchwork of terraces and clipped box in the renaissance style. They have charm but, after the ravishing beauty of the palace, they seem rather coarse: too many random pots of marigolds, cineraria, shrill petunias and other aimless ingredients. The *Torre de las Damas* lies to the north with an exquisite shady *mirador* overlooking the old city. A stately arcade frames a rectangular pool with two stone lions in the far corners.

Despite the tremendous crush of visitors, the serenity and power of the best parts of the Alhambra ensure that its magic is preserved. In the patios there is the irresistible attraction of the contrast between the richness of filigree arcades, many decorated with stylized floral motives, and the simplicity of what they contain.

Granada: Casa Morisca del Chapiz

Cuesta del Chapiz
Owner: Consejo de Investigaciones Cientificas
Opening times: By request during normal office hours
Admission charge: No

An anonymous passage leads down one side of the 16th-century house and opens out into a handsome patio with, on two sides, an Islamic arcade with a gallery above. A long, simple pool runs down the middle, flanked by box hedges with an orange tree at each end. The ground falls away abruptly to the valley of the Darro with views over the roof-tops of the lower city. A narrow path leads through a cypress screen to a beautiful secret garden lying on a long thin terrace, with exquisite views over the River Darro to the Alhambra. Formal beds are edged in box and planted with palms, oranges, many almond trees, oleanders, scented roses and philadelphus. Half-way along, a high *glorieta* of clipped cypress provides a welcome moment of shade.

Granada: Palacio de los Cordova

Cuesta del Chapiz
Owner: Ayuntamiento de Granada
Opening times: By request during normal office hours
Admission charge: No

A small patio with pebble-mosaic in patterns of interlacing squares, and with a fountain and pomegranate tree, is guarded by symmetrically arranged sentinel cypresses. Beyond, a stately avenue of cypresses leads to the building housing the archives of the city of Granada. It is a perfectly executed example of the Granadan *carmen*.

Granada: Generalife ★

E of the Alhambra
Owner: Patrimonio Nacional
Opening times: As for Alhambra
Admission charge: Included with Alhambra

The Generalife on the steep slopes to the east of the Alhambra was the summer palace of the sultans of Granada in the 14th century. In character it is very much a rural pleasure house – more intimate and private than the Alhambra, from which it can be reached. On the way there is a rare and seductive sight: the original kitchen gardens, still gardened and as tidy as an allotment, spread out on the slopes.

At the centre of the palace is a famous, but still breathtaking, showpiece – the Patio de la Acequia. A long thin canal runs straight down the patio with jets of water splashing in on either side, forming watery interlocking arches. *Magnolia grandiflora*, orange trees and many roses flank the canal, which is overlooked at either end by a charming *mirador*. Numerous terraced parterres and patios form an intricate patchwork about the palace and to the south extensive formal gardens with crenellated cypress hedges lead to the new gardens and a rather unhappy open-air theatre. Above the Patio de la Acequia a series of giant steps edged with water channels runs diagonally up the hill on the site of the original 14th-century garden. Visitors leave through a dramatic shady walk of overarching oleanders and giant pencil cypresses. The American writer Washington Irving wrote of the Generalife in 1829: 'Here is everything to delight a southern voluptuary: fruits, flowers, fragrance, green arbours and myrtle hedges, delicate air and gushing waters.' Few would quarrel with that.

Granada: Carmen de los Martíres ★

Campo de los Martíres
Owner: Ayuntamiento de Granada
Opening times: Daily 9–19
Admission charge: No

On the southern slopes of the Alhambra hill, with wonderful views, this 19th-century terraced garden with its handsome 1845 classical villa is in the process of impeccable restoration by the city of Granada. At the entrance the visitor is greeted by water nymphs lurking in the shade of a ferny grotto. A gravel path with informal planting sweeps round to the house, to the left of which is an entrance to a patio with a long pool and a cascade. Beyond it a terrace overlooks a formal garden where tall-trunked palms provide shade round a handsome three-tiered fountain. Steps lead up to a grand parterre with ravishing views; here four paths meet at a large circular pool overlooked by a statue of Neptune fringed with arum lilies. Each box-edged segment of the parterre is richly planted with palms (*Phoenix canariensis*), *Magnolia grandiflora*, roses, peonies and orange trees. Above it a romantic woodland garden is still to be restored. Beautifully maintained, with its exquisite setting, this is one of the finest Granadan gardens.

Medina Azahara ★

8km W of Córdoba off C431
Owner: Junta de Andalucía
Opening times: Daily, May–Sept 10–14, 18–20;
Oct–Apr 10–14, 16–18
Admission charge: Yes

This is one of the most bewitching garden sites in Spain. Medina Azahara was built in the late 10th century, by the great caliph Abdur Rahman III, as a kind of city-palace on the outskirts of Córdoba in the Guadalquivir valley. The remains of the exquisite palace buildings have been painstakingly pieced together and attractive formal gardens have been made with hedges of cypress and pomegranate punctuated by strawberry trees (*Arbutus unedo*), oleanders and oleasters (*Elaeagnus angustifolia*). There are date palms everywhere, giving the powerful feeling of a Near Eastern oasis.

Palacio La Moratalla

Moratalla, 45km W of Córdoba on C431
Owner: Duque de Pañaranda
Opening times: By appointment, Moratalla, Córdoba, Provincia de Córdoba

The *palacio* is a handsome 15th-century stucco house at the centre of a great citrus farm. Behind the house

there is a formal garden designed by J. C. N. Forestier, a happy mixture of French formality with
touches of Islamic influence. A dramatic double oval
of plane trees surrounds a fountain fringed with arum
lilies. Radiating from the fountain are segments of
box hedging filled with massed agapanthus (blue and
white) and bergenias. Leading away from the house

**Orange trees and cypresses in the Lindaraja patio in
the Alhambra.**

**Plane trees shade a pool in the garden of La Morat-
alla designed by J. C. N. Forestier.**

is a vista with a thin runnel of water, statues, pairs of
Irish yews and immensely long myrtle hedges backed
by a profusion of shrubs – philadelphus, oleaster,
chaenomeles, oleanders and many others – punctuated by pencil cypresses. The land rises gently and
then falls towards a pair of superb, richly ornate
wrought-iron gates.

135

Jardines de Narváez

24km E of Antequera on N342; take C334 Rute road; after
2.3km turn right on to track
Owner: Doña Julia Díaz Bertel
Opening times: Daily, on request at house
Admission charge: No

A garden of unusual charm attached to a handsome
farmhouse. Serpentine box hedges meander about an
octagonal moated fountain surrounded by blue and
white irises. Sheets of scented violets spread under
fruit and nut trees – pomegranates, mulberries,
loquats and almonds. A giant hive-shaped hollow
mound of box with stone benches makes a summer-
house. To the north large palms, *Magnolia grandiflora* and *Abies pinsapo* provide shelter and seclusion.

Jardín del Retiro ★

Alhaurín de la Torre, 12km SW of Málaga on C344
Owner: Duque de Aveyro
Opening times: Daily 9–12.30, 14–17.30, except Sun
Admission charge: No

An avenue of young eucalyptus marks the drive
leading to the edge of an escarpment overlooking
Málaga airport – an apparently unpromising site for
what is, in fact, a wonderful garden. The house was
built in the 18th century as the place of retirement of
a Bishop of Málaga and the garden lies on the very
edge of the escarpment, with an exotic orchard of
oranges, lemons and loquats on the slopes. Behind
the house a long terrace with parterres of clipped box
and cypress lies parallel to the contours of the land.
There is also a large fountain surrounded with
grotesque figures. Steps lead down abruptly into the
formal early 18th-century water garden ('excellent
water-works', as Loudon notes in his *Encyclopaedia*)
– rills and water-spouts gush down vertiginous
flights of steps linking terraces ornamented with a
profusion of shell-work, urns and statues. It is an
abrupt change of mood – from formal calm to
baroque exuberance with an Italianate note. On
either side rise screens of substantial nettle trees
(*Celtis australis*). Above all this a long, wide canal,
which may be Islamic in origin, separates a wild
garden in which jacarandas, Judas trees, mulberries
and magnolias are planted in rough grass.

Ronda: Casa del Rey Moro

Calle de Marques de Paradas
Owner: Doña Carmela Hernández
Opening times: By appointment, Calle del Rey Moro,
Ronda, Provincia de Málaga
Admission charge: No

This small and seductive formal garden in the centre
of the beautiful town of Ronda was designed in 1912
by the French architect J. C. N. Forestier. It hugs a
narrow terrace overhanging a spectacular gorge with
remarkable views. Although quite small the garden
has a firm central axis – a runnel with box domes on
either side flanked by small parterres. It is Le Nôtre
in a pocket handkerchief – but with Islamic under-
tones. Now sadly neglected, it is still worth seeing as
an instructive example of the brilliant use of an
exceptional site.

Ronda: La Alameda del Tajo

Town centre
Owner: Ciudad de Ronda
Opening times: At all times
Admission charge: No

An attractive municipal garden on the edge of a
spectacular gorge with commanding views west.
Judas trees, palms and orange trees give shade to beds
planted with roses and peonies. On the north side
there is an especially fine Spanish fir (*Abies pinsapo*),
which is native to the hills round Ronda.

Seville: Palacio de las Dueñas ★

Calle Dueñas, NE of Plaza de la Encarnación
Owner: Duque de Alba
Opening times: By appointment not less than one month
beforehand, Calle Dueñas, Sevilla, Provincia de Sevilla
Admission charge: No

The imposing entrance, of white and orange stucco,
is crowned with a pediment bearing the Alba arms in
tiles, although the *palacio* was built in the 15th
century by the Pinedas family. It is *mudejar* work of
the finest quality, in which dramatic contrasts of
brilliant light and soothing shade make a distinctively
Andalusian harmony.

A path to the house is flanked by low myrtle hedges with oranges and lemons underplanted with canna lilies. The entrance leads directly into the main patio, a place of great beauty where deep arcades of richly carved stone surround a tiled fountain planted with arum lilies and orange clivia under tall palms. Beyond a beautiful wrought-iron gate is a formal arrangement of rose beds bordered with box hedges under a profusion of oranges and lemons. From here an arbour covered in the yellow banksian rose leads up steps, past a smaller patio and the ancient cistern that supplies the water for the garden, to a large shady garden lying between the house and a high wall. A huge *Ficus elastica* stands guard over beds edged in clipped euonymus whose shiny leaves provide a lively note in this shady area. Here are many ornamental trees and shrubs – loquats, hibiscus and citrus – and some much less familiar, including the coral tree (*Erythrina crista-galli*) and *Xanthoceras sorbifolium*. The walls of the house are festooned with climbing bignonia, bougainvillea, white solanum, wisteria and the richly-scented white banksian rose. Other smaller courtyards cluster round the house. All are impeccably kept and perfectly in keeping with the exceptional charm and beauty of the house – an oasis in the midst of city bustle.

Seville: Parque de María Luisa

SE of the city centre
Owner: Ciudad de Sevilla
Opening times: At all times
Admission charge: No

This great public park was made in the 19th century and added to in 1929 by the French architect and garden designer J. C. N. Forestier. It is an attractive blend of informal landscape design, with many fine trees, and charming formal elements. Avenues of *Magnolia grandiflora* or orange trees, and paths edged with shiny-leaved euonymus give structure to a jungle-like richness of planting.

Seville: Casa de Pilatos ★

Plaza Pilatos, E city centre
Owner: Duquesa de Medinaceli
Opening times: Daily 10–13, 14–19; Oct to Feb closes 18
Admission charge: Yes

The beautiful house was built in the 15th century in refined *mudejar* style for the Marqués de Tarifa. At its centre there is an exquisite patio with arcades, busts of Roman emperors and a white marble fountain. The chief garden lies beyond it, a formal arrangement with euonymus hedges and a shady central arbour covered in a yellow banksian rose. In the beds are clivia, roses, lemons, pomegranates and philadelphus. A smaller patio, on the other side of the *patio principal*, has a rectangular pool, fig trees and climbing heliotrope scaling a high wall. Entrance to these patios, of which tantalizing glimpses are seen through grilles, is gained through open rooms which are lined with magnificent *azulejos*.

Seville: Jardines de las Reales Alcázares ★

Alcázar
Owner: Ayuntamiento de Sevilla
Opening times: Weekdays 9–12.45, 15–17.45, Sat, Sun, public hols 9–13
Admission charge: Yes

On this site, as archaeology has shown, there was once a great Muslim garden in the late 12th and early 13th centuries. The garden today, despite the odd Islamic detail, is emphatically of the Renaissance and is chiefly of the 17th century and later. The entrance courtyard has high myrtle hedges with domes at each corner and mounded bushes of *Pittosporum tobira*; on the right is a fine floss silk tree, *Chorisia speciosa*. Tantalizing glimpses of greenery can be seen through iron grilles in the shady passages of the palace. A handsome square pool on a terrace, with a bronze figure of Mercury and a richly arcaded Italianate screen, is the prelude to the formal gardens that spread below. This part of the garden is entirely enclosed by walls and railings with ornamental piers flanking decorative *clairvoyées* and gates. Myrtle hedges line straight paths and the beds are sufficiently spacious to accommodate very large trees with no feeling of constraint – palms, huge specimens of *Magnolia grandiflora* – as well as a profusion of peaches, almonds, bay, philadelphus, roses and *Pittosporum tobira*. Wherever the paths intersect, a fountain plays.

The main gate leads to a further formal garden and the charming Charles V pavilion with fine arcades and tiles. Two columnar cypresses mark the entrance to the rest of the garden, where there is a change of

The early 18th-century baroque water garden of El Retiro is ornamented with statues and elaborate *rocaille* work.

mood: here, in spite of a series of straight walks, the planting is so rich that it gives the impression of a luxuriant jungle. There are many groves of bitter oranges where fallen fruit lying on the warm ground in spring smell like marmalade in the making. On the south side are huge mulberries and giant eucalyptus. Only the occasional distant noise of traffic spoils the impression of having wandered into a painting by Douanier Rousseau.

The Islands

Canary Islands: Jardín de la Marquesa de Arucas
Gran Canaria: 0.5km W of Arucas off C810
Owner: Marquesa de Arucas
Opening times: Weekdays 10–18
Admission charge: Yes

A romantic 19th-century garden is set in lavish plantations of strelitzia and banana. There is a grotto, statues and an exotic summer-house and many rare plants flourishing in a subtropical climate. It is maintained with great judgement and care.

Canary Islands: Jardín Canario
Gran Canaria: Tafira Alta, 9km from Las Palmas on C811
Owner: Cabildo Insular de Gran Canario
Opening times: Daily, summer 9–18; winter 9–19
Admission charge: No

One of the first and most outstanding examples in the world of a botanic garden established to further plant conservation (in this case the flora of the Spanish and Portuguese Atlantic Islands). Founded in 1952, it was designed by the Swedish botanist Eric Sventenius in the natural setting of the Guiniquada valley and is being superbly maintained and expanded to provide suitable habitats for yet more of the islands' flora.

Canary Islands: Jardín de Aclimatación de la Orotava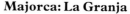

Tenerife: off the Autopiste del Norta at the entrance to Puerto de la Cruz
Owner: Instituto Nacional de Investigaciones Agrarias
Opening times: Daily, summer 9–19; winter 9–18; Sun, public hols 11–18/19
Admission charge: Yes

A 2ha walled garden on a formal plan, founded in 1788 by command of King Carlos III to acclimatize the many and useful plants discovered by Spanish explorers in Asia and the Americas. There are extensive collections of tropical fruit trees, araucarias, daturas, figs, palms, plumerias, and brightly-coloured foliage plants, many of them very old and enormous specimens.

Majorca: Jardín de la Alfabia

Buñola, 16km N of Palma on C711
Owner: Villalonga family
Opening times: Daily 9.30–13, 15–18, except public hols
Admission charge: Yes

The garden is a green oasis in a flat plain. Fine plane trees form the approach to the 17th-century stucco facade of the country house, which has Islamic origins. A stepped avenue of limes leads to a wall fountain flanked by covered reservoirs, the start of a ramped pergola with stone columns and a pebbled floor which is cooled by fountains and sprays. Adjoining it is a romantic 19th-century garden with fine trees and winding paths about an informal pond.

Majorca: La Granja

Esporlas, 15km NW of Palma on PM112
Owner: Fortuny family
Opening times: Daily 10–sunset
Admission charge: Yes

This ancient private estate with Islamic origins has one of the most beautiful houses on Majorca. It is sited by a stream which feeds in turn a waterfall, a reservoir shaded by an ancient yew tree, a fountain jet which tops the house in height, and miniature fountains lining a ramped pergola. Behind the house is a fey romantic garden with grotto and *glorieta*, or stately outdoor sitting-room, also cooled by fountain springs.

Majorca: Son Marroig

Deja, 15km W of Presto de Soller on C710
Owner: Donna Luisa Vives Ripoll
Opening times: Daily 9–14, 15.30–19 (winter–17.30)
Admission charge: Yes

This is the former seaside residence of the Habsburg Archduke Ludwig Salvator who first visited Majorca in 1867. The small garden, shaded by palm trees, has a pillared *glorieta* and a covered reservoir. A walk leads to the cliff face above which the archduke built a domed rotunda, with a view of the natural rock formation of Sa Foredada.

Majorca: Sa Torre Cega

Cala Ratjada, on the E tip of the island off C715
Owner: Don Bartolome March
Opening times: Easter to Oct, Tues–Fri from 9.30 by prior arrangement with the Officina d'Informacio Turistica
Admission charge: No

This impeccably-maintained 8ha garden on a hilltop above Cala Ratjada Bay was begun twenty years ago to a plan by the English garden designer Russell Page. Pine trees and flowering shrubs (chiefly forms of bougainvillea and hibiscus) provide a setting for an important collection of modern sculpture.

Portugal

Quinta da Aveleda ★

2.5km W of Paredes off N15, 30km E of Oporto
Owner: Sociedade Agricola e Comercial da Quinta da Aveleda
Opening times: Weekdays 10–17, except public hols
Admission charge: Yes

This informal woodland garden is approached by an avenue of majestic trees underplanted with camellia hedges which, despite years of clipping, are set solid in February and March with bright rosettes of scarlet, pink and white. The woodland is full of 19th-century picturesque incident – a miniature lake with boat-house, rustic bridges and rockwork, small-scale ruins, an aviary, thatched lodges, duck house and goat house, all in the style popularized in England by Shirley Hibberd's book *Rustic Adornments for Homes of Taste* (1856).

In recent years, the garden has been revitalized, many buildings restored, and the oak woods thinned to let light in on massed azaleas, rhododendrons, hydrangeas and Japanese maples which colour its shade in season. Large areas of ground-cover have been started and traditional bedding of begonias, calceolarias and pelargoniums make pretty patterns near the house. This is one of the most interesting and best-maintained gardens in Portugal.

Quinta da Bacalhôa ★

Vila Nogueira, 12km W of Setúbal off N10
Owner: Thomas Scoville
Opening times: Daily 13–17, except Sun and hols, by arrangement with the caretaker, Vila Nogueira, Azcitão, 2900 Setúbal
Admission charge: No

By the late 14th century Bacalhôa was already a royal residence. Its present aspect is the creation of the son of the first Viceroy of India, Afonso de Albuquerque, who was a notable connoisseur and travelled in Italy. He acquired the house in 1528 and laid out the garden in a renaissance style.

The house is situated in a huge walled enclosure from which there is a wide view towards Lisbon and the Tagus to the north. Of the garden's three shallow terraces, two are vineyards producing excellent wine. Every corner and change of level is marked by a melon-domed tower matching those at the corners of the house.

The garden next to the house is in three compartments – a box parterre, sunken orange grove and raised water-tank. The last, in the north-west corner of the site, balances the house and is linked to it by a wide promenade lined with tiled seats, parapet walls and flowerbeds.

On one edge of the water is a long pavilion of three square high-roofed rooms linked by open arcades, the walls of which are lined with rare 16th-century tiles. The sunken orange grove is irrigated from the tank and planted with collections of flowering shrubs and bulbs. These were introduced and the garden restored by Mrs Herbert Scoville of Connecticut, who bought the place, then long neglected, in 1936. 'For sheer boldness and simplicity of plan,' wrote the English garden designer Russell Page after his visit in 1935, 'this garden is one of the most striking in all European garden art.'

Bom Jesus do Monte

5km E of Braga on N103–3
Owner: Patrimonio Nacional
Opening times: Daily
Admission charge: No

This is a hilltop pilgrimage church reached by a grand architectural staircase with decorative fountains rising through oak woods. It was built between 1723 and c.1800, the last stage by the architect Carlos Amarante, and is divided into two parts – the *Stairway of the Three Virtues* and the *Stairway of the Five Senses*. 'All the stonework here is of the finest quality; the water is used with great skill and the whole place is in perfect repair,' wrote Russell Page in 1935. The same could be said today.

On either side of the staircase are large camellias, grown naturally or clipped. Rhododendrons and mimosas brighten the woods in March and neatly clipped parterres surround the church (1784–1811), also designed by Amarante.

Braga: Casa dos Biscaínhos

Rua D. Diego de Sousa
Owner: Municipality of Braga
Opening times: Daily 10–12, 14–17, except Mon, public hols
Admission charge: Yes

Behind the mainly 18th-century palace, now a museum, is a contemporary garden surrounded by one of the most delightful garden walls in Portugal, incorporating raised flowerbeds and alcove seats. Its tiled surfaces are capped with a granite coping whose rippling silhouette rises to entrance gates crowned with angels and trumpets. In one corner stands an octagonal pavilion with a tiled cupola above and a grotto beneath. The centre is occupied by a traditional box parterre of special interest because it contains arbours of clipped camellias in which fountains play. Beyond the wall, an orchard and an aviary are not well maintained, but Russell Page noted in 1935 that the paths were edged with blue and white irises and that the aviary (reserved for white peacocks) was 'curiously Indian' to look at.

In the nearby public Jardim de Santa Barbara there are dazzling displays of annuals in summer.

Parco dos Duques de Bragança

On Terreiro do Paco, Vila Viçosa on N254, 50km W of Badajoz
Owner: Fundação de Casa de Bragança
Opening times: Daily, summer 9–19; winter 9–18
Admission charge: Yes

Dating from 1501, and a royal palace from 1640, this complex of buildings, once the seat of the ducal family of Bragança, has a suite of small formal gardens dating from many periods. From the cloister garden of Dom Jaime I (15th-century), through a 17th-century pergola, there are the Box and Lady's gardens (both 18th-century), the woodland walk (19th-century) and finally an ornamental tank enclosure of the 20th century. Despite the different periods of these features, the styles are not strikingly dissimilar, which illustrates the often conservative taste of the Portuguese gardener.

Maze-like 18th-century box parterres in the Parco dos Duques de Bragança.

Tapada da Buçaco

Buçaco, 10km E of Mealhada on N235, 25km NE of Coimbra
Owner: Servicios Florestais
Opening times: Daily
Admission charge: No

A native forest of oak, phillyrea, laurustinus and tree heather, with spreading groves of *Rhododendron ponticum*, was walled in in the 17th century by monks from the Carmelite monastery established here in 1268. In 1643, Pope Urban VIII published a Papal Bull threatening with excommunication anyone who cut down or damaged any of its trees, which has ensured its remarkable survival.

Many exotic trees also date from the 17th century and are now over 30m tall, including what is described by W. J. Bean, author of the standard reference work on woody plants, as the 'most celebrated

PORTUGAL

plantation' of the Mexican *Cupressus lusitanica*. Underneath the trees are large camellias, rhododendrons, hydrangeas and tree ferns and a carpet of wild flowers, scillas and narcissi. Fountains, pools, alcoves and shrines enliven the shade.

Since 1850 Tapada da Buçaco has been in the charge of the forestry service. A large palace (now a hotel) was built 1887–1907 to the design of the Italian stage designer Luigi Manini. In front, a sloping parterre is overlooked by a terrace on which weeping oak, elm and *Sophora japonica* have been superbly trained into arbours.

Castelo Branco: Jardim dos Bispos (Gardens of the Bishop's Palace)
Rua de Frei Bartolomeu da Costa, Castelo Branco on N18
Owner: Municipality of Castelo Branco
Opening times: Daily, sunrise–12, 13–sunset
Admission charge: Yes

Box hedges, statuary and water compose the great formal terraced garden laid out *c*.1725 by the Bishop of Guarda beneath the windows of his palace. The statuary is set out thematically, with sculpture representing the signs of the Zodiac, the Virtues and the Four Seasons. Of particular interest is the pair of staircases linking the terraces, one of which is decorated with statues of Portuguese kings and queens (those who suffered Spanish domination being shown reduced in size) and the other with representations of the Apostles and Fathers of the Church.

The upper levels are filled with ornamental water tanks, each with a fountain in the form of a twisted column surmounted by a crown. One has flowerbeds set in arabesques of stone. Another is in the shape of a flower. Also unique is the balustrading in the form of widely-spaced, free-standing balusters connected only by the thinnest of metal handrails.

Coimbra: Botanic Garden ❀
Alameda Dr Julio Henriques
Owner: University of Coimbra
Opening times: Daily 8–sunset
Admission charge: No

The oldest and largest botanic garden in Portugal, founded in 1774, was laid out by the English engineer Colonel William Elsden. It extends over 80ha on a hillside below the university in the centre of Coimbra, though only the upper, formal part is open to the public. Here a sunken garden, with box-edged beds of flowering trees and shrubs and a central fountain, is overlooked by six terraces. The greenhouse, the largest in Portugal and still well-stocked, was completed in 1867.

Its greatest director, Julio Henriques (director 1873–1918), was responsible for the garden's present appearance. He corresponded and exchanged seed with the Director of the Melbourne Botanic Garden, Baron von Mueller, resulting in the present magnificent collection of over forty eucalyptus species and outstanding specimens of Moreton Bay fig and Norfolk Island pine. There are also extensive collections of palms, succulents and conifers, together with plants from the Portuguese islands of Madeira and the Azores.

Lisbon: Botanic Garden of Ajuda ❀
Calçada da Ajuda
Owner: Instituto Superior de Agronomia
Opening times: Daily, summer 9–19; winter 8–17
Admission charge: No

Founded as the Royal Botanic Garden in 1772 under the direction of the Italians Vandelli and Mattiazzi, the garden lost much of its importance on the foundation *c*.1840 of the University Faculty of Sciences Botanic Garden (q.v.).

Located in the shadow of the 19th-century Palace of Ajuda with a wide view of the Tagus, it is now an immense box parterre around a central fountain embellished with many carved sea creatures celebrating Portugal's maritime links. Fine trees on the upper parterre include a dragon tree (*Dracaena draco*), 6m high and 12m across, a 20m *Grevillea robusta*, an *Acacia armata* and *Schotia latifolia*.

Lisbon: Botanic Garden of Lisbon University Faculty of Sciences ❀
Rua da Escola Politécnica
Owner: Faculty of Sciences, Lisbon University
Opening times: Daily 10–17
Admission charge: No

Covering 4ha in the centre of Lisbon, the garden was founded *c*.1840 under the direction of the Austrian botanist F. Weltwitsch to replace the Royal Botanic Garden of Ajuda (q.v.). The present planting dates mainly from this time.

The upper part, with its observatory and School of Botany, is devoted to small flowering trees, shrubs and other plants in broad, box-edged beds. Steps lead down to a palm avenue composed of 35 species and a succulent garden with two giant dragon trees (*Dracaena draco*). (Although a native of the Canary Islands, the dragon tree was first described by the great botanist Clusius in the 16th century from a specimen at Belém on the outskirts of Lisbon.) Below is mixed woodland of exotic trees, including very large specimens of the Australian banyan (*Ficus benghalensis*), South African dombeya, Brazilian coral tree and a 30m *Chorisia speciosa*, its bole covered in warty prickles.

Lisbon: Estufa Fria ✽

Rua Castilho
Owner: Câmara Municipal de Lisboa
Opening times: Daily 10–18, except Dec 25
Admission charge: Yes

In 1906, a competition was held for the landscape design of an old quarry which formed part of the then new Edward VII park. It was won by the architect Raul Carapinha with a proposal to roof the quarry with wooden laths under which, protected from climatic extremes, tropical and subtropical plants might flourish. The result was the creation of the largest wooden lath house in the world, *c*.280m long and covering nearly 1ha, which opened to the public in 1930.

Ferns, tree ferns, figs and camellias flourish on the shady side of the quarry floor, while palms, bananas and mimosas are among the plants which enjoy the sunny side. The filtered light on the foliage, the sound of running water in streams and falls, the grotto-like spaces, and the vast leaves of many tropical plants give the visitor the impression of being in a jungle.

A heated greenhouse was added in 1975. Here a large collection of succulents is grown on high ledges and terraces around a pool with a flock of pink flamingos.

Lisbon: Palácio de Fronteira ★

Largo de São Domingos de Benfica, off Estrada de Benfico
Owner: Fundação das Casas de Fronteira e Alorna
Opening times: Nov to Mar, Mon 10–12, 14–16; Apr to Oct, Mon, Wed 10–12, Sat 15–18.30
Admission charge: Yes

A most splendid formal garden was laid out *c*.1668 by the powerful politician, the Marquês de Fronteira. It was visited in 1669 by the Florentines Cosimo de' Medici and the Marchese Corsini who described it as having 'diverse parterres, statues and bas reliefs'. So one might describe it today.

A fine fountained parterre, its intricate geometry derived from the engravings of French gardens by J. A. du Cerceau in 1576, is flanked by the most ornamental water-tank in Portugal. Fourteen huge tile panels of knights on horseback are reflected in its waters, stone figures besport themselves on its surface and three grottoes lie in shadowy recesses. On either side, stone staircases rise to the terrace walk above where corner pavilions are roofed with lustre-glazed tiles. The walk contains an outdoor gallery of Portuguese kings whose busts are set in niches of tiles, many modelled three-dimensionally as pine cones.

The shady Garden of Venus, now memorable for its beautiful bunya-bunya pine (*Araucaria bidwilli*), leads to a sunken garden with a spectacular domed grotto described by Corsini as 'adorned with mother of pearl, fragments of porcelain, various coloured glasses and diverse marble pieces'. In front is a pool of sinuous arabesque outline surrounded by seats faced with tilework in a charming naïve manner. Above the pool is a chapel with a grotto-like entrance and one of the glories of the garden, the Chapel Walk. Also in the form of an outdoor gallery, this walk is flanked by tiled panels that represent allegories of the arts and sciences, and by statues of deities set in niches. Raised flowerbeds, seats and shell fountains in the pavement complete the well-designed ensemble.

A seldom-visited woodland garden with pavilions set amidst rare trees stretches behind the palace.

Lisbon: Parque do Museu Calouste Gulbenkian

Avenida de Berna
Owner: Calouste Gulbenkian Foundation
Opening times: Daily 9–19
Admission charge: No

A modern landscape park around the museum and cultural centre of the Calouste Gulbenkian Foundation, completed in 1969. Lawns sloping to an artificial lake are surrounded by rose gardens, shrubberies, water gardens, sculpture gardens and an open-air theatre.

Lisbon: Quinta do Monteiro-Môr

Largo Julio de Castilho, Lumiar
Owner: Museo de Traje
Opening times: Daily 9–18, except Mon
Admission charge: Yes

The site of one of the earliest botanic gardens in Portugal, this is now mainly of interest to the tree enthusiast. On the terrace below the house (now a costume museum) successive Dukes of Palmela planted, from 1840, an important collection of trees, some now of immense size and well cared for. They were advised by a distinguished series of garden directors – Rosenfelder and Weiss from Paris and the Austrian, F. Weltwitsch. Among the notable trees are a huge hybrid plane (*Platanus × acerifolia*), a New Zealand Christmas tree (*Metrosideros excelsa*), a false magnolia (*Michelia figo*), a Mexican cypress (*Cupressus lusitanica*) and a Norfolk Island pine, many with an underplanting of the liliaceous ophiopogon.

Lisbon: Palácio das Necessidades

Largo das Necessidades
Owner: Ministerio dos Negocios Estangeiros
Opening times: Daily 10–18, except Sat, Sun, public hols
Admission charge: No

The mid 18th-century royal palace was designed by Caetano Tomás de Sousa. In front, on the terrace overlooking the Tagus, is one of the finest fountains in Lisbon. Behind is an extensive wooded park with fine trees – cedars, redwoods, magnolias and a dragon tree. There is an impressive domed conservatory and an ornamental zoo.

Lisbon: Jardim do Ultramar ❀

Calçada do Galvão, Belém, SW of city centre
Owner: Instituto de Investigação Cientifica Tropical
Opening times: Daily 11–12, 14–17, except Tues, public hols
Admission charge: No

The garden was founded in 1912 in the grounds of the 18th-century royal palace of Belém (now the official residence of the President of Portugal) for the study of plants from Portugal's former colonies. The exotic note is struck immediately with an island of banana trees on a lake by the entrance. Within the garden are avenues of palms, Brazilian coral trees (*Erythrina crista-galli*) and *Chorisia speciosa*.

The formal garden of the palace, occasionally open to the public, boasts an 18th-century aviary which is one of the finest garden buildings in Portugal.

Solar de Mateus

Mateus, 3km E of Vila Real on N322
Owner: Fundação da Casa de Mateus
Opening times: Summer 9–13, 14–18; winter 8–12, 13–17
Admission charge: Yes

The silhouette of Mateus is known throughout the world from the label on the rosé wine that bears its name. Built in the early 18th century, it and its adjoining chapel completed in 1750 are adorned with elaborate architectural ornament which is doubled by reflection in a large modern pool.

On the garden front, no less than four box parterres descend the hillside. The first and largest is divided into small box-edged beds in a classic Portuguese design; the furthest has a French pattern of swirling box arabesques, its boundary graced by a characteristic wall fountain in carved granite at one point and at another by a cypress hedge clipped to a curving baroque outline.

The garden is bisected by two features which were once the pride of northern Portuguese gardens but are now practically unknown – a clipped tunnel (of cypress or box) and a pergola supported on granite pillars carved as obelisks or giant balusters.

To the south is an ornamental orchard, its large plots bounded by cypress hedges which arch over the paths at intervals. Both paths and plots are crossed by irrigation channels of carved granite, their water flowing from the ornamental storage tank on a higher level.

Oporto: Quinta do Meio

211 Rua Entre Quintas, off Rua D. Manuel II
Owner: Câmara Municipal da Porto
Opening times: By appointment, Rua Entre Quintas 211, 4000 Oporto
Admission charge: No

This garden was created from 1881 by William Tait, an English merchant of Oporto, who was also an amateur ornithologist and botanist. On one of the terraces overlooking the Douro is a venerable tulip tree, the tallest in Europe before its crown was blown out by a gale in 1968. It is listed as a national monument. Magnificent specimens of sassafras, a Judas tree, a red-flowering gum and a southern magnolia grow amongst a collection of camellias, some of them rare Portuguese hybrids.

Two gardens adjoin. That of the *Museu Romantico* lies in the green shade of a mixed canopy of Portuguese and Australasian trees. The *Jardim do Palácio de Cristal*, the principal public garden of Oporto, was laid out by the local landscape gardener Emilio David with a 19th-century parterre, fountain and statuary, but it is now mostly devoted to public entertainment.

Oporto: Casa de Serralves

977 Rua de Serralves, off Avenida da Boavista
Owner: Secretaria do Estado da Cultura
Opening times: Daily 14–17.30, except Mon
Admission charge: Yes

Now a museum of 20th-century Portuguese art, the Casa de Serralves is one of the most important Modernist houses in Portugal. It was built during the 1930s for a noted patron of the arts, the Count of Vizela, to the design of the Oporto architect, Marquês de Silva.

The garden was laid out by the French architect and landscape designer Jacques Greber, chief de-signer of the Great Paris Exhibition of 1937, who carried out many projects on both sides of the Atlantic. His drawings are displayed in the house. The principal garden is designed around a long central canal in the Muslim tradition, which leads to a rock garden and landscaped pond. Formal rose gardens, kitchen gardens, herbaceous plants and shrubs are sheltered by the oakwoods of this large estate in the centre of Oporto.

Palácio de Marquês de Pombal

Oeiras, 10km W of Lisbon off N6
Owner: Instituto Nacional de Administração
Opening times: By appointment, Instituto Nacional de Administração, 2780 Oeiras
Admission charge: No

The rose-pink 18th-century palace, built by Carlos Mardel for the powerful prime minister, the Marquês de Pombal, has formal gardens famous for their statuary and tilework. Reached by bridges across the River Lage are further flower gardens and ornamental orchards, recently planted with shrubs, and the magnificent grotto-like Cascade of the Poets.

In the park stretching up the Oeiras valley is a delightful fishing complex consisting of pavilion, cascade and huge formal fish-tank plastered with statuary and splendid panels of tiles. Further on are an ornamental dairy, dovecote and a house for raising silkworms.

Palácio Nacional de Queluz ★

Queluz, 5km W of Lisbon off N117
Owner: Instituto Portugues do Patrimonio Cultural
Opening times: Daily 10–18, except Tues, Dec 25
Admission charge: Yes

The garden of the summer palace of Queluz was laid out 1753–82 for the future king, Pedro III, by the Frenchman Jean-Baptiste Robillon. Two elaborately designed box parterres, each forming a double square, were used in summer as outdoor reception rooms for the court. Balustraded terraces designed for the evening promenade surround them. Rococo fountains are still operated by the original hydraulic system devised by the king's engineer-in-chief, Manuel da Maia. There are English and Italian sculptures, many of which were originally gilded and painted in polychrome, and faience vases from the Rato factory in Lisbon. Here in hot weather in the late 18th century the Infanta Carlota Joaquina would sit on the edge of a fountain with her legs plunged into the water. Statues of Pegasus bearing an Allegory of Fame by the sculptors Manuel Alves and Felipe da Costa guard the entrance to the formal

Jungle-like plantings of tender exotic plants surround a pool at Estufa Fria.

woodland – the shade a contrast to the sunlit parterre. The park is crossed by hedged walks down which the Infanta commanded William Beckford, the English aesthete, to run a race with her ladies-in-waiting.

On the river bank below the formal gardens is the great feature of the garden – a canal, lined, balustraded and bridged with polychrome tiles. 'Built when the extravagances of the Braganza kings were astonishing Europe,' wrote Russell Page, 'this canal, with its exuberance of shape and colour, expresses all that is best in Portuguese gardens.'

Sintra: Quinta de Monserrate

3km W of Sintra on N375
Owner: Instituto Portugues do Patrimonio Cultural
Opening times: Daily 9–18, except Dec 25
Admission charge: Yes

Sintra, long famous for the luxurious vegetation of its mountains and the fantastic ruins and follies which crown its hills and line its roads, was pictured by Byron as a landscape of 'horrid crags by toppling convents crowned'.

William Beckford, the English writer and connoisseur of romantic landscape, lived at Monserrate from 1795–9, occupying himself entirely with creating much of the existing romantic garden of ruins, cataracts and pools. In 1856, Monserrate was bought by an English linen merchant, Sir Francis Cook, who had the house transformed into an arab-gothic fantasy by the English architect J. S. Knowles. The English landscape painter W. Stockdale advised him on the creation of romantic landscape views and W. Nevill from the Royal Botanic Gardens at Kew (q.v.) offered him botanical advice.

Integrated unobtrusively into the native woodland of oak, cork oak, arbutus and phillyrea are whole groves of tree camellias and tree ferns, collections of 25 palm species, rare southern hemisphere conifers and flowering trees, some of them, like the New Zealand Christmas tree (*Metrosideros excelsa*), now enormous specimens.

Sintra: Castelo da Pena

1km W of Sintra off N247–3
Owner: Servicios Forestais
Opening times: Daily, except Tues, summer 9–18; winter 10–15
Admission charge: No

A 200ha park in the Sintra mountains where, in *c*.1840, Ferdinand of Saxe-Coburg-Gotha, King-Consort of Portugal, built a palace to the design of the German architect Baron von Eschwege. Perched romantically on a crag, and a pastiche of several styles, it is built round the remains of a 16th-century monastery.

Drives wind sinuously across the park through a labyrinth of exotic conifers and natural vegetation, passing several springs covered with Islamic canopies and dipping to lakes romantically shaded by spreading conifers. There are camellias and rose gardens (the latter needing restoration) and a rustic cottage with a fernery by a stream.

Matching the extravagance of the architecture is an eclectic collection of trees, including giant tulip trees, the rimu tree (*Dacrydium cupressinum*) and a collection of the genus *Podocarpus*.

Sintra: Palácio de Seteais

1.5km W of Sintra on N375
Owner: Hotel Palacio de Seteais
Opening times: By appointment with the hotel, 2710 Sintra
Admission charge: No

The palace was built in the 1780s by the Dutch consul Daniel Gildemeester, but was later owned by the Marquês de Marialva who, in 1802, added a matching building linked to the existing one by a triumphal arch – a unique architectural composition. The entrance front has a setting of lawns and lime trees unusual for Portugal, but the garden front is typically Portuguese. Here a parterre of box-edged beds filled with cubes and spheres of box enjoys sensational views to the distant Atlantic.

Quinta das Torres

Vila Fresca de Azeitão, 11km W of Setúbal on N10
Owner: De Sousa family
Opening times: By appointment with the hotel manager, Quinta das Torres, Vila Fresca de Azeitão, 2400 Setúbal
Admission charge: Yes

The 16th-century manor house, now partly a hotel, is approached by an avenue of plane trees underplanted with hedges of *Spiraea cantoniensis* which flower magnificently in March. Built round a courtyard with orange trees and a central fountain, its Palladian loggia and high pyramid roofs make it one of the best examples of renaissance domestic architecture in Portugal.

A great ornamental tank provides water for the extensive orange groves below the house. It is fed by two fountains in the form of shells and in the middle is a cool pavilion with a cupola and twelve columns, which can be reached by boat.

Madeira

Funchal: Botanic Garden of Madeira

Quinta do Bom Sucesso, Rua Carlos Azevedo de Menezes
Owner: Região Antonomia de Madeira
Opening times: Daily 10–18
Admission charge: Yes

The house, originally belonging to the Reid family, is now a natural history museum. The garden is laid out on a series of informal terraces leading to the edge of a steep gorge, and is devoted to both the flora of Madeira and exotics.

Funchal: Quinta das Cruzas

Calçada de Santa Clara
Owner: Junte Geral do Funchal
Opening times: Daily 10–18, except Mon
Admission charge: Yes

The house, now a decorative arts museum, is surrounded by a garden of fine exotic trees – including a tall kauri pine (*Agathis australis*), a *Schefflera digitata* and a tree cycad (*Encephalartos altensteinii*) – among which are assembled antique architectural and sculptural fragments. At the top of the garden is a shaded orchid house.

Funchal: Quinta de Palmeira

Rua de Levada de Santa Luzia
Owner: Welch family
Opening times: By appointment, Rua de Levada de Santa Luzia, 9000 Funchal, Madeira
Admission charge: No

The present appearance of both house and garden dates from 1908, when an English family started developing a series of outdoor 'rooms' on terraces overlooking the harbour of Funchal, and building up an excellent plant collection.

Quinta do Palheiro Ferreiro ⊛

8km NE of Funchal off Camacha road
Owner: Blandy family
Opening times: Daily 8.30–12.30, except Sat, Sun, public hols
Admission charge: Yes

The estate was originally developed in 1804 by the Conde de Carvalhal, who built the chapel and manor house and laid out the series of formal pools leading to a majestic avenue of planes. When the property was purchased by the Blandy family in 1885, a new house was built on a higher site to the design of J. S. Clark, architect of Reid's Hotel in Funchal.

The new house is approached by an avenue 1km long, one side of which is entirely lined with many varieties of old camellias, 10–13m in height, which flower over a long season from December to April. The new garden (1885) of lawns sloping to woodland and distant prospects of the sea is divided by paths of the small black seashore pebbles characteristic of Madeira. Old redwoods, cedars, magnolias and tulip trees shelter great masses of agapanthus, arum lilies, nerines, wild lupin, belladonna lilies and even cymbidium orchids.

There are mixed borders of a most unusual kind in that all the plants are too tender to survive in northern Europe. To the east the Lady's Garden is a delightful old-fashioned mixture of roses, lilies and daturas around lily pools, with many of the whimsical topiary figures at which the Portuguese excel. To the west is the Inferno, a lush and shadowy dell with dripping rocks, tall tree ferns and a tangle of climbing aroids and morning glories. The gardens are famous for their splendid collections, from bulbs to trees, of South African, South American and Australasian plants, together with many endemic to Madeira or the neighbouring Canary Islands.

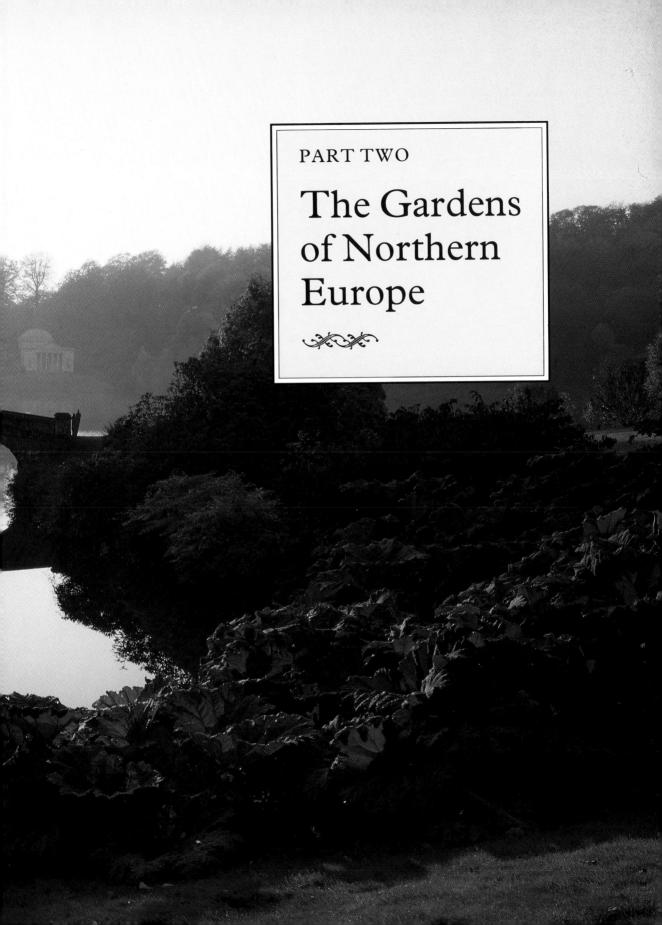

PART TWO

The Gardens of Northern Europe

Great Britain

*'The British isles are naturally and politically more favorable to the
practice of horticulture in all its branches than any other country; in no
country is so great a proportion of the surface covered with gardens.'*
J. C. Loudon, *An Encyclopaedia of Gardening* (1822)

England does not have great extremes of climate, but there are striking
variations across the country. Parts of the Lake District, for example, may
have more than 1,500mm of rain per annum; whereas an annual rainfall of
more than 750mm is rare in East Anglia. Sunshine varies considerably.
Yorkshire has an average over the whole year of 3.56 hours of bright sunshine
per day (which is only slightly more than Norway); Worthing, on the south
coast of England, has five hours, or an annual total of 1,825 hours (compared
with, say, Italy which has 2,600). Variations in temperature are not great.
From a gardening point of view the overriding factor is the occasional very
severe winter, with temperatures falling to below −15°C. Such minimum
temperatures may occur almost anywhere in Great Britain except in the Isles
of Scilly and in those western parts of Cornwall and Devon which are
strikingly tempered by the Gulf Stream drift. The lack of temperature
extremes does produce some problems; the young growth of woody plants
from climates with hotter summers does not ripen during British summers
and is vulnerable to frosts, while the mild winters, with recurrent warm
spells, during which sap rises or herbaceous plants put out shoots, may be
followed by successive periods of damaging cold.

PREVIOUS PAGES **Water and sky frame architectural
details in the sublime gardens at Stourhead. The
gardens were first laid out in the middle of the 18th
century.**

**Leonard Knyff's engraving (1702) of Hampton Court
shows the baroque layout.**

With this mild climate England grows a larger range of garden plants than any other country and has sought plants from all over the temperate world. New plants arrived before the Romans and from the 18th century onwards large-scale plant-hunting expeditions have resulted in vast numbers of new introductions. The 20th-century gardener in England has to reconcile his collector's instinct with a balanced design. This has not by any means always been so. The formal gardens of the 17th century, while sometimes containing small collections of 'florist's' flowers, depended in general on a restricted range of plants. 'Capability' Brown in the 18th century used only a few species of trees and shrubs in his great landscapes; other garden designers of his time, who encouraged flowerbed planting, were slow to experiment with newly-introduced, untried material, although individuals such as Bishop Compton, Peter Collinson and Philip Miller, the Director of the Chelsea Physic Garden (q.v.), and many other private collectors, grew a wide range of plants.

The Romans gardened in England, but although the excavations at Fishbourne have revealed details of what was probably a typical garden layout, little is known for certain about the plants they introduced. Periwinkle survived and naturalized, but most other introductions disappeared during the Dark Ages. The earliest documentary evidence of gardening comes from the Middle Ages and concerns monastic layouts and other gardens connected with the church. Friar Henry Daniel, for example, grew 252 different sorts of herbs in his garden at Stepney in London in the late 14th century, and wrote knowledgeably about botany and horticulture, showing a lively interest in the aesthetic qualities of plants as well as in their practical uses. During the reign of Henry VIII in the early 16th century there was a great increase in ornamental gardening associated with the lavish court life; Sir Roy Strong writes: 'Pleasure gardens are seen to pertain to the king and to the court as outward signs of regal magnificence.' Rivalry with Henry's French contemporary, Francis I, extended also to gardens. The royal palaces of Richmond and Hampton Court (q.v.) and the Duke of Buckingham's garden at Thornbury Castle were on a grandiose scale – formal, enclosed gardens rich in heraldry and ornamentation. In the later Tudor period there was continuing Italian and French influence, and architecture played an important role in the garden. The late Elizabethan gazebos at Montacute, looking both at the garden and the deer park, are typical of the period.

In the first half of the 17th century the careers of the Tradescants, father and son, show a discerning and passionate plantsmanship – an early sign of what was to become a decisive path of English gardening. The elder Tradescant was gardener to the Cecil family (see Hatfield House) and to Charles I, and travelled in Europe collecting fruit trees and other plants, while receiving others from North America through the Virginia Company. His son searched for plants in Virginia in 1638 and was responsible for many introductions which have proved important in gardens.

As far as garden design was concerned, the prevailing atmosphere was one of intricate formality. The 4th Earl of Pembroke's garden at Wilton House, of which little sign survives, was one of the horticultural wonders of the early 17th century. Wilton saw a collaboration of the rare talents of Inigo Jones and Isaac de Caus. The gardens, with elaborate parterres, statues, waterworks and a fabulous grotto, were a late-flowering version of the gardens of the Italian Renaissance. André Mollet came to Wilton from France and, although his role there is uncertain, he undoubtedly designed elaborate *parterres de broderie* for Charles I at St James's Palace, and at Wimbledon House. André Le Nôtre, the decisive European influence in the latter half of

The Gardens of Great Britain

N

Wick

Ullapool
Dunrobin Castle

Inverewe
Dundonnell
House

Inverness

Pitmedden Garden

Scotland

Crathes Castle
Aberdeen

Fort William

Cluny House
Brechin Castle

Bolfracks
Brankly Dundee
Drummond Perth
Castle
Kellie Castle

Oban
Arduaine
Falkland Palace
Crarae Glen Garden
Stirling

Achamore House
Glasgow
Royal Botanic Garden, Edinburgh
Edinburgh
Little Sparta

Culzean Castle and
Country Park
Galashiels

Bargany
Howick Hall

Stranraer
Arbigland
Newcastle

Logan Botanic Garden
Carlisle

Darlington

Kendal Sizergh Castle
Levens Hall
Holker Hall
Newby Hall
York

Northern England Hull

Manchester

Tatton Park Sheffield
Arley Hall
Chatsworth

Bodnant
Garden
Stoke
Nottingham

Hodnet Hall

East Anglia, the Midlands
Blickling Hall
Powis **and Wales**
Castle
Norwich
Birmingham
Packwood House

Wales
Hergest Croft
Northampton
Cambridge
Worcester
Hidcote Manor
The Priory, Kemerton
Ipswich
Fishguard
Sezincote
Stowe
Saling Hall
Westbury Court Garden
Gloucester
Rousham House
Painswick Rococo Garden
Blenheim Palace
Barnsley House
Oxford Oxford Botanic
Cardiff
Pusey Garden
Westonbirt House
Arboretum Reading
Bristol
London
Heale
House
Jenkyn Place
Hestercombe
Wakehurst
House
Stourhead
Place
Sissinghurst Castle
Rosemoor
Nymans
Dover
Mottisfont
Great Dixter
Knightshayes
Abbey
Court
Cranborne
Sheffield Park
Lanhydrock
Exeter
Manor
Brighton
The Garden
Southern England
Trewithen House
House
Tintinhull House
Penzance
East Lambrook Manor

South-West England and Isles of Scilly

Tresco
Abbey

Isles of Scilly

0   50   100   150 km

Hatfield House

Hampton
Court
Palace
Chelsea Physic
Garden

Royal Botanic
Gardens, Kew

Wisley Garden

An engraving from *Le Jardin de Wilton* by Isaac de
Caus shows his layout for the garden at Wilton House
in 1645.

the 17th century, did designs for Greenwich Park which survive but were not
executed. A few gardens showing the influence of the French baroque style
survive; Bramham Park, St Paul's Waldenbury, Melbourne Hall and much
of the layout of Hampton Court (q.v.), including the great axial vista, are fine
examples.

In the early 18th century English gardens were divided into compartments
with, when scale allowed, avenues radiating into the countryside. Kip's
engravings of the period are useful records. These gardens, even if on a grand
scale, frequently reveal a characteristically English intimacy. But already in
the early 18th century there were signs of the revolt against formality and the
start of the revolution that produced the landscape garden. A group of writers
– Alexander Pope and Joseph Addison among them – mocked the excesses of
the formal garden and prepared the way for William Kent (who made
Rousham (q.v.) from 1738 onwards), Charles Bridgeman (Stowe (q.v.), 1713
onwards) and Lancelot 'Capability' Brown (active from the 1740s onwards).

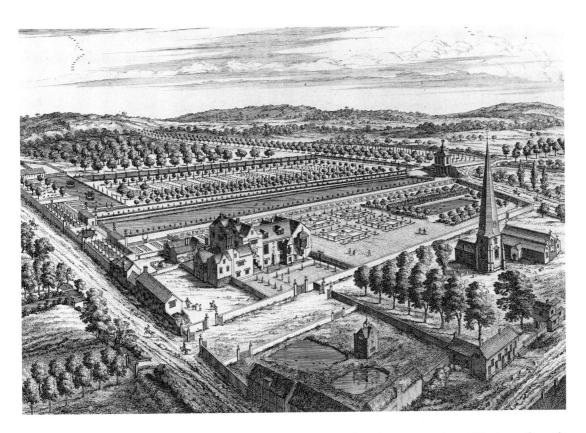

The Dutch-style water garden at Westbury Court is
shown in Kip's early 18th-century engraving.

Brown developed an easily imitated 'natural' style of landscape, with
clumped trees and serpentine lakes, that became internationally influential
and effectively destroyed the formal garden tradition in England. Brown's
successor, Humphry Repton, worked on a more intimate scale and used
rustic and picturesque buildings and ornaments rather than the classical
types preferred by Brown; towards the end of his life he reintroduced
flowerbeds and rosaries on terraces by the house or in enclosed garden areas.

The 19th century was restlessly eclectic with many backward glances at old
traditions. J. C. Loudon's 'gardenesque' style encouraged an emphasis on
winding walks and a self-conscious display of tree and plant specimens. By
the middle of the century elaborate parterres, with colourful summer
bedding (usually recently introduced annuals or tender plants which were
grown in the new glasshouses), were ostentatious features. The great
practitioners such as W. A. Nesfield and Sir Charles Barry showed a brilliant
command of historical styles on an immensely grand scale. Nesfield, in

particular, designed elaborate scroll and feather gravel and box patterns (his design at Broughton Hall still exists).

The 'natural' style of William Robinson, who hated topiary and architectural gardens, and laid emphasis on 'wild' gardening, was of great influence in the last half of the century and has continued to inspire both the large gardens of plant collectors as well as more humble cottage-style layouts. Gertrude Jekyll was one of a group of garden designers of the late 19th and early 20th centuries referred to as 'Arts and Crafts' gardeners, characterized by a particular interest in vernacular architecture and building materials and the traditional crafts of the countryside. Their gardens were divided into compartments with a strong architectural character that was emphasized by structural planting. Inside these 'rooms', planting was relaxed and free-flowing. In addition, Miss Jekyll's carefully controlled borders with subtle colour harmonies and contrasts influenced by contemporary colour theory (she had been trained as a painter) and her discerning interest in plants became dominant themes. In collaboration with the architect Edwin Lutyens, she produced some of the finest English gardens. She also influenced a generation of amateur gardeners including Lawrence Johnston (at Hidcote, q.v.) and Vita Sackville-West (at Sissinghurst, q.v.). That tradition, now perhaps in a rather decadent phase, still influences contemporary gardening.

Of the early history of gardening in Scotland very little is known. Monastic and royal gardens certainly existed; the remains of the orchard of the great Cistercian abbey at Melrose were still visible in 1797 and King David I had a garden at the base of Edinburgh Castle in the early 12th century. But nothing survives that gives any detailed account of the appearance of these gardens. Apart from several descriptions of vegetable gardens and orchards, we have no clear picture of Scottish gardens before the 17th century, when the connections between the royal houses of France and Scotland were an important influence. Surviving designs for 17th-century parterres at Holyrood House were used in the restoration of the Great Garden at Pitmedden (q.v.), whose owner in the 17th century, Sir Alexander Seton, had learned the latest French ideas from the architect William Bruce. Bruce himself made gardens at Balcaskie and Kinross with striking axial compositions in the spirit of Le Nôtre.

The Act of Union with England in 1707 allowed greater influence from south of the border, and later in the century the great Scottish estates followed English ideas in the making of landscape gardens. It was William Adam, of that great family of architects, who wrote in 1716, 'the rising and fallings of ground are to be humoured and generally make the greatest

Beautys in gardens.' Sir John Clerk of Penicuik from 1735 onwards made a landscape garden replete with classical allusions. There was nothing in Scotland quite like the landscape revolution associatd with 'Capability' Brown in England, but Thomas White, father and son, coming from Durham and practising widely in the Brownian style, were later much criticized by J. C. Loudon, himself a Scot from Edinburgh, for their insensitivity to the wild Scottish landscape.

In the 19th century Scotland produced several distinguished plant hunters, including David Douglas and Robert Fortune. Sir William Hooker, as Professor of Botany at Glasgow University from 1820–41, recognized that the west coast, with very high rainfall and temperatures influenced by the Gulf Stream drift, provided ideal habitats for many exotics. In this period the stream of new introductions became a flood and a new kind of gardening emerged characterized by assiduous plantsmanship. In 1862 Osgood Mackenzie started the garden at Inverewe (q.v.) and many other notable collections were built up on the west coast. Other gardens, like Drummond Castle (q.v.) and Dunrobin (q.v.), followed the English tradition for revived formal layouts.

The influence of English Arts and Crafts gardening is seen at Crathes Castle (q.v.), where from 1926 onwards Sir James and Lady Burnett of Leys introduced magnificent borders into a much earlier formal framework. In the early part of the 20th century, the architect Robert Lorimer, also influenced by the Arts and Crafts movement, designed several gardens – at Kellie Castle (q.v.), Earlshall and Hill of Tarvit – showing a discerning historicism and love of formality. Ian Hamilton Finlay's garden at Little Sparta (q.v.), made from 1976 onwards, seems distinctively 20th-century but, with its meticulously placed statues and inscriptions, draws deeply on past traditions.

The horticultural scene in Britain today is a vigorous one, with flourishing nursery gardens, an intense interest in garden visiting and an energetic movement for the conservation of gardens and garden plants. There is also a renewed interest, led by the National Trust and many owners of historic gardens, in authentic historical restoration. However, no distinctive modern style of garden has emerged. Individual owners rather than professional designers seem to set trends, and new gardens today tend to be based on a hesitant eclecticism rather than looking towards any brave new world.

South-West England and Isles of Scilly

East Lambrook Manor

East Lambrook, N of the A303, 2 miles N of South
Petherton on B3165
Owner: Mr and Mrs Andrew Norton
Opening times: Daily 9–17, except Sun
Admission charge: Yes

The manor is an Elizabethan house of Ham stone set
in a village of tranquil charm. The garden was created
by Margery Fish from 1938 and made famous by her
many influential books. She invented a style of
inspired cottage-gardening in which a fastidious taste
in plants, many of them wild, was allied to an
intuitive understanding of the conditions that suited
them best. After Mrs Fish's death in 1966 the garden
fell into some neglect. New owners are now restoring
it with energy and sensitivity.

Less than 0.5ha in area, the garden lies behind and
above the house. The design seems inconsequential,
but it makes virtues of the sloping site and natural
gullies. Paths amble about intensively planted mixed
borders and some structure is given by pollarded
willows and a curving avenue of *Chamaecyparis
lawsoniana* 'Fletcheri', clipped into tall domes. The
real distinction of the garden, however, lies in the
plants. There is something of horticultural interest in
every season. In summer the rich planting comes into
its own, but amid the luxuriance the firm hand of the
plant connoisseur is always evident.

The Garden House

Buckland Monachorum, 10 miles N of Plymouth off A386
Owner: The Fortescue Charitable Trust
Opening times: Daily, Apr to Sept 12–17
Admission charge: Yes

This garden, set on the side of a steep valley on the
south-western fringes of Dartmoor, has two faces.
The first, less interesting, provides a tranquil setting
for the house – impeccable lawns flow into the edges
of woodland planted with many azaleas and other
woodland shrubs. The second, descending into the
valley below the house, is a most remarkable 0.8ha

walled garden on the site of a medieval monastery.
Here, on terraced slopes, the maker of the garden, the
late Lionel Fortescue, built up a collection of fastidi-
ously chosen herbaceous perennials and ornamental
shrubs and disposed them charmingly among the
monastery ruins.

Hestercombe House ★

Cheddon Fitzpaine, 4½ miles NW of Taunton off A361
Owner: Somerset County Council
Opening times: Tues, Wed, Thurs 12–17; Jul, Aug,
occasional Sun
Admission charge: Yes

Hestercombe House is an ungainly 19th-century
mansion built for the Portman family. Its garden,
now beautifully restored, is a masterpiece by Gertrude Jekyll and Edwin Lutyens, created from 1904
onwards. With his back to the house, the visitor looks
down on an irresistible formal layout of stone paths,
balustrades, formal beds, straight rills and ornamental stonework of exquisite quality. The planting
is understated and harmonious; in summer, many
grey-leaved plants, delphiniums, roses of different
shades of pink, and purple irises; in winter, the
garden sparkles with the shiny leaves of evergreen
bergenias, the brilliant berries of *Skimmia japonica*
and the fragrance of wintersweet. Along the south
side, a pergola provides a decorative frame for views
of the unspoilt rural landscape beyond. To the north-
east there is a ravishing orangery by Lutyens, built of
lovely golden Ham stone.

Knightshayes Court ★

Bolham, 2 miles N of Tiverton off A396
Owner: The National Trust
Opening times: Daily, Apr to Sept 11–18, Oct 11–17
Admission charge: Yes

This garden, built round William Burges's red
sandstone mansion of 1870–3, is substantially the
creation of Sir John and Lady Heathcoat Amory

since World War II. Its great glory is the woodland garden in which an outstanding collection of ornamental trees and shrubs – including dogwoods, rhododendrons, rowans, magnolias, *Nothofagus betuloides* and *N. dombeyi* – is harmoniously disposed in ancient woodland. Nearer the house are fine mixed borders, a pool enclosed in yew hedges, a paved garden with silver plants, many old roses and superb views to the south over the Devon countryside.

Lanhydrock

3 miles SE of Bodmin via B3268
Owner: The National Trust
Opening times: Daily, Apr to Oct 11–18; rest of year, sunrise–sunset
Admission charge: Yes

Part of the house and its distinguished towered and turreted gatehouse are of the 17th century, built by the Robartes family. The setting is extremely beautiful – densely wooded slopes to the west and south with, to the east, wonderful views across old parkland

The 17th-century gatehouse at Lanhydrock is framed by rhododendrons and fine trees which grow on the surrounding slopes.

and a double avenue of beech, in which some old sycamores survive from the original 17th-century planting. In front of the house is a formal arrangement of giant clipped Irish yews and rose beds. Magnificent bronze urns are 17th-century French, identical to others at Versailles (q.v.). From a charming box-edged parterre there is access to the woodland garden with its growing collection of rhododendrons (mostly hybrids), splendid magnolias (some of great size) and other ornamental trees and shrubs. The ensemble of natural setting, park, garden and house is one of unusual perfection.

Rosemoor ⊛

1 mile SE of Great Torrington via B3220
Owner: The Royal Horticultural Society
Opening times: Daily, sunrise–sunset
Admission charge: Yes

Lady Anne Palmer made this garden from 1959 onwards, and in 1988 it was transferred to the Royal Horticultural Society. A very large collection of trees, shrubs and herbaceous plants, many of them exceedingly rare and grown from seed collected in the wild, flourish in an informal setting on a richly wooded slope in the sheltered valley of the River

Torridge. There are many flowering cherries, a collection of rare hollies, magnolias, stewartias and many other woody plants.

Tintinhull House ★

Tintinhull, 5 miles NW of Yeovil, S of A303
Owner: The National Trust
Opening times: Apr to Sept, Wed, Thurs, Sat, bank hol Mon 14–18
Admission charge: Yes

The garden at Tintinhull – made up of separate compartments in the tradition of Hidcote and Sissinghurst (q.v.), but more intimate than either – is principally the creation of Mrs P. F. Reiss, who came here in 1933 and gave the estate to the National Trust in 1953. On this fairly small (0.3ha) and flat walled

LEFT **The ruins of the old abbey at Tresco are draped with exotic climbers and other plants which thrive in this semi-tropical garden.**

BELOW **At Tintinhull House, variegated, glaucous and silver-leaved plants decorate a small garden 'room'.**

site there is great diversity of planting and atmosphere in different garden 'rooms'. But the rooms are linked together – by carefully planned axes and by a logical progression of paths and entrances. Above all there is harmony of planting. 'This is achieved,' as Margery Fish wrote, 'by choosing plants that fit in with a preconceived plan and not because of their individual attraction. This does not mean there are not unusual plants in the garden. There are, but they have been chosen so cleverly that one sees the garden as a whole first and discovers the many treasures in it afterwards.' There are mixed borders of finely-judged colour harmony, a fountain at the centre of a green-and-white enclosure, a decorative but unpretentious kitchen garden, a rectangular pool with a temple-like summer-house and carefully planted pots. A few mature trees (holm oaks and a cedar of Lebanon) emphasize by contrast the intricacy of what lies beneath them. It is a model of variety and liveliness contained within a relatively modest – but disciplined – space.

Tresco Abbey ★ ❀

SW corner of the island of Tresco in the Isles of Scilly; access by boat from St Mary's or by helicopter from Penzance
Owner: Mr Robert Dorrien-Smith
Opening times: Daily 10–18; tel. 0720 22849 for more information
Admission charge: Yes

This garden, laid out on a grid system on a south-facing slope and protected by a ring of woodland, is unique in the British Isles. Although unusually damaging frosts have recently cut back many of the rare tender plants and gales have opened funnels in the shelter belt, Tresco still has a superb collection of rare subtropical plants. Gardened by generations of the Dorrien-Smith family since Augustus Smith came here in 1834, the collection includes metrosideros, melaleuca, South African leucodendrons (including the silver *L. argenteum*), proteas and banksias, as well as the soaring Mexican *Furcraea longaeva*, acacias and eucalypts. Many plants, tender on the mainland, have naturalized on the steep sunny hillside. Between the ruined walls of an ancient abbey blue-flowered *Convolvulus sativus*, agapanthus and echiums in quantity, yellow aeoniums and the florist's broom from Madeira, all seed and multiply.

In the shade at the bottom of the slope tree ferns and bamboos flourish to make a cool green jungle. Tresco is not only a plantsman's paradise, it is also a garden with a strong formal layout which gives a structural frame to the exotic flora.

Trewithen House ❀

1 mile E of Probus off A390, E of Truro
Owner: Mr and Mrs Michael Galsworthy
Opening times: Daily, Mar-Sept 10–16.30, except Sun
Admission charge: Yes

The elegant stone house was started in the early 18th century but the great woodland garden which frames the house so beautifully is an entirely 20th-century creation. The grandfather of the present owner, Major George Johnstone, who inherited the estate in 1905, was largely responsible. Only ten miles from the sea and benefiting from a favoured microclimate, here is one of the finest collections of ornamental trees and shrubs in England. Superb magnolias, many rhododendrons, camellias, the rare Chinese *Rehderodendron macrocarpum* (one of two surviving in England from the first planting in 1934) and many

At Tresco Abbey, exotic palms and undergrowth frame views to the sea on Neptune's Walk.

other treasures are disposed in a harmonious setting. This is a great plantsman's garden which contains strong elements of design. Nearer the house an ornamental walled garden with good borders provides a note of formal contrast to the woodland garden.

Westbury Court Garden ★

9 miles SW of Gloucester on A48
Owner: The National Trust
Opening times: Apr to Oct, Wed–Sun, bank hol Mon 11–18; closed Good Fri
Admission charge: Yes

There is no longer a house at Westbury Court but the exquisite garden remains. It is a unique example of a lost type, a formal water garden influenced by Dutch ideas at the end of the 17th century. It was laid out by Maynard Colchester 1698–1705, with later additions by his nephew. Two parallel canals divide the enclosed garden, which is embellished by yew hedges with ornamental topiary, a box parterre, fine old brick walls with espaliered fruit trees (old varieties that could have been in the garden before 1700) and elegant *clairvoyées* that pierce the walls and allow

glimpses of water-meadows beyond. A dashing pillared pavilion in the Dutch style presides over all this, with a golden ball gleaming on top of its steeply-pitched roof. There is a charming secret walled garden in one corner, planted with old varieties of flowering plants. All has been superbly restored since 1973 when the National Trust acquired the garden.

Westonbirt Arboretum ❀

Westonbirt, 3 miles SW of Tetbury via A433
Owner: The Forestry Commission
Opening times: Daily 10–20 (or sunset)
Admission charge: Yes

This great arboretum on gently undulating ground was started as a private collection by Robert Holford in 1829. It is now one of the finest arboreta in Europe with very large holdings of the major groups of hardy trees and specialist collections of Japanese maples, beeches, willows, oaks and cherries. Strikingly effective groups of trees contain some fine specimens going back to the original planting. It is well worth visiting on any day of the year, but especially for autumn colour.

Southern England

Barnsley House ★

Barnsley, 4 miles NE of Cirencester on A433
Owner: Mrs D. C. W. Verey
Opening times: Mon–Fri 10–18 (or dusk)
Admission charge: Yes

Barnsley House is a 17th-century gabled house sheltered from the main village street by walls and fine old trees. Rosemary Verey and her husband came here in 1951 and started to make the garden that is seen today. Her garden is, in effect, a wonderful anthology of garden styles, put together with panache and good sense. Although only just over 1ha, it encompasses a very wide range of plants, excellent garden buildings and compositions of great variety. The effect is one of abundance – but firmly disci-

plined by a gardener with an eagle eye for a distinguished plant and a striking arrangement.

On the south side of the house a path leading from a garden door provides a firm axis. It is flanked by clipped Irish yews, and a profusion of rock roses – white, pink and red – grows between the stone flags. On the left at the end of the path is a pool overlooked by a classical temple. To the right a pleached lime walk leads into a spectacular laburnum tunnel. Mixed borders and impeccable lawns are disposed about these formal features. To the west a 'wilderness' contains a collection of choice ornamental trees. Beyond the garden walls there is a pretty formal *jardin potager* with brick paths where regimented lettuces, strawberries, ornamental cabbages and herbs luxuriate about the stems of apples trained in goblet shapes.

Blenheim Palace

Woodstock, 8 miles NW of Oxford on A34
Owner: His Grace the Duke of Marlborough
Opening times: *Park* daily; *gardens* mid Mar to Oct
11–18
Admission charge: Yes

Blenheim is every inch the ducal palace – a spectacular baroque house (1705–19, by Sir John Vanbrugh) with turrets and pinnacles enclosed in a garden of appropriate splendour. Alexander Pope visited the palace and wrote: ''Tis mighty fine/But where d'ye sleep/ And where d'ye dine?' Neither the house nor the garden are on a remotely domestic scale, but they are intensely romantic.

Many famous hands worked on the design of the garden and park – Vanbrugh, Bridgeman, Wise, 'Capability' Brown and the French neo-classical designer Achille Duchêne. The last two are responsible for Blenheim's magical atmosphere. Duchêne's formal gardens lie to the west and east of the north front. On the west are the water terraces (1925–30), rich in statues and ornamental masonry and with a fountain copied from Bernini's in the Piazza Navona in Rome. At the east end of the north front is the Italian garden, also by Duchêne (1908), with box and gravel *parterres de broderie* surrounded

At Barnsley House, water-gates and fine planting frame the 18th-century temple.

by yew hedges. The fountain at the centre, with bronze mermaids and gilt dolphins (*c.*1900–10), was made for the parterre by Waldo Story.

The view to the north is ruled by an axis centred on the house, which crosses Vanbrugh's monumental bridge over the lake and sweeps up towards the Column of Victory on the skyline. Brown's ravishing landscape undulates about this axis in a Claude-like scene, rising and falling on the slopes around the great serpentine lake.

Cranborne Manor

Cranborne, 10 miles NE of Wimborne Minster on B3078
Owner: The Viscount and Viscountess Cranborne
Opening times: Apr to Sept, Wed 9–17
Admission charge: Yes

The house, full of charm, was rebuilt in the early 17th century by the 1st Earl of Salisbury, an ancestor of the present owners. It is, however, a very ancient site, having been a hunting lodge of King John's. The present Lady Salisbury, conscious of the historical context, has restored the gardens with renaissance panache. There is much topiary and formality – a pollarded lime walk, old espaliered apple trees underplanted with old-fashioned pinks, a knot garden whose compartments of box are filled with decorative plants, and magnificent borders. All this is surrounded by ancient woodland through which there are occasional extended views.

Great Dixter ★

On the N edge of Northiam, 12 miles N of Hastings via A28
Owner: Quentin Lloyd
Opening times: Daily, Apr to mid Oct 14–17, except Mon (open bank hols)
Admission charge: Yes

The house is a beautiful half-timbered 15th-century manor which was added to by Edwin Lutyens in the early 20th century. Lutyens also gave firm bones to the garden which today is gardened by Christopher

At Great Dixter, Christopher Lloyd uses mixed planting of shrubs, roses, perennials, annuals and bulbs in his borders.

Lloyd, one of the most admired of all contemporary garden-writers.

The garden proper is entered from the north-east past a meadow garden that makes a satisfying setting for the ancient house. To the right is the sunken garden with a pool and many tender climbing plants. Beyond the house is the famous Long Border planted with tremendous exuberance. Across an orchard to one side of the Long Border is the rose garden and, beyond, the topiary lawn, with giant chessmen clipped out of yew. Throughout the garden are fine and carefully-chosen plants strikingly arranged. Mr Lloyd continues to experiment – and the excitement is felt by the visitor.

Hatfield House ★ ⊛

Hatfield, 30 miles N of London via A1M
Owner: The Marquess of Salisbury
Opening times: Late Mar to early Oct, Mon 14–17, Tues-Sat 12–18, Sun 14–17.30
Admission charge: Yes

The gardens at Hatfield are amongst the finest in England. Recent restorations by the present Marchioness of Salisbury, wife of the 6th Marquess, emphasize the historical layout and planting detail. The garden framework, a series of large horizontal terraces on different levels surrounding the Jacobean palace, remains 17th-century in spirit; lime pergolas, formal avenues of clipped trees and patterned flower-beds reflect the formality of the age. Inside this structure Lady Salisbury has planted old roses, peonies and summer-flowering perennials in Jekyll-style profusion. In a further garden, an orchard area when the house was built, a central herb garden is surrounded by fragrant flowers and leaves. To the east a Victorian labyrinth in yew (designed for a visit of the young Queen Victoria in 1848) lies on the lower terrace, its pattern visible from the windows above. In a sunken area by the old Tudor palace Lady Salisbury has introduced a labyrinth of low-cut box and a knot garden which lie at the base of sloping wild-flower banks. The knots are filled with flowers known during the 15th, 16th and 17th centuries, many of which were introduced to England by John Tradescant the Elder, the gardener at Hatfield in the years after it was built, or his son, another John, who travelled to the New World in the 1630s. In recent years new orchards, espaliered fruit and structured vegetable plots have been laid out under the east facade of the Jacobean house.

Heale House

Upper Woodford, 5 miles N of Salisbury via A345
Owner: Major David and Lady Anne Rasch
Opening times: Daily, Easter to autumn 10–17, except 2nd, 3rd, 4th Sun in month
Admission charge: Yes

Built on a flat site by the Wiltshire Avon, Heale House is a mainly 17th-century house of rosy brick. The garden is quintessentially English – masses of old roses (especially musks), exuberant mixed borders, an old vegetable garden turned to ornamental use, flagstone paths and drifts of *Alchemilla mollis*. A Japanese tea-house and bridge add an agreeably exotic note.

Jenkyn Place

Bentley, N of A31, 4 miles W of Farnham
Owner: Mr and Mrs Gerald Coke
Opening times: Mid Apr to Sept, Thurs, Fri, Sat, Sun and bank hols 14–18. (times may vary; tel. 0420 23118)
Admission charge: Yes

One of the charms of the compartmental layout at Jenkyn Place, which dates only from 1945, is the way in which garden planning and exciting planting on the hospitable greensand have been harmonized with the atmosphere of the elegant William and Mary brick house and the series of walled yards, overlooked by mature trees, which surround it. The garden is very similar in style to Sissinghurst (q.v.) and Hidcote (q.v.); a rose garden, a formal pool, fine herbaceous borders, a herb garden, an alley of green and copper beech centred on a marble reclining lion, beds for lupins and crinums and areas of flowing lawn drift together to make an imposing whole. The garden the Cokes have created is not only beautiful, but also full of botanical interest. Rare climbers such as *Caesalpinia japonica*, *Trachelospermum jasminoides* and *Holboellia latifolia* twine and clamber over old walls. A selection of magnolias, a flowering *Cladrastis sinensis* and many other rarely-seen trees are becoming fine specimens.

Kew: Royal Botanic Gardens ★ ⊛

6 miles SW of central London via A4 and A205
Owner: Royal Botanic Gardens
Opening times: Daily 9.30–17.30 (earlier in winter)
Admission charge: Yes

Lying hard by the Thames, covering an area of 120ha, Kew was founded as a botanic garden in 1772 under the direction of Sir Joseph Banks. But before that date it had been the garden of Princess Augusta, widow of Frederick, Prince of Wales, who died in 1751, and both during this period and under George III it was in the charge of William Aiton, whose *Hortus Kewensis* (1789) lists 5,600 species known at Kew. At the western extremity of the present site lie the famous buildings and landscape designed for the princess by Sir William Chambers. Here are Chambers's picturesque ruined Roman arch and his irresistible pagoda of 1761. Later buildings of exceptional quality include the glass palm house (1844–8), by Richard Turner (*see* Botanic Gardens of Dublin and Belfast) and Decimus Burton, now beautifully restored.

Most of the garden is informal, with paths leading across expanses of lawn; everywhere there are magnificent specimen trees, some of which date back to the early 18th century. Within this framework are many specialist collections – of grasses, bulbs, bamboos, heathers, rhododendrons and so on. All these are maintained to exceptional standards and plants are impeccably labelled. Kew is simultaneously a leading botanical research institution and one of the most attractive and fascinating gardens for the ordinary garden visitor.

London: Chelsea Physic Garden ★ ⊛

Access from Royal Hospital Road or Swan Walk, Chelsea
Owner: Trustees of the Chelsea Physic Garden
Opening times: Mid Apr to mid Oct, Wed, Sun 14–17; daily during Chelsea Flower Show week
Admission charge: Yes

Founded in 1673 by the Society of Apothecaries, the garden came into prominence after 1712 when it was acquired by Sir Hans Sloane, the Irish plant collector and physician, who appointed Philip Miller as curator in 1722. Sloane's library and natural history collections became the nucleus of the British Museum when it opened in 1759. The garden, where many new exotics were first grown, remained under Miller's guidance for fifty years; its importance to medicinal research and to 18th-century horticulture in general cannot be overstressed. Miller's famous *Gardeners' Dictionary* (including the 6th edition in which he employed Linnaeus's scheme of botanical nomenclature) remains an important source for both the study of contemporary gardening and for the history of plant introductions. In 1685 the diarist John Evelyn visited the 'garden of simples at Chelsea' and found 'innumerable rarities', including 'the tree bearing Jesuit's bark' (the invaluable *Cinchona* (quinine) which was found to cure malaria) growing in a stove-heated conservatory. In 1771 Miller's successor William Forsyth constructed the first recorded rock garden in England, using blocks of lava brought from Iceland by Sir Joseph Banks; these are still visible. Alterations to the layout of the garden were made when water gates and steps to the Thames disappeared in 1875 to make way for the embankment.

Laid out with systematic order beds for 'teaching', but with many fine trees and collections of plant genera, this historic oasis retains its link with botanical education.

London: Hampton Court Palace

6 miles SW of the centre of London via A308
Owner: Department of the Environment
Opening times: Daily 7–sunset
Admission charge: No

The great royal palace, partly Tudor and partly the work of Sir Christopher Wren (1689 onwards), occupies a spectacular site on a curve of the Thames. From the time it was built by Cardinal Wolsey it has had important gardens. But it was under William III (after 1689) that the gardens were at their finest; contemporary pictures show a garden on the scale of Versailles (q.v.). To the north was a great 'Wilderness', a formal, maze-like arrangement (designed by Wren) of which the surviving yew-maze is the last vestige. 'Nothing of that kind,' wrote Daniel Defoe in 1724, 'can be more beautiful.' To the east, there was a vast semi-circle with thirteen fountains, a central canal and radiating avenues of lime trees – the essential layout of all this survives. The original lively parterres which were part of this scheme have

On the east terrace at Hatfield House the layout is traditional, with broad, box-edged beds planted with summer-flowering shrubs and perennials. Flanking avenues of mop-headed evergreen oak are a recent addition.

been replaced by clipped yew and holly and rectangular beds with tulips in spring, followed by summer bedding. To the south is the 'Privy' garden, under King William a charming arrangement of parterres and fountains culminating in a refreshing view of the Thames glimpsed through the lovely wrought-iron screens made in 1692 by the Frenchman Jean Tijou. The screens survive, but the garden here is planted with a dense and dispiriting Victorian shrubbery. West of this is the 'Pond' garden, the vestiges of a Tudor arrangement – charming but rather lifeless. Here, overlooking the river, is Wren's ravishing banqueting house (*c*. 1700) with an exquisitely decorated interior and an old-fashioned Tudor appearance.

Mottisfont Abbey

4 miles N of Romsey off A3507
Owner: The National Trust
Opening times: Daily, Apr to Sept 14–18, except Fri, Sat; *rose garden* also open during the rose season, Tues, Wed, Thurs, Sun 19–21
Admission charge: Yes

The stone house formed out of a 13th-century priory on a wooded site by the River Test has 18th-century additions of pink brick. The walled former vegetable garden contains a large and beautiful collection of old roses, established by the Trust since 1971, skilfully planted in ornamental box-edged borders with gravel walks. Many climbing roses decorate the handsome old brick walls. A garden of roses only can be very dull for most of the year. Here, with a few old apple trees and some well-chosen herbaceous plantings, the decorative season is extended. Also, the formal ingredients of hedges and Irish yews, walls and walks, are so well contrived as to be ornamental in their own right. Nearer the house there is an elegant pleached lime walk designed by Geoffrey Jellicoe and a charming knot garden, designed by Norah Lindsay in the 1930s, planted with annuals. The grandest sight in the garden, however, is the giant London plane (*Platanus × acerifolia*) on the extensive, shady lawns by the river.

Nymans
Crawley, 4½ miles S of Crawley via A23 and B2114
Owner: The National Trust
Opening times: Daily, Apr to Oct 11–19, except Mon, Fri (open bank hol Mon and Good Fri)
Admission charge: Yes

The house and garden were made by Ludwig Messel from 1890. The house, an effective anthology of architectural styles from the Middle Ages onwards, was grafted on to an existing Georgian building and is now partly ruined, an attractive romantic backdrop to the planting. The garden is the remarkable creation of three generations of the Messel family. Very fine collections of plants, outstanding borders and ornamental effects that never seem contrived contribute to a distinctive character. The arboretum suffered grievously in the storm of October 1987. No less than 80 per cent of all the trees were lost – even some of those in the protection of the Wall Garden (including the largest specimens in Britain of *Nothofagus fusca* and *N. solanderi*). In addition, the famous wisteria pergola, newly restored, was demolished by falling branches.

The Wall Garden at the heart of Nymans, planted originally with advice from William Robinson, has double borders of annuals. At the centre are four crown-shaped topiary yews. About this rather formal arrangement there is a profusion of ornamental trees and shrubs planted in grass. To the south-east are lawns fringed with fine trees, beyond which are a rock garden and a heather garden. A long laurel walk leads north of the house to the rose garden, which was replanted in 1989. The Messels were pioneer collectors of Old Roses. Of the great pinetum almost nothing remains since the storm, but many fine rhododendrons were spared. Despite these disasters, the garden has recovered with remarkable speed and there is still much to see and delight in.

In the walled garden at Mottisfont Abbey, the rose 'Adélaide d'Orléans' drapes a simple pergola archway.

Brought back from the brink of extinction by the present devoted owner, this garden is a unique survival of a rococo garden of the 1740s. Hidden behind the house, the garden lies in a slender combe with 'walks through woods and adorn'd with water and buildings', as Bishop Pococke wrote after a visit in 1757. All this survives – terraced walks leading to fine gothic pavilions and seats, pools, ornamental fruit trees and a permanent atmosphere of the *fête champêtre*. Restoration has been possible because of the survival of exquisitely detailed paintings by Thomas Robins the Elder, showing the garden in its heyday.

Pusey House

Pusey, 5 miles NE of Faringdon via A420 and B4508
Owner: Pusey Garden Trust
Opening times: Daily, Apr to Oct 14–18, except Mon, Fri (open bank hol Mon)
Admission charge: Yes

The pale stone house was built in 1748, but the garden is a much more recent creation. It was made by Mr and Mrs Michael Hornby after they bought the house in 1935. They inherited a handsome lake and some fine trees and set about making the exceptional borders that are the chief glory of Pusey today. The garden is entered between a double herbaceous border in the old kitchen garden which leads to a wrought-iron gate. Beyond is a magnificent herbaceous border backed by brick walls festooned with climbing plants. By the house is a paved terrace and beds with many shrub roses. To the south-east lies a serpentine lake with a decorative chinoiserie bridge over the narrowest point. Beyond the lake are informal groups of trees and shrubs and mixed borders.

Oxford: University Botanic Garden ⊛

Rose Lane, opposite Magdalen College
Owner: The University of Oxford
Opening times: Daily, Mar to Oct 8.30–17; Nov to Feb 9–16.30 (Sun, closed 12–14)
Admission charge: Yes

The Oxford Botanic Garden, 'a repository of curious plants', was founded in 1621 – the first in Britain. The three superb entrance gateways were built 1632–3. The garden is entirely walled and a profusion of climbers clothes the walls. There are specialist collections of rock plants in a handsome rockery, a charming fernery by a shady wall, water plants, and greenhouses protecting a wide range of tender plants. Everywhere there are fine trees and shrubs and the whole is beautifully maintained.

Painswick Rococo Garden

Painswick, 4 miles NE of Stroud on A46
Owner: Lord Dickinson
Opening times: May to Sept, Wed, Thurs, Sun, bank hol Mon 11–17
Admission charge: Yes

Rousham House ★

Steeple Aston, 12 miles N of Oxford via A423 and B4030
Owner: C. Cottrell-Dormer
Opening times: Daily 10–16.30
Admission charge: Yes

This famous garden – a forerunner of the English landscape movement – was created 1737–41 by William Kent out of an earlier layout by Charles Bridgeman. In it, wrote Horace Walpole in 1760, are 'the sweetest little groves, streams, glades, porticoes, cascades, and river imaginable; all the scenes are perfectly classic'. It is one of those rare gardens that is both historically important and a delight to the visitor. In front of the house a rectangular apron of turf ends in a fine contemporary statue by the Dutch sculptor Pieter Scheemakers of a lion attacking a horse. Beyond, the land falls steeply away to the River Cherwell, with broad views of the rural landscape. On these slopes are disposed statues, urns, sitting places and temples carefully placed in relation to the attractive countryside. Virtually all the statues look outwards and the arcaded *praeneste* facing the river has subtly different views framed in each of its arches. Here are no borders, no rare plants; it is a composition of grass, trees, water, buildings and ornaments in which garden and countryside mingle in Elysian calm.

Saling Hall ❀

Great Saling, 6 miles NW of Braintree off A120
Owners: Mr and Mrs Hugh Johnson
Opening times: May, Jun, Jul, Wed 14–17
Admission charge: Yes

A 17th-century gabled brick house sits comfortably in a setting that resembles a village green. Lombardy poplars and pleached limes are the prelude to the garden which lies through a door in an old brick wall. Here is a walled garden (dated 1698) where formality is tempered by rural exuberance – box edging, herringbone brick paths, columns of *Chamaecyparis lawsoniana* 'Pottenii' and clipped apple trees rise above richly-planted borders. A further door leads out towards the arboretum where a choice collection of trees – some very unusual – has been made over the last twenty years in a setting of mature woodland. Here also is a charming Japanese garden, deftly infiltrated among the trees, with a serenely oriental pool. All about the house there are areas full of interest – including a shady water garden planted with Robinsonian abandon. The present owners have transformed an interesting old garden – making it their own with liveliness, wit and a discerning plantsmanship.

Sheffield Park ❀

5 miles NW of Uckfield, E of A275
Owner: The National Trust
Opening times: Apr to early Nov, Tues–Sat 11–18, or sunset, Sun and bank hol Mon 14–18, or sunset)
Admission charge: Yes

Sheffield Park is both a landscape garden and a notable arboretum (although severely damaged during the gales of October 1987). The park, on which both 'Capability' Brown and Repton advised in the 18th century, incorporates a T-shaped chain of lakes around which Mr Arthur Soames planted trees in the early 1900s. Brilliant autumn colour from North American tupelos, maples, and swamp cypress intermingled with pines and cedars is reflected in the still waters. Rhododendrons and azaleas in spring, a wildflower meadow garden and a stream garden are additional attractions and so is the National Collection of Ghent Azaleas. Wyatt's neo-gothic fantasy of 1775 standing high above the top lake is not owned by the National Trust.

Sissinghurst Castle ★

Sissinghurst, 2½ miles NE of Cranbrook on A262
Owner: The National Trust
Opening times: April to mid Oct, Tues–Fri 13–18. 30, Sat, Sun, Good Fri 10–18.30
Admission charge: Yes

This garden, made by Vita Sackville-West and her husband Harold Nicolson from 1930 onwards, is the most famous and influential of English 20th-century gardens. No longer in private ownership, it has nevertheless preserved its magic and each visit reveals more of its inexhaustible pleasures. Writing about the making of the garden, Vita Sackville-West set out the aims: 'Profusion, even extravagance and exuberance, within the confines of the utmost linear severity.' Disposed among the remains of a great Tudor house, intensely atmospheric buildings of old brick, the garden is based on a strong framework: the yew walk, the pleached lime alley and a firm grid of paths and gates. Within this pattern there is a great richness of planting with, in almost every part of the garden, an immense collection of shrub roses. Although there is exuberance in the planting there is also great restraint in colour harmony – the restricted palette of the formal White Garden, pale and green, or the warmer note of the yellows and oranges in the South Cottage garden. There is simplicity, too, in the orchard with its old apple trees festooned with rambling roses, bulbs in long grass and an unadorned gazebo. Everywhere there is discerning use of ornaments – some very simple earthenware pots, others the grandest 18th-century bronze urns. These are used as eye-catchers to terminate a vista, or in pairs to frame an entrance or a bench. Underlying all this is a fiercely selective choice of plants. And above everything rises the soaring gatehouse of 1535, from the top of which there are marvellous views of the garden. There is still no more beautiful garden in England.

Stourhead ★

Stourton, 3 miles NW of Mere via B3092
Owner: The National Trust
Opening times: Daily 8–19 (or sunset)
Admission charge: Yes

The garden is quite separate from the stately Palladian house (by Colen Campbell, 1721). It was started in about 1743 by the banker Henry Hoare who made the present lake, built temples and planted the trees which now shelter the combe and set off the buildings that ornament the slopes. It is an idealized landscape, a cultivated 18th-century gentleman's vision of Arcadia. Horace Walpole thought it resembled Milton's description of the Garden of Eden: 'umbrageous Grots and Caves/Of cool recess, o're which the mantling vine/Lays forth her purple Grape.' Despite subsequent changes, including the introduction of many new plants, in particular rhododendrons and conifers, the atmosphere is still idyllic. Paths wind about the shores of the lake (too obscured by recent planting) across which are delicious views of classical temples, a half-submerged grotto (with a figure of a river god), ornamental bridges, or a gothic cottage. Above all, the trees, many of which survive from 18th-century plantings, provide a superlative backdrop to the architectural conceits among them.

Wakehurst Place ★ ✿

1½ miles NW of Ardingly, on B2028
Owner: The National Trust, on loan to Kew Gardens
Opening times: Daily, Jan, Nov, Dec 10–16; Feb, Oct 10–17; Mar 10–18; Apr to Sept 10–19; closed Dec 25, Jan 1
Admission charge: Yes

The garden round the Elizabethan house was created after 1903 by Gerald Loder, 1st Lord Wakehurst. Rhododendrons and plants indigenous to New Zealand and Chile are special features. Two valleys provide frost drainage and give favourable microclimatic conditions so that it is possible to grow unusually tender plants. More formal schemes near the house give way to natural-style woodland planting in the horseshoe-shaped valley curving round it, with many fine specimens of introduced trees as well as native yew, beech and oak. Since 1974 the walled gardens have contained herbaceous borders and an area for South American plants. Wakehurst was given to the National Trust in 1963 and leased to the Royal Botanic Gardens, Kew (q.v.) in 1965. The sandy acid loam in the upper garden and the acid clay in the valleys promote the growth of many plants which cannot flourish at Kew. The woodland garden was severely damaged in the gale of 1987.

Wisley Garden

Wisley, 7 miles NE of Guildford off A3
Owner: The Royal Horticultural Society
Opening times: Daily 10–19 (or sunset), except Sun; Sun for members of the RHS
Admission charge: Yes

This very large garden (some 100ha in all) has many ingredients. Among other things, it is an important centre for horticultural research and education. There are demonstration areas showing different types of gardening; large collections of plants – a fine pinetum, an alpine meadow, many rhododendrons and azaleas and collections of tender plants in glasshouses; and large-scale horticultural laboratories. Near the laboratory buildings are formal areas – some designed by Lanning Roper and Geoffrey Jellicoe. But, to the visitor, the overwhelming value of Wisley is as a kind of encyclopaedic reference centre which exemplifies the highest standards of practical gardening.

East Anglia, the Midlands and Wales

Arley Hall ★

7 miles SE of Warrington on A50 or turn off M6 at Knutsford
Owner: The Hon M. L. Flower
Opening times: Daily, except Mon, Easter to early Oct 14–18; Jun to Aug 12–18 (open bank hol Mon)
Admission charge: Yes

The Arley gardens are famous for the historic herbaceous borders which have existed since 1846, laid out nearly half a century before William Robinson and Gertrude Jekyll made growing hardy plants fashionable. There are many other interesting garden features. Some of these, such as the yew topiary and buttresses and a walk of clipped ilex, are also 19th-century; others were introduced by Lady Ashbrook who tended the garden from 1939 until recently, during a period when rationalization of large gardens was essential. Today a rock garden, part of the earlier design, grows shrubs and ground-cover plants instead of alpines, and the old walled kitchen garden has become ornamental with central grass dominated by fastigiate Dawyck beech trees and mixed planting round the edge. Miss Jekyll visited the garden at the end of the 19th century and her contemporary George Elgood painted several views. The Italianate parterre by W. A. Nesfield which lay under the walls of the neo-Jacobean house has now vanished, but Mr and Mrs Flower plan a new garden in its place.

The famous perennial borders at Arley Hall were first laid out in the 1840s.

Blickling Hall

1½ miles NW of Aylsham, on B1354, 21 miles N of
Norwich
Owner: The National Trust
Opening times: Daily, Apr to Oct 13–17, except Mon,
Thurs (open bank hol Mon; closed Good Fri)
Admission charge: Yes

Blickling Hall is a romantic moated brick mansion,
gabled and turreted, built 1616–27 for the Hobart
family by Robert Lyminge, the architect of Hatfield
House (q.v.). In 1777 the pioneer feminist Hannah
More wrote, 'The situation is highly pleasing: more
so to me than any other I have seen in the east. You
admire Houghton, but you wish for Blickling; you
look at Houghton with astonishment, at Blickling
with desire . . . the park, wood and water of this place,
are superior to those of any of the neighbouring
estates.' Blickling today is every bit as seductive.

The broad approach to the house is flanked by
giant yew hedges, now attractively blowsy with age.
To the east of the house a 19th-century parterre was
simplified in the 1930s by Norah Lindsay. With a
fountain at its centre, it is arranged in four squares
marked with yew topiary at the corners. Each square
is planted with herbaceous plants in careful colour
harmonies and edged with cat-mint and the grey-
leaved *Stachys byzantina*. Further from the house are
slabs of yew topiary resembling grand pianos. From
the parterre, steps lead to a long vista through
woodland, interrupted by an 18th-century temple
and continued across the parkland that lies beyond.

Bodnant Garden ★ ⊛

Tal-y-Cafn, 8 miles S of Llandudno via A470
Owner: The National Trust
Opening times: Daily, mid Mar to Oct 10–17
Admission charge: Yes

The garden, commanding a superb site over the
River Conwy, was started in 1874 by Lord
Aberconway's great-grandfather. The Aberconway
family still live in the house and are deeply involved
in the running of the garden, which broadly speaking
falls into two parts – formal arrangements about the
house and a vast woodland garden in the canyon-like
valley of the Hiraethlyn, a tributary of the Conwy,

below. Both parts are superlatively well kept and
filled with major collections of plants. To the south-
west of the house a series of five Italianate terraces
descending the valley end in a huge rectangular lily
pond overlooked by a charming pavilion, the Pin
Mill. Fine trees and shrubs on these terraces include
a vast and beautiful *Arbutus × andrachnoides* and
many tender plants. To the south of all this lies the
woodland garden with magnificent collections of
ornamental shrubs and trees in a dramatically beautiful natural setting. The rhododendron collection is
one of the finest in Britain. Near the house, in the
East Garden, is one of Bodnant's show-pieces, an
enormous, gently curved tunnel of laburnum, hung
with thousands of golden flowers in June.

Chatsworth

Bakewell, 16 miles from Junction 29 on M1 via A617 and
619, 10 miles W of Chesterfield
Owner: Chatsworth House Trust
Opening times: Daily, Apr to Oct 11.30–16.30
Admission charge: Yes

Chatsworth is the home of the Duke of Devonshire
whose ancestor, the 1st Duke, had the present house
built 1687–1707 by William Talman. The setting, on
one side of the valley of the River Derwent, is
exceptionally beautiful. Horace Walpole noted in
1760, 'It is a glorious situation; the vale rich in corn
and verdure, vast woods hang down the hills . . . and
the immense rocks only serve to dignify the prospect.' The park (by 'Capability' Brown) and the
gardens (first designed by George London and
Henry Wise 1690–4 and much changed by Joseph
Paxton from 1826 onwards) are of an appropriate
grandeur for the vast palace which they surround.
Near the house there is much formality; to the west,
on a lower level, are the remains of the original
parterres (not open to the public); to the south a
pleached lime alley with a fountain and a vast canal
beyond; to the east a spectacular cascade of 1696,
with water tumbling from an ornamental pavilion
down precipitous steps. Of Paxton's time there
survives the very modern-looking 'Conservative
Wall' (1848), an immensely long conservatory
backed by a wall. Further from the house are many
other features of exceptional interest – a serpentine
hedge of beech, a substantial pinetum and arboretum, a lake with a grotto, a maze and attractive

woodland walks. Much of this is splendid, but the visitor may agree with J. C. Loudon's reservations about the garden's features, 'they no where combine in forming one grand artificial effect. They want concentration' (1831).

Hergest Croft ❀

On W outskirts of Kington, on the A44 Rhayader road
Owner: W. L. Banks and R. A. Banks
Opening times: Daily, May to mid Sept 13.30–18.30
Admission charge: Yes

Two separate gardens at Hergest were both created in the early years of this century, mainly as collections of trees and shrubs; many of the species planted here were introduced to cultivation during that period. Near the house are herbaceous borders and a fine kitchen garden. The wilder parts contain most of the notable woody specimens. Rhododendrons and azaleas predominate in an oak woodland known as Park Wood, and Hergest Croft has the National Acer Collection (except for *Acer japonicum* and its forms).

Hidcote Manor ★

Hidcote Bartrim, 4 miles NE of Chipping Campden via B4081
Owner: The National Trust
Opening times: Daily, Apr to Oct 11–20, except Tues, Fri
Admission charge: Yes

This is a justly famous garden, one of the most influential of all 20th-century English gardens. It was made by an American, Major Lawrence Johnston, who came to live here in 1907, although this cold site high up in the Cotswolds – the garden is 180m above sea-level – cannot have been an inviting prospect. It is this setting, however, that influenced the garden's design – a series of hedged enclosures giving protection and seclusion. Vita Sackville-West called it 'a jungle of beauty; a jungle controlled by a single mind.' Within the formality of immaculate hedges and arches of yew, topiary, box-edged parterres and an alley of pleached hornbeam there are explosions of richly diverse planting. But even here there is discipline in the colour harmony – a pair of glowing red borders, an enclosure of white plants among yew

topiary, the greens and yellows of the garden called after Johnston's mother, Mrs Winthrop. So many things like these are now to be found in other English gardens, it is hard to realize how revolutionary were Lawrence Johnston's gardening ideas. Hidcote, their model, still possesses a newly minted freshness of irresistible vitality.

Hodnet Hall ❀

6 miles SW of Market Drayton, 12 miles NE of Shrewsbury, at junction of A53 and A442
Owner: The Hon Mr and Mrs Algernon Heber-Percy
Opening times: Apr or Easter to Sept, Mon–Sat 14–17; Sun and bank hols 12–18
Admission charge: Yes

The Victorian mansion (now reduced to a more manageable size) built by Anthony Salvin in 1870 rises above steep terraces and looks south and west over a series of hanging ponds to the Shropshire hills and Long Mynd. The gardens were laid out after 1922 by Brigadier Heber-Percy, the father of the present owner. The flat terraces immediately under the house have conventional borders, wall shrubs and climbers; as the slope becomes more abrupt so planting, reaching into the water landscape below, becomes less formal to join up with lakeside vegetation. To the west hanging woods protect rhododendrons, azaleas, trilliums and astilbes which are massed beside pools and streams in naturalistic style. In the eastern part of the valley an avenue of magnolias, gnarled robinias, davidias and cornus shelters the earlier Tudor house (now tea rooms). Lysichitons and gunnera spread on the banks of smaller pools; hostas and rare woodlanders grow in the shade of maples and cercidiphyllums. This is a plantsman's garden where attention has been paid to plant and colour association. It is well maintained by the owners with a staff of only four men.

Packwood House

Hockley Heath, 12 miles SE of Birmingham off A34
Owner: The National Trust
Opening times: Daily, Apr to Sept 14–18, except Mon, Tues; Oct 12.30–16
Admission charge: Yes

ABOVE **At The Priory, Kemerton, Peter Healing has designed a border with flowers and foliage in deep subtle reds.**

LEFT **The late 17th-century terraces at Powis Castle look down on the lower garden, which has been recently restored.**

Although on the southern fringes of Birmingham, Packwood seems remote from anything urban. The house at its heart is a gabled Elizabethan manor whose south facade overlooks the garden – a wonderful extravaganza of yew topiary with some fine borders. Immediately to the south of the house is a sunken garden enclosed with handsome brick walls. At each corner raised gazebos survey the scene – lawns, a sunken pool flanked by mixed herbaceous borders and, on the east side, rose beds boxed in with yew walls. On the south side a raised terrace with a long narrow herbaceous border links two gazebos. Beyond lies the famous congregation of ancient clipped yews leading up to a mount where a helical path edged with box ascends to the culminating yew on the summit. The tradition that this arrangement represents the Sermon on the Mount and the yews below the Apostles and the Multitude is a modern one. The layout, some of the yews themselves and the immense wavy-topped box hedges on either side date from the second half of the 17th century and have an irresistible charm and presence.

Powis Castle ★ ⊛

1 mile S of Welshpool off A483
Owner: The National Trust
Opening times: Daily, Apr to Jun, Sept, Oct 12–17,
except Mon, Tues (open bank hol Mon); Jul, Aug 11–18,
except Mon (open bank hol Mon)
Admission charge: Yes

The pink stone castle, rearing up on its fortified
promontory, has scarcely changed since the early
Middle Ages. With one short interruption, it has
been the home of the Princes, later the Earls, of Powis
ever since. The most individual part of the garden is a
series of great terraces (152m long) that descend the
south-east slopes in front of the castle. The original
design of these terraces dates from around 1700 and
they are a rare formal survival from that time.
Attractively ornamented with urns, balustrades and
lead figures, they command ravishing views over the
remainder of the garden and the country beyond.
There are outstanding borders, chiefly of herbaceous
plants, backed by climbers taking advantage of the
terrace walls. Among these are many tender plants,
such as the pomegranate and the mysterious 'cruel
plant', *Araujia sericofera*. To the north-east rears a
giant yew hedge, blowsy with age, and now 15m high.
Steps lead down to a stately yew alley with, to the
north, the old kitchen gardens. Here is a charming
avenue of old pyramid-trained apples and pears. On a
ridge to the south-west is a fine woodland garden
with grassy walks and glades.

The Priory

Kemerton, NE of Tewkesbury, off A435
Owner: Mr and the Hon Mrs Peter Healing
Opening times: May to Sept, Thurs, some Suns 14–19
Admission charge: Yes

The garden, planted since 1945 by the present
owners, has some of the finest mixed and herbaceous
borders in England. They are mainly in strict colour
schemes. Mr Healing has designed one border with a
Jekyll range of rainbow colours; another has red
flowers set off with purple- and bronze-leaved
shrubs. There are also some rare tender plants which
are displayed outside during the summer.

Sezincote

2 miles SW of Moreton-in-Marsh off A44
Owner: Mr and Mrs D. Peake
Opening times: Jan to Nov, Thurs, Fri, bank hol Mon
Admission charge: Yes

Sir Charles Cockerell built the wonderful Indian
fantasy-house, with a garden to match, completing
both by about 1810. The present owners and their
predecessors have restored and extended the garden.
To the south of the house a curving conservatory
with Mogul overtones sweeps round a recently made
formal garden – with an octagonal pond, a central
canal and slender Irish yews. To the north of the
house a lake fed by a spring is overlooked by an
Indian temple and surrounded by fine ornamental
trees and shrubs. The stream flowing from the lake is
richly planted on both sides and spanned by a bridge
decorated with sacred bulls; mown turf set with trees
and shrubs flanks it on either side. A backdrop of
mature trees includes some magnificent cedars of
Lebanon contemporary with the house. The exotic
orientalism is accommodated with perfect harmony.

Stowe Landscape Gardens

4 miles N of Buckingham
Owner: The National Trust
Opening times: Daily during school holidays, 10–18 (or
sunset)
Admission charge: Yes

This is a landscape of exceptional interest. In 1713
Viscount Cobham engaged Charles Bridgeman to
incorporate the terraces south of his new house in a
garden which was eventually to extend to a 100ha
park. The plan was not symmetrical and used
diagonal walks and a French invention, the ha-ha, to
avoid a surrounding wall and allow a prospect of the
countryside beyond. In 1730 William Kent with
James Gibbs began to add buildings and removed
any vestiges of formality by linking the garden
visually with the landscape around. Horace Walpole,
writing of Kent in *On Modern Gardening* in the
middle of the century, coined the famous saying: 'He
leap'd the fence and saw that all nature was a garden.'
Kent introduced a series of classical temples, bridges,

statues and columns, many of which, after restoration, remain in the layout today.

In 1741 Lancelot 'Capability' Brown was employed and soon became head gardener, contributing a new dimension to the garden by planting woodland and creating lakes under the patronage of Richard Grenville, Lord Temple, who succeeded his father, Viscount Cobham, in 1749. Around 1790 the layout was almost complete. From that time it and the house have remained unaltered. Inevitably new buildings have been needed since Stowe School opened here in 1923 but these have been sited with consideration for the 18th-century plan. This landscape garden has recently been taken over by the National Trust.

Tatton Park

2 miles N of Knutsford, signposted in town
Owner: The National Trust
Opening times: Daily, Apr to Oct 11 or 11.30–17 or 17.30 (Sun, bank hol Mon 10.30–17.30); Nov to Mar 13–16 (Sun, bank hol Mon 12–16)
Admission charge: Yes

The house was remodelled for the Egerton family in the early 19th century by Lewis Wyatt, who also designed the handsome orangery. The gardens, covering 20ha, incorporate a rich diversity of styles. To the south of the house a pair of parterres designed by Joseph Paxton in 1856 (and beautifully restored in 1987) are spread out on a terrace which overlooks tree-scattered lawns sweeping down the hill. Here are informally planted groups of trees including outstanding old cedars of Lebanon, a lovely and unusual wingnut (*Pterocarya fraxinifolia*) and many other fine specimens. To the west are L-shaped borders divided into sections by buttresses of yew, with mixed shrubs and herbaceous planting. Very large clipped yew hedges, planted in the early 19th century, shield Her Ladyship's Garden, a charming sunken garden with a pool, rosebeds and an elegant pergola. Immediately north of all this is a grove of the dawn redwood (*Metasequoia glyptostroboides*), planted from the first seeds distributed in 1948. The Broad Walk, an avenue of beech trees planted in the early 18th century, leads past an elaborate Japanese garden and a Shinto temple on an island in a lake. The whole garden is kept to very high standards.

Northern England

Holker Hall ❀

Holker, near Cark-in-Cartmel on B5278 from Haverthwaite, 4 miles from Grange-over-Sands
Owner: Mr and Mrs Hugh Cavendish
Opening times: Daily, Easter to Oct 10.30–18, except Sat
Admission charge: Yes

There are two gardens at Holker. Near the house, in a new formal summer garden on the south lawn, clipped evergreens, trellis-work arbours and border colour orchestration enliven Edwardian patterns of yew hedging planted by the landscape designer Thomas Mawson, who also designed a rose garden with a curving pergola in the outer garden. The informal woodland and rhododendron garden was first laid out with Joseph Paxton's advice in the middle of the 19th century. Conifers, including the first monkey puzzles, came from both North and South America and by the end of the century rhododendrons from Joseph Hooker's expeditions to the Himalayas were added. Today some of Paxton's trees, as well as fine oaks, ilex and beech, have grown to large proportions and provide a protective shield for exciting new collections of different genera. Developments in both garden areas reflect the enthusiasm of knowledgeable owners who take advantage of the mild climate, abundant rainfall and rich acid soil to experiment with plants from many areas of the world.

Howick Hall ★ ❀

6 miles NE of Alnwick, E of B1339
Owner: Howick Trustees Ltd
Opening times: Daily, Apr to Oct 14–19
Admission charge: Yes

With the sea barely a mile away and protected from gales by shelter belts of mature woodland, Howick Hall enjoys an exceptional microclimate, which is reflected in the planting. There are two distinct gardens here. To the east of the house there is a glorious woodland in acid soil which was planted from 1920 by Lord Grey and after World War II by his daughter, Lady Mary Howick. In this garden trees, shrubs and smaller woodlanders grow in informal layers; magnolias and hoherias, rhododendrons and eucryphias, trilliums and meconopsis all flourish, reflecting the plantsman's skill and discernment and an artist's sure eye for arrangement. The other much more formal garden, on an alkaline-based soil, frames the 18th-century house and terraces. Planting here dates from the 19th century; Victorian horticultural journals describe the elaborate bedding on the sunny terraces. Today the design is much simplified with hedges of lavender, roses and agapanthus and borders which overflow with tender shrubs and herbaceous plants. Lord Howick, Lady Mary's son, is further extending the garden with collections of trees and shrubs grown from seed collected in the wild.

Levens Hall ★

6 miles SW of Kendal off A6, just after junction with A590
Owner: Mr C. H. Bagot
Opening times: Daily, Easter to mid Oct 11–17, except Fri, Sat
Admission charge: Yes

The house, gaunt and gabled in grey stone, was started in the 13th century and has scarcely changed since the late 17th century. More remarkable still is the garden. Its layout was designed by a Frenchman, Guillaume Beaumont, in the late 17th century and remains substantially the same as the garden plan of *c.*1730 that hangs in the house. Because Beaumont was French, it is supposed that he was influenced by Le Nôtre. But Levens is distinctly intimate and full of charm, quite different from the grandiose schemes of 17th-century France. It is famous for its yew topiary – a profusion of fantastic shapes full of whimsy. These are disposed in box-edged beds with, at their feet, swathes of single-coloured spring and summer plantings. To the north of the house there is a remarkable beech alley, planted in the late 17th century, and on the western edge of the garden there

is a ha-ha – probably the first made in England. Across the road from the house lies a landscaped park, of the same period as Beaumont, and an extraordinary forerunner of the 18th-century landscape style – 'the sweetest spot that Fancy can imagine', as Thomas West wrote in his *Guide to the Lakes* (1790). Garden and park, unspoilt and beautifully maintained, have a character of exceptional distinction.

Newby Hall ★ ❀

4 miles SE of Ripon, on Boroughbridge road; 3 miles W of M1
Owner: Mr R. E. Compton
Opening times: Daily, Apr to Oct 11–17.30, except Mon (open bank hol Mon)
Admission charge: Yes

The detailed planting in the gardens at Newby, which frame a late 17th-century house, was largely the work of Major Edward Compton between 1920 and his death in 1977. Since then his son, Robin Compton, has restored and extended the mature planting and added garden themes. Near the house earlier terraced walks, contemporary with it, were embellished with balustrading and Irish yews by William Burges in the 19th century; this area remains formal. The garden has a main axial view down a grassy slope edged by herbaceous borders, and across the valley of the River Ure. On either side it is divided into compartments with colour, plant or seasonal themes. A rock garden, the brain-child of Miss Ellen Willmott early in the 1900s, a winding pergola, a modern garden patterned with silvery foliage portraying a fine plasterwork ceiling from the Adam decoration in the house, a shrub rose garden, a white garden, a June garden, a July garden and a garden with 'tropical' foliage are amongst these garden rooms. They are each furnished with unusual plants, evidence of Mr and Mrs Robin Compton's continued interest and knowledge. On the outer edges the garden compartments drift into woodland groves and reveal views to the countryside.

Massed annuals in box-edged beds frame the golden and green topiary shapes at Levens Hall. Some of the topiary dates back to the 1690s, but many pieces were re-established in the Victorian period.

Sizergh Castle

4 miles S of Kendal off A591

Owner: The National Trust

Opening times: Daily, Apr to Oct 13.30–17.30, except Tues, Fri, Sat

Admission charge: Yes

The 14th-century pele tower at the heart of the castle is surrounded by Tudor and Georgian additions. To the north of the house is an exceptional large rock garden planted in the 1920s with many small conifers and a collection of 120 species of hardy ferns. To the east the land slopes down to a formal lake with a stone balustrade. A garden of shrub roses to the south has an attractive avenue of the ornamental rowan *Sorbus aucuparia* 'Beissneri'.

Scotland

Achamore House ❀

SW Isle of Gigha; ferry from Tayinloan, 17 miles S of
Tarbert on A83, weather permitting
Owner: Mr D. W. N. Landale
Opening times: Daily, Apr to late Oct 8–21
Admission charge: Yes

On this small Inner Hebridean island, benefiting
from the benign effects of the Gulf Stream drift, Sir
James Horlick started the present garden in 1944. It
is 20ha in area and contains one of the best collections
of rhododendrons in Britain. In addition there is a
bewildering richness of decorative trees and shrubs,
especially of those from the Southern Hemisphere,
many of which will survive in very few other gardens
in Britain; among the shrubs are *Olearia chathamica*
(from the Chatham Islands), the handsome large-
leaved griselinia, *G. lucida* (from New Zealand), and
the beautiful Tasmanian waratah (*Telopea truncata*),
with vivid scarlet flowers. In addition there are many
bulbs and herbaceous plants – hostas, Asiatic primulas, rodgersias – flourishing in the rich acid soil and
the relatively high rainfall.

Arbigland

Kirkbean, on Solway coast road, A710, from New Abbey
Owner: Captain J. B. Blackett
Opening times: May to Sept, Tues, Thurs, Sun 14–18;
also Whit week and Aug bank hol
Admission charge: Yes

A broad tree-lined walk leads from the house directly
down to the sea-shore and the gardens which shelter
behind a solid belt of woodland. First laid out in the
late 18th century, they have been revitalized since
1974. Away from the sea breezes, there is an immediate air of tranquillity and peace in the sunken garden,
with its colourful borders, shrubs and lawns. Paths
lead on to the Japanese garden and water gardens
with ponds and running burns. The overall effect is
one of constantly changing colours as light shafts
through the trees. Often the only sound is the sighing
of the sea in the background.

Arduaine ❀

Kilmelford, on A816 S of Oban, via entrance to Loch
Melfort Hotel
Owner: Mr H. C. and Mr E. A. T. Wright
Opening times: Apr to Sept, Wed, Sat 10–18
Admission charge: Yes

Entered by a grass path leading from the Loch
Melfort Hotel, the garden sits on a promontory
looking out to sea across Loch Melfort. Sheltered by
larch, the mild west coast climate and high rainfall
have helped to create one of the finest rhododendron
and azalea collections in Scotland. Rescued from
neglect in 1971 by the present owners, who carried
out extensive replanting, this 10ha garden has well-
stocked beds and borders and a water garden at the
lower levels. Paths climb past *Rhododendron giganteum* 7m high, and out of the woodland belt to give
outstanding views of the coast and garden.

Bargany

4 miles E of Girvan on B734 Girvan–Dailly road
Owner: Captain N. Dalrymple-Hamilton RN
Opening times: Daily, Mar to Oct; summer 10–19;
winter 10–16
Admission charge: Yes

A woodland garden with fine trees surrounding a
large lily pond, and superb spring and autumn
colour. Tall ponticum azaleas, many other rhododendrons and maples crowd around the pond, and
paths wind between banks of flowers in May and
June. There are rock gardens at each end of the
walled garden with flowering cherries and daffodils.

Bolfracks

2 miles S of Aberfeldy, on A827 to Kenmore
Owner: Mr J. D. Hutchison CBE
Opening times: Daily, mid Apr to mid Oct 10–18
Admission charge: Yes

Grass paths meander through borders of trees, hardy
shrubs and perennials in the walled garden on a steep

north-facing slope with lovely views across the Tay valley. Up the hill behind the house there are peat walls and a stream garden. Masses of bulbs flower in spring and there are fine autumn colours.

Brechin Castle

SW outskirts of Brechin on A94
Owner: The Earl of Dalhousie
Opening times: Occasionally for Scotland's Garden Scheme and at other times by appointment, Brechin, Angus
Admission charge: Yes

The 13th/14th-century fortress which occupied this fine site overlooking the River South Esk was rebuilt in about 1700. Here is a rare and charming survival – a great walled garden, lying, as was the custom in Scottish gardens, at some distance from the house, its 18th-century layout still preserved. Old yew hedges with rounded tops divide the garden and there are good borders, gravel paths and many ornamental trees and shrubs, including rhododendrons, *Magnolia sieboldii* and *Trochodendron aralioides*. An uncontrived formality associates harmoniously with a spectacular background of trees, some of which survive from 18th-century plantings.

Cluny House ❀

3½ miles NW of Aberfeldy on the Weem to Strathtay road
Owner: Mr and Mrs W. Mattingley
Opening times: Mar to Oct 10–18
Admission charge: Yes

At a height of 180m above sea-level, with extensive views to Ben Lawers, this 20th-century woodland garden is filled with specimen trees and many rare plants of Himalayan origin. Marked trails from the lawns around the house lead down through the woods and open out into hidden clearings of colour. Vantage points give spectacular views of the countryside and there is wonderful spring and autumn colour. Borders surround the lawns by the house.

Crarae Glen Garden ❀

Crarae, 10 miles SW of Inverary on A83
Owner: The Crarae Garden Charitable Trust
Opening times: Daily; summer 9–18; winter sunrise–sunset
Admission charge: Yes

The garden in its present form was first laid out in 1912 by Lady Campbell of Succoth, an aunt of the great plant hunter Reginald Farrer. She started the distinguished collection of species rhododendrons that flourishes today. The 16ha garden lies on the shores of Loch Fyne with a fast-flowing burn in a precipitous ravine at its centre. From the lower slopes, where the garden is entered, steep paths climb the glen which has been skilfully planted with many rarities that provide spectacular spring and autumn colour. Here are rare conifers (such as *Pinus koraiensis*), and tender plants from Australasia (including many species of eucalyptus) and from South America (such as *Gevuina avellana*).

Crathes Castle ★ ❀

3 miles E of Banchory and 15 miles W of Aberdeen on A93
Owner: The National Trust for Scotland
Opening times: Daily 9.30–sunset
Admission charge: Yes

The late 16th-century castle, turreted and romantic, commands wide views over the countryside and the intricate garden below. The Burnett family were granted the land in 1323 and continued to own the estate until it was given to the National Trust for Scotland in 1951. The walled garden lies down a slope to the south of the castle. Yew hedges dating from 1702, clipped trees of Portugal laurel and fine stone walls and terraces provide a firm structure, dividing the garden into many compartments. Exceptionally fine borders, both mixed and exclusively herbaceous, date from between the wars and show a fastidious sense of colour harmony. Extended hours of summer daylight in these northern parts prolong the flowering season and these borders are still full of exuberance deep into the autumn. More formal elements – such as the box-edged parterre surrounding the Italian fountain in the Fountain Garden – are isolated with walls of yew. There are

At Inverewe, tender exotics thrive in the exceptional climate on the west coast of Scotland, tempered by the Gulf Stream.

many rarities and an immensely wide range of plants but they are all happily accommodated in a harmonious structure.

Culzean Castle and Country Park
4 miles W of Maybole on A719
Owner: The National Trust for Scotland and Culzean Country Park Joint Committee
Opening times: Daily 9–sunset
Admission charge: Yes

Culzean Castle, an exotic gothic-revival mansion designed by Robert Adam, sits above a sheer drop to the sea on the Strathclyde coast, sheltering the formal Fountain Court garden with its orangery to one side. Here, extensive borders and lawns make an impressive entrance to the castle. As is often the case in Scottish gardens, the walled garden lies some way from the house. It is divided centrally by glasshouses,

with the kitchen garden on one side and formal borders and lawns on the other. In the woodland garden, many of the trees from America were collected by Archibald Menzies and David Douglas and there are also species from the Himalayas. Lovely woodland walks wind through the policies, many of them leading down to the sea-shore. First laid out in the 18th and 19th centuries, the gardens have been extensively restored since 1960.

Drummond Castle ★
On A822 between Crieff (3 miles) and Muthill (3 miles)
Owner: The Grimsthorpe and Drummond Castle Trust
Opening times: Daily, May to Aug 14–18; Sept, Wed, Sun 14–18
Admission charge: Yes

Rearing up dramatically on its ridge, Drummond Castle was started in the late 15th century, the seat of the Drummond family, later Earls of Perth. A fine sundial survives from the early 17th century when the 2nd Earl took a keen interest in gardening and created a famous garden here. The heart of the garden today, one of the showpieces of formal gardening in Scotland, is the vast and intricate parterre laid out in 1839 below the southern terraces of the castle. Segmental beds edged in box and filled with roses fan out from the central 17th-century sundial, also the focus of diagonal grass paths forming a St Andrew's cross. Formality is continued in the clipped shapes of many trees and shrubs – yew, holly, *Prunus pissardii* and Portugal laurel – and in the profusion of fine statues and urns.

Dundonnell House

At the head of Little Loch Broom on A832, 24 miles S of Ullapool
Owner: Mr Alan Roger and Mr Neil Roger
Opening times: Four times a year for Scotland's Garden Scheme; horticultural groups by appointment, Dundonnell House, by Ullapool, Ross and Cromarty
Admission charge: Yes

Although the elegant 18th-century house in the valley of the Dundonnell river faces south-east across

The reconstructed 17th-century parterres in the sunken garden at Pitmedden.

lawns, this is a garden of enclosures and enticing box-edged paths where many rare and distinguished plants relish the mild climate. The present owners have added enormously to its interest – a handsome tunnel of laburnum, good mixed borders, a discerning collection of bonsai (on which Alan Roger is an expert). A more ancient and astonishing feature is an immensely venerable yew in the centre of the garden.

Dunrobin Castle

1 mile NE of Golspie via A9
Owner: The Sutherland Trust
Opening times: Daily, Jun to mid Sept, Mon–Sat 10.30–17.30, Sun 13–17.30
Admission charge: Yes

The castle, with wonderful views south-east across the Dornoch Firth, was rebuilt by Sir Charles Barry in the 1830s and 1840s. It is an exuberant pastiche of a Loire château seen through tartan-coloured spectacles. Barry also designed the circular parterre at the foot of the castle terraces, with box-edged segments filled with red floribunda roses and cones of clipped yew giving vertical accents. One of the parterres inspired those in the Italian garden at Mount Stewart

(q.v.). On the lowest terrace, protected by its walls, is a very fine herbaceous border, broken by buttresses of yew.

Edinburgh: Royal Botanic Garden

Inverleith Row, N of city centre
Owner: The Crown
Opening times: Daily, Mon–Sat 9–sunset, Sun 11–sunset
Admission charge: Yes

The botanic garden was founded, on a different site, in 1670. It moved to its present attractively undulating site, with fine views of the city, in 1820. Its primary purpose is, of course, botanical research, but it is attractively laid out and maintained to exemplary standards. Paths wind up a hill with countless specimen trees disposed on mown grass. Different areas provide special habitats for groups of plants – a heath garden, rock garden, woodland garden and so on. There are major collections of tender plants in glasshouses, including an elegant temperate palm house built in 1858.

Falkland Palace ★

Falkland, 11 miles N of Kirkcaldy on A912
Owner: The National Trust for Scotland
Opening times: Daily, Apr to Sept, Mon–Sat 10–18, Sun 14–18; Oct, Sat 10–18, Sun 14–18
Admission charge: Yes

The 16th-century royal palace is in the centre of the ancient burgh of Falkland. Hidden behind high stone walls that run along the high street, the gardens owe their present appearance to Percy Cane, who re-designed them after World War II with outstandingly successful borders. A giant mixed border 163m long faces west across a great expanse of lawn where island beds are filled with mixed plantings of shrubs and ornamental trees (including an exceptional *Acer griseum*). On the other side of the lawn a new border of delphiniums running along a terrace wall is continued with a harmonious herbaceous border of blue and white. A profusion of fine old stone walls provides homes for many climbing shrubs. Beyond all this, monumental yew hedges enclose a calm pool.

Inverewe ★ ⊛

On A832, just N of Poolewe, 6 miles NE of Gairloch
Owner: The National Trust for Scotland
Opening times: Daily 9.30–sunset
Admission charge: Yes

This is one of the most remarkable gardens in Scotland. It was started from scratch in 1862 by Osgood Mackenzie on a site where the only protection from the westerly gales was afforded by offshore islands. He planted windbreaks and, taking advantage of the benefits of the Gulf Stream drift, built up a vast collection of marginally hardy plants. Although Inverewe lies on a more northerly latitude than Moscow, the Chatham Island forget-me-not, the lovely tree-fern *Dicksonia antarctica* from eastern Australia, and *Geranium palmatum* from Madeira all grow here. Other generally hardy plants flourish with exceptional vigour. In spring the garden is rich with meconopsis, primulas, trilliums and erythroniums. Near the house there is a fine walled kitchen garden and some good borders. But the overwhelming reason for coming to Inverewe is to see the jungle-like profusion of rare plants introduced from many parts of the world and seemingly perfectly at home.

Kellie Castle

3 miles NW of Pittenweem on B9171, 47 miles NE of Edinburgh
Owner: The National Trust for Scotland
Opening times: Daily 10–sunset
Admission charge: Yes

The castle is a seductive late medieval and renaissance fortified house with views to the south across land that slopes to the sea. It was the home of the architect Robert Lorimer who made plans for the garden in 1880 as a boy of sixteen. Quite small (0.4ha), and lying immediately to the north of the castle, the garden is entirely walled. It is divided with paths and box hedges, roses are trained over arches, and shrubs and herbaceous plants flourish in well-kept borders.

Little Sparta ★

1½ miles NW of Dunsyre, 20 miles SW of Edinburgh via
A702
Owner: Ian Hamilton Finlay and Sue Finlay
Opening times: By appointment, Stonypath, Dunsyre,
Lanark
Admission charge: No

There is no other garden quite like this in the world.
Ian Hamilton Finlay is a poet and his garden is full of
references to classical literature and mythology,
painters of romantic landscapes and revolutionary
philosophers. It is also full of humour, but this
always has some deeper horticultural and/or philosophical reverberation. The first, and lasting, impression is one of exhilaration – a new kind of garden
remarkably in harmony with the dramatic and lovely
scenery that surrounds it. It is built on a wild
Pentland hillside where pasture becomes bleak
heathland. Richly planted compartments are linked
with paths and studded with beautifully made objects
which have both ornamental and contemplative
purposes – sundials, model ships (and many other
references to the sea), pyramids, plaques and statues.
Where the garden merges into the open heath, slabs
of stone with an inscription from the French revolutionary Saint-Just overlook a pool in which even
the black swan seems perfectly placed.

Logan Botanic Garden ✺

Just N of Port Logan, on B7065, 14 miles S of Stranraer
Opening times: Apr to Sept 10–17
Admission charge: Yes
Owner: Edinburgh Royal Botanic Garden

The mild west-coast climate, balmy westerly winds
and a virtually frost-free microclimate enable tender
plants, many native to the southern hemisphere, to be
grown in the walled garden here, created this century. Evergreen tree ferns (*Dicksonia antarctica*),
avenues of cabbage trees (*Cordyline australis*) and
Chusan palms (*Trachycarpus fortunei*) all flourish,
and give the whole garden an attractively exotic air.
There is, in addition, a woodland garden and an
impressive water garden – all contained in some 5ha.

Perth: Branklyn ✺

¼ mile from Queen's Bridge on A85 Dundee road
Owner: The National Trust for Scotland
Opening times: Daily, Mar to Oct 9.30–sunset
Admission charge: Yes

This 0.8ha garden was started in 1922 by John and
Dorothy Renton, who had a particular interest in
alpine and ericaceous plants, especially heathers and
rhododendrons. It is now one of the finest gardens in
Scotland, filled with rare and beautiful plants. From
the lawns around the house paths lead through
informal borders filled with colour and interest. A
vast range of alpine plants is cultivated in rockeries,
scree gardens and raised troughs. Height is given
throughout the garden by many good ornamental
trees and shrubs, including several maples.

Pitmedden Garden ★

1 mile W of Pitmedden off the A920, 14 miles N of
Aberdeen
Owner: The National Trust for Scotland
Opening times: Daily 9.30–sunset
Admission charge: Yes

The great 17th-century house of the Seton family
was destroyed by fire in the 19th century. But the
garden walls, fine double staircase and charming
garden pavilions survived. In this enclosure the
National Trust for Scotland has, since 1952, recreated parterres to give something of the flavour of
the original garden which was completed in 1675.
Purists may balk at the modern cultivars used as
bedding plants in the box-edged ornamental parterres. Others will relish the colourful formality of
these four great beds spread out like eastern rugs
below the terrace that overlooks them.

Ireland

Ireland is an island washed by warm waters. Warm westerly winds prevail and provide the high rainfall and equable conditions which make it possible to grow plants from many corners of the world, rare and tender plants in coastal locations quickly maturing to great size. Plants chosen for their qualities of form, colour and texture are usually arranged in a natural style and seldom restrained or pruned into artificial shapes. Irish gardens, more than any in Europe, give a hint of the meaning of a natural paradise. The Irish union of man-made gardens with the landscape is unique.

Not all gardens in Ireland originated as natural landscapes. In Tudor and Jacobean times formal parterres existed but, due to the troubled state of the country, only inside a curtilage wall. Plans exist of early 17th-century layouts for Carrickfergus Castle in Co Antrim and Lismore (q.v.) in Co Waterford. The remains of some later 17th-century layouts, similar to French-style English restoration gardens, can be seen at Kilkenny Castle and at Kilruddery (q.v.) in Co Wicklow. After the Revolution of 1688–90, leading to the accession of William of Orange and Queen Mary to the English throne, several gardens were designed in a patriotic Dutch style, with water canals and small garden rooms of intricate formal planting – such as Stillorgan, Co Dublin, which was laid out in 1695. More baroque French-style gardens were planned at the beginning of the 18th century with radiating avenues stretching into the countryside. Few of these remain, but there are traces at Castletown and Carton, both in Co Kildare; the best preserved is at Kilruddery. The English landscape style, introduced to Ireland through Dean Swift and Mrs Delany at Delville in the suburbs of Dublin, seemed to adapt perfectly to the beautiful natural scenery of mountains, loughs and rivers. Travellers from England who admired Irish landscape included Richard Colt Hoare (from Stourhead, q.v.) and Prince Pückler-Muskau, who was to introduce the landscape-style to his estates in East Germany (*see* Introduction to East Germany) in the 1820s. The grand Italianate designs of the 19th century are rarely found, although it is said that the terraces of Powerscourt (q.v.) are based on those of the Villa Butera in Sicily. The remains of Victorian balustrading, parterres and statuary are found at Adare (Co Limerick), Baron's Court (Co Tyrone) and at Clandeboye in Co Down.

William Robinson, born in Ireland, and writing in the 1870s and 1880s on 'wild' gardening, had a marked influence on the development of the

The Gardens of Ireland

N

Northern Ireland

Glenveagh Castle
Brook Hall Londonderry
Belfast Botanic Garden
Lough Neagh
Belfast
Mount Stewart
Lough Erne
Rowallane Seaforde
Castle Ward
Sligo
Castlewellan Forest Park
Dundalk

Eire

Butterstream
Athlone
Belvedere
Galway
Liffey
Dublin
Tully House Japanese Garden
Powerscourt
Killruddery
Birr Castle
Emo Court
Kildare
Mount Usher
Kilmacurragh
Wicklow
Avondale Forest Park
Carlow
Wicklow Mountains
Shannon
Kilkenny
Limerick
J.F. Kennedy Park
Clonmel
Kilmokea
Wexford
Johnstown Castle
Tralee
Anne's Grove
Mount Congreve
Lismore
Waterford
Dunloe Castle Hotel
Lismore Castle
Killarney
Muckross Park
Cork
Fota
Derreen
Ilnacullin
Bantry House
Bantry

Malahide Castle
National Botanic Garden
Beech Park
Liffey
45 Sandford Road
Fernhill

0   50   100 km

woodland gardens which are Ireland's greatest glory today. Many of the choice plants introduced at the turn of the century proved especially suitable in the Irish climate. It is these Robinsonian or plantsmen's gardens, on both a large and small scale, which are most typical of modern Irish gardening. Many Irish garden owners subscribed to late 19th- and early 20th-century plant-hunting expeditions, including those of Ernest Wilson, George Forrest, Frank Kingdon-Ward and the Combers.

No organization such as the National Trust in England, Wales and Northern Ireland, and in Scotland, exists in the Republic of Ireland to take over the care of gardens in a country where owners and upkeep are threatened by high taxation and maintenance costs. However, the National Parks and Monuments Service of the Office of Public Works and some County Councils do now maintain some heritage gardens. Despite this, some of Ireland's greatest plant collections remain at risk.

Eire

Anne's Grove ✿

1½ miles N of Castletownroche off N72
Owner: Patrick Grove Annesley
Opening times: Easter to Sept, Mon–Sat 10–17, Sun 13–18
Admission charge: Yes

Richard Grove Annesley began the garden in 1907, influenced by William Robinson. Walled, water and woodland gardens lie within parkland in a secluded valley setting. The woodland garden has many introductions of the period: rhododendrons from Frank Kingdon-Ward and George Forrest's plant-collecting expeditions; embothriums, crinodendrons and eucryphias from South America; olearias from New Zealand and Tasmania; and dogwoods from North America. The famous river garden has waterside plantings of native and exotic plants. Yellow flag iris, giant gunnera, skunk cabbage, bamboos, willows and poplars combine with pampas grass, New Zealand flax, Tibetan poppies and clumps of water-lilies to create the atmosphere of a Claude Monet or Douanier Rousseau painting. A Victorian walled garden nearer the house is divided into compartments with walks, Irish yews, flower borders, a pool and a Victorian summer-house.

Avondale Forest Park ✿

½ mile S of Rathdrum off R752
Owner: Department of Fisheries and Forestry
Opening times: Daily 8–sunset
Admission charge: No

Planting on the estate and around the 18th-century house on this magnificent site bordering the River Avoca was begun by Samuel Hayes, author of *A Practical Treatise on Planting* (1794). It was continued a century later by the great Irish plant hunter Augustine Henry in collaboration with the Director of Forestry, A. C. Forbes. Along the river bank and Great Ride are 0.5ha groves of huge trees such as giant eucalyptus, and many introductions, such as *Lilium henryi*, from Henry's travels in China. There is also an Augustine Henry Memorial Grove.

Bantry House

W of Bantry on N71
Owner: Egerton Shelswell-White
Opening times: Daily 9–18, except Dec 25
Admission charge: Yes

Formal, balustraded terraces were laid out c.1850 overlooking Bantry Bay. A sunken box garden behind the 18th-century house is in French renaissance style with an arcaded gallery to one side, its layout based on a plate from Dezallier d'Argenville's *The Theory and Practice of Gardening* (1709). The garden and house are at present undergoing extensive restoration.

Beech Park ⊛

2 miles W of Clonsilla off R121, 9 miles NW of Dublin
Owner: Jonathan Shackleton
Opening times: Mar to Nov, 1st Sun in month 14–18
Admission charge: Yes

The borders in this 0.5ha walled garden, the longest well over 100m, contain an outstanding collection of the best of hardy perennial plants, including meconopsis, kniphofia and phlox. Many rare plants including dwarf rhododendrons, hardy orchids and 34 different species of celmisia, the New Zealand mountain daisy, grow in raised alpine beds.

Belvedere

2 miles S of Mullingar on N52
Owner: Westmeath County Council
Opening times: Daily 12–17.30
Admission charge: Yes

An 18th-century landscape park on the shores of Lough Ennell, with a fine tree collection, a grotto, a sham ruin and a folly from a design in Thomas Wright's *Universal Architecture* (1755). It also has terraces of 1906, based on those at Haddon Hall in Derbyshire, and a walled garden with modern planting.

Birr Castle ★ ⊛

NE Birr, on N52/62, 60 miles W of Dublin
Owner: The Earl of Rosse
Opening times: Daily 9.30–13, 14–17.30
Admission charge: Yes

The 60ha park, watered by two rivers and a lake, has gardens, terraces, an arboretum and outstanding

buildings. Crenellated ramparts were added to the 17th-century castle during the Great Famine of 1845–9; the suspension bridge is of 1820; and the huge shell of the Rosse telescope (1845) has lost its speculum to the London Science Museum. Anne, Countess of Rosse, designed the formal gardens in the 1930s: a charming *giardino segreto* in the castle courtyard, with roses, clipped edges of germander and climbers; and a walled garden with pleached hornbeam *allées*, statues and planted urns. There are huge, ancient box hedges. Terraces with herbaceous borders, topiary, statuary and tubs lead to a lovely Robinsonian river walk under flowering trees, including many different magnolias. The arboretum, one of the finest in Ireland, and the parkland itself contain outstanding trees introduced by plant hunters in the early years of this century: conifers, eucryphias, magnolias and maples are planted among old forest trees.

Butterstream

N of Trim off R154, 25 miles NW of Dublin
Owner: Jim Reynolds
Opening times: By appointment for horticultural groups, Trim, Co Meath
Admission charge: Yes

This modern garden on a modest scale is composed of a series of hedged and walled compartments in the style of Sissinghurst (q.v.). Each garden 'room' is expertly planted on a different theme with a variety of architectural and sculptural focal points. There is a collection of old shrub roses and the borders are arranged in striking colour schemes.

Derreen ⊛

Lauragh, 15 miles SW of Kenmare on R571
Owner: Hon. David Bigham
Opening times: May to Sept, Wed, Sat 14–18
Admission charge: Yes

The Victorian villa sits high on a promontory above Kenmare Bay and sheltered glades have vistas to the sea. The woodland garden with its natural rock outcrops was begun c.1880 by the 5th Marquess of Lansdowne; it was revived in the 1950s. The mild, moist climate favours the growth of giant rhododendrons, tree ferns, myrtles, arbutus and other plants from the southern hemisphere, many of which self-seed, forming huge clumps along the rides.

Dublin: National Botanic Garden ★ ⊛

Glasnevin, 2 miles N of city centre on R108
Owner: Department of Agriculture
Opening times: Daily, summer 10–17.30, winter 10–16.30
Admission charge: No

Founded in 1795, Glasnevin owes its survival to Ninian Niven, the Irish garden architect who became Curator of the Botanic Gardens in 1834 and laid out the 20ha site here in the formal French style which was his trademark. This layout, although much altered, remains today. Four years later he entrusted

Philippe Jullien designed the conservatory at Glenveagh in the 1960s.

the garden to the care of the botanist David Moore. Glasnevin contains one of the most comprehensive and mature plant collections in Europe. Its principal ornaments include a curvilinear greenhouse (1834–69) by the Dublin ironmaster Richard Turner (*see* Belfast Botanic Garden and Kew), a chain tent (*c.*1835) and the palm house of 1884.

Dublin: 45 Sandford Road ⊛

Ranelagh, 1 mile S of city centre
Owner: Mrs V. Dillon
Opening times: By appointment for groups, 45 Sandford Road, Ranelagh, Dublin 6
Admission charge: Yes

An excellently maintained small town garden containing one of the most distinguished collections of perennials, alpines and bulbs in Ireland. It is designed in compartments, each with its own sculptural or architectural feature.

Dunloe Castle Hotel ❀

1½ miles S of Beaufort off R562, 4 miles W of Killarney
Owner: Dunloe Castle Hotel
Opening times: Daily 8–sunset
Admission charge: No

Within sight of one of Killarney's famous lakes and the picturesque mountain pass, the Gap of Dunloe, is a magnificent tree collection begun at the beginning of this century by the Pettit family, and later expanded with the advice of the dendrologists Dr Gerd Krussmann, Harold Hillier, and Roy Lancaster.

Emo Court

Emo on R422, 14 miles SW of Kildare
Owner: C. D. Cholmeley Harrison
Opening times: Daily 10–18
Admission charge: Yes

The domed porticoed house of 1790–1810 is surrounded by extensive 18th-century parkland in which flowering trees and shrubs for all seasons have recently been planted. There is a lake, a Victorian formal garden and an avenue of giant redwoods.

Fernhill ❀

½ mile S of Sandyford, on R117, 7m S of Dublin
Owner: Mrs Sally Walker and Mr Robert Walker
Opening times: Mar to Oct, weekdays 11–17, Sun 14–17
Admission charge: Yes

Laid out in the 1860s in the foothills of the Dublin mountains, 16ha of parkland, woodland, rock and water garden display a collection of plants from all over the temperate world. A Victorian pleasure ground, the last remaining laurel lawn in Ireland, a

The Victorian parterre and superb conservatory at Kilruddery.

traditional kitchen garden, a conifer walk, an alpine garden planted round huge boulders, and a stream with pools, all contribute to the setting of the Victorian villa. Long vistas edged with clipped laurel give views of Dublin Bay, and there is a new herb garden and nursery.

Fota ⊛
Fota Island, Carrigtohill, on R624 7½ miles E of Cork
Owner: University College, Cork
Opening times: Apr to Oct, weekdays 10–18, Sun 11–18
Admission charge: No

The sheltered shores of Queenstown Harbour were famous in the 18th century for subtropical plants. In the early 19th century Lord Barrymore and his gardener William Osborne developed this great ornamental estate on the island of Fota. The formal gardens have gone, but the 3ha arboretum of the 1820s remains, as do garden buildings, rock, walled and water gardens, and an historic collection of tender and semi-tender plants, mostly acquired from well-known horticultural and botanist friends of the period.

Glenveagh Castle ★ ⊛
14 miles NW of Letterkenny on R251
Owner: The Office of Public Works
Opening times: Daily, May to Oct 10.30–18.30
Admission charge: Yes

The Victorian castle sits on a rocky promontory above Loch Beagh in wild mountain scenery. The garden of the 900ha estate in this remote and sheltered valley was begun in the late 19th century. It was further developed and enlarged 1937–83 by its then owner, Henry McIlhenny, with advice from garden consultants James Russell and Lanning Roper. Everywhere there is sumptuous mixed planting. The kitchen garden has flowers, fruit, herbs and vegetables; in the woodland garden the rich variety of hardy and half-hardy trees, shrubs, perennials and bulbs includes crinodendrons, mimosas, olearias, hoherias and rhododendrons; the wild garden with its huge rock garden contains palm trees and tree ferns. There are formal elements as well: urns and

herms among the shrubs, a gothic conservatory by Philippe Jullien, and fine Italian statuary.

Ilnacullin ★ ⊛
Off Glengariff on R572
Owner: The Office of Public Works
Opening times: Mar to Oct, weekdays 10–16.30, Sun 13–17
Admission charge: Yes

From 1910 the centre of this barren, rocky island was transformed into an Italianate garden by the designer Harold Peto, and it is one of his finest gardens. The planting was done by the owner, Annan Bryce. Described as 'Robinsonian wild gardening held together by Italian formality', the garden has glorious views across the water from lookouts, belvederes and an Italian pavilion. Today the garden has one of the finest collections of tender exotics in Ireland.

Johnstown Castle
Murntown, 4 miles SW of Wexford off N25
Owner: Department of Agriculture
Opening times: Daily 9–17.30
Admission charge: Yes

A 19th-century gothic-revival castle adjoining a 13th-century stronghold has a contemporary park with lakes and glasshouses and a good collection of trees, camellias and rhododendrons.

J. F. Kennedy Park
6 miles S of New Ross on R733
Owner: Department of Fisheries and Forestry
Opening times: Daily, 10–sunset
Admission charge: No

The 20ha National Arboretum, established in 1968 as a memorial to the American President, now contains over 4,000 different plants. Shrubs are grouped according to species in front of forest trees in a splendid landscaped setting with streams, cascades and ponds and distant views of Waterford harbour.

Kilmacurragh

10 miles SW of Wicklow off R752
Owner: Department of Fisheries and Forestry
Opening times: By appointment, Rathdrum, Co
Wicklow
Admission charge: No

One of Ireland's earliest collections of woody plants,
including many tender species of remarkable size. It
was created 1850–1908 as a 'wild' garden by Thomas
Ball Acton and his sister. Now overgrown, it is still
beautiful.

Kilmokea ✤

Campile, 10 miles S of New Ross off R733
Owner: Mr and Mrs D. E. C. Price
Opening times: By appointment for horticultural groups,
Campile, New Ross, Co Wexford
Admission charge: Yes

Begun in 1951 around a Georgian rectory, the garden
now encompasses nearly 3ha. There are formal and
informal areas with statuary, water, topiary, and a
fine plant collection. Many of the plants are tender
and are being grown for the first time on the south-
east coast of Ireland in this garden.

Kilruddery ★

1 mile S of Bray on R761, 14 miles SE of Dublin via N11
Owner: The Earl of Meath
Opening times: Daily, May, Jun, Sept 13–17
Admission charge: Yes

The early 19th-century Tudor-revival seat of the
Earls of Meath has the most important late 17th-
century formal landscape garden surviving in
Ireland. The garden is laid out in the French style
with a design based on the layout at Courances (q.v.).
Twin canals and the famous 'Angles' – a pattern of
lime, hornbeam and beech hedges with statues at the
intersections – still survive. There is also a conservatory by William Burn, terraces by Daniel Robertson,
a dairy by Sir George Hodson, and a rock garden.

Lismore Castle

W of Lismore on N72, 16½ miles E of Fermoy
Owner: The Duke of Devonshire
Opening times: Daily, early May to early Sept
13.45–16.45, except Sat
Admission charge: Yes

The castle, rebuilt 1812–21 and enlarged for the
Duke of Devonshire by Sir Joseph Paxton and Henry
Stokes in 1848, has a walled garden of 1626, the
earliest surviving in Ireland, with towers, terraces
and battlements. This is a traditional kitchen garden,
now planted with yew hedges backing perennial and
shrub borders. The largely 18th-century outer park,
with a bridge by Thomas Ivory, was laid out round an
earlier yew avenue of 1717. Paxton later contributed
a glasshouse in the walled garden and other improvements in the pleasure ground nearby. There is a good
collection of magnolias and camellias and the setting
is one of Ireland's most beautiful river valleys.

Malahide Castle (The Talbot Botanic Garden) ✤

1 mile SW of Malahide on R107, 8 miles N of Dublin
Owner: Dublin County Council
Opening times: Daily, May to Sept 14–16.30
Admission charge: Yes

The 8ha garden, forming part of a 103ha park,
contains one of Europe's most outstanding collections of rare trees, shrubs and bulbs from the
southern hemisphere: acacias, albizias, banksias, lep-
tospermums, olearias and pittosporums. It was made
1948–73 by Lord Talbot de Malahide.

Mount Congreve ✤

Kilmeadan, 7 miles W of Waterford off N25
Owner: Ambrose Congreve
Opening times: By appointment, for groups only,
Kilmeadan, Co Waterford
Admission charge: Yes

One of the most outstanding of contemporary garden
projects, this 48.5ha romantic pleasure ground with

formal features is being created within an 18th-century walled demesne along the wooded banks of the River Suir. Some of the most extensive plantings ever made of magnolias, camellias, rhododendrons and tree ferns are supported by massed hydrangeas. A walled former kitchen garden with lawns has a restored 18th-century greenhouse and new propagating houses. The 18th-century house was completely remodelled and enlarged in 1965.

Mount Usher ⊛

4 miles NW of Wicklow on N11
Owner: Mrs Madeleine Jay
Opening times: Daily, mid Mar to Oct 11–18
Admission charge: Yes

Mount Usher lies in a sheltered valley between the Wicklow Mountains and the sea. In the latter part of the 19th century the 8ha garden on the banks of the River Vartrey became a prime example of Robinsonian layout, with native and exotic plants arranged in drifts and encouraged to thrive and spread in conditions closely allied to those of their native habitats. There are major collections of eucalyptus, eucryphia and southern beech (*Nothofagus* from New Zealand and South America). William Robinson often visited the Walpole brothers who made the garden, and the woodland area, acquired in 1888, was one of the first to be planted according to his precepts. Informal paths lead through open glades patterned with bulbs in spring and groves of flowering magnolias; trees and shrubs hanging over the river bank give an air of relaxed profusion. An engineer Walpole brother was responsible for the suspension bridge over the river.

Muckross Park

3 miles S of Killarney on N71
Owner: The Office of Public Works
Opening times: Daily 9–sunset
Admission charge: No

On the shore of the lake in the 8,000ha Killarney National Park is an Elizabethan revival mansion of 1840. Around it is a natural rock garden and collections of mainly tender trees and shrubs. Formal gardens include a 1906 parterre in early renaissance style and a later layout of *c*.1935.

Powerscourt ★

1 mile S of Enniskerry on R760, 14 miles S of Dublin
Owner: The Slazenger Family
Opening times: Daily, mid Mar to Oct 9–17.30
Admission charge: Yes

Powerscourt's elaborate and imposing formal terrace garden in the picturesque Wicklow Mountains was begun *c*.1740, but developed in its present form from 1841. Advice was sought by the 7th Viscount Powerscourt from many different architects and garden designers; inspiration for the original terracing is said to have come from the renaissance Villa Butera in Sicily, but the 7th Viscount scoured all of Europe for ideas. A central axis from the house (recently destroyed by fire), with views to the Sugar Loaf mountain, leads downhill via terraces and stairways to a central pond; fine 18th-century wrought-iron gates from Bavaria lead into an earlier walled garden. Successive Viscounts Powerscourt assembled the superb collections of statuary and garden architecture and planted the notable arboretum.

Tully House: Japanese Garden ★

½ mile S of Kildare off the N7
Owner: The National Stud
Opening times: Easter to Oct, weekdays 10.30–17, Sun 14–17.30
Admission charge: Yes

Lord Wavertree bequeathed Tully House to the National Stud of Ireland. The garden was designed for him in 1906 by the Japanese garden designer Tassa Eida, whom he imported to the estate along with his family. It is one of the oldest Japanese gardens in Europe, and its design, a horticultural and aesthetic mixture of East and West, and intended to induce tranquillity and meditation, takes its symbolism from man's journey through life. Planting includes azaleas, chaenomeles, kerrias, mahonias, wisterias, willows, maples and alpine plants. There are bridges, paths, stepping-stones and a tea-house.

Northern Ireland

Belfast: Botanic Garden
Malone Road or University Road
Owner: Belfast City Council
Opening times: Daily 8–sunset
Admission charge: No

Founded in 1829 as a botanic garden and now a public park, the outstanding features of the current layout include a recently restored glass-domed palm house of 1834, a tropical ravine house of 1886, and excellent rose gardens and herbaceous borders. The palm house was built by Richard Turner, the Dublin ironmaster (*see* Dublin: National Botanic Garden), who also partnered Decimus Burton in building the palm house at Kew (q.v.).

Brook Hall ❀
Culmore Road, Londonderry, on R238 1 mile N of city centre
Owner: David Gilliland
Opening times: By appointment for horticultural groups, 65 Culmore Road, Londonderry BT48 8JE
Admission charge: Yes

A well-maintained collection of rare trees and shrubs, many of outstanding size, is planted in an arboretum along the almost frost-free shores of Lough Foyle.

Castle Ward
1½ miles W of Strangford on A25, 7 miles NE of Downpatrick
Owner: The National Trust
Opening times: Estate and grounds daily all year
Admission charge: Yes

When Lord Bangor built Castle Ward in the 1760s he insisted on the classical front, his wife on the neo-gothic. The 290ha estate contains an early 18th-century formal water garden focused on the ruined keep of Audley's Castle of *c*.1500 and overlooked by Lady Anne's Temple of *c*.1753. (The earlier Castle Ward of 1610 is also in the grounds.) Near the present house is a terraced Victorian sunken garden with perennials and tender shrubs, a natural rock garden, a pinetum and extensive pleasure grounds

In the Italian garden at Mount Stewart, formal parterres are filled with varied, informal planting.

recently replanted with the advice of garden designer Lanning Roper.

Castlewellan Forest Park ✸

½ mile NW of Castlewellan on A50, 12 miles SW of Downpatrick
Owner: The Forest Service for Northern Ireland
Opening times: Daily 8–sunset
Admission charge: No

William Burn's 19th-century baronial castle looks down from its terraces to the lake below and to the Mountains of Mourne beyond. The garden was begun in the middle of the 19th century by the 4th Earl of Annesley, and planting was greatly extended in the 1870s by the 5th Earl in both the 5ha walled garden and in the park outside. In the walled garden, fine specimens of exotic conifers and other trees and shrubs include Montezuma pines, silver firs and a specimen *Dacrydium franklinii*, as well as large-leaved rhododendrons, Japanese maples, pitto-sporums, myrtles, cordylines and an avenue of eucry-phias, all of which demonstrate the rapid growth which occurs in the mild humid climate; Castle-wellan is only three miles from the sea, rainfall is 87cm per annum and frosts are rare. More conventional borders and flowerbeds lie around the Italia-nate central fountain with its tiered basin.

Mount Stewart ★ ✸

5 miles SE of Newtownards, on A20 12 miles E of Belfast
Owner: The National Trust
Opening times: Apr, May, Sept, Oct, Sat, Sun and bank hol Mon 12–18; Easter, Jun to Aug, daily, 12–18
Admission charge: Yes

Laid out around the late 18th-century house on the north-east shore of Strangford Lough, the gardens at Mount Stewart enjoy an exceptionally mild climate. Here, from 1921 onwards, Edith, Marchioness of Londonderry made dazzling and idiosyncratic formal gardens. These include the Italian terraced garden with 'colour' parterres, the blue and white Mairi garden with many Australasian plants, a Span-ish garden and a sunken garden with a pergola. Further planting in the outer pleasure grounds immensely enriched the existing 18th-century plant-ing; round the lake there are more tender trees, shrubs, perennials and bulbs from South America, South Africa and Australia. To the east of the garden is a beautiful Temple of the Winds designed in 1785 by James 'Athenian' Stuart.

Rowallane ✸

1 mile S of Saintfield on A7, 11 miles S of Belfast
Owner: The National Trust
Opening times: All year, Mon–Fri, 9 or 10.30–sunset; Easter to end Oct, also Sat, Sun 14–18
Admission charge: Yes

This 20ha woodland garden, with a natural rock garden on one of the outcrops of whinstone, is on the site of a farm and the original field walls are incorpo-rated in the design. Of great interest to a plantsman, the collection, including rare rhododendrons, was assembled by Hugh Armytage Moore from 1917, who obtained his seed from the E. H. Wilson, George Forrest and Frank Kingdon-Ward expeditions at the turn of the century. Some plants bear the garden's name: for example, *Hypericum* 'Rowallane' and *Vib-urnum plicatum* 'Rowallane'. The National Collec-tion of penstemons is held here in the walled garden. This area, with traditional kitchen garden cross axes, was originally used as a nursery by Mr Armytage Moore; it is now beautiful, with well-grown rare wall shrubs and climbers and small woodland-type plants growing at the base of tender shrubs such as azaras, hoherias and olearias.

Seaforde

2 miles N of Seaforde on A24, 6 miles W of Downpatrick
Owner: Patrick Forde
Opening times: By appointment for horticultural groups, Seaforde, Co Down
Admission charge: Yes

In a magnificent parkland setting with a lake and mountain views, a walled garden contains a maze, shrubbery, herb garden and gothic arbour. Pleasure grounds include a distinguished plant collection, at present being extended.

Holland is bordered on the west by the sea, while low-lying fens and river valleys mark its boundaries with Germany and Belgium on the east and south. Crossed by three major rivers (the Scheldt, the Meuse and the Rhine) and innumerable other waterways and drainage canals, much of its flat windswept terrain is below sea-level and subject to inundation. Avenues and hedges are essential windbreaks in gardens. South-west winds off the sea, which give the western seaboard the highest rainfall, generally prevent low winter temperatures, although cold winds from Continental Europe occasionally bring severe conditions. North-west winds in spring and summer keep temperatures cool, and 'wind-chill' factors often affect plants as growth commences. Humidity is high.

Belgium to the south consists of two very dissimilar areas: the north is flat, Flemish-speaking and rich in art and architecture; the south, hillier in the east, where winding valleys cut deep into the Ardennes, is Walloon French-speaking. As in Holland, the climate is tempered by the North Sea, with a more continental regime in the northern Ardennes where frosts occur for longer.

Holland and Belgium finally became autonomous in 1831, but the history of the two countries has many common threads. Both suffered repeatedly from invasions, with the Romans, Germans, Spanish, French and Austrians in turn exercising authority over their territories. As a result, the Low Countries became a crossroads of civilization, generating a creative energy which fuelled a blossoming of the arts; Flemish, Dutch and Walloon artists were commissioned by all the great European emperors, dukes and princes.

The history of gardening in Holland and Belgium, besides being similar, also has essential differences. Medieval gardens in both regions were like those of northern Europe: monastic enclosures mainly devoted to simples and herbs, or flowery meads with arbours, bowers, trellis and pots of flowers as depicted in the detail of many contemporary paintings. However, by the 16th and 17th centuries Flanders, under Spanish domination, was a bastion of Catholic orthodoxy and Jesuit militancy. Strong links with renaissance Italy ensured Flemish development of similar artistic precepts, but with additional 'gaiety and exuberance'. Gardens were enclosed and symmetrical, geometrically divided and surrounded by walls or hedges, although still, as in medieval times, adorned with bowers and arbours. The garden depicted in

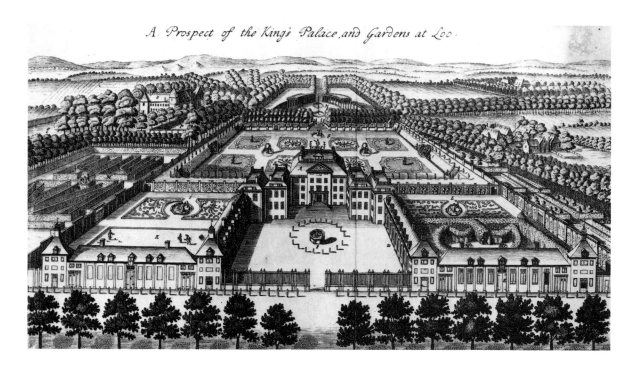

A. Prospect of the King's Palace, and Gardens at Loo.

An engraving from Walter Harris's *A Description of the King's Garden at Het Loo* (1699) shows the palace and gardens as they looked soon after being built for William and Mary between 1686–95.

Rubens's *La Promenade au Jardin* of 1631 shows this essentially local baroque sense of show. By the middle of the century French influence led to more ambitious baroque designs, especially in the hillier eastern provinces and notably at the royal palace of Mariemont (Belgium, q.v.), and above all at Enghien (Belgium, q.v.), where 50ha were divided into numerous separate sections. Neither of these extraordinary gardens remains. In Holland the essential characteristic is a form of neatness exemplified by Dutch Protestant frugality (and the influence of Erasmus), which made it difficult to accept luxury.

Basic ideas of garden art in the two regions thus found different expressions. This is further exemplified by Hans Vredeman de Vries's strictly delineated late 16th-century engravings, *Hortorum viridariorumque elegantes et multi plicis formae*, published in Antwerp in 1583, where he showed plans characterized by intricate parterre patterns laid out on a series of flat spaces separated by trellis or galleries, but with no overall integration or axial alignment with the house itself. Other dissimilarities may have been due to topographical features. In Holland, with much land below sea-level, there was an essential emphasis on holding waters at bay. This systematic control of the larger landscape, in which cultivated land in rectangles and

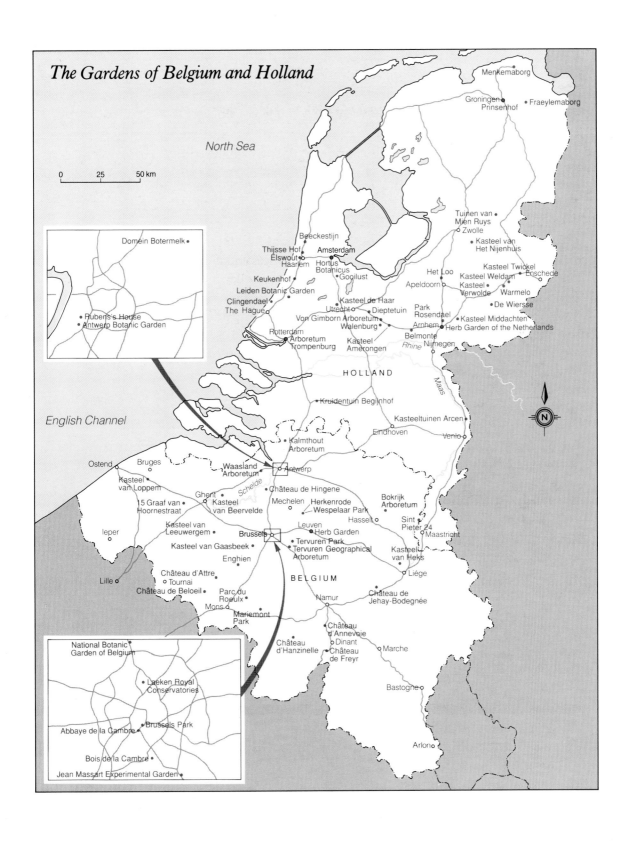

The Gardens of Belgium and Holland

North Sea

0   25   50 km

English Channel

Menkemaborg

Groningen
Prinsenhof
Fraeylemaborg

Tuinen van
Mien Ruys
Zwolle
Kasteel van
Het Nijenhuis

Beeckestijn
Thijsse Hof
Élswout
Haarlem
Amsterdam
Hortus
Botanicus
Gooilust
Het Loo
Apeldoorn
Kasteel Twickel
Kasteel Weldam
Kasteel
Verwolde
Enschede
Warmelo
De Wiersse

Keukenhof
Leiden Botanic Garden
Clingendael
The Hague
Kasteel de Haar
Utrecht
Dieptetuin
Park
Rosendael
Von Gimborn Arboretum
Walenburg
Arnhem
Kasteel Middachten
Herb Garden of the Netherlands
Rotterdam
Arboretum
Trompenburg
Kasteel
Amerongen
Belmonte
Nijmegen

HOLLAND

Rhine

Maas

Kruidentuin Beginhof

Kasteeltuinen Arcen
Eindhoven
Venlo

Domein Botermelk

Rubens's House
Antwerp Botanic Garden

Kalmthout
Arboretum

Ostend
Bruges
Waasland
Arboretum
Antwerp
Kasteel
van Loppem
Schelde
Château de Hingene
Ghent
Kasteel
van Beervelde
Mechelen
Herkenrode
Wespelaar Park
Bokrijk
Arboretum

15 Graaf van
Hoornestraat
Hasselt
Sint
Pieter 24
Ieper
Kasteel van
Leeuwergem
Brussels
Leuven
Herb Garden
Maastricht
Kasteel van Gaasbeek
Tervuren Park
Tervuren Geographical
Arboretum
Kasteel
van Heks
Enghien
Liège

Château d'Attre
Tournai
BELGIUM
Château de Beloeil
Parc du
Roeulx
Mons
Namur
Château de
Jehay-Bodegnée
Lille
Mariemont
Park
Château
d'Annevoie
Marche
Château
d'Hanzinelle
Dinant
Château
de Freyr

Bastogne

National Botanic
Garden of Belgium

Laeken Royal
Conservatories

Abbaye de la Cambre
Brussels Park

Bois de la Cambre

Jean Massart Experimental Garden

Arlon

N

squares was surrounded by drainage canals, will have influenced the development of the Dutch canal garden with the flat static qualities which reflected the ordered countryside. In the more hilly regions of Flanders there was less incentive for gardens to develop in this way.

By the middle of the 17th century, formal geometric layouts were still enclosed but richly decorated with topiary, statues and fountains. *Parterres de broderie* and ornamental *rocaille* work became fashionable. Later, under William and Mary, all these influences synthesized in the northern provinces into a hybrid style with a concentration on decorative detail (*see* Het Loo in Holland and Hampton Court in England). Dutch gardens of this period influenced garden design in England, Germany and Russia.

In the 16th and 17th centuries horticultural treatises and florilegiums from the Low Countries were setting new standards of excellence in scholarship and printing throughout Europe. De Vries, living at a time when many new plants were being introduced into Europe from the Middle East and the Americas, and a contemporary of the Flemish Dodoens (from whose original work the English herbalist Gerard took much of his material), the slightly younger Clusius (*see* Botanic Garden of Leiden, and Introduction to Austria) and L'Obel, all of whom were publishing important herbals and botanical works, also designed parterres specifically for the display of rare plants – *parterres de pièces coupées*. Clusius's work on the recently imported tulip, including his observations on the 'breaking' which caused so many different varieties, ultimately led to the speculative 'tulipomania' of the 1630s. Dutch tulip breeding began at this time, and like Dutch horticultural expertise, has remained influential to the present day.

The 18th century saw the emergence of the Dutch *Régence* garden, in which artificial elements became subordinate to natural ones, the house became subordinate to the garden, and 'useful' ingredients (orchards and kitchen gardens) were integrated with the beautiful. However, at the same time gardens such as Beloeil (q.v.) and Leeuwergem (q.v.) in what is now Belgium were also being laid out in accordance with the French classical ideal of linked garden vistas related to the house and stretching out into the countryside – nearly a hundred years after Vaux-le-Vicomte and Versailles in France.

Even before the French Revolution in 1789, these gardens and earlier baroque ones were being replaced or altered, influenced by the 'picturesque'

Citrus fruit trees in ornamental flower-pots decorate the garden behind the house at Soest Dyck towards the end of the 17th century.

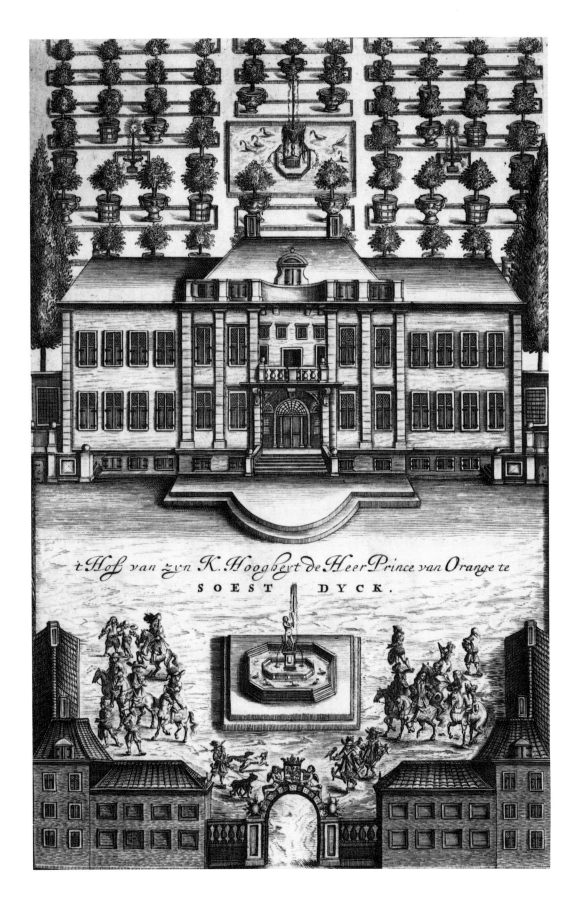

t'Hof van zyn K. Hooghyt de Heer Prince van Orange te
SOEST   DYCK.

interpretation of the English landscape and the French *anglo-chinois* style (*see* Kew in England). In the 19th century romantic landscape parks reflected English influence; and an informal gardening style evolved with parks (and greenhouses) in which new plant introductions could be grown. This was followed, as in England, by an 'historicist' revival: castles were gothicized and gardens redesigned with appropriate neo-baroque features (*see* Kasteel Weldam in Holland).

In this century Dutch gardens, usually on a small scale, combine classical elements of design with Jekyllesque (*see* Hestercombe in England) cottage-garden planting, executed with a fine degree of taste. A designer such as Mien Ruys (*see* Tuinen van Mien Ruys) advocates an architectural framework inside which flowerbeds framed by hedges and walls can overflow with good plants in carefully planned colour schemes. Others (*see* Thijsse Hof) with ecological interests emphasize preservation of the natural landscape. In 1980 the Nederlandse Tuinenstichting (Dutch Garden Society) was founded to record, conserve and restore 19th- and early 20th-century landscape gardens and to promote important contemporary gardens.

In Belgium modern designers provide for fine plant collections inside a firmly designed framework. Jules Buyssens (*see* Brussels: Abbaye de la Cambre) understood the importance of linking the garden with its site by the use of local material; the work of René Pechère (*see* Parc du Roeulx) has a philosophical bias, as evidenced by his designs for the Garden of Hearts and the Labyrinth adjoining the van Buuren Museum in Brussels. Jacques Wirtz (*see* Domein Botermelk) designs with formal box hedges which are geometrically arranged inside different garden 'rooms'.

Belgium

Château d'Annevoie

14km S of Namur via N92
Owner: Montpellier d'Annevoie family
Opening times: Daily, Apr to Oct 9–19

The gardens that we see at Annevoie today were laid out by the owner, Charles-Alexis de Montpellier, during the 1770s. Much travelled in Italy and France, where he admired the great gardens, the wealthy ironmaster transformed the surroundings of the modest manor house he had inherited into a highly original garden of renaissance formality. His use of water, inspired by the fountains of the Villa d'Este at Tivoli (q.v.) and the quieter *bassins* of Versailles (q.v.), is a dominant theme. A long (365m) canal, flanked by avenues of lime trees, is not only decorative; fed by three springs, it provides the essential water supply for the *buffet d'eau* and for many of the murmuring fountains, cascades and pools found on different levels throughout the garden. With long, straight avenues, carefully tended tall hedges (*charmilles*), box-edged flowerbeds and regularly-placed water features, the garden is basically formal in character, but its lines are softened by nature and planting adds greatly to its charms. Tall trees provide shelter and bulbs have naturalized in the grass, while the garden is framed by the wooded landscape of the Meuse valley. A ruin (complete with a model hermit, now in the château), and a summerhouse decorated with frescoes – 'picturesque' features introduced by Charles-Alexis's son Nicolas Charles – lie in a part of the garden not normally open to the public.

Since World War II Charles-Alexis's descendants have rejuvenated the garden with timely surgery on old trees and new planting, and have even extended it by another 2ha and introduced a rose garden. The garden has been further enriched by the acquisition of old statues from other European gardens.

Antwerp: Botanic Garden

24 Leopoldstraat
Owner: City of Antwerp
Opening times: Daily 8–17.30

Laid out in 1797 as the first herb garden in Antwerp, the botanic garden now covers .8ha and contains a remarkable collection of herbaceous plants and some fine trees.

Antwerp: Rubens's House ★

9–11 Rubenstraat, in city centre
Owner: City of Antwerp
Opening times: Daily 10–17, except Mon
Admission charge: Yes

In 1937 the city of Antwerp acquired Rubens's house in the centre of the city, where the painter had lived from 1615 until his death in 1640. The garden has been recreated, using views taken from Rubens's own paintings; *La Promenade au Jardin* shows the garden, and even the flowers, in great detail. An arcade leads to a terrace overlooking the simple layout, designed in renaissance style in accordance with Rubens's humanist philosophy, but also reflecting Flemish opulence. Four rectangular parterres – two with circles in the centre, two with lozenges – are edged with low yew hedges; there is also a pavilion of Hercules, a pool, and a wooden pergola.

Château d'Attre ★

Attre, on N56 5km S of Ath, SW of Brussels via N7
Owner: B. de Meester de Heyndonck
Opening times: Apr to Oct, Sat, Sun, hols 10–12, 14–18; Jul, Aug, daily
Admission charge: Yes

The château of Attre was rebuilt in 1752 in classical style and still retains a remarkable architectural unity, although the forecourt was remodelled in 1909. The landscaped park at the rear, with its fine trees, has never been altered; its features are true to the taste of the period: a tower named after a spurious hermit, a Swiss chalet, and a bathing pavilion in the form of an ancient temple. Most spectacular of all is a rock 'folly', 24m high, like a vast cave topped by a ruined tower, which was built on the edge of a pool from enormous blocks of stone in the 1780s. Hair-raising pathways lead up to several different levels and a room at the top of the tower has a grotto exotically decorated with bark, roots and wood.

Kasteel van Beervelde

Beervelde, 20km NE of Ghent via N70
Owner: Comte Renaud de Kerchove de Denterghem
Opening times: By appointment, Beervelde-Dorp 75, B–9131 Lochristi

The 20ha park, originally designed and planted by L. Fuchs (*see* Château d'Hanzinelle) after 1870, is in the English landscape style. Lakes and ponds, linked by bridges and pathways, make a romantic setting for woodland and gardens. In April naturalized daffodils spread through the grass, while Ghent and other deciduous azaleas are a special feature in May.

Château de Beloeil ★

10km SE of Leuze on N7 SW of Brussels
Owner: Prince de Ligne
Opening times: Daily, Apr to Oct 10–17
Admission charge: Yes

The Beloeil estate has existed since 1146, and has belonged to the family of the Prince de Ligne since 1511, when Antoine de Ligne owned what was then a primitive fortress surrounded on three sides by water. The château was remodelled by Prince Claude-Lamoral de Ligne in the 17th century, and rebuilt after it was burnt down in 1900; the superb French-style gardens were laid out in the first part of the 18th century by the prince's grandson, Claude-Lamoral II, with the help of the French architect Jean-Baptiste Bergé. The great water basin – almost 6ha in extent – is the most arresting feature at Beloeil.

Although very long, it appears almost square when seen from the terrace in front of the château. The gardens at either side of the *bassin* are not seen from this point, as they would have been if designed by Le Nôtre; instead they unfold as a procession of secret enclosed garden 'rooms', each with a separate theme and formal arrangements of paths and ponds. 10km of tall clipped hedges, sometimes to a height of 8m, and lines of pleached limes, make the living green 'walls' which surround them. To the right of the main gardens is a *potager*, laid out in 1721 and divided into rectangles; in the centre is a pavilion to Pomona. The deer park was landscaped in 1775 by Prince Charles-Joseph de Ligne but is not open to the public. Author of *Coup d'oeil sur Beloeil et sur une grande partie des jardins de l'Europe* (1781), the prince also built several garden features: a ruin, an obelisk and Morpheus' Temple. At the end of the 18th century he put on fashionably lavish entertainments, with boats on the *bassin* and firework displays.

Bokrijk Arboretum

N of N75 Hasselt to Genk road, E of Brussels
Owner: Province of Limburg
Opening times: Daily, Apr to Oct 10–18
Admission charge: No

Until 1797 Bokrijk belonged to the abbey of Herkenrode; it was then privately owned until acquired by the Province of Limburg in 1938. This important plant collection, which includes over 3,000 species of trees, is partly laid out in systematic order beds and partly as a 13ha landscape park. A herb garden and rose garden have recently been added.

Domein Botermelk

Schoten, NE of Antwerp
Owner: Jacques Wirtz
Opening times: By appointment, B–2120 Schoten, tel. 03 658 4670

Now owned by the landscape gardener Jacques Wirtz, the garden was originally the vegetable area of the 200ha estate of a nearby château. A compartmental layout, with box-edged beds, lawns, borders and trees, is surrounded by an old beech hedge and a wall with espaliered fruit.

Brussels: Abbaye de la Cambre

Junction of the Avenue Louise and the Ring boulevard
Owner: City of Brussels
Opening times: At all times
Admission charge: No

The Cistercian nunnery founded on this site on the edge of the Forêt de Soignes was dissolved in 1796. Formal gardens, with a *cour d'honneur*, terraces and stairways, date from the 1720s and were restored by the garden designer Jules Buyssens in the 1930s. He copied details of the garden from contemporary engravings.

Brussels: Bois de la Cambre

Via Avenue Louise and the Ring boulevard
Owner: City of Brussels
Opening times: At all times
Admission charge: No

Once part of the Forêt de Soignes, the Bois de la Cambre was acquired by the city in 1862 and transformed into an exceptionally attractive 125ha park by the German architect Edouard Keilig. From the city centre the Avenue Louise leads past two neo-classical pavilions into the park, where it forms a distorted figure-of-eight. Forest trees surround this area and are grouped round lawns, a monumental bridge and an artificial lake with a wooded island.

Brussels: Jean Massart Experimental Garden

1850 Chaussée de Wavre
Owner: Université Libre de Bruxelles
Opening times: Mon–Fri 7–17
Admission charge: No

Created in 1922 by the botanist Jean Massart, this garden is mainly devoted to conifers, wild flowers and medicinal and other useful plants.

Brussels: Laeken Royal Conservatories

In the grounds of the Royal Palace, Laeken, on the N outskirts of the city
Owner: King of Belgium
Opening times: Annually, one week in May
Admission charge: Yes

The glasshouses, the *Serres Royales*, built under the direction of J. P. Barillet-Deschamps for King Leopold II during the second half of the 19th century, are only open for a few days each spring. They contain mainly tropical plants, but pelargoniums, azaleas and orchids are also displayed.

Brussels: Park

NE of Place Royale in city centre
Owner: City of Brussels
Opening times: At all times

This huge public square was laid out 1774–87 on a symmetrical Y-shaped plan by the Frenchman Barnabé Guimard, who was brought in to redesign the whole Place Royale area after the royal palace was destroyed by fire some forty years earlier. It was the last great formal park to be created in Belgium; after this date new landscapes were created in the fashionable more naturalistic style. Avenues bordered by trees radiate as a *patte d'oie* from a large circular water basin surrounded by pleached limes at the Allée du Parlement end; tightly clipped tall hedges, *charmilles*, edge the *allées* which run round the perimeter of the park; wooded areas are criss-crossed by paths. Features include a small theatre, and a 'Vauxhall' (based on the pleasure gardens in London) built in 1783. Many of the fine sculptures were originally at Tervuren (q.v.).

Enghien

Enghien on N7, 26km SW of Brussels
Owner: City of Enghien
Opening times: Daily
Admission charge: Yes

Henry IV of France sold Enghien in 1607 to Count Charles d'Arenberg and the count's eldest son Phil-

ippe and his Capuchin architect brother redesigned the grounds on a vast and grandiose scale. The garden, which covered about 50ha at its height, became one of the most splendid of the 17th century, 'the most beautiful and extraordinary thing in the world', according to Mademoiselle de Monpensier who visited the Louis XIV's court in 1671. Alas, little remains of the former glory: changed into a romantic park later in the 18th century, Enghien was then destroyed during the French Revolution. Some buildings, and a scheme of converging avenues and various water features, including a 2km-long canal, are of interest to the enthusiastic historian.

Château de Freyr ★

On the left bank of the Meuse at Waulsort on the N95, 10km S of Dinant
Owner: Baron Francis Bonaert
Opening times: Jul, Aug, Sat, Sun, public hols 14–18
Admission charge: Yes

The 7ha 18th-century French-style garden at Freyr, laid out in 1760 by the brothers Count Guillaume and Count Philippe de Beaufort Spontin, lies beside the River Meuse. The main axis, marked by a canal punctuated with *bassins*, runs for 2km parallel to the river, continuing beyond the 16th- and 17th-century château. The layout is perfectly symmetrical. Near the château, parterres and *bassins* with simple jets of water are repeated in mirror images, followed by four cubes of clipped limes round an ornamental pool (the only remnant of an earlier renaissance garden), and then by more *bassins*, this time surrounded by tubs, 33 of them containing 300-year-old orange trees. The whole terminates in two 18th-century orangeries.

A second axis, formed by a huge oval *bassin* and a cascade, crosses the first, running up the slope from the river and culminating in Frederick's Hall, a rococo domed pavilion, from where there is a fine view of the whole garden. Built in 1774–5, the pavilion was decorated by the Italian Moretti brothers who also worked at Annevoie (q.v.). On the slopes below the pavilion are hedges laid out in the shape of the suits on playing cards.

At Beloeil, hornbeam hedges and frames are conceived as architectural features.

Kasteel van Gaasbeek

5km S of N8, 10km W of Brussels
Owner: Belgian State (Ministerie van de Vlaamse Gemeenschap)
Opening times: Daily, Jul, Aug 10–17, except Fri; Apr to Jun, Sept to Oct 10–17, except Mon, Fri
Admission charge: Yes

The fortified renaissance palace created from a castle in the 16th century was given a more fortified appearance in the 1880s and 1890s, along the lines made fashionable at the time by that great gothic-revival architect and restorer of fortifications, Eugène Viollet-le-Duc. The early 17th-century pleasure garden was also restored, but is no longer open to the public. A 17th-century fountain returned to the *cour d'honneur* retains some of the renaissance atmosphere, as do the box hedging and topiary of the courtyard inside the castle. A triumphal arch erected at the edge of the park in 1803 in honour of Napoleon Bonaparte still remains, and the extensive park itself contains fine trees, some of them 200 to 300 years old.

Château d'Hanzinelle

17km S of Charleroi
Owner: Baron Fallon
Opening times: Jul to Aug, Sat, Sun, hols 10–18
Admission charge: Yes

The 18th-century château, which once had a symmetrical French-style garden, is now framed by a charming romantic landscape which includes a lake and a curious rocky mound above a subterranean cave and galleries, created in 1885 by L. Fuchs (*see* Beervelde) for the then owner, Madame Emile Pirmez. A hornbeam arbour and clipped yews are a reminder of the earlier formality.

Château de Hex

Heks, 10km W of Tongeren near the Dutch border, via Brussels-Liège motorway E40
Owner: Comtesse D'Ursel
Opening times: By appointment, B–3877 Heers
Admission charge: Yes

The grand and beautiful park was laid out in the 18th century when the house was built. There are French-style formal gardens, a vegetable garden which was remodelled from the original in the early 1900s, and a collection of old and species roses.

Herkenrode

Haacht, N of N26 Mechelen to Leuven road, 25km NE of Brussels
Owner: Vicomte Philippe de Spoelberch
Opening times: By appointment, Vijverbos 6, B–2990 Haacht (Wespelaar), tel. 016 602311

The 3ha 19th-century landscape garden (originally part of the Wespelaar estate), with some remarkable trees, has been extended into the surrounding oak and larch woodland with plantings of rhododendron, acer, magnolia, dogwood, stewartia and styrax. Meadows have been drained and landscaped in the last few years for a 4ha arboretum in addition to the woodland garden. To the east of the house a formal kitchen garden, divided into hedged 'rooms', was designed by Jacques Wirtz (*see* Domein Botermelk) in 1979.

Château de Hingene

40km from Brussels between Antwerp, Ghent and Brussels
Owner: Municipality of Bornem
Opening times: Tel. 03 889 1280
Admission charge: Yes

Built in the 1760s for the Duc d'Ursel by Giovanni Niccolò Servadoni (*see* Dobříš in Czechoslovakia), a theatre set-designer as well as an architect, Hingene has recently been restored. The original contemporary plans show parterres of various designs on both sides of the lake. The present layout is simpler and wide paths lead through the wooded parkland.

15 Graaf van Hoornestraat ❋

Nevele, 3km from Brussels to Ostend motorway, exit 12
Owner: Dr A. De Clercq
Opening times: By appointment, Graaf van Hoornestraat 15, B – 9850 Nevele, tel. 09 171 5535 (after 22)

This 1.5ha garden of great botanical interest belongs to a plant enthusiast. The specialities are rhododendrons, including deciduous azaleas and the hardy Ghent azaleas, as well as a collection of prunus and sorbus. Dr De Clercq is interested in trees of columnar habit; some of the recent plantings are his own grafting. The garden is best visited in the first two weeks of May.

Château de Jehay-Bodegnée

Jehay, 4km N of Amay on N90, SW of Liège
Owner: Comte Guy van den Steen de Jehay
Opening times: Easter Sat to mid Sept, Sat, Sun 14–18

The 16th-century château, with chequer-board facade, is surrounded by water. The gardens, restored since World War II, are reached by a bridge from the courtyard and are formal in style with *charmilles*, topiary, water and sculptures – many of them by the owner.

Kalmthout Arboretum ❋

Kalmthout, 20km N of Antwerp; N1 to Maria ter Heide then NW
Owner: Foundation Arboretum Kalmthout
Opening times: Mar to mid Nov, Mon–Fri 9–17; Sat, Sun, hols 10–17
Admission charge: Yes

In 1856 Charles Van Geert moved his nursery from Antwerp to Kalmthout, where the soil was more favourable for growing newly-introduced conifers from western America as well as desirable ericaceous plants. After Van Geert's death the nursery became the Société Horticole de Calmpthout. It thrived at first but declined during the 1930s. In 1952 it was acquired by MM. Georges and Robert de Belder and from that date has steadily increased its importance as a tree and shrub collection, concentrating on hamamelis, acer and prunus. The arboretum lies alongside the Kalmthouts Heide, a large nature reserve open to the public.

Kasteel van Leeuwergem ★

2km NE of Zottegem, 18km W of Aalst via E40 Brussels-Ghent road
Owner: Baron Baudouin della Faille d'Huysse
Opening times: *Château and garden* by appointment; groups only, B–9620 Zottegem
Admission charge: Yes

Leeuwergem, though less grandiose, has many similarities with Beloeil (q.v.), notably the large rectangular-shaped pond in which the château is reflected.

The estate was created by Count d'Hane Steenhuyse in 1745. By the end of the 18th century a landscape park, with numerous man-made features, had been added. Several features still exist: an obelisk, a lodge in the vegetable garden and an island with a tomb bearing the inscription '*Carpe Diem*'. However, it is for the *théâtre de verdure*, a green theatre, that Leeuwergem is justly famous. Made from trained and pruned hornbeam, the theatre seats about 1,200, has a stage measuring 12m across, and is still in regular use. Baron Baudouin della Faille d'Huysse, a descendant of the Hane Steenhuyse family, has ensured that this 18th-century jewel remains intact.

Leuven: Herb Garden

30 Capucijnenvoer, Leuven, 23km E of Brussels via N2 or A3 motorway
Owner: Stad Leuven
Opening times: Daily 7.30–sunset
Admission charge: No

The present 2ha garden is the extension of a herb garden created in 1738 in the oldest part of the city. The garden now contains an important collection of herbs and other plants, a neo-classical orangery of 1821 and a semi-circular pond of 1827.

Kasteel van Loppem

Loppem, 7km S of Bruges, 2km E of A32, S of motorway
Owner: *Castle* Fonds van Caloen ASBL; *park* Municipality of Loppem
Opening times: Daily, sunrise–sunset

The important feature here is the large rectangular maze. It was laid out in 1859, when an 18th-century country house with a picturesque anglo-chinese garden (of which no traces survive) was replaced by the 40ha park and the neo-gothic château. The hedges of the labyrinth, which has a succession of false trails, are cut to below head height. Some fine old oak trees and two grottoes can be seen in the park.

Mariemont Park

Morlanwelz, 3km SE of La Louvière, 15km E of Mons, S of motorway E19
Owner: Ministère des Travaux Publics
Opening times: Daily, sunrise–sunset
Admission charge: No

Mariemont was named after Mary of Hungary, sister of the Holy Roman Emperor Charles V and regent of the Netherlands. In 1546 she had a moated hunting lodge built here on the edge of the Morlanwelz woods overlooking the River Haine, and laid out a great Italian-style terraced garden on the slopes below the house. In the early 17th century the 'Archdukes' Isabella (daughter of Philip II of Spain) and Albert of Austria turned Mariemont into a royal residence and created new gardens inspired by those at Aranjuez in Spain (q.v.). A painting by Alsloot of *c.*1630 shows their layout and the many fountains, and Mariemont was also depicted in the Gobelin tapestries of *Les Maisons Royales* following Louis XIV's appropriation of the estate in 1668. In the mid 18th century Charles de Lorraine laid out gardens in the French classical style with broad *allées*, terraces and huge parterres, but nothing of these or the earlier layout survived destruction during the French Revolution. In 1830 part of the property was acquired by the industrialist Nicolas Warocqué who, with the help of the English (or Swedish) garden designer C. A. Petersen, designed the 40ha romantic landscape that we see today. Fine trees in the park date from this period, among them a large cedar, some redwoods, oaks, ash, and a selection of lime species. There is also an important rose garden, and part of the beech avenue which replaced the 1km elm avenue planted in the 17th century.

National Botanic Garden of Belgium ✸

Meise-Bouchout, 10km N of Brussels via motorway
Brussels–Boom A12 and N177
Owner: Belgian State
Opening times: Daily 9–sunset
Admission charge: *Botanic garden* no; *Palais des Plantes*
yes

King Leopold II gave the Domein Bouchout to his
sister Charlotte after Tervuren (q.v.) was destroyed
in 1879. In 1882 more land was acquired and the park
extended to cover 90ha. In 1938 the Belgian government took it over and made it into a new botanic
garden, beautifully laid out with ponds, grass and
superb trees. The Palais des Plantes (1966) includes
several large hothouses open to the public, one of
which is devoted to tropical water plants. The 18th-
century orangery is now a restaurant.

**Rich planting in the woodland at Kalmthout
Arboretum.**

Parc du Roeulx

Le Roeulx, 14km E of Mons on N55, N of motorway E19
Owner: Prince de Croy-Roeulx
Opening times: Daily, Easter to Sept 10–12, 13.30–18,
except Wed (currently closed for restoration)
Admission charge: Yes

The 18th-century house is famous for its 1ha pentagonal walled rose garden, its orangery and its
romantic 45ha park. The rose garden, restored in
1960 by the garden designer René Pechère, contains
many roses from Monsieur et Madame Robert de
Belder's collection at Kalmthout (q.v.).

Sint Pieter 24

Rekem, on N17 S of E314, 10km NNW of Maastricht on
the Dutch border
Owner: Patricia van Roosmalen
Opening times: Jun, Fri and one weekend; also by
appointment, tel. 01 171 4692

A small, formal, compartmental garden with
herbaceous borders, roses, espaliered fruit and herbs.

Tervuren Geographical Arboretum
Jezus-Eiklaan, S of Tervuren on N3, 13km E of centre of Brussels
Owner: De Koninklijke Schenking
Opening times: Daily, sunrise–sunset; tours by appointment, Eikestraat 104, B–1980 Tervuren *or* tel. 02 767 9242

The end of the 19th century saw new ideas being applied in forestry. In 1897 the Belgian Secretary for Agriculture ordered the creation of experimental arboreta in different regions of the country to find out how new plant introductions adapted to local conditions. The most extensive project was started in Tervuren in the north-east corner of the Forêt de Soignes. Its instigator was Professor Charles Bommer of the Free University of Brussels, who revised conventional planting schemes and grouped species according to their ecological affinities. Each of the forty groups in the 100ha arboretum represented a different ecological habitat; large trees were planted and also the shrubs and bushes normally associated with them in their country of origin. Tervuren is of great interest and importance in the teaching of plant geography.

Tervuren Park
E outskirts of Brussels on N3
Owner: Belgian State
Opening times: At all times
Admission charge: No

Charles de Lorraine, who took over the remains of the original 13th-century château on a promontory in Lake Hubert in 1749, was responsible for the grand formal layout of this lake-girded park, with eight avenues radiating from a central *rond-point*. (One avenue, widened in 1897 for the Brussels exhibition, now links Tervuren with Brussels.) The estate, including a new château built to the north of the old one at the beginning of the 19th century, was given by King Leopold II to his sister Charlotte, widow of the Emperor Maximilian of Mexico (*see* Castello di Miramare in Italy), in 1853, but the château burnt down and Charlotte moved to Meise-Bouchout (*see* National Botanic Garden). Forty years later the French architect Lainé was brought in to create a

garden to set off a temporary building for the Brussels exhibition constructed on the site of the château. His formal layout has two axes centred on a large oval *bassin*, one focused on the building of 1897, the other leading south along a canal into the park.

Waasland Arboretum
Beveren, 12km W of Antwerp on N70
Owner: Stad Beveren
Opening times: Mon–Sat, 2nd Sun in month 10–17
Admission charge: No

Michel Decalut started a private plant collection here in the early 1970s. As the collection rapidly increased, it was agreed with the town of Beveren that he should extend his tree planting into a newly restored public park. The ruined castle with an orangery and outhouses dates from 1790.

Wespelaar Park
Haacht, N of N26 Mechelen to Leuven road, 25km NE of Brussels
Owner: Vicomte Nicolas de Spoelberch
Opening times: By appointment, B – 2990 Haacht (Wespelaar)

The original 15ha French-style formal garden, acquired by brewer Artois in 1796, was transformed during the next twenty years into a romantic park with the help of the architect G. J. Henry and Professor M. Verlat of Leuven University. Some of the original picturesque features have vanished, but a grotto, an Egyptian pyramid, a Temple of Flora, an orangery and an obelisk still survive. The botanist Augustin de Candolle visited in 1810 and described the garden in his journal as being the best in Belgium. The 100ha park contains beautiful vistas over the lake and canals. A modern (1955) house, built on an island, is of 18th-century inspiration.

Holland

Kasteel Amerongen

Amerongen, 25km SE of Utrecht on N225
Owner: Stichting Kasteel Amerongen
Opening times: Apr to Oct, Tues–Fri 10–17; Sat, Sun, public hols 13–17
Admission charge: Yes

The gardens surrounding Amerongen Castle, which was rebuilt 1674–8, are not on a large scale, but include a variety of features. Moats, bastions and bridges have existed since about 1700, but the garden was redesigned in the late 19th century by the landscape architect Hugo A. C. Poortman for Count van Aldenburg Bentinck, who lived in the castle from 1879. Poortman designed the formal flower garden in the old kitchen garden, with herbaceous borders, clipped box and yew topiary, a conservatory for tubs of agapanthus and oleander, a little house for the count's children, and a pergola. In the park woodland is carpeted with aconites, wood anemones and European primroses.

Amsterdam: Hortus Botanicus

City centre, between Mr Visserplein and the Plantage
Owner: University of Amsterdam
Opening times: Mon–Fri 10–12, 13.30–16; Sat, Sun, hols 13–16
Admission charge: Yes

Founded in 1682, the garden originally had rectangular beds in which medicinal plants were grown. It was redesigned in the landscape style towards the end of the 19th century, and there are now over 6,000 different plants from all over the temperate, tropical and subtropical world.

Kasteeltuinen Arcen

Arcen, 6km N of Venlo on N271
Owner: Kasteeltuinen Arcen B. V.
Opening times: Apr to Oct, daily 10–18
Admission charge: Yes

New public gardens on three square moated islands in the grounds of the 18th-century castle at Arcen are intended to please non-gardening visitors as well as interest the specialist. The design combines natural planting and gardens in different styles. The scale is grand and planting lavish. The castle, orangery and outbuildings are on one island; on the second a baroque-style pool with shell-shaped waterfall is the centrepiece of a formal rose garden, where thousands of roses, all bred in the region, perform through the summer. On the third island a pinewood, populated with exotic birds, is underplanted with shade-loving hostas and ferns. The dome of a tropical glasshouse dominates the striking newer part of the garden where a lake and smaller pools, groves of birch and perennial beds are laid out. A canyon, part cement, part stone and planted with bamboo, cherry and maples, leads back to the castle.

Arnhem: Herb Garden of the Netherlands

In the Netherlands Open-air Museum just N of the city
Owner: Ministry of Cultural Affairs, Recreation and Social Welfare
Opening times: Apr to Oct, Tues–Fri 9–17; Sat, Sun 10–17; June to Aug closes 17.30
Admission charge: Yes

The botanical garden, established in 1927, is planted as a replica of the Benedictine monastery garden shown in the 9th-century plan found at St Gall in Switzerland (see Introduction to Switzerland). There are areas for culinary and medicinal herbs and for plants used for dyes.

Beeckestijn

Westelijke parallelweg, 134 Rijksweg, S Velsen, 4km N of Haarlem on motorway A9
Owner: Gemeente Velsen
Opening times: At all times
Admission charge: No

The garden of this 18th-century house shows a

unique blend of the Dutch baroque and English landscape styles. It was designed by J. G. Michael (*see* Elswout) in 1772 for Jacob Boreel, a frequent visitor to England, and restored in 1953 according to the original plans. From the circular entrance courtyard an axis runs through the house to the landscape park behind, where a broad walk is first interrupted by a shell basin surrounded by five marble statues, then by a sunken sculpted pool; framed by young lime trees and low beech hedges with clumps of rhododendrons behind, the walk finally disappears into the distance. On both sides of the house, where the old serpentine walls of former kitchen gardens remain, new gardens were planted during the restoration: to the right a formal herb garden contains only plants that were grown in the 18th century; to the left a flower garden designed in French baroque style includes a rose garden, flower borders, and beds laid out in the shape of violin sound-holes and filled with bedding plants.

Belmonte

94 Generaal Foulkesweg, Wageningen, 13km W of Arnhem on N225
Owner: Agricultural University of Wageningen
Opening times: Daily 8–sunset
Admission charge: No

Belmonte was a large 19th-century family estate on the Rhine, with lovely views over the river and marshes. Some of the original planting of the landscape park remains on the slopes down to the river, but the park was badly damaged during World War II and the Italianate house destroyed. In 1951 the Agricultural University took over the estate, and in 1953 started to plant the arboretum now sited in the western part of the park. A narrow strip of woodland, a remnant of the 19th-century planting, divides this from an eastern section that was laid out some years later with cherries and crab-apples. Spring blossom, some of it from a beautiful *Prunus* 'Ichiyo' arching over the path through the arboretum, is followed by the brilliant colours of hundreds of rhododendrons.

Breda: Kruidentuin Begijnhof

54 Catherinastraat
Owner: Stichting Begijnhof
Opening times: Daily 9–16.30
Admission charge: No

The herb garden of the 16th-century Begijnhof is a peaceful sanctuary in the centre of Breda. A rectangle of small almshouses, still occupied by a religious lay community, surrounds a courtyard where each nursing sister had her own small plot of medicinal and culinary herbs, and which also contained a common drying-green. In 1970 the town council had the herb garden restored to its 16th-century form. Low yew hedges, kept short by regular cutting and root trimming, surround twenty carefully labelled beds in which more than 300 medicinal and culinary herbs are grown, as well as herbs once thought to ward off the evil eye. Pebbled paths divide the beds.

Clingendael

Wassenaarseweg, Wassenaar, 6km N of The Hague (s'Gravenhage) on N44
Owner: Gemeente Den Haag
Opening times: At all times; *Japanese garden* May to mid June
Admission charge: No

Clingendael's original 17th-century formal layout was designed by its owner, an admirer of Le Nôtre and a close friend of William and Mary. The influence of the French baroque garden created here was felt throughout the Netherlands, leading ultimately to the garden at Het Loo (q.v.). This Versailles-type layout disappeared when the English landscape style became popular at the end of the 18th century, but a formal and colourful garden has now been restored, with low box parterres in red gravel complementing an elegant 17th-century staircase ascribed to Daniel Marot.

The highlight of the park beyond is a hidden Japanese garden. Inspired by a visit to Japan in 1895, the then owner, Baroness van Brienen, brought back an authentic tea-house, bridges, lanterns and rocks – all vital ingredients of symbolic meaning. More than fifty different mosses carpet the banks of quiet pools and curving streams that symbolize the river of life.

Wandering paths, edged with bright azaleas, maples and drifts of candelabra primulas, contrast with the quieter areas of green simplicity. Elsewhere, extensive areas of grass frame lakes with islands, and walks lead through woods of fine trees and a rhododendron shrubbery.

Dieptetuin

Van Tetslaan and Lindenlaan, Zeist, 8km E of Utrecht on N225
Owner: Gemeente Zeist
Opening times: Mid Apr to Sept 8–sunset
Admission charge: No

The Dieptetuin (sunken garden) may best be described as a botanical garden in an English cottage-garden setting. Originally it formed part of a larger garden designed in 1909 in the English cottage-garden style by the Dutch garden architect C. Smitskamp to complement the (now demolished) house. The original layout remains. From the entrance, where the fine rock garden was made in 1975, steps and pergolas lead to a pool set in a lawn in the centre of the garden. There is an extensive collection of perennials (including *Kirengeshoma palmata* and *Meconopsis betonicifolia*), but also annuals, biennials, climbers, tender plants in tubs, bulbs (such as alliums and fritillarias), tuberous plants, trees, shrubs and fine conifers, among them the incense cedar (*Calocedrus decurrens*), dawn redwood (*Metasequoia glyptostroboides*) and ginkgos.

Elswout

12–14 Elswoutlaan, Poourtgebouw, Overveen, just N of Haarlem on Ijmuiden road
Owner: Staatsbosbeheer
Opening times: At all times
Admission charge: Yes

Elswout lies near the sea, close to the Kennemer-duinen national park. In the mid 17th century the original owner excavated the sand dunes to create a terraced Italian-style formal garden, the cross axes of which can still be identified in the older, southern part of the garden. Here, balustraded terraces and a staircase descend from the present house, a neo-renaissance palace built in 1880, to a strip of grass-

The restored parterre at Kasteel Amerongen.

land bordered by formal avenues. The pastoral design of the more naturalistic garden to the north reflects the late 18th-century landscape work of J. G. Michael (*see* Beeckestijn). Here a Swiss bridge crosses a stream in a hidden valley; paths meander through beech and lime woods, wander over open meadows and encircle mossy hills; and small wooden summer houses are dotted over the park. An orangery crowned with cupolas houses a collection of cacti.

Fraeylemaborg

30–2 Hoofdweg, Slochteren, 16km E of Groningen via motorway A7; 5km N of Hoogezand
Owner: Gerrit van Houtenstichting and Gemeente Slochteren
Opening times: Daily, Mar to Sept 10–12, 13–16/17, except Mon
Admission charge: Yes

A formal garden and a landscape park behind the mid 16th-century fortified manor house (or *borg*) were already in existence by the end of the 18th century. In the first half of the 19th century Lucas Pieters Roodbaard, a well-known garden architect from the north Netherlands, swept away the formal layout and enlarged and replanted much of the park. The naturalistic garden still retains some 18th-century features, including a pond and summer-house, but baroque avenues were transformed into winding paths, formal pools were given curving banks, and even the terrain was made more undulating. The park contains some beautiful specimen trees, including an American walnut, an ash (*Fraxinus excelsior* 'Jaspidea') with golden young growth and golden leaves in autumn, and swamp cypresses. Beyond a road, a long avenue with meadows on either side crosses a wood.

Von Gimborn Arboretum ❁

Vossensteinsesteeg, Doorn, 16km SE of Utrecht on N225
Owner: Rijksuniversiteit Utrecht
Opening times: Mon–Fri 8.30–16.30, Sat, Sun, hols 10–16.30
Admission charge: Yes

In 1924 Max von Gimborn started to lay out an arboretum in the style of a landscape park. He planted a large variety of conifers, supplemented with broad-leaved trees, heathers and ground-cover plants, establishing what quickly became one of the most important collections in Europe. After his death in 1966 the University of Utrecht took it over and now concentrates on the collections of conifers, maples, birches, magnolias, heathers and euonymus. Most of the 4,500 plants are labelled and the beautiful heather garden and the Tsuga wood deserve special attention. Three different walks lead past remarkable trees such as a western red cedar about 20m high, and the rare weeping spruce (*Picea breweriana*).

Gooilust

's-Graveland, 22km SE of Amsterdam via the A2 and N201
Owner: Vereniging tot Behoud van Natuurmonumenten
Opening times: *Park* daily, sunrise–sunset; *gardens* Apr to Sept 14.30–17
Admission charge: Yes

Gooilust is one of a series of country estates in 's-Gravenhage. The house, built in 1780, was surrounded by a baroque garden whose formal *allées*, circular pond and *sterrebos* (a small wood cut by radiating paths) are still identifiable, although the pond was 'irregularized' when the garden was redesigned in the landscape style at the end of the century. The hillocks and richly-planted rhododendron valley in the south-east area of the garden also date from this period. The walled kitchen garden with a central pool, used by the last owner, F.E. Blaauw, for his collection of exotic plants and animals, is now partly a plant nursery, while the other half, grassed over, contains a collection of specimen trees. Here a massive ninety-year-old evergreen oak acts as a foil for groups of ginkgo and other rare trees, shrubs and climbers which provide colour and interest in every season.

Groningen: Prinsenhof

Turfsingel
Owner: Gemeente Groningen
Opening times: Daily, mid Mar to mid Oct, weekdays 8–sunset, Sat, Sun, public hols 10–sunset
Admission charge: No

The Prinsenhof, the residence of the 'stadthouders' or lieutenant-governors in the 17th century, is an imposing building lying just north of the Martinikerk. Its walled renaissance garden was recently reconstructed by E. A. Canneman (*see* Walenburg) from a print showing a bird's-eye view of the city in 1635. Connecting hornbeam tunnels encircle box-edged flowerbeds filled with tulips, hyacinths and narcissus in spring and African marigolds and ageratum in summer. High fences surround three other compartments: a rose garden where modern polyanthus flower all summer; a formal design shaded by a large chestnut tree where box set off by white shells outlines two coats of arms; and a third area, typical of the practical-minded Dutch, given over to grass, with fruit trees and herbs at the sides. Espaliered lime trees grow against the walls.

Kasteel De Haar

Haarzuilens, NW of Vleuten, 8km NW of Utrecht
Owner: Baron van Zuylen van Nijevelt van de Haar
Opening times: All year, except mid Aug to mid Oct; summer 9–18; winter 9–16
Admission charge: Yes

The park and gardens at the castle of De Haar provide a fairytale example of a late 19th-century romantic layout with formal overtones. The immense and impressive neo-gothic castle was built 1892–1912 by the garden architect Henri Copijn, when the little village of Haarzuilens, situated near the ruins of the old castle, was demolished and rebuilt at the entrance to the drive. Inspired by historical designs, Copijn incorporated features from many different periods in the gardens around the castle: there is a Roman garden, a French-style *parterre de broderie*, a *berceau*, a formal rose garden, and even a grand canal where classical urns are reflected in the water. A landscape park, creating an atmosphere of calm beauty, surrounds the whole of this formal area. Winding paths lead past reflecting lakes and massive trees, some of which were already sixty or seventy years old when they were planted in 1900.

Het Loo ★

2km NW of Apeldoorn off N344
Owner: Netherlands State
Opening times: Daily, Apr to Oct 10–17
Admission charge: Yes

Prince William of Orange bought the medieval castle of Het Loo as a hunting lodge in 1684 and employed Jacob Roman to build a house. Both Roman and Daniel Marot were responsible for details in the garden, but it is not known who designed the layout as a whole. After the coronation of William and Mary in England in 1688, Het Loo became a royal palace and Hans Willem Bentinck was put in charge of enlarging it and enormously extending the garden in their absence. (In London, William and Mary were creating similar 'Dutch' gardens at Kensington Palace and Hampton Court, q.v.) Het Loo remained the palace of the House of Orange until the death of Queen Wilhelmina in 1975, when it became a state museum. Since then, the Great Garden behind the palace, which had been destroyed when the grounds were landscaped in 1807, has been largely restored to its well-documented appearance of about 1690.

The glory of Het Loo lies partly in its magnificent baroque layout, but also in the ornamentation and use of water: sculpture, fountains, *bassins* and cascades abound. The garden is in four parts. The enclosed Great Garden, with its central axis on the palace, is divided into the sunken and terraced Lower Garden adjoining the house, and the Upper Garden, with a cross avenue leading to the castle of Het Oude Loo separating the two. The King's Garden and Queen's Garden lie under the wings at each side of the palace.

The Lower Garden, its walls and terraces now rebuilt, is divided into eight *parterres*, almost certainly designed by Daniel Marot, their detailed patterns formed by box, yew, stone chippings, grass and flowers. There are three basins with fountains, and cascades fall from the terraces into rows of garden vases. The only plants are those that would have been found in late 17th-century Dutch gardens, such as blue monkshood, rue, yellow flags, *Rosa gallica* 'Versicolor', nasturtiums and fritillaries. Each plant is isolated from the next, in the fashion of the time. In contrast, only four of the original twelve parterres in the Upper Garden have been restored, thus making it possible to keep a number of fine old trees, including a beech and a tulip tree, from the 19th-century layout. In the centre is the dramatic King's Fountain, with a jet spouting to a height of 13.8m, and this part of the garden is terminated by a curved colonnade, moved here from nearer the house when the garden was extended in the later 17th century. The Great Garden was originally surrounded by a number of *giardini segreti*; these no longer exist, but the early 19th-century parkland beyond the walls remains.

Only part of the original Queen's Garden survives, but wooden arbours covered in hornbeam and enclosing small parterres and fountains are as they were in the 17th century. The King's Garden consists of a bowling green and parterres filled with flowers, clipped box and juniper. Orange trees, bays and plants originating from South Africa are grown here, and espaliered fruit trees are trained along the south walls of both gardens.

Keukenhof

166a Stationsweg, Lisse, 14km S of Haarlem on N208
Owner: Stichting Keukenhof
Opening times: Daily, Apr to mid May 8–19.30
Admission charge: Yes

After World War II, Dutch bulb growers were looking for a more natural setting than the bulb fields in which to show their bulbs. They found it at the Keukenhof, a landscape park that in the 15th century formed the hunting grounds which provisioned the kitchen (the *keuken*) of Jacoba van Beieren. The informal, slightly sloping setting offsets the formality of the bulb beds which, set in annual grass and redesigned every year, contain five to six million tulips, narcissus, hyacinths and 'lesser' bulbs. Mature trees, underplanted with spring-flowering shrubs and smaller trees such as viburnums, rhododendrons, corylopsis and prunus, overshadow the flowers. Immense greenhouses are filled with out-of-season bulbs, and the Keukenhof is crossed by canals leading away from a large pond.

OVERLEAF **The restored parterres, orginally designed by Daniel Marot, at the 17th-century palace of Het Loo are in box and gravel. Plants from the period, including yews as accent plants, are used in the flowerbeds round the edges of the elaborate patterns.**

Leiden: Botanic Garden of Leiden University ★ ❀

Between the Rapenburg and the Witte Singel canal; entrance Rapenburg
Owner: State University of Leiden
Opening times: Apr to Oct, Mon–Sat 9–17, Sun 10–16; Nov to Mar, daily 9–12, 13.30–16, except Sun; *hothouses* closed 12.30–13.30

Founded in April 1587, the Hortus Academicus was amongst the earliest botanical gardens in Europe, and from the outset was planted with ornamental as well as useful plants. Carolus Clusius (*see* Introduction), the Flemish doctor and botanist, and perhaps the most influential of all 16th-century scientific horticulturists, was appointed professor at the university in 1594. In Dutch gardening history he will be remembered not only for his scholarship but for his observations on tulips 'breaking', a phenomenon, later discovered to be due to a virus, causing the many different varieties which led to the speculative tulipomania of the 1630s. Clusius laid the foundations of Dutch bulb breeding and the bulb industry today.

Detailed lists of plants and planting information from Clusius's time have made it possible to reconstruct his garden, which is sited near where it originally lay. In the systematic garden, plants arranged in families surround a bust of the Swedish botanist Linnaeus (*see* Linnaeus's Garden, Sweden), who lived and wrote in Leiden in the 1730s. A laburnum planted by Clusius survives and there are many good specimen trees, including a copper beech, a fern-leaved beech and a Caucasian wingnut that were planted in the early 19th century.

Menkemaborg

E of Uithuizen town centre, 22km NE of Groningen via N46 and N363
Owner: Stichting Groninger Museum voor Stad en Lande
Opening times: Daily, Apr to Sept 10–12, 13–17; Oct to Mar, Tues, Sat 10–12, 13–17, Sun 13–16; closed Jan
Admission charge: Yes

Menkemaborg is a 15th-century fortified manor house, or *borg*, altered in *c.*1700. The garden architect Henri Copijn (*see* Kasteel De Haar) began to restore the gardens in 1921, but some of his work is now being replaced and restoration is still in progress. Different sections around the house are either ornamental or utilitarian. In one, a parterre with a summer-house and six cupolas made of trellis-work is executed according to original 18th-century designs. Another contains a symmetrical rose garden punctuated with clipped yews, while a third is a box garden with a sundial. Behind the house, beyond a parterre of four triangles set in gravel, a maze leads to a *berceau* of pear trees and an apple orchard. The *berceau* develops into a path, spanned at regular intervals by rose arches and bordering a kitchen garden planted with soft fruit, vegetables and herbs.

Kasteel Middachten ★

De Steeg, 15km E of Arnhem on A48
Owner: Anon
Opening times: Variable; check VVV Velp,
tel. 085 610616/452921
Admission charge: Yes

The outlines of the garden laid out at the beginning of the 18th century still survive here. The walled garden was redesigned in formal 18th-century style in 1900 by Hugo A. C. Poortman, a pupil of the French garden and landscape architect Edouard André, and the gardens were again renovated in the 1980s. Different compartments – 'green rooms' – contain a rose garden, a sunken garden with annuals, and a garden in front of the orangery. Old-fashioned roses are trained along a wire framework, there are exotics such as a cedar of Lebanon and a ginkgo, and the orangery is still used in winter to protect a variety of potted plants, including orange trees and palms.

Tuinen van Mien Ruys

78 Moerheimstraat, Dedemsvaart, 30km NE of Zwolle on N377
Owner: Stichting Tuinen Mien Ruys
Opening times: Apr to Oct, Mon–Sat 10–17, Sun 13–17
Admission charge: Yes

Mien Ruys is one of the best known garden designers in the Netherlands today, and every plant or garden lover will find much of interest here. Mien Ruys first started an experimental garden in the grounds of her father's Moerheim nursery, where she set out to explore how perennials could be used, in which soil they grew best and how they could best be combined; the planting was allowed (within limits) to grow wild. Since then her experiments both with plants and the use of hard surfaces in the garden have increased and she is now responsible for some 25 gardens on this site. Apart from her first garden, there is a herb garden, a rose garden, a water garden, a woodland garden, a herbaceous border 30m long, and examples of roof gardens. Plants are combined according to colour, flowering season or their preference for dry or damp soil. There are also garden ornaments and statuary.

Kasteel van Het Nijenhuis

On Wijhe road, 3km SW of Heino on N35 SE of Zwolle
Owner: Province of Overijssel
Opening times: Daily 11–17; closed Dec 25, Jan 1
Admission charge: No

The house and farm buildings are surrounded by a landscape park with meandering paths, in which planting is mainly 19th-century. A 17th-century arrangement of avenues also remains, together with an irregularly-shaped 'grand canal', a walled garden and an arbour. There are also garden statues, a dovecote and an obelisk.

Park Rosendael

Kerklaan, Rozendaal, 5km NE of Arnhem via Velperweg across motorway A12 and N on Daalhuizerweg for 1.5km
Owner: Stichting het Gelders Landschap
Opening times: June to mid Sept, Tues–Fri 10–17, Sun 13–17; Sept, Oct, Sun 13–17
Admission charge: Yes

Rosendael's hilly site with its natural streams is unique in Holland and was put to full use by Jan van Arnhem in the baroque garden he created in the 1660s, and subsequently in the early 18th-century rococo embellishment of the park, when several elements of the existing garden were retained, including the straight lines of the former layout, the *bedriegertjes* or water tricks, for which the park was famous, and the shell grotto and shell gallery near the lake. In 1837 the landscape architect J. D. Zocher gave gentler and more natural lines to the paths and to the shapes of ponds and groups of trees. Among the fine specimen trees in the park are a 500-year-old oak, a huge pencil tree (*Calocedrus decurrens*), and a *Thuja plicata* with branches nearly as thick as the main trunk. The rose garden dates from the beginning of this century and has recently been refurbished with more than 1,500 roses, mostly old-fashioned varieties, but also some more modern hybrids to ensure a longer flowering season.

Rotterdam: Arboretum Trompenburg ❀

Entrance Honingerdijk, E of city centre near Erasmus University
Owner: Stichting Arboretum Trompenburg
Opening times: Daily 9–17, except Sun; closed Easter, Whit, Christmas
Admission charge: No (tickets free from VVV)

The beautifully laid out arboretum is an oasis in the middle of Rotterdam. Here five generations of the van Hoey Smith family have brought together outstanding trees from Europe, Africa, Asia and America, crowned by a collection of cedars. The oldest trees, the oaks, originate from plantings in 1820. Fifty years later, the landscape architect J. D. Zocher designed the western part of the arboretum, adding ash trees and maples, a ginkgo and a swamp cypress. Much of the planting also dates from the first half of this century, when many new trees were established after elm disease first struck in 1928. Trompenburg now lists 2,500 varieties of trees and shrubs, all carefully labelled, among them 750 rhododendrons, a notable weeping beech, and a weeping oak draped over a pergola. Yet even in 'conifer corner' the planting is never oppressive, and part of the arboretum is kept as open grass, with a goldfish pond edged with drifts of yellow lysichitum. There is also a hothouse, built in 1900, which houses the cactus Queen of the Night and a collection of succulent euphorbias.

Thijsse Hof

4 Mollaan, Bloemendaal, just W of Haarlem
Owner: Stichting Thijsse Hof
Opening times: Apr to Oct, Tues–Fri 9–12, 13.30–17, Sat, Sun 9–17; Nov to Mar, Tues–Fri 9–12, 13.30–16, Sat 9–16
Admission charge: No

The site of this garden, which lies close to the sea, was presented to the field biologist Jacques P. Thijsse on his sixtieth birthday in 1925. Leisure activities on the coast had increased alarmingly and Thijsse set out to create a wild garden where something could still be seen of the indigenous flora and fauna. The landscape architect Leonard Springer designed this dune valley to be a home for different communities of plant and bird life. In the wood, different layers of vegetation emerge in season; first the mosses, anemones and primroses, then the shrubs, and finally the trees – mostly oak, birch, beech, elm and maple – come into leaf. In places a scrub of spindle bushes, sea-buckthorn and wild roses has taken over. There is a slope overgrown with the burnet rose, a dry meadow with heather and broom, and near the pond a damp meadow where orchids and different grasses grow, and water-birds nest. The garden is at its most beautiful from May to the middle of July.

Kasteel Twickel

Delden, 14km NW of Enschede, 2km W of motorway on N346
Owner: Stichting Twickel
Opening times: Mid May to mid Oct, Wed, Sat 13.30–17
Admission charge: Yes

The grounds around the castle are in three distinct parts: a landscape park, a formal garden, and a flower garden. The park dates from the late 19th century, when Carl Eduard Adolf Petzold, a German garden and landscape architect, redesigned an earlier informal layout, creating new paths, opening up views, and importing trees and other plants from Germany by rail.

The formal layout near the orangery, with a large number of well-grown orange trees, old fuchsias and palm trees in tubs and old yews clipped into the shapes of birds and spirals, was designed in about

1900 by Edouard André and executed by his pupil Hugo A. C. Poortman.

The richly coloured flower garden is the most recent addition. Laid out in 1925 and improved subsequently by the then owner, Baroness van Heeckeren, it is designed in the cottage-garden style.

Kasteel Verwolde

Between Laren and Markelo, 7km N of Lochem, 22km NE of Zutphen via N346
Owner: Stichting Vrieden der Geldersche Kasteelen
Opening times: Apr to Oct, Tues–Sat 9–17, Sun 13–17
Admission charge: Yes

The neo-baroque garden was redesigned by Hugo A. C. Poortman in 1926–7 at the same time as the 18th-century house was rebuilt. Two axes, centred on the house, run through two symmetrically placed gardens: one a sunken garden with a box *parterre de broderie*; the other a lawn bordered with perennial flowerbeds backed by yew hedges, where green niches set off statues and vases. The gardens were renovated in 1979–82 when the borders were re-designed and replanted with 'mixed' schemes of shrubs, roses and perennials forming a repeated pattern. The small landscape park, which Poortman also created, contains beautiful rhododendrons, a big *Catalpa bignonioides*, and a variety of broad-leaved trees and conifers.

Walenburg ★

Langbroek, 14km S of Amersfoort on N227
Owner: Under management of Nederlandse Tuinenstichting
Opening times: 6 days each year 10–17 and by appointment; enquire Nederlandse Tuinenstichting, Prinsengracht 624, 1017 KT Amsterdam, tel. 020 235058
Admission charge: Yes

The garden of Walenburg, a 13th-century tower with a 16th-century house attached to it, is the creation of an architect, the late E. A. Canneman, and his wife, a landscape architect, who both contributed much to gardening in Holland. When they came to live here in 1965 they found the garden as it had been in medieval times: a rectangular plot leading from the moat below the house to an outer moat, where there is a wind-break of oaks. The Cannemans divided the garden symmetrically into small, hedged compartments, each with its own character, and with two marble statues as focal points of the dividing paths. *Viburnum plicatum* 'Mariesii' mark each corner of the white garden, which is centred on a Roman column surrounded by six *Hydrangea paniculata* 'Grandiflora'. In the rose garden old-fashioned varieties flourish on the heavy clay and climbing species are supported by apple trees. The flower garden features two large borders filled with 'plantsmen's plants', and the fourth compartment, through which the garden is now reached, is a herb garden, where there is also a hothouse and a number of rare plants.

Warmelo ★

S of Diepenheim, 18km SW of Enschede via N346
Owner: Avenarius family
Opening times: Mid May to mid Oct, Tues, Thurs 13.30–17, Sun, public hols 10–17
Admission charge: Yes

Yew topiary, clipped thujas and box-edged parterres in front of the 18th-century house are framed by its mulberry-clad walls. A geometrical French garden, with a view to the 19th-century landscape park, lies behind the house, while in another area scented roses grow in a symmetrically-planned layout and yews frame a rococo pool. Also near the house is the garden room designed in 1920 by Baroness F. Creutz, where part of the great fuchsia collection – 350 varieties totalling 3,000 plants – is displayed. Bridges and mossy paths lead to the 19th-century pinetum planned by Princess Armgard von Lippe Biesterfeld, who planted exotic pines and other conifers to create a theatrical setting.

Kasteel Weldam

2km NE of Diepenheim, 16km NW of Enschede via N346
Owner: A. Graaf zu Solms Sonnervalde
Opening times: Mon–Sat 10–12, 13–16
Admission charge: Yes

The moated gardens surrounding the castle at Weldam are an idealized version of an early 18th-century baroque layout, with an emphasis on architectural elements. Dating only from 1886, when they were

Modern boarder planting at De Wiersse, with lilies and blue-and-white agapanthus in flower.

designed and created by Hugo A. C. Poortman, they have since been hardly altered, and are a good example of late 19th-century Dutch interest in 'historical' reconstructions. The principal motif is 'green' architecture, with garden rooms dominated by clipped yew and box hedges and very few flowers, except for rhododendrons, roses and annuals. A thuja maze embraces a raised platform from which there is a view over a boxwood *parterre de broderie*, its corners marked by single, pillar-shaped conifers, and over a hornbeam-covered walk. Statues stand above two long canals and stare into the water, and there are views over the moat to the countryside around. Ancient oaks and an avenue of chestnuts line the approaches to the castle and gardens.

De Wiersse ★

6.5km E of Vorden on N319, SE of Zutphen
Owner: E. V. Gatacre
Opening times: May to Oct, 5 to 7 times; enquiries to
VVV Achterhoek, tel. 05750 19355, or VVV Vorden,
tel. 05752 3222; groups, tel. 05752 6693
Admission charge: Yes

De Wiersse is one of a group of small country houses round Vorden and lies in woodland in the centre of a modest 300ha estate. Most of the layout was the work of the owner's parents, Alice de Stuers and her English husband W. E. Gatacre, who created a variety of features within a relatively small area. A series of intimate inner gardens close to the house includes a sunken garden framed by flower borders and a rose pergola, and the rose parterre, designed by Alice de Stuers after an old French pattern and set off by topiary in box and yew. In the romantic woodland garden beyond, where banks of rhododendrons and azaleas screen one area from another, paths lead past pools to vistas punctuated by benches, topiary and statues; a birch grove is bright with daffodils and erythroniums in spring. Though not a plantsman's garden, much thought has been given to plant associations.

At Kasteel Weldam, the hornbeam-covered walk in the late 19th-century garden was inspired by baroque designs.

The decisive factor in gardening in Norway and Sweden is geography. Most of their landmass lies north of latitude 60°N and extends at its northern extremity into the Arctic Circle. Even in the south, the monthly mean temperature in Stockholm and Oslo from December to March is below zero. The minimum temperature in those months is occasionally below $-20°C$ and will occasionally drop below zero in nine months of the year. Denmark, between the same latitudes as northern Britain, has a much less severe climate, but it is hard enough greatly to restrict the range of garden plants that may be cultivated. On the west coast of Norway the severity of the climate is in certain places mitigated by the effects of the Gulf Stream drift. The garden of the State Horticultural School at Râ (q.v.), nearly 69°N and thus well into the Arctic Circle, must be one of the most northerly gardens in the world.

The earliest detailed accounts of horticulture in Scandinavia relate to monastic gardens. In Sweden there are records of gardening at the Cistercian monastery of Alvastra in 1143. In 1165 a French monk, William, became Abbot of Eskilsø in Denmark and ordered plants and cuttings from Paris. In Norway the tradition of monastic orchard farming, originating in the 12th century, is still continued in the regions of Hardanger and Sogn.

But it was not until the Renaissance that gardening flourished in Scandinavia, particularly in Sweden where kings of the Vasa dynasty were great builders and garden lovers. Substantial records of garden making in Scandinavia, and many examples, survive from the 17th century, and specifically from the decades of peace following the end of the Thirty Years' War in 1648. This period saw an international exchange of gardening ideas. André Mollet came to Sweden from France and worked for Queen Christina. His book *Le Jardin de Plaisir*, published in Stockholm in 1651, appeared in French, German and Swedish. In Sweden, Nicodemus Tessin, father and son, introduced the latest ideas of French formal gardening at the great royal garden of Drottningholm (q.v.). The younger Tessin was a typical figure of his age – an international architect-designer who travelled widely and came to the admiring attention of his great contemporaries, who included André Le Nôtre and Christopher Wren. The tradition of the formal baroque garden is also found in Norway at Rosendal Barony (q.v.) (laid out by a Flemish gardener in about 1670) and in Denmark, where King Frederick IV, having seen Le Nôtre's gardens in France, imported his ideas in the making of the garden at Frederiksborg Castle (q.v.). Linnaeus, too, was an essential figure in attracting European horticultural attention to Scandinavia. He was appointed director of the botanic garden at Uppsala (founded in the 1650s, q.v.) in 1741 and here, and at his charming summer house at Hammarby (q.v.), he received many of the greatest botanical and horticultural figures of the day.

The tradition of the romantic landscape garden, an international style of gardening that succeeded the French formal style, struck a deep chord in the Scandinavian sensibility. The Swedish architect F. M. Piper travelled widely and made an especial study of England where he was particularly impressed by the landscape garden of Stourhead (q.v.), of which he made many exquisite drawings. In Sweden he drew on these inspirations for the gardens he made at Drottningholm (q.v.) and at Haga (q.v.). This tradition was seen also in Denmark, where the garden at Liselund (q.v.) shows Rousseau-esque influence. The 19th-century Danish landscape designer R. Rothe visited many gardens in Europe and made the park at Fredensborg (q.v.). In Norway, a landscaped park of about 1780 survives at Bogstad Manor near Oslo.

In the 19th and 20th centuries the distinctive development in Scandinavian gardening has been the importance of public parks. In Norway major public gardens were made at Ravnedalen in Kristiansand (q.v.) in the 1870s and at Nygård in Bergen (q.v.) in 1880. In Denmark there is the remarkable Geographic Garden at Kolding (q.v.), which was started in 1920. The sculpture garden at Rottneros (1945) (q.v.) in Sweden is, perhaps, the pre-eminent example of the distinctive style of the 20th-century public garden – an open-air museum and place of recreation in which plants are not the chief interest.

Because of the limitations of the climate, Scandinavia does not possess large numbers of distinguished gardens accessible to the public. The garden visitor will nevertheless find gardens of a distinctive Scandinavian character, sometimes influenced by international styles, and frequently set in scenery of spectacular natural beauty.

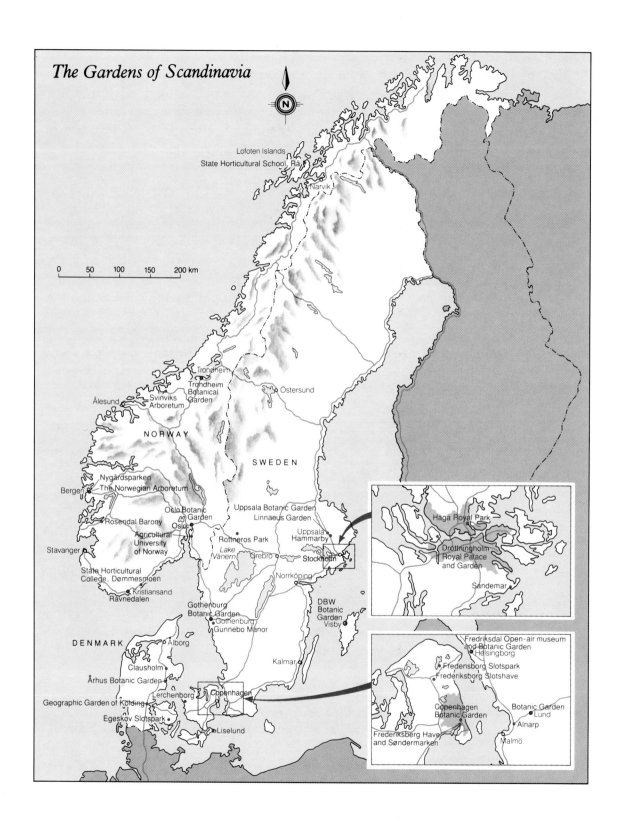

The Gardens of Scandinavia

N

0 50 100 150 200 km

Lofoten Islands
State Horticultural School, Rå

Narvik

NORWAY

Trondheim
Trondheim
Botanical
Garden

Østersund

Ålesund
Svinviks
Arboretum

SWEDEN

Nygårdsparken
The Norwegian Arboretum
Bergen

Uppsala Botanic Garden
Linnaeus Garden

Oslo Botanic
Garden
Oslo
Rottneros Park
Uppsala
Hammarby

Rosendal Barony
Agricultural
University
of Norway

Lake
Vänern
Örebro

Stockholm

Stavanger

State Horticultural
College. Dømmesmoen
Kristiansand
Rävnedalen

Norrköping

DBW
Botanic
Garden
Visby

Gothenburg
Botanic Garden
Gothenburg
Gunnebo Manor

DENMARK

Ålborg

Kalmar

Clausholm

Århus Botanic Garden

Geographic Garden of Kolding
Lerchenborg
Copenhagen

Egeskov Slotspark

Liselund

Stockholm inset

Haga Royal Park

Drottningholm
Royal Palace
and Garden

Sandemar

Copenhagen inset

Fredriksdal Open-air museum
and Botanic Garden
Helsingborg
Fredensborg Slotspark
Frederiksborg Slotshave

Copenhagen
Botanic Garden

Botanic Garden
Lund

Alnarp

Frederiksberg Have
and Søndermarken

Malmö

Denmark

Århus: Botanic Garden

Peter Holm Vej-Vestre Ringgade, Eugen Warmingsvej, W of town centre
Owner: City of Århus
Opening times: Daily
Admission charge: No

A natural valley which cuts through the western part of Århus has been used as the site of the botanic garden. Trees and shrubs of botanical interest are planted on grassy slopes and a stream running through the valley is attractively edged with native Danish vegetation. A good collection of herbaceous perennials and of annuals is contained in beds on the slopes of a large natural 'bowl'.

In the 20th-century landscape garden at Århus, willows fringe a formal pool with modern sculpture.

Clausholm

Near the village of Voldum, 10km S of Randers
Owner: Kim A. Berner
Opening times: Easter to May, mid Aug to mid Oct, Sat, Sun, public hols 10–12, 14–17; June to mid Aug, daily 10–12, 14–17.30
Admission charge: No

The late 17th-century castle of Clausholm, surrounded by a moat, lies at the foot of a steep hill. A cascade tumbling from the very top of the slope through gullies and pools on the terraced hillside to the moat below is a 20th-century version of an original baroque feature, and despite the modern materials and techniques the result is charming. Nothing of the gardens round the castle has survived except for a few old limes.

Copenhagen: Botanic Garden of Copenhagen University ✷

126 Gothersgade
Owner: University of Copenhagen
Opening times: Daily, May to Aug 8.30–18; winter 8.30–16
Admission charge: No

The medieval part of Copenhagen is surrounded by a ring of parks which were created on the site of Christian IV's 17th-century fortifications. In 1870 the botanical garden of the University of Copenhagen was moved here from the inner city, the first park to be made in this area. Today it has the appearance of a typical public park. A low-lying lake, part of the old system of moats, and the undulations of the old fortification mounds give a romantic feeling. There is also a substantial botanical garden with large rockeries, splendid greenhouses, and beds containing a collection of plant species gathered from all parts of the world. As the garden is now more than 100 years old, many of the trees and shrubs are fine specimens, and their underplanting is lush and varied. The greenhouses have recently been restored and contain collections of tropical, subtropical and arctic plants.

Copenhagen: Frederiksberg Have and Søndermarken ★

Frederiksberg Runddel
Owner: The State
Opening times: Daily sunrise–sunset
Admission charge: No

Fine trees, woodland, open meadows and gentle expanses of water are the chief elements to be seen in the park on arriving by the Frederiksberg alley. However, this is more than a landscape park – it is a royal garden. In the 18th century Frederick IV visited France and fell under the spell of Le Nôtre. Long vistas through woodland, the remains of alleys, and not least the castle itself rising on a terraced hill, are evidence of French influence. From the magnificent entrance gate winding paths lead the visitor about the garden. Elegant bridges cross meandering channels to romantic islands (one with a charming Chinese pavilion dating from the late 18th century); a

grotto, a mound, a Swiss cottage and a classical temple also contribute to the dream-like atmosphere.

Søndermarken, which is south of the castle, is also part of the garden. Here two alleys survive from the baroque garden and further alleys about a pool on the main axis have recently been replanted. Here, too, are features of the romantic style that superseded the baroque – including a timber 'Norwegian' cottage overlooking a precipitous slope.

Egeskov Slotspark

3km W of Kvaerndrup on Route 8, 25km S of Odense
Owner: Claus Count Ahlefeldt-Laurvig-Bille
Opening times: Daily, May, Sept 10–17; Jun to Aug 9–18
Admission charge: Yes

Egeskov, a gem among Danish renaissance castles, has an outstanding formal garden with alleys, clipped hedges, a maze and topiary. Deceptively, it was designed 200 years later than the castle, which was built in 1554. One of the hedged enclosures contains a charming kitchen garden with elegant pavilions in each corner. In another enclosed area there is an excellent collection of fuchsias planted decoratively among old apple trees. In 1960 the French garden designer Ferdinand Duprat laid out the elegant box parterre to the east of the castle, which makes a formal link with an obelisk placed in the open field beyond. A rose garden and a collection of herbaceous plants are more recent additions.

Fredensborg Slotspark ★

Fredensborg, 45km N of Copenhagen, Route 6
Owner: The State
Opening times: Daily; *Marble Garden* Jul 9–16
Admission charge: No

Fredensborg is the favourite residence of the Danish royal family. The estate with its fine early 18th-century castle is positioned high above forest and lake in the beautiful North Sealand. The entrance is from the south through a short alley flanked by service buildings and an octagonal forecourt. The castle lies at the centre of a semi-circular formal garden from which seven lime alleys radiate out into woodland, glimpses of Lake Esrum visible through the trees.

This corresponds to the original layout designed in 1720 by Johan Cornelius Krieger. Old limes bordering the semi-circle have sculptures behind them, chiefly the work of Johannes Wiedewelt in the 1760s. The richest ornamentation is found west of the castle in the Italian-inspired Marble Garden (*Marmorhave*), created by Wiedewelt and the French architect N. H. Jardin. This part of the garden is private and is normally open to the public only in July.

A terraced valley, the *Normandsdalen* (Norman valley), in the woods between the Marble Garden and the lake has a number of sandstone carvings by J. G. Grund depicting Nordic peasants and fishermen. This is one of the few French-inspired *bosquets* surviving in Denmark. Beyond, by the shores of the lake, are two decorative summer-houses (the Eremitage Pavilions), several memorials and an idealized boatman's hut, the *Skipperhuset*.

The garden today is a most attractive mixture of garden styles – the formal style of the early 18th century and the romantic style of 1800 – blended in striking harmony. Later in the 19th century, Rudolf Rothe was head gardener at Fredensborg and added to the woodland garden.

Frederiksborg Slotshave ★
Hillerød, 39km N of Copenhagen
Owner: The State
Opening times: Daily
Admission charge: No

The castle, dating from the 16th and 17th centuries, was built on three islands in a small lake and is separated from the garden, which is on a terraced slope to the north-east. There are beautiful views of the garden from the upper floors of the castle, but the best prospect is from the topmost terrace looking down over the lake. The garden is the creation of J. C. Krieger and was laid out 1720–6. From the north entrance, by an oval pool, the castle in its lake has the appearance of an enchanted stage set. The approach is flanked with pleached lime alleys and the castle is reflected in the serene surface of the lake. From this upper level visitors can walk down from terrace to terrace through the alleys. There are no retaining walls or steps, only attractive grassy slopes. The neatly trimmed turf edges are emphasized by old box hedges overhanging the slopes – the remains of those which surrounded the *bosquets* and parterres of

Krieger's original scheme. On the lowest terrace, at the edge of the lake, box hedges and topiary provide an appropriate formal setting for the renaissance castle. In the garden's great days this terrace also had French-inspired parterres and a fine cascade cut through the central axis of the garden. The cascade was demolished but plans are afoot to reinstate it.

Kolding: Geographic Garden of Kolding ❀
Vej, centre of town
Owner: City of Kolding
Opening times: Daily, Apr to May 10–18; Jun to Jul 9–20; Aug 10–19; Sept 10–18
Admission charge: Yes

More than fifty years of intensive and inspired research lies behind this garden. In 1920 the nurseryman Aksel Olsen started collecting plants in geographical groups. 6,000 species were introduced from China, Burma, the Himalayas and North and South America, of which 2,000 species survived. Today the collection occupies 12ha, and is run by the municipality of Kolding, who have added a herb garden, a rose garden, a garden of herbaceous plants and a display garden.

Lerchenborg
4km S of Kalundborg, on coast W of Copenhagen via Route 23
Owner: Chr. C. K. Count Lerche-Lerchenborg
Opening times: Mid Jun to mid Aug, Mon–Sat 13–17, except Fri, Sun 13–18
Admission charge: No

The garden of the mid 18th-century manor house of Lerchenborg, designed by J. B. de Longueville, is one of the most perfect examples in Denmark of the French baroque style. It is composed along an east-west axis, extended far into the countryside by 200-year-old lime avenues. These, and the ingeniously shaped lime arcades, survived when a landscape garden was added in the 19th century. There is a continuing programme of restoration – the lime avenues have been trimmed, the arcades reshaped using a new steel frame, paths and courtyards repaired and a handsome new fountain erected.

Norway

Liselund ★

E of Borre, NE coast of the Isle of Møn
Owner: Niels Henrick Count Rosencrantz
Opening times: Daily
Admission charge: No

This outstanding example of a late 18th-century romantic garden lies close to one of the most dramatic coastlines of Denmark, the chalk cliffs of the Isle of Møn. Hidden within a glade in the beech woods at the top of the cliffs, in a spectacular setting, are four pavilions. The 'castle', with columns and a spire, lies on the banks of a stream which feeds a series of ornamental lakes. Opposite the lakes, on the crest of the cliff, is the 'Norwegian' house, partly built of wood. The 'Swiss' house, low and white, has heavy granite foundations. Most exotic of all is a charming octagonal Chinese pavilion with a curved roof. A winding path crosses a flimsy bridge over a ravine, passing monuments with symbolic inscriptions, to a cross on the cliff.

Rustic thatched houses ornament the 18th-century landscape garden of Liselund.

Agricultural University of Norway

Ås, 30km S of Oslo, W of E18
Owner: Agricultural University of Norway
Opening times: Daily
Admission charge: No

The development of the park began shortly after the foundation of the original college in 1859, and several big trees survive from that period, among them a common lime, now 34m high, in the centre of the campus. Today the park covers 60ha and is chiefly laid out according to the plans of Professor Olav L. Moens, made in the 1920s. The central area is neo-classical in spirit, with an axial composition and a

RIGHT **An avenue of oaks in the early 19th-century landscape park which is now the Oslo Botanic Garden.**

reflecting pool. Other parts have a more informal character with views over undulating ground. There are systematic collections of more than 600 species of trees and shrubs and a colourful azalea garden.

Bergen: The Norwegian Arboretum ❀
In town centre
Owner: The Norwegian Arboretum Foundation
Opening times: Daily
Admission charge: No

The arboretum, founded in 1971, is situated in a very attractive fjord landscape with forest-covered hills and shifting views. Special emphasis is being put on growing trees and shrubs that thrive in the mild climate of the west Norwegian coast. These include monkey puzzles, *Cryptomeria*, *Nothofagus*, and rhododendrons.

Bergen: Nygårdsparken
Bergen
Owner: City of Bergen
Opening times: Daily
Admission charge: No

The public park at Nygård in Bergen was established by a private society in 1880. It covers nearly 7.5ha of undulating terrain with man-made lakes crossed by arching bridges, lush groves of rhododendrons, and many specimen trees of exotic origin such as monkey puzzles, cedars, *Betula ermanii* and others. In 1947 the park was given to the municipal parks department of Bergen.

Kristiansand: Ravnedalen
Owner: Municipality of Kristiansand
Opening times: Daily
Admission charge: No

This public park was established in the 1870s by General Oscar Wergeland, who used his soldiers for much of the landscaping. It is laid out around man-made lakes in a steep gorge enclosed by granite cliffs, an unusually romantic setting for the exceptionally fine trees – chiefly beeches and firs.

Oslo: Botanic Garden of Oslo University
23 Trondheimsvn, in W suburbs of city
Owner: University of Oslo
Opening times: Daily, summer 7–20; winter 7–17
Admission charge: No

The grounds were given to the university by King Frederick VI in 1812 and the botanic garden established in 1814. Many features of the original layout remain. There are 3,000 species and cultivars of trees and shrubs, an old palm house and a newly constructed rock garden with a great variety of alpine plants.

Rosendal Barony
Kvinnherad in Hardanger
Owner: University of Oslo
Opening times: Daily in summer
Admission charge: No

The old garden at Rosendal was laid out by a Flemish gardener around 1670 on the western side of a small baroque palace. This is one of the few gardens of its date to have survived in the north of Europe without major alterations. The parterre with its geometric patterns outlined by *c*.300-year-old box hedges is now a rose garden. A park in the gardenesque style was added to the estate in the middle of the 19th century and includes several large specimens of purple-leaved beech, holly, pine and cypress. The surrounding mountain scenery with glaciers and waterfalls provides a powerful contrast to the palace and gardens.

State Horticultural College
Dömmesmoen, near Grimstad, 50km NE of Kristiansand via E18
Owner: The State
Opening times: Daily
Admission charge: No

These well-kept gardens include herbaceous borders, rock gardens and an interesting collection of conifers and other trees and shrubs.

State Horticultural School

Râ, near Harstad in the Vesterålen Islands, NW of Narvik
Owner: The State
Opening times: Daily
Admission charge: No

Taking advantage of the mild coastal climate, this garden, one of the northernmost in the world, is situated far into the Arctic Circle at a latitude of nearly 69°N. It contains trees, shrubs and perennials suitable for sub-arctic conditions.

Svinviks Arboretum

Todalen, 50km E of Kristiansund, SW of Trondheim
Owner: University of Trondheim
Opening times: Daily, May to Sept
Admission charge: No

This 1ha woodland garden, set in the fjord country of north-west Norway, has a collection of conifers, bamboos and rhododendrons that is unique for such a northerly garden (63°N). The surroundings are dramatic, with fine views over the fjords.

Trondheim: Botanic Garden of Trondheim University

Ringve
Owner: University of Trondheim
Opening times: Daily
Admission charge: No

This botanical garden, newly designed by Professor Egil Gabrielsen, is still under construction. A series of garden compartments enclosed by a network of hedges has been completed for the systematic collections. The garden is surrounded by gently rolling country overlooking the sea. In the adjacent Ringve manor garden there are old beech trees of a remarkable size.

Sweden

Alnarp

10km N of Malmö
Owner: Agricultural University of Sweden
Opening times: Daily
Admission charge: No

A horticultural school was started here in the 1870s and the park and gardens originated at that time.

There is a woodland garden which benefits from naturally rich soil favourable for the growth of exotic trees and shrubs. Some of the specimens are the biggest examples in Sweden: *Sorbus domestica*, a swamp cypress (*Taxodium distichum*), *Magnolia × soulangeana* 'Alexandrina', *Magnolia acuminata*, and a weeping oak (*Quercus robur* 'Pendula'). In addition there are specialist gardens of fruit, vegetables and ornamental plants where scientific trials are carried out.

DBW Botanic Garden

Centre of Visby on island of Gotland
Owner: DBW Society
Opening times: Daily
Admission charge: No

DBW – 'The Bathing Friends' – is an old society in medieval Visby on the Baltic island of Gotland. In 1855 the society founded a botanic garden which, although small, is well stocked with interesting trees, shrubs and other plants which thrive in the relatively mild climate. Among the many curiosities is a tree unique in Sweden, the ash *Fraxinus excelsior coarctata*. The garden is ornamented with a ruined medieval building which gives it a romantic air.

Drottningholm ★

8km W of Stockholm
Owner: The State
Opening times: Daily
Admission charge: No

Drottningholm on the shores of Lake Mälaren has been the residence of queens since the 16th century. The palace and French-style baroque garden that are seen today were commissioned by the Dowager Queen Hedvig Eleonora in the late 17th century and were designed by Nicodemus Tessin, father and son. Although many details – not least the water parterre – are borrowed from foreign models, they nevertheless have the unity and beauty of a coherent work of art. The sculptures, both figures and urns, are of high quality. A superb 17th-century figure of Hercules, decorating a fountain, is by the Flemish sculptor Adrien de Vries. It and others were removed from the Wallenstein Garden in Prague (q.v.) in 1648.

South-east of the palace, in woodland laced with avenues and walks, there is 'Kina', a chinoiserie folly, with exquisite original interiors, made in 1763. It was visited by an English traveller, A. L. Hamilton, in 1767: 'Their majesties, with a select entourage, made their way at noon most days to China, a little pleasure palace ... The King worked at his lathe, the Queen listened to her reader ... the Princesses made lace, Prince Karl sailed a frigate, Prince Fredrik ran about in the fields, the guards smoked.'

After 1780 an English-style landscape park was designed by F. M. Piper on his return from England, where he had seen Stourhead (q.v.) and other landscape gardens. It is a good example of this style on a grand scale and adapted to northern conditions. It has winding streams, pools and a gothic tower. A novelty is a hill with rows of limes radiating from the top, a formal planting visible only from certain positions.

The king and queen now reside permanently in the palace and part of the garden is periodically closed to the public. The main area, however, is an immensely popular place of public recreation all the year round. A further attraction is the court theatre where opera is performed in the summer.

Fredriksdal Open-air Museum and Botanic Garden ❀

In outskirts of Helsingborg
Owner: Helsingborg Town
Opening times: Daily, 10–18
Admission charge: Yes

Fredriksdal is a combination of open-air museum and botanic garden, the latter consisting chiefly of the indigenous flora of Scania, grown partly by habitat and partly in systematic order. A charming rose garden, with many old shrub roses, shows what may be grown in southern Scandinavia. The museum contains different types of buildings – rural and urban.

Gothenburg: Botanic Garden ❀

In outskirts of the city
Owner: Gothenburg Town
Opening times: Daily 9–sunset
Admission charge: No

The botanical garden, founded in 1916 on attractive, undulating land, covers a vast area and has a varied and interesting collection of plants in both a garden proper and a nature park. The *garden* is divided into different collections – a pinetum, roses, a bamboo grove – linked by lawns with fine trees and shrubs. A valley of rhododendrons leads to a rock garden with many alpine plants – campanulas, gentians, saxifrages and lewisias – as well as primulas and meconopsis. Another valley is devoted to plants from Japan, many of which were collected by the botanic garden itself. Here are carefully-selected hardy plants. Hydrangeas, stewartias, trochodendrons, schizophragmas and many others show what may be grown successfully in this part of Sweden.

The *nature park* is partly uncultivated meadow, but an outer area contains many types of plants characteristic of the west coast of Sweden where the climate is relatively mild. Part of this is an arboretum with several exotic trees and shrubs including *Cercid-*

iphyllum japonicum, *Metasequoia glyptostroboides* and other species of great horticultural interest.

There are also systematic beds and modern glasshouses with tropical and subtropical plants (including a fine collection of orchids). The whole garden not only serves scientific and educational purposes but is at the same time a very beautiful and popular pleasure garden.

The old botanic garden at Uppsala showing the house where Linnaeus lived.

Gunnebo Manor

Mölndal, 6km S of Gothenburg (Göteborg) on E6
Owner: Mölndal Town
Opening times: Daily
Admission charge: No

In the last decades of the 18th century a wealthy Scottish merchant in Gothenburg, John Hall, commissioned a country house near the town. It was the creation of Carl Wilhelm Carlberg, an accomplished architect who designed a fine neo-classical house, all its contents and an extremely elegant baroque garden to go with it. All this has been restored since the 1950s with the help of hundreds of original drawings. The garden, on an axis with the house, consists of a series of formal enclosures, *bosquets* and pleached lime alleys and culminates, to the north, in a handsome oval pool with a fountain. It is embellished with many fine statues and urns. At Gunnebo, the garden, the house and its contents are all of high quality and should be seen as a single, remarkable whole.

Hammarby ★ ❀

6km SE of Uppsala via E4
Owner: The State
Opening times: Daily
Admission charge: No

Hammarby, the summer resort of Linnaeus (*see* Linnaeus Garden in Uppsala), still looks very much as it did in his day. He built the wooden manor house in 1769 and a small museum on a hilltop – 'my museum in the air', as he called it. Here he made a garden with the plants he specially loved, including an area called 'Siberia' in which Russian plants (a present from Catherine the Great) flourished. Among these are naturalized *Corydalis nobilis* with decorative yellow flowers that change to orange as they fade. All this is charming and unpretentious, but in Linnaeus's time scientists came here from all over Europe to visit the great naturalist.

Lund: Botanic Garden of Lund University ❀

Centre of town
Owner: The University of Lund
Opening times: Daily; *greenhouses* 12–15
Admission charge: No

The botanical garden of Lund University, in the centre of the old cathedral town, was founded in the late 17th century. Although chiefly intended for educational purposes and research, it is also a popular public garden. It contains about 7,000 species of plants from all parts of the world, outdoors and in conservatories. The collection of trees and shrubs is very good and thrives in the relatively mild climate of this southern province. Among noteworthy specimens are a *Ginkgo biloba* – the second biggest in the country – some tulip trees and Caucasian wingnuts (*Pterocarya fraxinifolia*). Bog, rock and herb gardens add to the interest of this charming place.

Rottneros Park

Rottneros, 5km S of Sunne, 60km N of Karlstad via Routes 61 and 234
Owner: A private trust
Opening times: Daily, May 9–17; June 9–19; Jul 8–19; Aug 9–18
Admission charge: Yes

Rottneros Park is situated high up with views over undulating countryside and an extensive lake. Laid out for the most part after 1945, it is an unusual mixture of styles, with formal vistas in a park in the English landscape tradition. Sculptures, mostly of a very high quality, are a great attraction. These are principally by 20th-century Scandinavian artists, but there are also some excellent copies of classical works.

Sandemar

30km east of Stockholm near the shores of the Baltic
Owner: Claes Braunerhjelm
Opening times: Daily
Admission charge: No

After the Thirty Years' War (1618–48), Sweden

enjoyed a period of affluent peace and noblemen built palaces with elaborate gardens. Owners of more modest estates followed the fashion but their houses were built of wood and their gardens were much smaller and few survived. Sandemar is a miraculously well-preserved example of such a place. It is approached by an *allée* aligned with the centre of the house, on the other side of which a terrace overlooks a baroque parterre edged with five rows of clipped limes. In the parterre the pyramids of clipped spruce (*Picea abies*) are now giants but little else has changed in 300 years. An imposing white-painted wooden figure of Neptune, insolent-looking *putti* and well-raked gravel help to convey a vivid impression of what a gentleman of that time could achieve with modest means in a harsh climate, while the reflected light of the sea nearby gives the place a special quality.

Stockholm: Haga Royal Park

N of city
Owner: The State
Opening times: Daily
Admission charge: No

Beautifully situated near a bay on the Baltic Sea, Haga was a favourite resort of the young king Gustavus III, who reigned from 1771–92. In this attractive countryside he found the ideal site for creating an English-style landscape garden and in 1785 he commissioned F. M. Piper to make a design. It is, after Drottningholm (q.v.), the second such garden to have been made in Sweden. In the taste of the time the park was embellished with several garden buildings, of which only a few survive – a Chinese pavilion, a Turkish kiosk, a *salon de treillage* and the ruined foundations of a never completed palace. The king's *Maison de Plaisance*, designed by O. Tempelman, is where Gustavus III spent his last night before being assassinated. These surviving buildings contribute much to the intended romantic and picturesque atmosphere.

Uppsala: Botanic Garden of Uppsala University ✳

8 Villavägen, town centre
Owner: Uppsala University
Opening times: Daily, summer 9–19; winter 9–15; *glasshouses* 10–12
Admission charge: No

Five terraces lead down from the royal palace, started in the 16th century, to a garden originally laid out in the 1660s. A century later it was reconstructed in the French baroque style and in 1787 Gustavus III gave it to Uppsala University to be used as a botanic garden to replace the Linnaeus garden (q.v.), which had become too small. It was stipulated that no change in the design should be allowed, so that to this day it has preserved formal beds arranged in systematic order, surrounded by hedges and pyramids of Norway spruce. A neo-classical orangery and greenhouses, part of the original gift, have also survived.

The adjoining modern botanic garden contains good collections of hostas, saxifrages and geraniums.

Uppsala: The Linnaeus Garden ✳

27 Svartbäcksgatan, near town centre
Owner: Uppsala University
Opening times: Daily
Admission charge: No

The Linnaeus garden, the Linnéträdgården, founded in the 1650s, was the first botanic garden in Uppsala. It was the most northerly botanic garden in the world. Under the directorship of Carl Linnaeus it became from 1741 a European centre of plant studies. Linnaeus devised a system of rigorously scientific nomenclature for all living organisms; in the realm of botany his *Species plantarum* (1753) is a foundation stone of plant classification.

In its heyday, the garden had about 4,000 species of plants and a small zoo, but by the end of the 18th century it had become too small and another botanic garden was created. In the 1920s and 1930s the site was partly reconstructed to resemble its appearance in Linnaeus's time. The adjoining house, where he lived and died, is now a museum. The garden today, redolent of the genius of Linnaeus, is of great historic interest.

Austria

With two-thirds of the country in the eastern Alps, where peaks rise to over 3,000m, Austria's gardens are concentrated in the western lowlands of Vorarlberg, in the hilly, wooded countryside which merges eastward with the Hungarian plain, and in the gently undulating landscape of northern Austria which rises on the other side of the Danube to the mountains of Bohemia. The climate is mainly continental with hot summers (cooler in the mountains), a long autumn and snowy, cold winters. The average rainfall is 1,200–1,500mm per annum. Yew and box have always been used for hedging and typical avenues are of chestnut, hornbeam and lime, with more varied parkland planting that includes maples, *Robinia pseudacacia* (which has become naturalized here as in most of the rest of Europe), oak, ash, beech and elm. Conifers are restricted to Siberian pines, larch and fir. The climate is too cold for the Italian cypress.

The development of gardens in Austria dates from the renaissance period when the Habsburgs were not only Holy Roman emperors, influential in all Catholic countries, but had world-wide connections with access to new plant introductions. Towards the end of the 16th century the botanist Clusius (Charles de l'Ecluse) was prefect of the imperial gardens in Vienna. It was he who introduced the horse chestnut and the potato and first described the flora of Austria and Hungary. Through his contacts and those of the Empire, lilacs and lilies from the Middle East were grown in Vienna for the first time in Europe. The first gardens made in Austria were influenced by Italian styles, in particular the famous garden at Hellbrunn in Salzburg (q.v.), built 1615–18, and gardens in Carinthia (Kärnten) and Vorarlberg. Later, after the expulsion of the Turks in 1699 and the end of the subsequent wars, Austrian baroque architecture and garden design reached its peak, with grander French-style layouts becoming all the rage. Architects such as J. B. Fischer von Erlach and Lukas von Hildebrandt built palaces, and the gardens which were firmly linked with them, for the aristocracy. In the second half of the 18th century a more naturalistic style was adopted, based on a French interpretation of the English landscape movement. The larger gardens often contained a series of eclectic picturesque buildings, while new

PREVIOUS PAGES **The restored *bosquet* with clipped yew pyramids and gilt statues in the formal baroque garden at Herrenhausen.**

244

planting of trees and shrubs throughout the 19th century followed a 'romantic' theme. Social changes after World Wars I and II led to a decline in the condition of many gardens, although the most important have become tourist attractions. Recently, gardens deemed to be of historic importance have been listed and there are encouraging signs of a new interest in historical restoration.

Doblhoffpark

Baden town centre, 32km S of Vienna, off A2 or Route 17
Owner: Stadtgemeinde Baden
Opening times: At all times
Admission charge: No

The once formal garden of Schloss Weikersdorf (now a hotel) was partially landscaped by its Doblhoff owners at the beginning of the 19th century. The parterre in front of the orangery is now planted with roses and the garden itself holds the national rose collection.

Schloss Ehrnegg

St Kollmann, S of Griffen, 30km E of Klagenfurt
Owner: Edgar Piskernik
Opening times: By appointment, St Kollmann, A9112 Griffen, Kärnten
Admission charge: No

None of the gardens for which Carinthia was famous in the 16th and 17th centuries has survived and they are known only from prints and descriptions (Valvasor praised the beauty of this garden in the 17th century). So a private restoration is a major undertaking, and work has begun. The site belongs to one of those little renaissance castles typical of the region. The original wall, terraces and two gazebos still exist, and excavation has revealed the outline of the garden.

Schlosspark Eisenstadt

Eisenstadt, 50km S of Vienna
Owner: Paul Fürst Esterházy
Opening times: At all times
Admission charge: No

This romantic landscape park stretching up the hill from Schloss Eisenstadt dates from 1805, when Prince Anton Esterházy first landscaped his formal gardens. It became the most famous garden in Hungary (to which it belonged until 1919). The facade of the palace was classicized to harmonize with the Leopoldinentempel built high on a rock in honour of Esterházy's daughter. From here a cascade, crossed by bridges, tumbles across the park to an informal pond which was once a geometric *bassin* in the original design. An orangery on a high terrace is another survival from this earlier period. The landscape, although neglected, still retains much that is beautiful, with surprise views and groups of mature trees. Haydn spent many of his last years at Eisenstadt and in 1792–3 he introduced the young Beethoven to Prince Anton Esterházy. A full restoration of the park has begun.

Graz: Schloss Eggenberg

3km W of city centre
Owner: Land Steiermark
Opening times: 8–sunset
Admission charge: Yes

At the end of the long Eggenberger Allee a delightful rococo gate opens into a landscape park with deer, peacocks and other colourful birds. Contemporary prints show a rectangular renaissance garden separated from the palace (begun 1625), but a new baroque garden was laid out in 1750. A simple forecourt, the twelve gates in the encircling wall and a pavilion date from after 1763; these survived when the garden was remodelled in 1860. The landscape park has fine specimen trees which were planted only in the middle of the 19th century, although an earlier apocryphal painting in the Hunting Room shows Eggenberg framed and half hidden behind mighty trees.

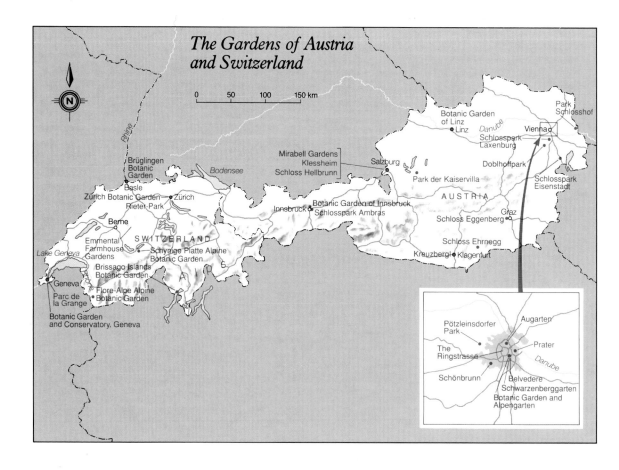

The Gardens of Austria and Switzerland

Innsbruck: Schlosspark Ambras

In the SE outskirts of the city on road to Aldrans; E of
River Inn
Owner: Republik Österreich
Opening times: 6–sunset
Admission charge: No

The renaissance castle of Ambras, dominating the
romantic scenery, lies at the foot of the mountain
range south-east of Innsbruck. Built 1564–7 by the
Archduke Ferdinand II for his consort Philippine
Welser, it was his summer residence as well as
housing his art collections. A formal garden must
have existed at this time (see 17th-century engravings by Merian), but the park was remodelled from
1854 and now has two distinct schemes: a romantic
landscape park complete with a grotto and a cascade

in a gorge; and formal lawns, box-edged flowerbeds
and roses near the entrance to the lower castle
courtyard.

Innsbruck: Botanic Garden of Innsbruck University

W suburb of Innsbruck-Hötting
Owner: Innsbruck University
Opening times: Daily sunrise–sunset; *conservatories*
Thurs 13–16, 1st Sun in month
Admission charge: No

Innsbruck's first botanic garden was established in
1793 in the old Jesuit Collegium. It was revived in the
second half of the 19th century when Anton Kerner
von Marilaun installed a miniature Tyrolean landscape; by 1880 it contained the most complete

collection of alpine plants in Europe. The garden was moved to its present suburban site in 1909. Here, in a restricted space, medicinal, culinary and poisonous plants grow in beds in front of a new conservatory (not always open); the alpinum has been recently reorganized.

Park der Kaiservilla

On S slope of Mount Jainzen, Bad Ischl, 56km SE of
Salzburg on Route 158
Owner: Private
Opening times: Daily 8–17
Admission charge: Yes

In 1854 the Archduchess Sophie gave this Bieder-meier villa to her son, the Emperor Franz-Josef, as a wedding present. From 1855–80 the Emperor and his gardener Franz Rauch developed the garden in naturalistic style on the slopes of Mount Jainzen. Indigenous and exotic trees frame mountain views. A small 19th-century lattice-work pavilion, a kiosk and the picturesque Marmorschlössl, a *cottage orné* of 1869, are hidden among the groves of trees. The Emperor's intention was not to compete with the grandeur of the mountain views, but rather to enhance their splendour.

Klagenfurt: Kreuzbergl

Neuer Platz
Owner: Landeshauptstadt Klagenfurt
Opening times: At all times
Admission charge: No

For 400 years the site of the little chapel (Kreuzbergl) at the foot of the hill at the end of Radetzky Strasse was praised for its natural beauty and the views to the Karawanken mountains. In 1850 terraces were built to celebrate a visit from the Emperor. A Swiss cottage was added in 1852. Today, the informal park with its ponds and woodland is a popular spot. There is an interesting small botanical rock garden in an old quarry, where Mediterranean plants thrive in a favourable microclimate.

The Temple of Diana at Schlosspark Laxenburg, one of many garden features.

Schlosspark Laxenburg

16km S of Vienna, E of Mödling on Route 16 to Eisenstadt
Owner: Stadt Wien
Opening times: Daily sunrise–sunset
Admission charge: Yes

South of Vienna at the foot of the Wienerwald the Laxenburg park stretches into the flat Pannonian plain. From the 14th century it was a favourite imperial hunting ground. The moated castle suffered during the Turkish invasions and gardening on a grand scale only became possible after 1700 as the Turks retreated. Of the formal gardens created under Maria Theresa, only the mall, marching rigidly through the now landscaped park, and the trellis-work pavilion of 1753 in the centre of the radial hunting alleys are left. The formal garden was redesigned from 1780–1811, first by Le Februe d'Archambault in 1782–3, with winding paths and natural plantings reminiscent of Ermenonville (q.v.) in France, and then, 1794–1811, by Ludwig de Traux, who added ponds and streamlets, cascades and bridges, a grotto and other garden buildings. The little River Schwechat runs through the grounds and feeds the vast lake where the neo-gothic Fran-

zensburg (1798–1801) on an island now provides the main focus of the garden. The grotto, the gothic bridge, the tournament field, the Knight's Column and the Knight's Bury symbolize romantic ideals of medieval chivalry. Everything is immaculately maintained and run as a commercial enterprise. The garden tends to be overcrowded on fine weekends.

Linz: Botanic Garden

W part of town
Owner: Stadt Linz
Opening times: Daily 8–sunset; *conservatories* 8–12, 13–16
Admission charge: Yes

Opened only in 1952, the garden has an interesting layout and a romantic charm. Typical Austrian plants, orchids, other tropical specimens, and a collection of cacti flourish here. There is also a 12ha arboretum.

The marble Knight's Column at Schlosspark Laxenburg.

Salzburg: Schloss Hellbrunn ★

SE of city centre via Hellbrunner Strasse and Hellbrunn Allee
Owner: Stadt Salzburg
Opening times: Daily, *park* 9–sunset; *waterworks* (guided tours only) Apr, Oct 9–16.30; May, Sept 9–17.30; Jun to Aug 9–18.30
Admission charge: *park* no; *waterworks* yes

This was the only notable garden to be built in Austria before the defeat of the Turks in 1699. Markus Sittikus von Hohenems, Archbishop of Salzburg, had spent many years in Italy before commissioning Santino Solari to build the palace (1613–15), which resembles an Italian villa. The garden was laid out 1615–18 and Markus Sittikus also enlarged a pre-1425 *Tiergarten* (menagerie) and built a series of temples and grottoes with concealed water jokes (*Wasserspiele*), many of which survive, a Neptune grotto containing singing birds, a Midas grotto like that at the Eremitage in West Germany (q.v.), and a Roman theatre with a stone table and central water channel like that of the Villa Lante in Italy (q.v.). An amphitheatre, the Felsentheater, was carved out of the quarry from which stone for the castle was obtained (here the first open-air opera to be performed north of the Alps was presented in 1617 – Monteverdi's *L'Orfeo*). The style of the amphitheatre was copied at the Eremitage (q.v.) and at Sanspareil (q.v.) near Bayreuth in the 1740s.

In the 1730s the gardens were simplified by F. A. Danreiter, and at the end of the century an English landscape park was laid out to one side of the castle. All is in good condition today, with surviving pools, parterres, orangery and statuary.

Salzburg: Klessheim

W outskirts of city between autobahn and Saalach river
Owner: Land Salzburg
Opening times: At all times
Admission charge: No

The palace was built 1700–32 to plans by J. B. Fischer von Erlach. The formal garden was restored after World War II and the statuary gathered from other gardens.

Salzburg: Mirabell Gardens (N part now the Kurgarten)

Mirabellplatz and Makartplatz
Owner: Stadt Salzburg
Opening times: Daily sunrise–sunset
Admission charge: Yes

For many visitors the view over this colourful formal garden to Salzburg's medieval fortress on its rocky hill captures the essence of the city. The garden was first laid out for Salome Alt, mistress of Archbishop Wolfdietrich von Raitenau, in 1606. A new palace and garden were designed in about 1690, probably by J. B. Fischer von Erlach and Ottavio Mosto, and this baroque layout with parterres, statuary, fountains, pools and a maze was again remodelled, 1721–7, by Lukas von Hildebrandt, the most distinguished Austrian exponent of the grander French style. The early 18th-century architectural framework still survives and fine contemporary statues and vases are set off by bright bedding-out schemes (pansies in spring and begonias in summer). An open-air theatre, designed 1710–18 by Matthias Diesl, is still used for performances.

Park Schlosshof

70km E of Vienna, on Route 49 N of Hainburg/Niederösterreich crossing of the River Danube
Owner: Republik Österreich
Opening times: By appointment, Bundesbaudirektion Wien, Kärntner Ring 9–13, A 1015 Wien

The splendour of the garden designed by Lukas von Hildebrandt in 1725 is best seen in the paintings of Bernardo Bellotto. Only the terrace in front of the *sala terrena*, with its *nymphaeum*, has been restored. From here can be seen the main axis leading down to the wrought-iron gates, 1731, by J. G. Oegg.

Vienna: Augarten

Across the Danube canal by the Schwedenbrücke
Owner: Republik Österreich
Opening times: 6–sunset
Admission charge: No

The old imperial hunting ground was opened to the public in 1775 after being planted with 400 lime trees and 200 beeches. The park next to it became the first garden in landscape style to be designed for the Emperor Joseph II.

Vienna: Belvedere ★

Main entrances Rennweg or Prinz Eugenstrasse, SE of city centre
Owner: Republik Österreich
Opening times: 6–sunset
Admission charge: No

This, the most important of Austria's baroque gardens, links the two palaces built outside the city walls as a summer retreat for Prince Eugene of Savoy. Designed by Lukas von Hildebrandt in collaboration with Dominique Girard, a pupil of André Le Nôtre, the Lower Belvedere was erected 1713–16 as private apartments, and the Upper Belvedere 1721–32 for official entertaining. To understand fully the symbolism of the whole scheme (gardens and buildings), it is important to visit the splendid interiors of these princely palaces and appreciate the fine views from their windows, as well as the garden itself. The underlying theme is man's journey from darkness to the divine light of eternity. From a parterre and shady *bosquet* on the flat ground in front of the Lower Belvedere, a central cascade leads the eye up the slope to the Upper Belvedere. Flights of steps framing the water are copies of the famous Stairs to Heaven in Peking. Statues support the theme and a vast *bassin* provides water for the cascade and reflects the south facade of the upper palace. There are plans for much-needed restoration.

Vienna: Botanic Garden and Alpengarten

Botanic garden: Mechelgasse off Rennweg; *Alpengarten*: Landstrasser Gürtel
Owner: Republik Österreich
Opening times: Mid Apr to Sept 9–sunset
Admission charge: *Botanic garden* no; *Alpengarten* yes

The *botanic garden* is traditionally associated with the botanist Clusius (*see* Botanic Garden of Leiden) who, while prefect of the imperial gardens in Vienna from 1573–7, received seeds and bulbs of tulips and other

Bellotto's painting (1759–60) shows the parterres at the palace of Schönbrunn.

rarities through Ogier Ghiselin de Busbecq, imperial ambassador to the Turkish court in Constantinople, and distributed them widely throughout Europe. The Empress Maria Theresa bought the present site outside the city walls near the Belvedere (q.v.) in 1754; she installed Nikolaus von Jacquin as director in 1768, and he was succeeded by his son. The regular-shaped flowerbeds from this period have been replaced by a more naturalistic style. There are 19th-century conservatories and a modern rock garden is under construction. One area, the charming Host'sche Garten, belonged to Nikolaus Wilhelm Host, physician to the emperor and a keen collector of Austrian native flowers.

The famous *Alpengarten* next door was originally in the Tyrolean garden on the hill of the Gloriette at Schönbrunn (q.v.), where a Swiss cottage marks the position; it was started by the Habsburg Archduke Johann in 1803, and in 1865 was moved to the present site. Miniature mountain scenery was constructed to simulate alpine conditions. Some plants survive from 1803 in spite of wartime neglect. Today there are displays of European alpine flora and of appropriate plants from other regions of the world.

Vienna: Pötzleinsdorfer Park
Entrance from Geymullergasse or Potzleinsdorfer Strasse; NW of city centre
Owner: Stadt Wien
Opening times: Daily 7–sunset
Admission charge: No

The park was redesigned by Konrad Rosenthal in the early 19th century. Some lovely sculptures and obelisks enhance the woodland garden with its alleys, groves and huge specimen trees.

Vienna: The Ringstrasse

Encircling the old city centre
Owner: Republik Österreich
Opening times: Daily sunrise–sunset
Admission charge: No

A remarkable project started in 1857 to provide public parks on the site of the old city walls, which were razed to the ground on the orders of the Emperor Franz-Josef so the city could be linked to its suburbs. Ludwig Forster was responsible for the earliest plans for the Ringstrasse, which includes the Burggarten, the Rathauspark, the Stadtpark and the Volksgarten.

CENTRE **The cascade linking the two palaces in Vienna's baroque Belvedere gardens.**

BELOW **The 17th-century garden at Schloss Hellbrunn was inspired by Italian renaissance layouts. Although simplified in the 1730s, some of the original features survive.**

Vienna: Prater

On an island in the Danube; NE of city centre via Schwedenbrücke and Praterstrasse; U1 to Praterstern
Owner: Stadt Wien
Opening times: At all times
Admission charge: No

The Prater is laid out on an island encircled by two arms of the Danube. Originally the emperor's hunting ground, it is traversed by an avenue 4.5km long for which the first chestnuts were planted in 1537. The octagonal Lusthaus at the end of this avenue, and the central focus of other radiating alleys, was originally a hunting lodge but was remodelled in 1781, fifteen years after the park was opened to the public. Today most visitors see only the main park, much of which is used for sport and exhibitions, but round the perimeter there is a quiet hidden landscape of trees, meadows and water.

Vienna: Schönbrunn ★

SW of city centre; U4 from Karlsplatz
Owner: Republik Österreich
Opening times: 6–sunset; *conservatory* summer 9–18;
winter 10–16.30
Admission charge: *Conservatory* yes

The Habsburgs had a hunting lodge here from 1540, but the castle and garden of Schönbrunn were not begun until after the Turkish defeat in 1699. Franz I commissioned J. B. Fischer von Erlach to create an imitation of Versailles and Von Erlach's plan of 1695 was carried out, with the help of the French garden designer Jean Trehet, by 1714. The original *parterre de broderie*, although planted now in bright 19th-century style, retains Trehet's basic outline. During Maria Theresa's reign Trehet's garden was further extended in the French manner: a *Tiergarten* or menagerie was added in 1752, and the Gloriette as a focal point on the hill to the south in 1775. This classical colonnade is set in woods cut by

An 18th-century engraving by Le Rouge shows the intricate baroque detail of the French-style parterres at the Schwartzenberggarten in Vienna.

formal avenues lined with walls of trees. Less well-known are the gardens on either side of the palace – an orangery to the east and the still important botanical garden to the west, started as a Dutch garden in 1753 where Nikolaus von Jacquin, Richard van der Schott and Franz Boos planted newly-introduced exotics. A huge 19th-century palm house is being restored.

Vienna: Schwarzenberggarten

Schwarzenbergplatz, SE of city centre
Owner: Fürst Schwarzenberg
Opening times: For guests of Palais Schwarzenberg Hotel or by appointment, Fürst-Schwarzenbergische Verwaltung, Rennweg 2, A 1030 Wien

First laid out by Jean Trehet in 1697, the garden was altered by J. B. Fischer von Erlach in 1720. The formal terraces and great water basin (spoiled by a tennis court) escaped the late 18th-century craze for landscaping. The garden appears in Bernardo Bellotto's *View from the Upper Belvedere* in the Kunsthistorisches Museum in Vienna. Much of the garden is overlooked by the Palais Schwarzenberg Hotel in a wing of the baroque palace.

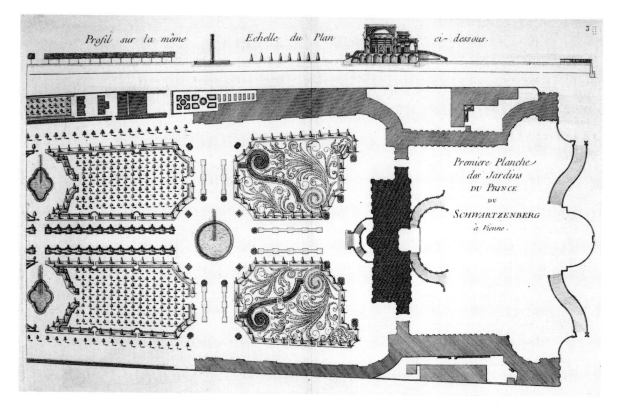

Profil sur la même *Echelle du Plan* *ci-dessous.*

Premiere Planche des Jardins DU PRINCE DU SCHWARTZENBERG à Vienne.

Switzerland

For map, see p.246.

Switzerland has never been a garden country. This is partly a reflection of the geography and climate, since the major part of the country consists of mountains and the climate is extreme, with hot summers and very cold winters. Nor have there been princely courts or large landed-gentry estates. Of the few baroque gardens created under the influence of neighbouring France, practically none has survived; most were swept away in the first half of the 19th century by the fashion for English landscape parks. Towards the end of the century numerous public parks and promenades were laid out in the same style, and these still adorn towns and lakeside resorts. Around Berne and in other parts of central Switzerland, typical farmhouse gardens going back to renaissance and baroque traditions are still well preserved.

The Swiss Alps with their wonderful flora have always attracted plant enthusiasts from near and far – so much so that many alpines are now threatened with extinction. Thus alpine gardens and the alpine sections of Swiss botanic gardens today also play an important part in conservation.

The plan preserved in the St Gall abbey library, dated AD 816, is the earliest evidence of garden design in Switzerland. This famous Carolingian master plan for monastic settlements shows the layout and plants of a vegetable garden, orchard and medicinal herb garden. Swiss garden design today reflects limited and high-priced building space. There is an increasing interest in wild gardens as a reaction to the pressure on the natural environment and enthusiasm for plants and gardening in general is lively.

Basle: Brüglingen Botanic Garden ✺
5 St Alban Vorstadt, Brüglingen
Owner: AG Botanischer Garten in Brüglingen
Opening times: Daily 8–sunset
Admission charge: No

Brüglingen Botanic Garden was created in 1968 in part of the Brüglingen estate bequeathed to the city of Basle by its last owner, Christoph Merian, in 1858. An area of 13ha includes the Vorder-Brüglingen farm as well as the Villa Merian, a 19th-century summer residence with its English landscape park.

Among the many features of this beautiful site are a maze designed for plant identification, a garden showing culinary plants, a bog garden, dry banks with silver-leaved plants, and collections of roses, *Campanulaceae* and *Umbelliferae*. A shady valley accommodates a large number of rhododendrons, and some 120 different clematis are displayed in a meadow meandering between tall trees. The iris collection presented by Baroness von Stein-Zeppelin, with some 1,400 species and varieties, is outstanding.

Christoph Merian's favourite garden features were

ornamental pot plants, and an impressive number of large tubs filled with non-hardy flowering and fruiting plants still adorn the farm buildings built by Melchior Berri in the last century. The citrus fruits, small palm trees, myrtles, laurels, figs, pomegranates, eucalyptus and oleanders, as well as countless geraniums, fuchsias and begonias, were already listed in an inventory of the Brüglingen orangery in Christoph Merian's day.

The adjoining Unter-Brüglingen farm is another complex of beautiful historic buildings with an old mill and an orangery. There is also a large medicinal and herb garden with some 300 species and varieties, which was created for the Swiss Horticultural Exhibition held here in 1980.

Brissago Islands: Botanic Garden ❀

Lake Maggiore; boat from Locarno or Ronco
Owner: Canton of Ticino
Opening times: Daily, Apr to mid Oct 9–18
Admission charge: Yes

This is the only Swiss botanical garden south of the Alps. It lies in the region around the Italian lakes known as Insubria, where the particularly mild climate reflects a sheltered position at the southern foot of the Alps and the moderating effect of the lakes, which warm their surroundings in winter and cool them in summer. Brissago's annual mean temperature is 12.8°C, with an average of fifteen days of frost when the temperature falls to − 5°C at most.

In 1885 the Russian-born Baroness St Leger bought the islands and laid out the gardens on the larger San Pancrazio (c.25ha), creating botanical landscapes according to the geographical provenance of the plants. This original intention is still followed when new plantings are added. The Canton of Ticino purchased the islands in 1950 and opened San Pancrazio to the public.

The neo-classical villa, on the highest point of the island, gives on to a terrace with a splendid collection of citrus trees. Below it lies a pond with subtropical aquatic plants surrounded by a jungle of palm trees. A path through rhododendrons and azaleas leads to a walled pool garden with herb borders, beyond which grow bamboos, 100-year-old eucalyptus, proteas, grevilleas, agaves and opuntias. From the eastern end of the island a long pergola walk leads back to the villa past swamp cypresses growing by the lakeside.

Emmental Farmhouse Gardens

Emmental, Canton of Berne

The traditional Swiss farmhouse garden with its formal box-edged beds still survives in the Emmental valley. Its roots lie in the medieval monastery garden, the *giardino segreto* of the Italian Renaissance and the French baroque garden.

A rectangular piece of land in front of the house

was fenced off from the surrounding farmland to protect the vegetables and medicinal and culinary herbs grown in it. Eventually it became more ornamental through the addition of cottage flowers. Similarly, a simple layout with four squares sep-

At Schynige Platte, only Swiss native plants are grown in the calcareous scree. At an altitude of 2,000 m, the view of the Alps is breathtaking.

arated by a cross path gradually became more elaborate, with more intricate divisions, although always symmetrical in design. The semi-circular gable of the house was often reflected in a central round flower-bed. Today, low wooden fences allow the passer-by to admire vegetables, herbs and flowers grown in beautiful patterns and neat rows.

In the area around Burgdorf and Langnau the following villages have particularly attractive farmhouse gardens: Heimiswil, Busswil, Lützelflüh, Rüderswil, Ranflüh, Zollbrück, Signau and Trub.

Flore-Alpe Alpine Botanic Garden ⊛
Above Champex-Lac, S of Martigny, Valais
Owner: Fondation J. M. Aubert. Responsibility for
garden: Universities of Geneva and Neufchâtel
Opening times: May to Sept, Tues–Sat 10–12
Admission charge: Yes

Flore-Alpe, situated above the picturesque small lake
of Champex at a height of 1,500m, was created by the
industrialist J. M. Aubert in 1927 as a private garden
to surround his mountain chalet. For the last thirty
years Egidio Anchisi, an outstanding and dedicated
alpine specialist, has been in charge of the garden and
responsible for the very high standard of upkeep.

Flore-Alpe's dramatically steep site has been exploited by sophisticated waterworks feeding several
pools connected by cascades, with bridges leading
from one to another, and by elaborate man-made
rockeries and ornamental details. The 1ha site is
superbly planted with over 3,000 species, with alpines from all over the world growing in spectacular
combinations. The garden's two most important
collections are the comprehensive European sections
of auriculas and sempervivums. There are also
substantial collections of gentians, saxifrages,
conifers, alpine rhododendrons and species roses, all
grown from seed collected in the wild. The sound of
running water is heard throughout the garden and
adds to the many visual delights.

Geneva: Botanic Garden and Conservatory ⊛
1 Chemin de l'Impératrice, Chambésy
Owner: City of Geneva
Opening times: *Garden* daily, summer 7–18.30, winter
9–17; *glasshouses* daily 9–11, 14–16.30, except Fri;
conservatory daily 7.45–12, 13.30–17
Admission charge: No

The first botanical garden in Geneva was founded in
1817 by the botanist Augustin de Candolle on the site
of the present Parc des Bastions. At the turn of the
century it was moved to Chambésy, where, following
the garden's long tradition of outstanding alpine
collections, a new alpine garden was opened to the
public in 1902. In the 1880s the expert alpine
gardener Henry Correvon was in charge of the alpine
garden and to this day the alpine section is the most
attractive feature of the garden. It covers 1ha, with
some 115 geographical groups grown on different
types of rockeries, ravines and slopes, separated by
countless meandering rivulets and small tracks. One
particularly interesting hillock shows all the protected plants of the Swiss alpine flora.

The botanic garden, extending over 12ha, commands impressive views to the lake and mountains
beyond. Its many features include an arboretum, a
collection of rhododendrons, a pond with aquatic
plants, borders showing culinary and medicinal
plants, an orangery and various glasshouses, including the spectacular round Mediterranean house,
covered in glass resembling shiny soap bubbles.

Geneva: Parc de la Grange
Quai Gustave Ador
Owner: City of Geneva
Opening times: Daily sunrise–sunset
Admission charge: No

In the last century remnants of a Roman habitation
were found in the upper part of La Grange. The
present Louis XV-style house dates from *c.*1770 and
its French classical gardens were fashionably remodelled in the first half of the 19th century as an English
landscape park. William Favre, the last owner of La
Grange, bequeathed the whole estate of some 20ha to
the city of Geneva in 1917, with the proviso that it
should remain unaltered and become a public park.

Owing to a plentiful supply of underground water,
the trees of La Grange have reached exceptionally
large dimensions; among them a cedar of Lebanon
near the house, and imposing groups of sophoras,
planes, pines and oaks. Behind the farm buildings a
large area has been turned into a nursery garden,
which provides most of the bedding-out plants for
Geneva's municipal gardens.

In 1945 a hexagonal rose garden, the largest in
Switzerland, was established in the lower part of the
estate, with 12,000 plants of some 200 varieties.
Attractive pergolas and pools enhance the layout.
The international rose growers' competition takes
place every June on the rose trial grounds in the
upper park.

La Grange is separated from the lake shore by the
main road, but many vantage points offer superb
views over Lake Geneva.

Schynige Platte Alpine Botanic Garden ❀

Schynige Platte, next to rack-railway station; 1 hr via rack-railway from Wilderswil S of Interlaken
Owner: Verein Alpengarten Schynige Platte
Opening times: Daily, mid Jun to mid Sept (depending on snow conditions) 8–18
Admission charge: Yes

The Alpine Garden was opened in 1929 and is unique in as much as it contains Swiss native alpines only, assembled here on a site of outstanding natural beauty. Several plant groups were present before the garden was created and now form the nucleus of the collection, to which flowering Swiss alpines not native to the Schynige Platte area have been added, together representing some 500 species out of the 620 known flowering plants and ferns found above the treeline in the Swiss Alps.

At an altitude of 1,950–2,000m, the garden covers an area of 8,300sq m, with a breathtaking view across the valley to the peaks of the Bernese Alps. On average it is without snow for 150 days in the year. The most spectacular time to visit is during the alpine spring in early July, though early August sees the greatest number of flowering plants in bloom.

Zürich: Botanic Garden of Zürich University ❀

107 Zollikerstrasse
Owner: Zürich University
Opening times: Mar to Sept, weekdays 7–18, Sat, Sun 8–18; Oct to Feb, weekdays 8–18, Sat, Sun 8–17; *glasshouses* daily 9.30–11.30, 13–16
Admission charge: No

The earliest botanical garden known in Zürich was that of Konrad Gesner, created *c.*1560. Gesner, one of the founders of scientific botany, historian and doctor, wrote *Horti Germaniae* in 1559. In 1834 the first University Botanic Garden was established in the Park zur Katz, from where it was moved to its present more spacious site, the old Schönau park, in 1977. The 5.3ha area is now dominated by the modern building housing the university's Institutes of Systematic Botany and Plant Biology.

The plant collections were carefully integrated into the existing garden with its old trees and undulating site. A brook cascades across an alpine garden arranged in geographical sections behind the Institutes' building, the pond into which it runs is now home to a large number of aquatic plants. Mediterranean plants – rock roses, wormwood, lavender, sage, thyme, rosemary, tarragon and hyssop – thrive on the sheltered south-facing slope in front of the building. There is also a dry, stony river-bed for other drought-loving plants, with striking specimens of the bitter orange, *Poncirus trifoliata*, the only citrus plant which can survive Swiss winters in the open. Other parts of the garden include a copse and flower meadows, a heather garden, and comprehensive collections of medicinal and culinary plants and plants used for dyeing. Three spectacular dome-shaped glasshouses of American design shelter tropical plants, subtropical species and plants of the savannah.

Zürich: Rieter-Park

Seestrasse
Owner: Municipality of Zürich
Opening times: Daily sunrise–sunset
Admission charge: No

Zürich's most beautiful English landscape garden was laid out in the 1850s by Theodor Froebel. The neo-classical villa was built at the same time by Leonhard Zeugheer for Froebel's employer, the Rhenish silk merchant Otto Wesendonck. The house became a centre of Zürich social and cultural life. Richard Wagner was a neighbour and a close friend and here Mathilde Wesendonck inspired him to write and compose *Tristan und Isolde*, which he is known to have read to her in a secluded corner of the garden.

Froebel laid out a large pleasure-ground with gently curving paths south of the house and planted clumps of trees on the slopes of the Rietberg hill beyond, a former vineyard. The original vistas over the lake and, on clear days, views to the snow-covered Alps down the main axis towards the south are now concealed by trees, but the terraces at the far corners of the pleasure ground remind one of these earlier delights. Today the park represents one of Zürich's most precious dendrological collections, with many rare specimens. The villa houses the Rietberg Museum of non-European figurative art.

West Germany

The Federal Republic of Germany stretches a vast distance from the North and Baltic seas in the north to the Alps in the south. The climate is maritime in north-west Germany and up to the border with Denmark; in the south-east, east and in the mountains it shows continental extremes, with average mean temperatures in January and February below 0°C. The mildest climates for gardening are in the southern river valleys, along the Rhine and the Main. Spring travels north down the Rhine from Lake Constance (and the Island of Mainau, q.v.), arriving four weeks later in the north-eastern part of the country.

One of the earliest sources of an aesthetic attitude towards flowers and gardening is Walafrid Strabo's poem *Hortulus*, written at Reichenau on Lake Constance in 840. Charlemagne's *Capitulare de Villis*, drawn up in about 800, provides us with a list of plants which could have been grown in early German gardens. In about 1260 Albertus Magnus, Count of Bollstadt in Swabia, who had studied at the university in Padua and entered the Dominican order, wrote a treatise on vegetables and plants to which he appended a chapter on designing pleasure gardens. Details in 13th- and 14th-century illuminated manuscripts, tapestries and paintings show flowers growing in turf (flowery meads) inside castle enclosures, with rose arbours and trellis-work features. By the 16th century botany had become a subject of interest to princes as well as to scholars and doctors.

The first great renaissance garden was the Hortus Palatinus at Heidelberg (q.v.). From 1615, terraces, grottoes, fountains, water parterres and elaborate musical hydraulic systems that were essentially Italian renaissance in spirit were designed and described by Salomon de Caus above the River Neckar. After the Thirty Years War (1618–48), the new baroque style of Vaux-le-Vicomte (q.v.) and Versailles (q.v.) was imported from France, but without slavish imitation. Many of the surviving great early 18th-century German gardens have highly individualistic features with radiating star shapes, transverse axes, or even circular designs which prepared the way for a change of emphasis towards the end of the century, when strict formality gave way to more naturalistic and picturesque motifs. Amongst the most important designers of English landscape-type gardens were Friedrich Ludwig von Sckell, Peter Josef Lenné and Prince Hermann Pückler-Muskau (*see* Introduction to East Germany), all of whom have had lasting

The Gardens of West Germany

0   50   100   150 km

N

Louisenlund

Kiel
Kiel
Botanic
Garden

Rosarium Uetersen
Hamburg
Schlosspark
Lütetsburg
Hamburg
Botanic Garden

Schlosspark Rastede

Rhododendron
Waldpark
Nursery Hobbie
Bremen
Botanic Garden and
Rhododendron Park

Clemenswerth
Bürgerpark

North Germany

West Berlin
Schlosspark Tegel
Berlin
Bundes-Gartenschaupark
1985
Schlosspark Charlottenburg
Pfaueninsel
Klein-Glienicke
Berlin-Dahlem
Botanic Garden

Hanover
Herrenhausen

Schlosspark Ahaus
Münster

Schlosspark Nordkirchen

Dortmund
Old Botanic Garden, Göttingen
Göttingen

Düsseldorf
Schloss
Dyck
Schloss Benrath
Kassel
Karlsaue
Cologne
Flora and Botanic Garden
of Cologne
Bergpark Wilhelmshöhe

Bonn
Bonn Botanic Garden
The Harle Garden and Arboretum
Giessen
Botanic Garden

Burggarten Stolzenfels

South-West and
West
Germany
Kurpark, Bad Homburg
Palmengarten
Frankfurt

Prinz-Georg Garten
Darmstadt
Schönbusch
Felsengarten Sanspareil
Bamberg
Bayreuth
Eremitage
Schloss Veitshöchheim
Rosengarten
Neue Residenz
Hofgarten
Hofgarten Würzburg
Würzburg

Schlosspark
Weinheim and Exotenwald
Mannheim
Heidelberg
Schlossgarten Weikersheim
Nuremberg

Europas Rosengarten
Schlossgarten
Schwetzingen
Schlossgarten Heidelberg
Hofgarten Ansbach

Karlsruhe
Schlosspark Karlsruhe
Alpengarten Pforzheim

Stuttgart
Höhenpark Killesberg
Wilhelma Park
Bavaria

Schlosspark Hohenheim

Munich Botanic Garden
Englischer Garten
Hofgarten
Weihenstephan
Horticultural Garden
Schlosspark Nymphenburg
Munich
Park Schloss Schleissheim

Mainau Island

Bodensee
Schlosspark Linderhof
Alpengarten 'Schachen'

Danube

Rhine

Rhine

influence on German garden development. Romantic landscape parks were laid out all through the 19th century and many trees, newly introduced from North America and Asia, have grown to make fine specimens even in regions of extreme continental climate.

By the early years of the 20th century Erwin Barth (1880–1933), who was primarily a designer of private gardens in the Jugendstil style (historically equivalent to art nouveau in Britain), began to influence public park layouts. Gradually this architectural approach gave way to more naturalistic landscapes, no longer based on the English romantic park, but clearly directed towards ecological and sociological needs, making use of native plant communities and the geological aspect of each site. Karl Foerster, nurseryman, plant-breeder and garden writer, stressed the importance of plants, encouraging the use of perennials, alpines, ferns and grasses. His influence and that of Hermann Mattern extended to the wider field of design around road networks and attempts to integrate such schemes into the landscape. Many designers were involved in the nursery business. Perhaps because of this, since World War II, when many famous gardens such as the Tiergarten in Berlin were completely destroyed and food crops grown on the land, West Germany has led the world in setting up a series of influential *Gartenschauen* (National Garden Shows), where visitors can study trends in both design and plant breeding. In 1950 the *Gartenschau* at the Höhenpark Killesberg in Stuttgart (q.v.) marked the completion of a design begun by Hermann Mattern in 1939. At Karlsaue in Kassel (q.v.) the 18th-century baroque garden had its formal layout thoroughly restored for the 1981 *Gartenschau*.

Modern gardening trends lean towards the naturalistic and the use of native plants. On the other hand, it is only comparatively recently that broad-leaved evergreen shrubs have been proved to be hardy in many areas and there is today, for instance, interest in hardy rhododendrons and a corresponding increase in the number of nurseries with a wide range of both woody and perennial plants. It is also only in recent years that many important historic gardens, originally owned by aristocratic rulers but now the property of each state, have been successfully restored. There are still important private gardens, but few of these are accessible to the public.

The Octagon, surmounted by the Farnese statue of Hercules, dominates the cascades at Wilhelmshöhe.

North Germany

Schlosspark Ahaus

Ahaus town centre, 100km N of Essen, 5km W of A31
motorway to Gronau
Owner: Kreis Borken
Opening times: At all times
Admission charge: No

The once famous formal garden was landscaped
mainly after 1745. Fortunately the 1767 double flight
of steps by Johann Conrad Schlaun survives, and
many fine old trees enhance the views to the moated
Schloss.

Bremen: Botanic Garden and Rhododendron Park ❀

60 Marcusallee, NE of town centre
Owner: Stadt Bremen
Opening times: *Rhododendron park* daily 7.30–sunset
(best end Apr to early Jun); *botanic garden* daily, Apr to
Sept 7.30–sunset; *rhododendron house* Mon–Fri, Sun
10–16, Sat 12–16
Admission charge: No

Founded in 1936 by the German Rhododendron
Society, with planting in an old oak wood, the 36ha

Rhododendron Park is now the largest in the world
and has an international reputation. The park was
extended 1949–51 into the *Botanic Garden*, which
now contains 8,000 plant varieties. It is divided into
geographical sections demonstrating plants from
every continent, with one area devoted to Mediterranean flora. There is a heather garden, an azalea
museum, a display house for a collection of fuchsias
and glasshouses for tropical and subtropical rhododendrons. This is not just another botanic teaching
garden, but is laid out with style and taste.

Bremen: Bürgerpark

Between Holler-Allee (main entrance) and the university
Owner: Bürgerpark-Verein
Opening times: At all times
Admission charge: No

Although designed as a public park in 1866 by the
German Wilhelm Benque (who collaborated with
F. L. Olmsted in laying out Central Park in New
York), the Bürgerpark nevertheless has the elegance
of a private garden, with a formal area at the entrance
and a charming English-style landscape behind,
where a winding stream widens to lakes.

Clemenswerth ★

E of Sögel, 85km NW of Osnabrück via B68
Owner: *Park*: Herzog von Arenberg; *buildings*: Landkreis
Emsland
Opening times: At all times
Admission charge: No

This 17ha 18th-century park was first laid out in the
form of a star in 1736 by Johann Conrad Schlaun as a
hunting park for Elector Clemens August, with
wooded rides and formal fishponds. Eight avenues
radiate from the main lodge in a central roundel, with
eight pavilions set between them. Schlaun's original
drawings for the park still exist. As well as the formal
lime avenues, one of which stretches for 800m, there
is a monastery garden with old yew topiary shapes
and hedges. (A fine porcelain collection can be seen in
one of the pavilions.)

Göttingen: Old Botanic Garden of Göttingen University

Untere Karspüle, close to town centre; 42km NE of Kassel
Owner: Göttingen University
Opening times: Mon–Fri 8–18, Sat, Sun and public hols 8–13
Admission charge: No

Founded in 1736, at the same time as the university, the botanic garden prospered in the 18th and early 19th centuries owing to its connection with Kew Gardens (q.v.) in England (monarchs of the House of Hanover ruled both the electorate of Hanover and Great Britain 1714–1837, and Kew was royal property until 1837). Of special beauty is the landscape around the pond and the alpinum. Some of the conservatories are late 19th-century. There is also a new botanic garden in Grisebachstrasse.

Hamburg: Botanic Garden of Hamburg University ❀

Flottbek, W of city centre
Owner: University of Hamburg
Opening times: Daily, summer 9–19; winter 9–17
Admission charge: No

Founded in 1971 and opened to the public in 1979, the gardens are among the most important teaching collections in West Germany. They contain a great number of different plant varieties, including tropical and subtropical plants in heated glasshouses. There are areas where plants are arranged in systematic beds, an alpinum, collections of roses, irises, lilies and perennials as well as medicinal plants and a pinetum.

Hanover: Herrenhausen ★

NW outskirts of the city
Owner: Landeshauptstadt Hannover
Opening times: *Grosser Garten* daily 8–sunset; *Berggarten* daily 7–sunset; *glasshouses* 8–sunset
Admission charge: No

At Herrenhausen, terracotta pots ornament the reconstructed chequerboard parterre with its patterns of gravel and coal dust.

Much of the Herrenhausen, including the castle, was destroyed during World War II, but the vast 50ha baroque garden, the *Grosser Garten*, planned and laid out 1680–1714, was restored in 1945, and the orangery survives. The summer residence of the Electors of Hanover, Herrenhausen was developed by Sophie, wife of Ernst August, daughter of Frederick V of the Palatinate and mother of George I of England. Sophie had spent much of her youth in the Netherlands; she sent her gardener, Martin Charbonnier, to study garden design there. Her garden, a large rectangle extended in 1692, is surrounded on three sides by a canal. A central axis bisects the main hedged parterre which is divided into smaller garden 'rooms'. These small hedged gardens have each a different pattern. A star-shaped *bosquet*, with a central pool where a water jet rises 80m, is surrounded by more ornate lateral *bosquets* with fountains and multiple basins with decorative statues. A trapezoid-shaped theatre of clipped beech is today again used for performances.

A great cascade built in 1676, one of the oldest features in the garden, has a *buffet d'eau* with water rippling over open shell-work.

A garden existed on the site of the *Berggarten* from 1666 when it was the kitchen garden of the Herrenhausen. Before 1700 the Electress Sophie began to

collect rare plants here, an orangery was built in 1686, and both tobacco and white mulberry trees were grown in a trial ground. After 1750 it developed as a botanical garden and the 'useful' plants became less important, although the white mulberry was cultivated to supply the silkworms for the royal silk manufactory at Hameln until this was closed by Napoleon. Queen Victoria's water lily (*Victoria amazonica*) flowered for the first time in Europe in the greenhouses, and the African violet was first cultivated and described here in 1893. The mausoleum contains the tomb of Sophie's son, George I of England.

Kassel: Karlsaue

Between the theatre and River Fulda
Owner: Land Hessen
Opening times: At all times
Admission charge: No

This 150ha public park, stretching through the centre of the city, was begun in 1568, but many of its present features date either from formal baroque development *c.*1710 by the Landgrave Karl von Hessen-Kassel or to the more naturalistic landscape style imposed on the layout at the end of the 18th century. Canals, an orangery and a marble pavilion date from 1710. An island, Siebenbergen, has many good trees, plants and flowerbeds. The garden was redesigned for the 1955 *Gartenschau*.

Kassel: Bergpark Wilhelmshöhe ★

W of city centre
Owner: Land Hessen
Opening times: At all times
Admission charge: No

Landgrave Karl von Hessen-Kassel ordered Giovanni Guerniero to design him this Italian-style baroque garden (unique in Germany) after a visit to the Villa Aldobrandini (q.v.) at Frascati in 1699–1700. Designed round the hunting lodge of Weissenstein on the wooded slopes of the Habichtswald outside Kassel, where the land drops 200m over a distance of only 1,000m, the precipitous site was intended for a series of dramatic cascades and grottoes. Only a third of the ambitious plan was finally implemented, but the completed waterworks are still in operation and a colossal bronze copy of the Farnese statue of Hercules is set on the Octagon at the head of the cascades. Guerniero left in 1715 but compiled a fine collection of engravings for Weissenstein.

Taste changed, and pagodas, temples and hermitages date from later in the 18th century. At the end of the century the garden was landscaped in the English style, and H. C. Jussow built the Schloss Löwenburg as a 'medieval' ruin between 1794 and 1798. The 900ha park has interesting trees and shrubs as well as an 1822 glasshouse with camellias, palms, ferns and orchids. It is also known for the *Rose Garden* (Roseninsel Park Wilhelmshöhe). A rosary was first established here in 1765, and many rose species and other shrub roses have again been planted in the garden areas round the lake. In the years 1806–15 the royal painter Salomon Pinhas produced 134 watercolours of these roses, some of which were the 'parents' of the Empress Josephine's collection at Malmaison (q.v.)

Kiel: Botanic Garden of Kiel University
Main entrance, Leibnitzstrasse
Owner: Land Schleswig-Holstein
Opening times: Daily, Apr to Oct 9–18; *conservatories* 9.30–11.30, 14–17.30
Admission charge: No

Kiel has had a botanic garden since 1669, but it has been moved several times. The old one at Düsterbrooker Weg, opened in 1878, still holds remarkable plants. But the world-famous collection of succulents, in particular a collection of the genus *Lithops* (known as living stones), came here in 1985. There are lovely views over the bay.

Louisenlund
Güby, between Schleswig and Eckernförde on A76
Owner: Herzog von Schleswig-Holstein
Opening times: Daily sunrise–sunset
Admission charge: No

The landscaped park was designed in 1770, at the same time as the house. The layout was based on the ideals of Freemasonry; the lodge and hermitage have gone, but a Norwegian hut of 1774 is still used as a chapel and there are many masonic memorials distributed throughout the grounds. There is a breathtaking view, framed by enormous old trees, down to the River Schlei.

Schlosspark Lütetsburg
Lütetsburg bei Norden, SE of Norden, 30km NE of Emden via A72 and B70
Owner: Huberta Gräfin zu Innhausen und Knyphausen
Opening times: Daily 9–19
Admission charge: No

A formal garden was redesigned by Carl Ferdinand Bosse in 1790. He kept the avenues and the canals in the Dutch manner as the framework of his landscape park.

Schlosspark Nordkirchen
Edge of village of Nordkirchen, 30km SW of Münster
Owner: Land Nordrhein-Westfalen
Opening times: At all times
Admission charge: No

The elegant formal garden of this 'Westphalian Versailles' was designed in 1725 by Johann Conrad Schlaun and part of his layout in front of the Oranienburg and orangery in the Westgarten has been restored. The Nordgarten was redesigned by Achille Duchêne in 1906. Further careful restoration is still in progress.

Schlosspark Rastede
Oldenburger Strasse, Rastede, 12km N of Oldenburg
Owner: Grossherzog von Oldenburg
Opening times: At all times
Admission charge: No

Begun in 1777, this extensive forest-like park was developed over a hundred years as more land was acquired. Oaks planted in the 18th century partly surround the huge lake. A famous rhododendron hedge 270m long separates the park from the private garden next to the Schloss. Both were designed by Carl Ferdinand Bosse. Opposite the Schloss is the well-kept little Palaisgarten with its rare trees.

Rhododendron Waldpark Nursery Hobbie ✤

Westerstede-Linswege, 23km NW of Oldenburg via A28
Owner: Elizabeth Hobbie
Opening times: Daily 8–19
Admission charge: Apr to early Jul, yes;
mid-Jul to Mar, no

Originally the private estate of the Hobbie family, the 65ha rhododendron park was laid out in a pine forest by Dietrich C. Hobbie in 1929. It comprises a vast collection of rhododendron species and cultivars, as well as other plants brought back from expeditions to Asia in 1939, Alaska in 1945, and from the high Himalayas in the post-war years.

Rosarium Uetersen

Uetersen, 35km NW of Hamburg on B431
Owner: Stadt Uetersen
Opening times: Daily 7–22
Admission charge: No

The formal rose garden of 1934 is now park-like, with mature trees backing about 30,000 roses, mostly Kordes, Tantau and Strobel/Meilland.

Bavaria

Hofgarten Ansbach

Ansbach, opposite the palace; 42km SW of Nuremberg on A14
Owner: Bayerische Verwaltung der staatlichen Schlösser, Gärten und Seen
Opening times: Daily sunrise–sunset
Admission charge: No

Originally a formal baroque layout dating from 1723–50, only the east–west lime avenue was retained when the grounds were landscaped in 1780. The formal gardens in front of the 18th-century orangery have now been restored and the flowerbeds are planted with pansies and tulips for spring and with colourful annuals in summer.

Rosengarten Neue Residenz Bamberg

Bamberg, 47km N of Nuremberg. Through doorway of the Neue Residenz in the Domplatz
Owner: Bayerische Verwaltung der staatlichen Schlösser, Gärten und Seen
Opening times: Daily sunrise–sunset
Admission charge: No

This is a formal garden, designed in 1733 by Balthasar Neumann, with a Chinese pavilion added in 1757. Pleached lime trees encircle a fountain, and box-edged beds are filled with modern roses. There are 18th-century garden statues by Ferdinand Tietz.

Bayreuth: Eremitage

4km E of centre of town
Owner: Bayerische Verwaltung der staatlichen Schlösser, Gärten und Seen
Opening times: Daily
Admission charge: No

The 47ha gardens are laid out around two castles, one built in 1715 for the Margrave Georg Wilhelm von Brandenburg-Bayreuth as a country retreat and designed like a Carthusian monastery, and the second, the semi-circular Neues Schloss, to the west of the Altes Schloss, built 1749–53 for the Margravine Wilhelmine (sister of Frederick the Great of Prussia). The first gardens, conceived by Gabriel Luck, contained other small hermitages hidden in the woodland and reached by winding paths. The Margravine started to remodel the gardens in 1736; the new plans included a number of buildings, some 'ruined' (like the Roman theatre for open-air operatic performances), an impressive lower grotto surrounded by nymphs, and a system of water jets. Even the Neues Schloss started life as a bird house and orangery, only later becoming a residence. After the Margravine's death the gardens were turned into an English-style park; in her lifetime, although the garden seemed a collection of unintegrated features with no obvious pattern, a tour of the whole area revealed unexpected avenues, features and axial views.

Bayreuth: Hofgarten

Neues Schloss, centre of town
Owner: Bayerische Verwaltung der staatlichen Schlösser, Gärten und Seen
Opening times: Daily sunrise–sunset
Admission charge: No

Gardens have existed here since 1580 when fruit and vegetables were grown. By 1610 the Hofgarten was laid out as a pleasure garden, with a grotto and other features added in 1680. A lime avenue was then the main axis, extending to the Eremitage (q.v.). A fire destroyed the old palace in 1753 and the garden was enlarged when the new palace was constructed out of several existing buildings. A canal became the new axis for the garden, but was not linked with the palace and had a rather uncompromising dog-leg at its further end. It contained four islands (two remain), which were planted with flowerbeds; the largest had *treillage* panels round an aviary. After 1789 the formal garden was converted into an informal landscape, which endures today in spite of some attempts to restore the earlier scheme. A number of statues, including parts of an original Neptune group of 1763, are dotted about the remaining islands in a charming way.

Schlosspark Linderhof

W of Ettal, 68km SW of Munich via A95
Owner: Bayerische Verwaltung der staatlichen Schlösser, Gärten und Seen
Opening times: At all times
Admission charge: No

Created in 1880, this palace and garden set in wooded countryside represent the 'mad' King Ludwig II of

Designed for the Margravine Wilhelmina after 1736, the formal gardens at the Eremitage in Bayreuth include grottoes and water jets.

Bavaria's vision of an Italian villa. The steep slopes round the castle are terraced, with elaborate staircases and cascades joining the separate levels. In front of the villa are a formal *bassin* and water jet and parterres are bedded out with colourful sweeps of annuals. There is a kiosk and a grotto in the 58ha park.

Munich: Botanic Garden ❀

Menzinger Strasse, adjoining the park of Schloss Nymphenburg, W of city centre
Owner: Freistaat Bayern
Opening times: Daily, summer 9–19; winter 9–17
Admission charge: No

The original 5ha garden belonged to the Bavarian Academy of Sciences and was laid out in 1812 on a site between Elisenstrasse and Sophienstrasse, now a green island surrounded by roaring traffic. It was moved to its present 20ha site adjoining Schloss Nymphenburg in 1914. It has a fine collection of ornamental plants as well as ecological and genetic study areas. An alpine house has two sections, one of which is not heated. The main arboretum contains a lake, a heather garden, an alpine area, a shady glen with ferns and a collection of rhododendrons. Glasshouses contain orchids, palms, cacti and succulents. (*See also* Alpengarten 'Schachen'.)

Munich: Englischer Garten

City centre, behind the Bavarian State Museum
Owner: Bayerische Verwaltung der staatlichen Schlösser, Gärten und Seen
Opening times: At all times
Admission charge: No

This 370ha park was laid out at the end of the 18th century in the English style by the garden designer F. L. von Sckell at the instigation of the Elector Carl Theodor and an American, Benjamin Thompson (later, as the Elector's minister, given the title of Count von Rumford). It was the first notable public park in Germany, opened in 1793 although not

completed until the 1800s. Paths lead through the parkland to a circular temple, the Monopteros, and a wooden Chinese tower; a large lake, the Kleinhesseloher, lies to the north. Along the river the park becomes less sophisticated as it gets further from the town; this stretch is unfortunately crossed by busy roads.

Munich: Hofgarten
City centre, beside the Residenz; main entrance Odeonsplatz
Owner: Bayerische Verwaltung der staatlichen Schlösser, Gärten und Seen
Opening times: At all times
Admission charge: No

The residence's island garden dating from 1613 still retains much of its original atmosphere and charm. Paths radiate from a 1615 fountain pavilion in the centre of a formal garden laid out in renaissance style, but the rectangular *bassin* was filled in and used as the site of a war memorial after World War I.

Munich: Schlosspark Nymphenburg ★
NW of city centre
Owner: Bayerische Verwaltung der staatlichen Schlösser, Gärten und Seen
Opening times: Daily, Apr to Sept 7–20; Oct to Mar 7–17
Admission charge: No

The early Schloss, begun in 1664 and now the central building at Nymphenburg, was designed by Agostino Barelli in Italian style for the Elector Ferdinand Maria; a small renaissance garden was laid out under the western facade in 1670. His son Max Emanuel inherited the estate, and after 1701 employed the architects Enrico Zuccalli and A. Viscardi to add two side pavilions, connected by galleries to Barelli's main structure. Later, 1715–30, he commissioned Joseph Effner to build a series of pavilions in the garden, including the Pagodenburg and the Badenburg, each with a baroque parterre and waterworks, and the Magdalenenklause which was intended as a hermitage. In 1739 the famous rococo Amalienburg hunting lodge was designed by François Cuvilliés for Max Emanuel's son Karl Albrecht and his wife the Electress Amalia.

Max Emanuel, who had spent ten years as Governor of the Spanish Netherlands and knew Versailles well, employed the Frenchmen Charles Carbonet and Dominique Girard to extend the gardens in baroque style. The latter, an architect from Versailles, had already played a part in the design of the garden at Schleissheim (q.v.). Although Friedrich Ludwig von Sckell turned most of the garden into a romantic park with natural-looking lakes in front of two pavilions in 1804–23, he incorporated some elements of the baroque layout in his wider scheme, including the *bassin* surrounded by fountains and the *parterre de broderie* under the west front. He also retained the canal on a central axis with the main building, a great stretch of water which plunges over a cascade (also designed by Effner) to the Wurm Canal beyond. More canals moat the Schloss. The still pools give the garden a distinctively Dutch atmosphere and reflect the facade of the great palace, which seems to float in the water.

Munich: Park Schloss Schleissheim ★
Just N of city; S-Bahn 1
Owner: Bayerische Verwaltung der staatlichen Schlösser, Gärten und Seen
Opening times: Daily sunrise–sunset
Admission charge: No

A genuine baroque concept of the early 18th century by Dominique Girard, with all the characteristic ingredients: hedges, canals, *bosquets*, and a low cascade tumbling down to the sunken parterre in front of the magnificent Neues Palais of 1701 (by Enrico Zuccalli and Joseph Effner). Commissioned by Max Emanuel, Elector of Bavaria, who had spent ten years as Governor of the Spanish Netherlands, the gardens clearly show Dutch influence, especially in the use of water features. They lie between the Neues Palais and the earlier Lustheim (1684 by Zuccalli) surrounded by its circular canal.

Felsengarten Sanspareil
N of the Fortress Zwernitz between Bayreuth and Bamberg, via A505
Opening times: Daily, Apr to Sept 9–12, 13.30–17, except Mon
Admission charge: Yes

Quite different in character from the Eremitage (q.v.), the Margravine Wilhelmine's other garden at Bayreuth, Sanspareil was essentially a hunting ground and its wild romantic landscape was completed in 1748. The design of the grove, where beech trees surround huge rocky outcrops, was inspired by Fénelon's *Les Aventures de Télémaque*, with the centre of the grove envisaged as the magical island of Ogygia where Telemachus was shipwrecked during his voyage in pursuit of Odysseus. By reliving the son's selfless search for his father, visitors were to experience the soul's purification. The Morgenland-ischer Bau or Hainbau, a rustic ornamental building with cupola and small open courtyard, was built around a beech tree for the Margravine by the Bavarian architect Josef Saint-Pierre in the 1740s. There is also a grotto embellished to resemble a ruined theatre.

Alpengarten 'Schachen' ❀

Wettersteingebirge, Garmisch Mt Schachen, S of Garmisch-Partenkirchen, 90km S of Munich via A95
Owner: Munich Botanic Garden
Opening times: Jul to Aug, Mon–Fri 7–18, Sat, Sun 8–18
Admission charge: Yes

This alpine garden is only reached after a three-hour walk through the mountains. It was originally laid out in 1900 at a height of 1,850m and is designed to resemble a real landscape, with native and threatened flora growing in natural conditions.

Schönbusch ★

3km W of Aschaffenburg on A26, in a loop of the River Main
Owner: Bayerische Verwaltung der staatlichen Schlösser, Gärten und Seen
Opening times: Daily
Admission charge: No

Schönbusch was the first landscape park in Germany to eschew the romantic and adopt a classical simplicity. The small castle was built and the old game reserve laid out as a park in 1778 for the Elector and Archbishop of Mainz, Friedrich Carl von Erthal, by his minister Wilhelm von Sickingen and a Por-

tuguese architect, Joseph Emanuel d'Herigoyen. After 1785 F. L. von Sckell worked on the design and was responsible for using the river as a perimeter or ha-ha. A lake in front of the castle reflects its facade, and across it there is a marvellous view to the castle of Aschaffenburg. A second lake, the Oberer See, has dried up and is now a meadow. Several classical buildings, a banqueting hall, Dutch cottages and shepherds' huts are scattered throughout the park. Some good specimen trees include a copper beech, a ginkgo and swamp cypress; there is an unusual maze of field maple.

Schloss Veitshöchheim ★

3km N of Würzburg via motorway
Owner: Bayerische Verwaltung der staatlichen Schlösser, Gärten und Seen
Opening times: Daily, summer 7.30–20; winter 8–16
Admission charge: No

Veitshöchheim is one of the most beautiful gardens in Germany, and certainly the country's greatest surviving rococo garden. It was completed after 1763 for Prince Bishop Adam Friedrich von Seinsheim (who was also responsible for the Hofgarten at Würzburg, q.v.), with the help of the master gardener J. Prokop Mayer. The highly original new hedged layout, surrounded by a wall, was located to the side of the palace with no axial connection with the building. Of regular design with a grid of hedges and walks, and small garden rooms with arbours and Chinese pavilions at intersections, the garden seems maze-like in its complexity. The Grosser See, a large formal *bassin*, is the central focus of the garden (already *in situ* in 1702–3); the statuary carved for it by Ferdinand Tietz in the 1760s includes a Mount Parnassus, surmounted by the winged horse Pegasus, who strains towards Olympus. Delightful statues of children, *putti* and ornamental vases decorate this garden area.

Gardens to complement the palace, built in the 1680s, had already been conceived earlier in the century by Balthasar Neumann; much of this more baroque design still remained as the rococo garden was embellished, and both elements can still be seen today. There are fine stairways from the palace down to the hedged garden.

Weihenstephan Horticultural Garden

Weihenstephan, 26km N of Munich via A11, S outskirts of Freising
Owner: Fachhochschule Weihenstephan
Opening times: Daily 7–18
Admission charge: No

Begun in 1948, together with a state Institute for Horticulture, the 5ha garden has collections of hardy perennials and some good ornamental trees. There are 250 *Paeonia lactiflora* cultivars, and 800 different roses. It is the headquarters of the International Shrub Register. The garden is the equivalent of the demonstration gardens at Wisley in England (q.v.), with scientific areas laid out with great charm.

BELOW RIGHT **The Temple of Friendship in the 18th-century park at Schönbusch.**

BELOW LEFT **Huge natural rocks have become part of the fantastic romantic landscape created at Sanspareil. The garden was finished in 1748.**

Würzburg: Hofgarten

Centre of town, behind the Residenz
Owner: Bayerische Verwaltung der staatlichen Schlösser, Gärten und Seen
Opening times: Daily sunrise–sunset
Admission charge: No

The east part of the garden had to fit in the angle of the old town fortifications behind Balthasar Neumann's charming early 18th-century Residenz for the prince bishops of Würzburg. Many designs were put forward and in 1774 those of J. Prokop Mayer were finally accepted by Prince Bishop Adam Friedrich von Seinsheim (*see* Veitshöchheim). Glorious three-dimensional effects are achieved by banked terraces connected by ramps and flights of steps, all lavishly decorated with balustrading and sculptures. Post-war planting includes white mulberries on the upper terraces. Laburnum and larch arbours are imaginatively backed with cornelian cherry. The south garden, also by Mayer, has 200-year-old pyramids of clipped yew, ivy-clad walls, a walk of flowering cherries and a formal parterre. The rest of the park was later remodelled in landscape style and there are fine specimens of yews, cypresses, magnolias, planes, limes and mulberries and an avenue of ginkgos.

South-West and West Germany

Bad Homburg: Kurpark

Town centre
Owner: Kur- und Kongress-GmbH, Bad Homburg
Opening times: At all times
Admission charge: No

The spa garden, begun in 1854, was designed by Peter Josef Lenné. Specimen trees and imaginative pavilions and temples for the many wells fill the site.

Bonn: Botanic Garden of Bonn University ❀

In the park of Poppelsdorf Schloss, Meckenheimer Allee
Owner: University of Bonn
Opening times: Summer, weekdays 8–19, Sat 8–12, Sun 10–13; winter, daily 8–17, except Sat, Sun
Admission charge: No

Laid out in 1818 when the university was founded, the 7ha botanic garden is on the site of a baroque garden of the 1720s. It has an interesting collection of rare trees, including a *Pinus bungeana*, the Chinese temple pine, with coloured scaly bark, and some fine swamp cypresses. Flowerbeds are arranged in systematic orders.

Bonn: The Harle Garden and Arboretum

40 Buchelstrasse, SE of city centre
Owners: Fräulein Regina Harle and Fräulein Maria Harle
Opening times: By appointment, Buchelstrasse 40, 5300 Bonn 3 (Oberkassel)

Almost surrounded by the industrial area of Bonn, the two gardens form an oasis on the northern slope of the Siebengebirge. The original 7ha park, first planted with exotic trees in 1870, included an orchard, woodland and a nursery and was acquired by the father of the Harle sisters in 1921. In 1977 3ha of the arboretum were taken for the autobahn A3, which also affected the water-table, but new forms of cedar, chamaecyparis, juniper and yew have since been added to the original plantings. In spite of air pollution the arboretum remains a fine collection. Of interest too are shade-loving ground-cover plants, and the nursery area has been turned into a beautiful flower garden with sensitive colour schemes and interesting plants.

Cologne: Flora and Botanic Garden

Amsterdamer Strasse, next to the zoological garden, NE of city centre
Owner: Stadt Köln
Opening times: Daily 8–sunset; *conservatories* 10–18
Admission charge: No

The part of this landscaped park called 'Flora' was designed by Peter Josef Lenné for the 'Flora AG' and opened in 1864. Later united with the botanical garden, the area contains about 10,000 species.

Darmstadt: Prinz-Georg Garten

City centre; entrance through Herrngarten
Owner: Land Hessen
Opening times: At all times
Admission charge: No

Laid out as a pleasure garden in 1625, the garden was redesigned in the rococo style during the 18th century. Combined with the Prettlack garden after 1743 (the Prettlack garden house is of 1710), both gardens remain essentially formal in design.

Düsseldorf: Schloss Benrath ★

Benrath, S of city centre
Owner: Stadt Düsseldorf
Opening times: Daily sunrise–sunset
Admission charge: No

The new Schloss was begun in 1756 by the Elector Karl Theodor, who employed Nicolas de Pigage (creator of the French baroque gardens at Schwetzingen, q.v., in 1752) as architect and garden designer. The main palace, with two curving wings making a semi-circle round a large formal pool, has a long canal as its southern axis. The east 'French' garden retains Pigage's geometric style with cascades and flowerbeds, while the 'flower garden' on the west was landscaped by M. F. Weyhe after 1841 and now contains rare trees. Pigage's huge square hunting park lies to the south-west of the Schloss, crossed by avenues in the form of a star. A hedged alley strikes through the woods from the corner by the palace, crossing avenues, winding pathways and a circular path to meet seven other alleys at a central rondel. Narrow canals almost surround the 64ha area.

Düsseldorf: Schloss Dyck ❀

Near Neuss, across the Rhine, SW of city centre
Owner: Fürstin zu Salm-Reifferscheidt-Dyck
Opening times: By appointment, 4053 Jülich
Admission charge: Yes

Dyck is mentioned in Loudon's *Encyclopaedia of Gardening* for its landscape laid out in 1820 by the Scotsman Thomas Blaikie, a garden designer who also had a good knowledge of plants, and had been working in France since before the Revolution. By 1834 the park was said to 'contain all the hardy plants which can be procured, arranged in groups, according to the Jussieuean system'. The owner of Dyck, the Prince of Salm, was also 'advantageously known by his work on succulents' and for his collection of these plants in the glasshouses (his orangery still survives). In his *Hortus Dyckensis*, published in 1834, the Prince explains how he made his collection from England, France, Holland and Brabant and his personal connections with William Aiton at Kew (q.v.) in England, the Swiss Augustin Pyramus de Candolle, and other botanists of the day. He took drawing lessons from Pierre Joseph Redouté (a copy of Redouté's *Liliacées* and his own *Hortus* are in the library at Dyck).

In order to make his new scientific landscape park, with trees and shrubs planted in families and genera, the prince swept away a baroque-style garden which had parterres on the flat area beyond the moat. For those with specialist botanic interests Dyck has more than twelve kinds of beech and ten different kinds of oak, with a good assembly of maples, limes, horse chestnuts and poplars. Wide, undulating lawns are surrounded by groves of magnificent trees to give natural effects. Unfortunately, open-cast mining in the area threatens the water-table, which has already dropped 10m; shallow-rooted trees may well not survive. One of the few private gardens open to the public, the park is immaculately kept.

A fine avenue of Spanish chestnut marks the approach to the moated castle; it was planted in 1811 as a link with the monastery of St Nikolaus, which contains the family vault.

Europas Rosengarten

Zweibrücken, 30km E of Saarbrücken; between Rosengartenstrasse and Saarlandstrasse
Owner: Stadt Zweibrücken
Opening times: Daily, Apr to Oct
Admission charge: Yes

The rose garden was opened in 1914, but was bombed in World War II. The new rose garden consists of a landscape garden with about 60,000 roses old and new, many of French origin.

Frankfurt: Palmengarten ❀

Siesmayer Strasse, W of city centre
Owner: Stadt Frankfurt
Opening times: Daily, summer 9–20; winter 9–16

Founded in 1869–71 by the Palm Garden Society, the Palmengarten acquired Duke Adolph von Nassau's plant collection after he was dethroned in 1866. The recently restored palm house is the oldest and largest in Germany and contains a good collection of cacti, succulents, *Bromeliaceae* and tropical plants. In 1932 the Society gave the garden to the municipality. It has been extended to cover 22ha, with lawns and a landscaped park. A greenhouse complex, including a remarkable tropicarium built in the 1980s, a rose garden, a collection of evergreens and collections of German irises and of hemerocallis make the Palmengarten one of the most interesting plant collections in Germany.

Giessen: Botanic Garden of Giessen University

Main entrance Sonnenstrasse; town centre next to castle
Owner: Justus-Liebig-Universität
Opening times: Weekdays 8–12, 14–sunset; Sat, Sun and public hols, summer 8–18, winter 8–12; *conservatories* daily, mid May to Aug 10–12, 13.30–15.45
Admission charge: No

Founded by the university in 1609, the 4ha botanical garden has remained on the same site ever since. It was joined to the 1802 forestry garden after 1817; hence most of the old trees. Over 1,000 species are grouped geographically and in other ways in this rather restricted area.

Heidelberg: Schlossgarten (Hortus Palatinus)

E of the castle
Owner: Land Baden-Württemberg
Opening times: At all times
Admission charge: No

Only terraces remain of this important garden, but fortunately restoration work is now in progress. The original renaissance design, illustrated in the *Hortus Palatinus* of Salomon de Caus (published in 1620), was never completed. In 1615 De Caus was invited by the Elector Frederick V of the Palatinate (by 1619, King of Bohemia) to lay out a new garden round Heidelberg castle for his wife, Elizabeth Stuart, the daughter of James I of England and Scotland (De Caus had been Elizabeth's drawing-master in England). In spite of work being interrupted by the Thirty Years' War (1618–48), the design, as portrayed in later engravings, remains influential. A maze, pergolas, gazebos and other ornamental features were typical of the period, but De Caus's grottoes and elaborate musical waterworks, inspired by his visits to Italy as a young man, were unique in Germany at this time.

Schlosspark Hohenheim

10km S of Stuttgart, off A312 to airport
Owner: Land Baden-Württemberg
Opening times: At all times
Admission charge: No

The garden, started in 1774, was once crammed with temples, churches, cottages and other buildings, as well as with trees from North America, introduced in the 18th and 19th centuries. Nearly all the buildings have gone, but many specimen trees survive. Watercolours showing the garden in its heyday are in the palace of Ludwigsburg.

Karlsruhe: Schlosspark

Town centre
Owner: Land Baden-Württemberg
Opening times: 6–sunset
Admission charge: No

During the 18th century the landscape park was developed from a former hunting ground, with the palace begun in 1715 as the hub of a series of radiating alleys. The layout of both park and town (also founded in 1715) forms two huge fans. The park was altered for the National Garden Show in 1967, particularly around the 19th-century lake.

Mainau Island

On W side of Bodensee, reached by a bridge 6km N of Konstanz
Owner: Count Lennart Bernadotte
Opening times: Daily, Apr to Oct 8–19
Admission charge: Yes

The island, originally occupied by a monastery, passed to the Grand Dukes of Baden in the 19th century and the Italianate gardens were laid out 1860–80 by Grand Duke Friedrich I of Baden, when cedars, giant redwoods and other trees were planted, and oranges and lemons in ornamental pots were introduced to decorate the terrace. In 1932 the island was inherited by Count Lennart Bernadotte, who continued to extend the planting. Now of great horticultural interest, the 30ha garden has displays of tulips, irises, rare lilies and dahlias besides a 'tropical' garden of bananas, eucalyptus and palms, all of which are given glasshouse protection in winter. A formal rose garden with pergolas has 30,000 rose plants. On the inland side of the site a spring garden with an avenue of sweet chestnuts leads to the Swede's Tower and the arboretum, where some of the trees, now over 100 years old, were planted by the Grand Duke. An avenue of dawn redwoods, *Metasequoia glyptostroboides*, is a recent addition.

Alpengarten Pforzheim

4km SE of Pforzheim on road to Weil der Stadt
Owner: Joachim Carl
Opening times: Daily, Apr to Oct 8–19
Admission charge: No

Started in 1927 and laid out following the principles of Karl Foerster (*see* Introduction), the garden now contains a remarkable collection of plants from mountainous regions all over the world. There is also a nursery.

Schlossgarten Schwetzingen ★

Town centre, 15km S of Mannheim on A6
Owner: Land Baden-Württemberg
Opening times: Daily 8–sunset
Admission charge: Yes

The palace, the summer residence of the Palatinate Court, was destroyed during the Thirty Years' War (1618–48) and rebuilt in the 18th century by the Elector Karl Theodor, who commissioned Alessandro Galli da Bibiena with Nicolas de Pigage (*see* Benrath). Behind the Schloss and at a lower level, two curving pavilions inspired a highly original circular parterre laid out by the court gardener, J. Ludwig Petri. Clipped hedges of box, coloured gravel and grass with borders of flowers are separated by paths edged by pleached limes. Statuary and

The recently-restored palm house in the Palmengarten in Frankfurt is the oldest in Germany.

rococo-style buildings include a stag fountain by the sculptor Peter Anton von Verschaffelt, a theatre for musical performances (still used between mid May and mid June for the Schwetzingen Festival) and a bath-house (in the wood), both by Pigage. After 1776 Friedrich Ludwig von Sckell created a separate English garden on the perimeter of the formal areas; he also used Pigage to design buildings, including an oriental mosque, as features in this more park-like area. The parterre gardens were restored in 1974, and are now planted with appropriate 18th-century flowers.

Burggarten Stolzenfels

Kapellen-Stolzenfels, 5km S of Koblenz on A9
Owner: Land Rheinland-Pfalz
Opening times: Daily, except Mon, Apr to Sept 9–13, 14–18; Oct to Mar 9–13, 14–17; closed Dec
Admission charge: Yes

This romantic dream of a medieval castle garden was designed about 1836 by K. F. Schinkel to match the rebuilt 13th-century castle. A pergola runs around the courtyard, which has regular box-edged flower-beds and a fountain in the centre. The woodland park round the castle was designed by Peter Josef Lenné.

Stuttgart: Höhenpark Killesberg

W of town centre
Owner: Stadt Stuttgart
Opening times: Daily, May to Sept 8–20; winter 8–sunset
Admission charge: No

This modern 50ha park was first laid out in a disused quarry on the Killesberg by Hermann Mattern (*see* Introduction) for the Reichs Garden Exhibition in 1939. Destroyed in World War II, it was reconstructed by Mattern in 1950 for the first National Garden Show. A parterre, spring gardens with primulas and naturalized bulbs, a rose garden, marsh and aquatic plants by a water-lily pond, besides seasonal displays of tulips and dahlias, make the park of interest for much of the year.

In the formal 18th-century garden at Schwetzingen, a marble figure of Neptune is glimpsed through the leaves of a horse chestnut.

Stuttgart: Wilhelma Park

Neckartalstrasse, N city centre
Owner: Land Baden-Württemberg
Opening times: Daily, summer 7–17.30; winter 8–16
Admission charge: Yes

The original palace and park were designed 1837–53 in the Moorish style for Wilhelm I of Württemberg. The path was opened as a botanic garden after World War I, then destroyed, and remodelled with the addition of a zoological garden after World War II. The Moorish garden contains the largest grove of magnolias in Europe and many camellias and azaleas. There is also an orchid collection in the conservatories.

Schlossgarten Weikersheim ★

44km S of Würzburg, E of A19
Owner: Land Baden-Württemberg
Opening times: Daily 8–sunset
Admission charge: Apr to Oct, yes

The baroque garden of the renaissance Schloss (originally a moated castle) is one of the finest in the country and was created at the beginning of the 18th century. The simple rectangular parterre has a central fountain with a statue of Hercules on the summit of a wild crag, and is decorated with clipped box and statues, including dwarf caricatures. Its central axis, providing a vista to hills across the valley, terminates dramatically in an impressive orangery, the semi-circular recess between its two wings once adorned by an equestrian statue.

Schlosspark Weinheim and Exotenwald

Centre of Weinheim, 16km NE of Mannheim
Owner: Stadt Weinheim
Opening times: At all times
Admission charge: No

An earlier formal garden surrounding the 16th-century Schloss was redesigned in the landscape style by F. L. von Sckell in about 1785. After 1868 Baron Christian von Berckheim began to use the garden as a trial ground for rare and exotic trees and extended the park to make the *Exotenwald*. Here today there are fine specimens of sweet chestnuts, tulip trees, American redwoods, incense cedars and Japanese umbrella pines.

West Berlin

Botanic Garden of Berlin-Dahlem

Königen-Luise-Strasse, Dahlem, SW of city centre
Owner: Land Berlin
Opening times: Mon–Sat 8–sunset, Sun and hols 9–sunset
Admission charge: No

Carl Ludwig Willdenow's collection of medicinal plants, started in 1801, became part of a botanical garden founded by Heinrich Friedrich Link in 1815. The systematic beds were laid out on the present site 1897-1903 by Adolf Engler, and today contain an internationally recognized collection of plants. There is a section for native German flora and for plants from the mountainous regions of the northern hemisphere laid out in woodland. There is a botanical museum in the northern corner of the grounds, and late 19th-century glasshouses and parterres.

Bundesgartenschaupark 1985

Mohringer Allee-Massinger Weg, Neukölln, SE of city centre
Owner: Land Berlin
Opening times: Daily, Oct to Apr 9–19; May to Sept 9–20
Admission charge: No

This new garden was created from scratch by Wolfgang Miller for the National Garden Show in

1985. Artificial lakes were dug out and the surrounding fields and hills modelled to give the impression of real countryside. Of the three hills, one is a wood, one a toboggan run and the third gives views over the whole garden layout.

Schlosspark Charlottenburg ★

Charlottenburg, W of city centre
Owner: Gartenbauamt Charlottenburg
Opening times: Daily, May to Sept 7–21; Oct to Apr 7–20
Admission charge: No

The oldest garden in Berlin, and the first in Germany to be laid out in the French baroque style, the Charlottenburg was begun in 1701 for Sophie Charlotte, wife of Frederick I of Prussia and daughter of the Electress Sophie of Hanover who laid out the Herrenhausen (q.v.). Designed by Simon Godeau, a pupil of Le Nôtre, in the formal French style, it is bordered on two sides by the River Spree, and water is an important element, revealing Dutch as well as French influence. Avenues formerly flanked a long parterre over which the distant countryside was visible through viewpoints cut into the woodland. Later, at the end of the 18th and in the early 19th century, the gardens were landscaped by J. F. Eyserbeck and Peter Josef Lenné and the formal *bassin* transformed into a natural lake. There are three important buildings: the late 18th-century belvedere, the mausoleum designed by K. F. Schinkel for Frederick-William III's wife Louise, and an Italianate pavilion, also by Schinkel, on the terrace to the east. Since 1950 the gardens have been restored to their baroque appearance in a pattern of box and gravel.

Klein-Glienicke

On Havel lakes, W of Zehlendorf, SW of city centre
Owner: Gartenbauamt Zehlendorf
Opening times: Daily sunrise–sunset
Admission charge: No

The pleasure grounds between K. F. Schinkel's classical Schloss and the River Havel were Peter Josef Lenné's first garden in Prussia; the round flowerbeds, meandering paths and views are as they were conceived in 1816. After 1822 the design of the park was extended in the direction of Potsdam and features were added to give the impression of an Italian estate. Schinkel designed a temple, a rotunda, a *casino* and a bridge, and converted existing buildings in an Italianate style; statues and other ornaments were brought from Italy by Prince Carl of Prussia. Klein-Glienicke is part of Lenné's overall scheme for improving the Potsdam landscape (*see* Introduction to East Germany). The area around the buildings has already been restored but it will take some time to restore the whole 116ha park.

Pfaueninsel (Peacock Island)

In the Havel lakes, W of Zehlendorf, SW of city centre
Owner: Staatliche Schlösser und Gärten
Opening times: Daily 8–18
Admission charge: Yes; includes ferry ticket

The Peacock Island, in the Havel lakes, 1,500m long and 500m wide, was laid out in 1822 as an English park by Peter Josef Lenné. It included plantings of exotics and many rare species. Exotic animals and birds were also introduced, which later formed the basis of the Berlin Tiergarten; in 1924 the island became a nature reserve. Some fine large trees include a Weymouth pine, a cedar of Lebanon, and a Caucasian wingnut. Other buildings followed a 'ruined castle' of 1796: a Swiss cottage and Kavalierhaus by K. F. Schinkel, a neo-gothic 'ruined' farm, a circular rustic pergola, and the famous Palmenhaus, later burnt down.

Schlosspark Tegel

19 Adelheidallee, Reinickendorf, NW city centre
Owner: Ulrich von Heinz
Opening times: By appointment, Adelheidallee 19, D 1000 Berlin 27

The park once belonged to the scientist Wilhelm von Humboldt and is still in the possession of his descendants. At the end of the 18th century it consisted mainly of a vineyard, to which Humboldt added a vast meadow between the hill and the manor house. K. F. Schinkel redesigned the garden as a landscape park early in the 19th century. The impressive lime avenue dates from 1792.

PART FOUR

The Gardens of the Balkans, East Europe and Russia

Bulgaria

Bulgaria is almost bisected by the east–west Balkan ridge, the Stara Planina, the southern half of the great horseshoe of the Carpathians. Oak and beech forests flourish on the slopes of the mountains, which rise to over 2,900m. Roses are cultivated for oil of attar in the deep valleys and vines, peaches, mulberries (for silk-worms) and tobacco have long been staple crops here. Between the Balkan ridge and the mountainous frontiers with Turkey, Greece and Yugoslavia to the south and west run the Maritsa plains, sloping east to the Black Sea and with a favourable climate, although swept by dry tropical winds. North of the Balkan ridge fertile plains extend towards the Danube and the frontier with Romania. The Black Sea coastline stretching from north of Varna (*see* the Palace of Balchik) to the south of Burgas enjoys a soft climate where Mediterranean and exotic flora thrive without protection.

Crossed by trading routes from the Russian grasslands and the Asian steppes to the Mediterranean, Bulgaria also lay on the Danube corridor between western Europe and Asia Minor. These old routes were used by both conquerors and pilgrims: for over five centuries, from 1396 to the late 19th century, Bulgaria was part of the Ottoman empire, while Crusaders *en route* for the Holy Land described the dark impenetrable forests of the *Silva Bulgarie*.

Only grass-covered ruins remain where the Romans gardened or where medieval cities once flourished with their terraced gardens thrown out above cobbled streets. From the Turkish occupation in 1396 until the end of the 19th century there was no rich land-owning class to construct pleasure parks. Turkish customs prevailed, and hidden inner courtyards with flowerbeds and shady vine arbours were on a small scale and followed traditional folk patterns. Simple monastery gardens in mountainous regions, typical of those in the rest of Europe, survived Turkish rule. Existing murals in the 10th-century Rila monastery, the 14th-century Bachkovo monastery, the 16th-century church at Rozhen and in the Troyan monastery in the north reveal contemporary garden layouts. The Turks were finally ousted, with Russian assistance, in 1878, and after 1887 the new royal family of Coburg employed

PREVIOUS PAGES **The 18th-century Chinese temple at Pushkin near Leningrad reflected in water.**

foreigners to lay out large city parks and their own estates in both formal and landscape styles. Many exotic plants were found to flourish in areas of particularly favourable climate. Since 1945 the city park tradition has been extended to provide the Bulgarian people with areas for recreation and enjoyment of nature.

Parks in Bulgaria are owned by the State and are usually open daily.

Palace of Balchik ★ ✿
Balchik, 30km N of Varna on the Black Sea, Route 9
Admission charge: Yes

Part of Romania after the Balkan war of 1912–13, Balchik was returned to Bulgaria in 1940. The palace was the residence of the English-born Queen Maria Regina of Romania and the gardens were designed for her 1926–36 in an oriental style by the Frenchman Julius Janine. The high walls, luxuriant greenery and picturesque cascades make an enchanting background to the well-preserved royal palace, rotunda and ancillary buildings. Terraces with canals provide settings for decorative jars and vases brought from Morocco. Roses, jasmine and honeysuckles clamber over the terrace walls. Notable exotics which thrive in the favoured climate of the Black Sea coast include magnolias, albizias, persimmons, *Melia azedarach* (the Indian bead tree), and pomegranates. The garden is now a branch of the Botanical Gardens of Sofia University.

Drouzhba Park
9km N of Varna on the Black Sea
Admission charge: No

The park provides an attractive and leafy background to the resort. The planting includes large specimen cedars, junipers, limes, horse chestnuts, plane trees, albizias and box.

OVERLEAF ABOVE **Queen Maria Regina's garden at Balchik on the shores of the Black Sea was laid out between 1926–36.**

Kazanlŭk
33km NW of Stara Zagora on E85/E772

The beds of roses cultivated for the production of attar of roses, a distilled fragrant oil, are not strictly 'gardens', but are of interest to any horticulturist. This cottage industry in the south-facing valleys of the mountainous central area of Bulgaria has been a traditional occupation for centuries. The Alba roses, Rugosas and Centifolias were at first the main source of the oils, but experiments proved that the Damask rose, *Rosa × damascena* 'Trigintipetala', with soft pink flowers, gives the highest yield. This rose was brought to Bulgaria in the 17th century and cultivated in the valleys near the town of Kazanlŭk – sheltered from the cold north winds and yet cool in summer.

Sofia: The City Garden
In front of the National Art Gallery

This 3ha garden, where trees were first planted in 1837, is Bulgaria's oldest park. It was designed as part of the square in front of the Turkish town hall and was planted with a variety of different trees, including fruit trees. After Bulgaria's liberation from the Turks in 1878 it was redesigned by the Czech architect Anton Kolar in front of what was now the royal palace, and included flowerbeds and a fountain.

After the socialist revolution in 1944, the palace was converted into the National Art Gallery and the

OVERLEAF BELOW **The Varna Maritime Park on the Black Sea was laid out in the 19th century and many specimen trees survive from this time. Today, bedded-out annuals decorate the long walks.**

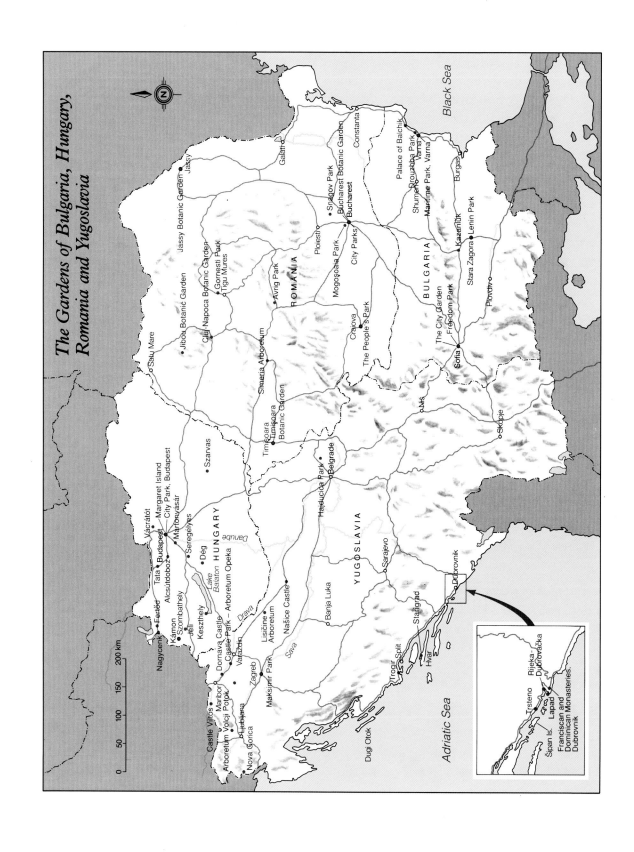

The Gardens of Bulgaria, Hungary, Romania and Yugoslavia

Black Sea

Palace of Balchik
Varna
Grouzdba Park, Varna
Shumen
Maritime Park, Varna
Burgas
BULGARIA
Kazanlik
Lenin Park
Stara Zagora
The City Garden
Freedom Park
Plovdiv
Sofia
Niš
Skopje

Constanta
Bucharest Botanic Garden
Bucharest
City Parks
Mogoşoaia Park
Ploieşti
Snagov Park
Galaţi
Avrig Park
Craiova
The People's Park
ROMANIA
Gorneşti Park
Tigu Mureş
Cluj-Napoca Botanic Garden
Jibou Botanic Garden
Jassy Botanic Garden
Jassy
Satu Mare

Simeria Arboretum
Timişoara
Timişoara Botanic Garden
Belgrade
Hajducica Park
Sarajevo
Dubrovnik
YUGOSLAVIA
Banja Luka
Našice Castle
Lisičine Arboretum
Castle Park – Arboretum Opeka
Varaždin
Zagreb
Maksimir Park
Nova Gorica
Ljubljana
Arboretum Volcji Potok
Maribor
Castle Vitos
Staigrad
Split
Trogir
Hvar
Dugi Otok

Szarvas
Szeged
HUNGARY
Lake Balaton
Danube
Drava
Sava
Dég
Keszthely
Jeli
Szombathely
Kámon
Nagycenk
Fertőd
Alcsútdoboz
Tata
Budapest
Margaret Island
City Park, Budapest
Martonvásár
Seregélyes
Vácrátót
Dornava Castle

Adriatic Sea

Rijeka – Dubrovačka
Trsteno
Lapad
Šipan Is.
Franciscan and Dominican Monasteries, Dubrovnik

0 50 100 150 200 km

N

garden was basically redesigned again. It consists of two parterre axes laid out in floral patterns and a huge rectangular fountain leading to the neo-baroque building of the Ivan Vazov National Theatre. The mausoleum of Georgi Dimitrov (the first Bulgarian prime minister after the 1944 revolution) is incorporated into the garden.

Sofia: Freedom Park
Entrance on Orlov Most Square (Eagle Bridge)

After 1878, when the Bulgarians finally shook off the Turkish yoke, Sofia became the capital city in place of the medieval Tirnovo. In 1882 a Swiss designer, Daniel Neff, laid out this 360ha English-style landscape park on what was then the outskirts of the city; it was named the Prince Boris Garden, after the crown prince born in 1894. Its present name comes from the dedication of a 41m obelisk ('Common Grave') to those who fell as partisans in the struggle for freedom from fascism in World War II. Neff made a large nursery garden which eventually became absorbed in the park. In 1906 Josef Fray extended the range of flower species. The layout today, prepared by Professor Sougarev in 1948, includes a Japanese garden, an English garden, roses and a rock garden and an open-air theatre. There are also recreational facilities.

Stara Zagora: The Lenin Park (formerly Ayazmo Park)★ ❀
89km NE of Plovdiv, on Route 66/E85

The Ayazmo, a holy spring believed to have curative properties, originally attracted people to what was a bare hillside. In 1895 Bishop Metodi Kousevich, Metropolitan of Stara Zagora, began to lay out a park with avenues commanding fine views over the town. The planting scheme benefited from a most favourable climatic situation (moderate minimum temperatures in winter, a hot dry summer and a warm autumn) with eight good growing months, and from an irrigation system. Today vegetation is lush and the park is of exceptional beauty. It has an alley of cypresses, groves of cedars and groups of Judas trees, besides many fine specimen trees.

Varna: Maritime Park
On the Black Sea, via A2/Route 9
Admission charge: No

Known as the 'Green Pearl' because of its collection of indigenous and foreign trees, this 116ha maritime park is more than a frame for a traditional holiday resort with promenade, former casino (now a restaurant) and open-air theatre. Already laid out in 1862 when Bulgaria was still under Turkish rule, the garden was extended after 1892 by a French engineer. Planting includes cedars, cypress, *Abies nobilis*, plane trees, pines, celtis, magnolias, albizias, tulip trees and liquidambars. The gardens continued to expand until the 1960s, when they merged with the neighbouring Saltanat gardens.

Czechoslovakia

Czechoslovakia, an area of great strategic and political importance in the heartland of Europe, is a long, narrow country made up since 1969 of two federal republics: the Czech Socialist Republic (consisting of Bohemia, Moravia and Silesia) with Prague (Praha) as its capital, and the Slovak Socialist Republic (Slovakia), with Bratislava as its capital.

The climate is continental, with warm, humid summers and cold, dry winters, but varies greatly with altitude and exposure; sheltered valleys in Moravia and in the foothills of the Carpathians can grow vines and fruit, while other regions, snowbound for much of the winter, have a more extreme regime.

There is a long, and continuing, tradition of gardening in Czechoslovakia, both formal and informal. The history of Czech garden style inevitably follows that of its neighbours – northern Austria, Germany (West and East), Poland and Hungary – and in the regions which were culturally aligned with Western Europe the pattern of garden development was similar: the contained gardens of the Italian Renaissance were followed by more ostentatious French baroque layouts which stretched into surrounding countryside and distant forests. In the east, in the more pastoral landscape of the Carpathians and their foothills, landowners were quicker to absorb the ideas behind the picturesque English style, and in the late 18th century adapted existing formal layouts to make new pleasure grounds in the winding valleys.

Unlike those in the rest of northern Europe, however, gardens in Czechoslovakia remained walled enclosures, connected to castles and monasteries, right into the renaissance period. Only at the end of the 16th century did new ideas spread gradually north from Italy. The Dutchman Hans Vredeman de Vries (*see* Introduction to Belgium and Holland) worked for the Habsburg Emperor Rudolph II in Prague in about 1596, extending the Royal Garden (q.v.) already laid out on Italian lines earlier in the century. Gardens at the royal seat of Brandýs (q.v.), just north of Prague on the Elbe, the moated garden at Kratochvíle (q.v.) in south Bohemia, and nearby Jindřichův Hradec (q.v.), all belong to the last quarter of the 16th century.

The prosperity of Bohemia and Moravia in the 17th century gave rise to castles with spacious pleasure gardens and hunting enclosures, such as the Wallenstein Garden (q.v.) in Prague. In the 18th century a number of remarkable baroque gardens were laid out. Buchlovice (q.v.) in Moravia is a beautiful example of Italian influence; Troja (q.v.), near Prague, shows a compromise between French and Italian styles; Jaroměřice nad Rokytnou (q.v.), also in Moravia, came very close to the French classical ideal – to which it has been partially restored after landscaping in the 19th century; and Dobříš (q.v.) in central Bohemia shows a strong French influence. The grand palaces in the Malá Strana below Prague Castle, with their staircases and terraces, also show European influences, but the workmanship is Czech.

Many of the gardens that can be visited today were originally baroque and were later altered to a more natural style. The English garden, or the French interpretation of the English garden, became fashionable towards the end of the 18th century. In 1769 the now lost garden at Červený Dvůr, a few kilometres west of Krumlov, possessed a grotto, a lake with an island and bridge, and Chinese and Dutch pavilions. In 1770 Count Albert von Hoditz entertained Frederick the Great at his new garden at Rosswald (now Rudoltice) in Silesia, where he provided dancing girls to perform as naiads among the grottoes and waterfalls. In 1755 the Auerspergs made an English-style garden in a winding steep-sided valley at Vlašim (q.v.), 52km south-east of Prague. Views by W. Berger and A. Pucherna, published 1802–5, show a

J. M. Fischer's 1691 engraving of Kroměříž shows the huge walled parterre garden and the long colonnade through which it was entered.

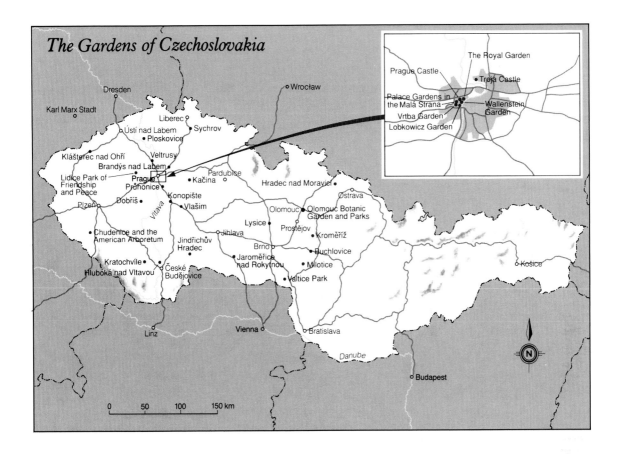

Chinese pavilion, a romantic grotto and an aviary, all set in picturesque scenery. In Slovakia, where castles remained fortified defence posts against repeated Turkish invasions and also protected trading routes until the end of the 18th century, English-style gardens were adopted with enthusiasm. 'Natural' parks with interesting planting of new introductions from both North America and then Asia continued to be created in different parts of the country throughout the 19th century.

The beginning of the 19th century also saw spa towns in Bohemia and Moravia laid out with spacious formal flowerbeds and specimen trees to give shade. Marienbad, made popular by Edward VII as Prince of Wales, Teplice and Franzensbad (all in west Bohemia), and Luhačovice in Moravia, are among the best known. In the 1850s municipal parks came to the fore, many of them built on old town fortifications.

Today, gardens originally made to frame palaces and castles for private landowners are well kept, and many historically important gardens have been or are being restored. The main buildings are often public institutions, such as museums, schools, offices or sanatoria. The many small private gardens and allotments are also carefully tended, with fruit, vegetables and flowers beautifully laid out, pruned and cherished.

Most gardens in Czechoslovakia are state-owned and open daily in summer from dawn to dusk with only a small admission charge. However, it would be wise to check with the nearest Čedok office as circumstances change and gardens may be closed for restoration.

Brandýs nad Labem
10km S of Stará Boleslav, 20km NE of Prague via E14

The original renaissance royal garden, with a summer house and terraces designed by H. de Vaccanni, was conceived in the late 1580s for Rudolph II and was designed to complement the massive castle romantically situated on a rock overlooking the Elbe. A place of great beauty, the garden was partly destroyed in 1639 during battles with the Turks. It is currently being restored.

Buchlovice ★ ⊛
In the Chřiby hills, 67km E of Brno on Route 50

The original terraced baroque garden, laid out on a slope in the Chřiby hills, was completely Italian in spirit to match the new castle built at the turn of the 17th century by Jan Dětřich of Petřvald for his Italian wife. Designed by a Roman, Domenico Martinelli, the axial garden had formal parterres and fountains. During the 18th century French influence became more important; balustrading, steps and statuary multiplied and topiary shapes were clipped on the terraces. In 1794 an obelisk was introduced to terminate the view beyond the fountain on the lowest level. In the middle of the 19th century, when another 50ha was attached to the garden, a park with interesting trees was laid out by the brothers Dr Leopold and Dr Friedrich Berchtold, both of whom were natural scientists and well-travelled. Today the park has 60 varieties of conifers and 143 species of deciduous trees. Both it and the formal gardens are well preserved.

Chudenice and the American Arboretum ⊛
Near Klatovy, 40km SW of Plzeň

Chudenice is a spa resort in Bohemia, established in the mid 19th century round the summer castle of the Černín family. A naturalistic landscape park was laid out by the landscape designer Blumenstang for Jan Rudolf Černín in the 1820s and planting continued all through the 19th century.

The *American Arboretum* is 700m from the spa. Influenced by the botanic garden founded by Count Sternberg near the Castle of Březina in about 1841, planting was mainly of rare foreign trees (not all, in spite of the name) from America. Trees came from Bubeneč Park in Prague and from the nurseryman J. Booth, and later from Vienna and from Erfurt in East Germany. They include the oldest Douglas fir (*Pseudotsuga menziesii*) in Czechoslovakia. The layout is geometric with a network of paths.

Dobříš ★
44km SW of Prague via Route 4
Owner: Czech Union of Writers

The large castle, built for Jindřich Pavel Mansfeld 1745–65, was designed by Robert de Cotte and G. N. Servadoni. The baroque garden layout with rococo elements was de Cotte's work and, completed in 1765, shows a strong French influence. Covering an area of 65ha, it extends over five terraces, with a fountain, statues on mythological themes, rococo *putti*, stone urns and clipped trees adorning the 200m main axis. An orangery with *trompe l'oeil* paintings and an Apollo statue in a niche is by I. F. Platzer, who also worked at Schönbrunn in Austria (q.v.) for the Empress Maria Theresa. In 1909 a rose garden, designed by M. Bertram from Dresden, was laid out near the castle. The original (and surviving) parterre and *bassin* were altered by Jean Touret in 1911.

Behind the formal garden, a 32ha English-style park with meadows, a lake and a valley, and planted with woodland groves as well as specimen trees, was created in about 1800 under the walls of the old Vargač fortress. Natural stone terraces with caves add a picturesque note and there are romantic views. In 1878 a 'new park' was laid out by the chief gardener of Opočno on the River Kněžňa, J. Liehm. Both landscape areas at Dobříš evolved without sweeping away any of the earlier formal design.

Hluboká nad Vltavou
15km NW of České Budějovice via Route 22

The mid 19th-century neo-gothic castle, inspired by Windsor Castle near London, stands in the middle of a 19th-century landscape park which replaced an early formal layout of rare fruit trees. Both castle and park were designed and built by a Viennese architect, Franz Beer. In 1851 11,597 trees and 2,180 shrubs were planted by the gardener Gervasius Immelin. Picturesque views with groves of exotic and native trees are a feature here. There are also huge fishponds and the River Vltava borders the park to the east.

Hradec nad Moravicí
9km S of Opava

The renaissance château created out of the original royal castle was altered in 1795 when a 40ha landscape park in the English style was laid out by Prince Karel Alois Lichnov, and again in 1860. The park was enlarged and planting continued through the 19th century, with use being made of picturesque buildings at selected spots and views extending into the natural countryside.

OVERLEAF LEFT **At Buchlovice, the baroque French-style parterres were added in the early 18th century to an existing Italian layout.**

Jaroměřice nad Rokytnou ★
Near Třebíč, 50km W of Brno

The medieval castle was rebuilt in baroque style 1700–37 and set off by a 15ha park with elaborate parterres and great vistas stretching to the horizon. The garden was probably designed by the Austrian Lukas von Hildebrandt and both it and the new castle are recorded in a drawing of 1710. A vast French-style *parterre de broderie*, statues and clipped trees occupied the central space, with avenues and orchards fanning out around. The Rokytna river was rechannelled and a theatre on an artificially created island was the setting for musical soirées through the 18th century. During the 19th century much of the elaborate baroque layout disappeared to make way for a naturalistic landscape park, but in spite of this traces of the earlier garden remain. Restoration based on the outlines revealed by an aerial photograph was begun in the 1950s and a formal knot garden in gravel and sand has been recreated.

Jindřichův Hradec
48km NE of České Budějovice via Route 34

Terraced gardens round the castle, focused on a central, star-shaped stone *bassin*, date from as early as 1590 and include a 'rondel', a jewel of Czech renaissance architecture, designed by G. M. Faconi. The single-storey arcade containing a grotto was built at the same period by Faconi, Baltazar Maio da Vomio and Antonio Cometa to enclose the castle garden.

There is also a fine mid 19th-century public park in the town.

Kačina
82km E of Prague via Route 38, between Kolin and Čáslav

A neo-classical house, designed by the Dresden architect C. F. Schuricht and built 1802–22 by a Czech professor of architecture, is surrounded by a public park which was begun before 1800. It was laid out by Count Jan Rudolf Chotek, a leading minister

OVERLEAF RIGHT **Annuals grow in the parterre at Kroměříž.**

of the Austro-Hungarian Empire, who became *Oberstburggraf* of Bohemia in 1802. He had previously worked on the park at Veltrusy (q.v.). The gardens at Kačina were partly conceived as a botanic garden, advice being given by Nikolaus von Jacquin and his son, keepers of the botanic garden at Schönbrunn in Vienna (q.v.). Grass lawns in the new English landscape style swept up to the mansion's windows and down to the lake. At the same time Chotek retained some formal elements: radiating avenues, centred on the house, stretched into the landscape, one avenue even continuing on the far side of the lake. Today a formal garden frames the building but the main planting is in a naturalistic style, although the remains of a lime avenue still exist by the side of the lake.

Klášterec nad Ohří
20km SW of Chomutov, Route 13

This landscape park, dating from the 1820s, was designed on the site of an earlier baroque garden belonging to the Thun family. Some statues of the seasons remain from the early garden as well as Rossi di Lucca's colonnaded *sala terrena* dating from 1666. There are scenic views over rolling countryside by the River Ohře, the mixed terrain – some hilly and some water-logged by the river – providing opportunities for planting trees requiring different sites.

Konopište ★ ❀
50km SE of Prague via Routes 1 and 3; 3km W of Benešov

The castle, built on a granite spur, belonged first to the leading Czech families of Beneš and Sternberk and then, in the 17th century, to Albrecht von Wallenstein (*see* Wallenstein Garden, Prague). It was bought in 1887 by the Habsburg Archduke Franz Ferdinand d'Este, the heir to the Austro-Hungarian throne, who was assassinated at Sarajevo in 1914. With his difficult political life and morganatic marriage, Franz Ferdinand found a refuge in gardening and spent his happiest days at Konopište. Formal terraces were laid out in place of the original moat, and a wide lake stretched away from the castle walls; small hills and meadows, trees and deer combine to

give the huge park a natural beauty. The Archduke laid out a geometrical rose garden and used species roses for hedges throughout the estate. He inherited the fabulous Villa d'Este in Tivoli (q.v.) from his cousin the Duke of Modena, and was able to enrich the Konopište gardens with many Italian renaissance statues.

Kaiser Wilhelm II and the German Admiral von Tirpitz visited Konopište in early June 1914, two weeks before the Sarajevo assassination. Thought at the time to have been a 'political' visit, his secretary's records prove that the Admiral wanted to see the 8ha rose garden at its peak.

Kratochvíle
Near Netolice, 70km SE of Plzeň

The Italian renaissance villa was built for William of Rožmberk by Baltazar Maio da Vomio in 1583–9. The rectangular garden was surrounded by an outer bailey and a moat, with a number of 'water machines'. It is at present being restored.

Kroměříž
On the Morava river, 68km E of Brno via Routes 46 and 47

The massive castle and surrounding complex of buildings in the main square dominate the whole town of Kroměříž; its garden, the Kvetna (Flower) Garden, lies outside the town walls. Engravings by J. van den Nypoort and J. M. Fischer published in 1691 show the palace and huge walled parterre garden, modelled on Versailles and with its entrance through a colonnade 230m long, later a gallery for statues representing mythological themes. An octagonal summer-house with lovely interior decoration dominates the garden. By 1727 the main parterre had been altered, the garden extended to reach the banks of the River Morava, and French-style avenues had been planted into the surrounding countryside.

From 1777–1811 the property was given a more romantic and picturesque flavour in the fashion of the time. A lake and fishing lodge, a hermitage, an artificial ruin with a waterfall, temples on an island and other romantic features were all added at this period. The naturalistic landscape was further extended in the middle of the century with the creation of another lake, with a Chinese pavilion on an island, and the introduction of Maximilian's Courtyard and a Pompey colonnade. There are some fine trees and shrubs. The garden has been under restoration since 1954, when P. Janák designed new parterres in front of the original colonnade and restored the baroque fountain. The whole area, including a large orangery, is open to the public.

Lednice: Valtice Park ★ ⊛
Near Břeclav and the Austrian border, 50km S of Brno, W of motorway and Route 2

Lednice castle belonged to the Liechtenstein family from 1249 until the end of World War II. Originally a gothic stronghold, frequent alterations culminated in the romantic neo-gothic castle seen today. Nothing now remains of the 17th-century garden designed in baroque style for Prince Karel Eusebius Liechtenstein by J. B. Fischer von Erlach, although its grandeur was captured in engravings by J. A. Delenbach. Instead, the two adjoining properties of Lednice and Valtice (acquired by the Liechtenstein family in 1395) demonstrate how successfully the English landscape style could be adapted to southern Moravia.

At the end of the 18th century Count Alois Josef von Liechtenstein swept away the terraces, sculpture, water basins and fountains which had been laid out in the marshland near Lednice castle, in order to make a romantic park in the form of a star. Picturesque buildings such as a minaret, an obelisk, a Chinese pavilion and an artificial ruin were designed by Joseph Hardtmuth and built 1798–1802. In the early 1800s, partly to reduce flooding, vast new water basins and lakes (the 'Lednice fishponds') were dug out in the flat terrain of the hunting park towards Valtice, 8km away on the border with Austria; fifteen islands in the 34ha of waterways were joined by bridges. As a concession to formality an avenue joined the two estates. Planting plans for the parks were devised with the help of the botanist Richard van der Schott, who introduced 36,000 exotics, mainly from North America.

At the beginning of the 19th century, further garden buildings were added, at first in neo-classical style, later in neo-gothic, to match the extensive alterations carried out at Lednice in 1842. An enormous glasshouse of light cast-iron, its pillars imitating bamboos, was added to the house in 1843 by an Englishman, E. Devien, in place of a theatre and winter garden; this structure leads to a terrace formed by the roof of a baroque orangery, famous in the late 17th century for its collection of exotic citrus fruits, figs and olives. After 1859 the head gardener laid out vast formal flowerbeds which still exist today. The parkland, some 270ha in extent, acquired its present appearance about 1880; many trees date from Van der Schott's planting and provide cover for rare birds which nest on the islets in the lakes.

Lidice Park of Friendship and Peace
22km NW of Prague via Route 7

The village of Lidice was annihilated by the Nazis in 1942, in retaliation for the murder of the German governor and police chief, R. Heydrich. The 'Park of Friendship and Peace', with terraces, rose beds and fountains, is a touching memorial. Thousands of roses were sent here from all over the world in March 1955.

Lysice
Near Blankso, W of Route 43, 30km N of Brno

The castle was renovated in the 1730s by Count Serényi, but Italianate terraces date from the early 17th century. Fine allegorical statues of the months of the year decorate niches on the top level. A colonnade and a box parterre inside an original walled garden date from the 19th century, when a number of alterations were made.

Milotice ★
10km N of Hodonín and 35km SW of Uherské Hradiště

A renaissance castle, of which parts of the ramparts and moat survive, was rebuilt in late baroque style from 1722–5 for Karl Anthony Serényi, probably by J. B. Fischer von Erlach. The castle, approached by a stone bridge, has formal gardens on three sides; behind, avenues of lime trees and maples stretch into the countryside. Fortunately, although threatened with 'anglicization' in the first half of the 19th century, most of this rare 4.5ha garden has survived in its original form, although planting behind the castle is naturalistic.

Olomouc Botanic Garden and Parks

Olomouc

Opening times: Daily all year; *flower shows* end Apr/early May and late Aug

The historic town of Olomouc, capital of Moravia 1187–1641, is also known today for its annual flower shows, Flora Olomouc. Three parks and the botanic garden, together covering some 50ha, lie to the south and west of the old town fortifications. Laid out in about 1820, their present appearance dates from the beginning of the 20th century and the great palm house was built in the 1930s. Since then a rose garden

RIGHT **At Lednice, 17th-century baroque parterres vanished when the park was landscaped at the end of that century. Today, a vast 19th-century layout of colourful flowerbeds strikes a formal note in the park. A glasshouse (BELOW), backing a box-hedged parterre, was designed by an Englishman in the mid 19th century.**

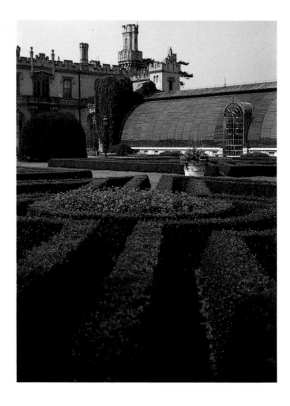

and alpine garden have been added and more glass-houses built: a cacti and succulent house, and a tropical house holding the largest collection of orchids in Czechoslovakia. Fine trees include a 710m lime avenue, a swamp cypress, a honey locust, koelreuterias, dawn redwoods, magnolias and a tulip tree.

Ploskovice
Near Litoměřice

There are gardens on two different levels of the baroque castle which, with arcaded galleries on both sides, was built in about 1730 by Octavio Broggio. Grottoes under the side terraces were covered in paintings and stucco decoration. In 1816 the geometric designs on the terraces were replaced with winding paths and irregularly-shaped flowerbeds, although a water pool with obelisks remained as part of the main central axis. Today the park to the east of the castle is planted in the landscape style.

Prague: Lobkowicz Garden
Vlašská Street; also entered from the monastery of Strahov or the seminary garden along the Observation Path

A terraced garden contemporary with the palace (now the West German embassy) was laid out in the early 18th century, but was converted after 1793 into the English park that we see today. J. V. Skalník, who designed the spa park at Marienbad, founded an alpine garden here in the 19th century, introducing the first collection of alpine plants in Bohemia. Only part of the garden is open to the public.

Prague: Palace Gardens in the Malá Strana ★
Entrance from Valdštejnská (Wallenstein) Street, Malá Strana, next to Kolowrat Palace
Opening times: Erratically during the summer months

Palaces were built in the Malá Strana on the left bank of the Vltava river from the 16th century onwards. Four 18th-century gardens, once attached to their own palaces but today joined together, lie on the steep south-facing terraced slopes (formerly occupied by vineyards) below the castle. All the top Czech architects of the period worked here, and 18th-century fountains, *bassins*, *gloriettes* and statues remain. The gardens were restored in the 1950s and there are good views of Prague from the upper terraces.

The terraced *Ledebour Gardens* were laid out in the early 1700s by the Trauttmannsdorff family in formal baroque style, but were modified in 1801 by I. J. Palliardi when the palace was enlarged and the *gloriette* built. Also of the 1700s, and restored, is the *sala terrena* with its walls and vaults painted with idealized landscapes. Open-air concerts take place here every summer.

The Pálffy Gardens, with terraces and loggias, were laid out by the Fürstenbergs in the mid 18th century.

The Černín Garden (also known as the Kolowrat Garden), the richest of these gardens, was built for Marie Barbora Černínová (*see* Chudenice) in 1874 by I. J. Palliardi, with a grand *sala terrena* on the top terrace. There are elaborate balustraded stone stairways, loggias, and fountains decorated with statues and vases.

The Fürstenberg Garden is now part of the Polish Embassy and not accessible to the public, but it is possible to obtain a glimpse of the mid 18th-century garden from Valdštejnská Street.

Prague: Prague Castle

Prague Castle, the former royal palace and now the residence of the President of the Republic, was first built in the 9th century, rebuilt as a romanesque palace in the 12th century, extended in gothic style in the 14th century by the Holy Roman Emperor Charles IV, and has been adapted frequently since. Three gardens created in the 1920s and 1930s were designed by J. Plečnik from a park of 1861, which itself marked the site of earlier layouts. *The Garden on the Bastion* lies at the western end of the castle between Hradčanské Square and the Second Courtyard of the castle, on the site of a rococo pavilion built by the Empress Maria Theresa (plans by N. Pacassi in 1762). Open-air concerts are held here in summer. *The Garden on the Ramparts* can be reached from Plečnik's staircase from the Third Courtyard of the castle and is linked to the Garden of Paradise. There are rockeries on the terraces below the Windischgrätz Wall and an observation terrace above. *The*

Garden of Paradise, occupying the western part of the southern slope below the castle, is on the site of a 16th-century garden, founded when the ramparts were filled in, and is reached from Hradčanské Square via Plečnik's open *sala terrena* and monumental staircase. The cylindrical Matthias Arbour in the south-east corner of the garden has a wooden renaissance ceiling and was built in 1617.

Prague: The Royal Garden

Between U Prašného mostu Street and the Summer Palace, N of Prague Castle

The Italian renaissance royal Summer Palace (also known as the Belvedere) was built 1538–52 for Ferdinand I in the form of an inverted ship's hull. In 1534 G. Spati laid out the large renaissance garden, which was later adorned with an aviary, a lion court and an orangery. It was further altered under Rudolph II in about 1596 by Hans Vredeman de Vries in the Dutch style, and is today separated from the palace.

P. O. Mattioli, the 16th-century Italian physician and botanist, introduced tulips from Turkey here, among the first to reach Europe (*see* Botanic Gardens of Vienna and Leiden). Original sculptures and vases from the 17th and 18th centuries adorn P. Janák's imaginative post-war restoration of the garden, which was largely destroyed in 1945.

In front of the Summer Palace itself a small 16th-century Italian-style box parterre was reconstructed by Janák in the late 1930s. There is also a charming Italian singing fountain of the 16th century, and the remains of a fig house of the same period can be seen below the terrace. This garden and the palace itself are at present closed for restoration.

Prague: Vrtba Garden

Karmelitska Street, Malá Strana
Opening times: Daily, May to Sept 8–19

Vrtba palace consists of two renaissance houses which were originally separated by a lane leading to vineyards on the slopes of Petrin, but were joined in about 1631. The lane became a passage and the vineyards were laid out as a terraced garden in about 1720, with classical and allegorical figures and stone

vases decorating the terraces. There are mythological paintings and statues in a *sala terrena* in the lower part of the garden, and magnificent views from the observation terrace at the top.

Prague: Wallenstein Garden

Next to Wallenstein Palace, entrance in Letenská Street, Malá Strana
Opening times: May to Sept 9–19

The palace and its walled garden were constructed for Albrecht von Wallenstein (*see* Konopiště) after 1623 when he demolished a medieval quarter of the town to accommodate them. The imposing *sala terrena* of the 1620s was designed by G. B. Pieroni, with stucco-work and painted ceilings by B. Bianco. The grotto nearby has a pool and artificial stalagmites and stalactites, and a small salon has frescoes depicting the story of the Golden Fleece. Formal pools reflect the palace facade. A bronze fountain with a Venus dates from the early 17th century, as does the avenue of statues (by the Dutch artist Adrien de Vries) leading across the terraced area – though the originals, removed in 1648, are now at Drottningholm Castle in Sweden (q.v.) and 19th-century copies take their place. A high wall with artificial stalactites has an aviary decorated in the style of the grotto. Open-air concerts are held here in summer.

Průhonice ✹

In the W suburbs of Prague, 16km from the centre of the city, via road to Chodonov or Prague–Benešov motorway
Opening times: Apr to Oct 7–19

Průhonice castle was reconstructed in pseudo-renaissance style in the 1890s and the park, one of Czechoslovakia's finest, was created by Count Ernst Emanuel Sylva-Taroucca at the same period (with advice from the notable dendrologist Camillo Schneider). Planted informally as an arboretum, it covers 260ha in hilly, rocky countryside where four streams meet, one of them, the Botič, forming three large lakes. The climate is mild and humid, providing excellent growing conditions for one of the most interesting collections of plants in Czechoslovakia. There are plants from all over the world, including kalmias, rhododendrons and azaleas, and the botanical institute in the castle has been responsible for introducing many new hybrids to the country.

Sychrov

Near Liberec, 7km N of Tornov

The original castle, on a plateau above the river Mohelka, was transformed into a neo-gothic palace by Prince Camille de Rohan in the middle of the 19th century, and the baroque garden redesigned as a landscape park. Most of the extensive planting dates from this time, but older avenues of oak and lime radiate diagonally from the castle to the park gates and beyond. A fountain dominates the courtyard garden in front of the castle, and from the terrace a central axis leads across a lawn to a renaissance-style orangery which forms a focal point to the east.

Troja Castle

N of Prague, reached from Stromorka park across the Vltava river or from U Trojeského Mostu

The terraced garden, marking the transition between the Italian renaissance and French baroque style, was originally laid out at the end of the 17th century. A grand garden staircase is decorated with classical deities, and terracotta vases adorn the balustrades. The garden has recently reopened after extensive restoration.

Veltrusy

On the River Vltava, 28km N of Prague via E55
Opening times: Daily, May to Aug 8–17; Sept to Apr 9–16

Count Václav Antonin Chotek bought the estate in 1698. His son extended the castle to create the present building and began a French-style baroque garden, which was in turn transformed into a 120ha landscape park by Count Jan Rudolf Chotek (*see* Kačina) after 1784. The botanist Richard van der Schott (*see* Lednice) collaborated in the planting, which today includes a large specimen ginkgo, white pines, tulip trees, a fine cut-leaved beech, sweet chestnuts, celtis and honeylocusts. Chotek built a chain of small buildings and monuments in an abandoned, sickle-shaped meander of the River Vltava. A square pavilion in honour of Field Marshal Laudon, the Temple of Friendship and a grotto between them (all dating from the very end of the 18th century) make a charming group. A Doric temple was added in 1811. Many neo-classical and neo-gothic garden buildings survive and provide focal points on walks through the woods. In the castle courtyard a small rococo parterre has recently been restored.

Vlašim

52km SE of Prague, via Routes 1 and 3

This romantic 75ha landscape, the oldest naturalistic garden in Bohemia, was created in a deer park and incorporates ancient forest trees. Lying behind the renaissance and baroque castle in the valley of the River Blanice, it was designed by Karel and Marie Auersperg in 1755. Many of the original features, including a Turkish minaret, no longer exist, but a neo-gothic entrance gate and a Chinese pavilion do remain. The park is being restored.

East Germany

The northern two-thirds of the German Democratic Republic consist of a low-lying plain, bounded by the Baltic Sea to the north and including a vast swampy area around Berlin which is fed by the Havel and Spree and drained by lakes and canals; the southern third is hilly, with the Thuringian Forest and the watershed of the Fichtelgebirge in the south-west and the Erzgebirge in the south-east. Summers are warm, though temperatures are lower than those of West Germany, and winter temperatures are often well below freezing for several months of the year. Average rain and snowfall is 700mm per annum in the low-lying north and more in the hilly south. Criss-crossed with rivers in the north, and with the Oder-Neisse forming the border with Poland to the east, it is nevertheless the Elbe that dominates, and on which many of the important gardens are built. Entering the country in the south near Dresden, it sweeps round to the west of Berlin and flows north to Hamburg in West Germany, and the sea.

The horticultural history of East Germany is intimately bound up with that of Germany as a whole – and indeed, since the boundaries of Germany have changed many times over the centuries, with the rest of Europe (*see* Introduction to West Germany). However, it is for the baroque gardens of the 18th century and the imaginative landscape designs of the early 19th that East Germany is best known. The beautiful Barockpark Grossedlitz (q.v.) on the Elbe near Dresden, begun in 1719 but never completely finished, was followed by Sanssouci (q.v.) at Potsdam, with its extraordinary curved terraces (recently restored), parterre and what J. C. Loudon described as 'every appendage and ornament of the Italian, French and Dutch taste'.

Towards the end of the 18th century the first of three great names in garden design appear: Prince Franz von Anhalt-Dessau began work on a huge scheme to turn 25km of land along the River Elbe between Dessau and Wörlitz into an 'arranged' landscape – the Gartenreich area – in which agriculture and forestry were to play a part. Influenced by visits to England, and in particular to Stourhead (q.v.), Stowe (q.v.) and Claremont, Prince von Anhalt-Dessau's work owed much to his travels. In the east of the country, at Muskau (q.v.), another landowner, Prince Hermann Pückler-Muskau, laid out a huge picturesque landscape garden in the valley of the Neisse after 1816. The Prince had also visited England and had admired the work of the English garden designer Humphry Repton. The garden at Muskau, together with the Prince's *Andeutungen über Landschaftsgärtnerei (Hints on Landscape*

Prince Pückler-Muskau was influenced by Humphry
Repton and English garden design in his own garden
at Muskau. In the 1820s he employed John Adey
Repton to give him further advice. The engraving is
from *Hints on Landscape Gardening* (1834) by
Prince Pückler-Muskau himself.

Gardening), published in 1834, became in turn an important influence on the
development of romantic parkland in Europe and North America. Landscape design in the first half of the 19th century was also profoundly
influenced by the work of Peter Josef Lenné. Lenné worked in Germany and
Austria on both public parks and private gardens, but is probably best known
for his work round Potsdam and the Havel lakes in Prussia, for which he drew
up an overall 'Plan to Embellish the Isle of Potsdam' in 1833. Lenné also
founded a school of gardening and formed an association for the encourage-
ment of gardening.

In East Germany today there is an energetic policy to restore historic
gardens of international importance and much has already been done. Many
of the palaces and houses round which these gardens lie are now used as
museums. Gardens are normally open during the hours of daylight and
admission is free.

Park Babelsberg

Babelsberg, 7km E of Potsdam; on the River Havel
Owner: Staatliche Schlösser und Gärten Potsdam-Sanssouci

From 1833 Peter Josef Lenné and Karl Friedrich Schinkel both worked on the plans for the park surrounding Schloss Babelsberg on the River Havel – part of an overall scheme for the Potsdam landscape (*see* Introduction). The designs, with broad drives leading from the castle, were influenced by Windsor Great Park in England. After 1843 Prince Hermann Pückler-Muskau (*see* Schlosspark Muskau and Introduction) took over the management of the gardens for the future Emperor William I and extended them to the south, increasing the area to over 200ha (now reduced to 110ha) and adding further garden features. The pleasure grounds with colourful flowerbeds, a Golden Rose Garden with a heron fountain (the *Reiherfontaine*), the Kleines Schloss and the Gerichtslaube (the Little Castle and Court Summerhouse), both important follies, lead on to extensive picturesque woodland where large specimen oaks and beeches still survive. Lakes and waterfalls abound, and follies added from the 1850s include the Flatow Tower surrounded by a water basin and built as a viewing-point, a coach house and various lodges. Between the Schloss and the River Havel lies a bowling green.

Berlin: Treptower Volkspark

SE of city centre
Owner: Berlin Municipal Council

These public gardens bordering the River Spree were constructed in 1876 to the designs of Gustav Meyer, the first director of municipal gardens for the city of Berlin. Large open spaces are framed by magnificent oak and lime trees shading broad rides. In one of these spaces stands a memorial to the Soviet soldiers who died during the battle for Berlin in World War II. There is a big carp pond in the southeast area of the park. A colourful summer flower garden also serves as an exhibition space for sculpture.

Park Branitz

Branitz, SE of Cottbus town centre
Owner: Cottbus Town Council

After Prince Hermann Pückler-Muskau sold Muskau (q.v.), he changed the layout of his manor house at Branitz, starting on the 70ha park in 1846. Terraces were built, existing buildings altered and a pergola erected. The Schmiedewiesen was laid out in front of the smithy, and elaborate enclosures contained flowerbeds, kiosks and statues. Prince Pückler-Muskau's nephew took over after his death in 1871 and completed the work by 1910. The high water-table made it possible to create artificial lakes and waterways which are an important feature. The park has beautiful specimen trees, mainly oak and beech, and high earth pyramids, and there are vistas from the castle through magnificent stands of trees. Cast-zinc sculptures and terracotta reliefs by the 18th-century Danish sculptor Bertel Thorwaldsen decorate the gardens near the castle.

One lake contains a pyramid tomb where the prince and his wife are buried. The inscription is from the Koran: 'Graves are the mountain tops of a distant, lovely land.'

Park Georgium

On the River Elbe between Dessau and Wörlitz
Owner: Dessau Town Council

The Georgium, named after its owner Johann Georg, Prince von Anhalt, was developed after 1780 5km west of Wörlitz Park (q.v.). The white classical building by F. W. von Erdmannsdorff (1780) is complemented by formal gardens, where long narrow vistas lead to decorative garden features including an Ionic temple, Roman ruins, the Sphinx Porticus, the House of Vases, a ruined bridge and many sculptures. In the woodland beyond the formal gardens there are other buildings: the Amalia Seat, an obelisk, the Elbe Pavilion, Wallwitz Castle and the Princes' Seat. The park has wide views of the River Elbe and the meadows which lie along its banks, and of the wooded parkland linking the landscape to Wörlitz.

Barockpark Grossedlitz

Grossedlitz-Heidenau, 21km SE of Dresden via Route 172
Owner: Heidenau Town Council

This baroque garden lies in a valley above the river Elbe, its lateral axis extending across a parterre and lawn, and over hedges and a ha-ha into the river landscape. It was started in 1719, worked on in two stages, but never completely finished. An orangery with a parterre, a grand cascade to the east with a beautiful sandstone staircase and softly playing fountains (known as *Stille Musik*), the many sculptures, all contribute to the sensitive beauty of this garden.

Park Luisium

Dessau-Waldersee; on the River Elbe between Dessau and Waldersee
Owner: Staatliche Schlösser und Gärten Wörlitz, Oranienbaum, Luisium

As part of his great plan for the Wörlitz area (*see* Wörlitz), Prince Franz von Anhalt-Dessau commissioned Johann Friedrich Eyserbeck from 1774 to enlarge and redesign the original park as a romantic landscape. Wilhelm Muller (nicknamed 'the Greek') praised it as the most beautiful garden in Germany. The manor house on the shore of a lake forms the centre of a star, with great vistas which lead out into the park and beyond to a church and obelisk. As well as an interesting orangery (1782–4), there are several decorative buildings and sculptures, including a Palladian bridge, the Pegasus Fountain, a grotto and a triumphal gate with a statue of Hermes. Many of the enormous old oaks, yews, sweet chestnuts and tulip trees date back to the first planting of the garden. As at Georgium (q.v.), there are fine views to the Elbe.

Moritzburg

16km NW of Dresden

The 18th-century Schloss, with its terracing, hunting statues and four small gardens with clipped trees,

At Grossedlitz the gardens, beautifully situated above the River Elbe, have extensive views into the landscape. The fine sandstone staircase terminates one of the axial vistas.

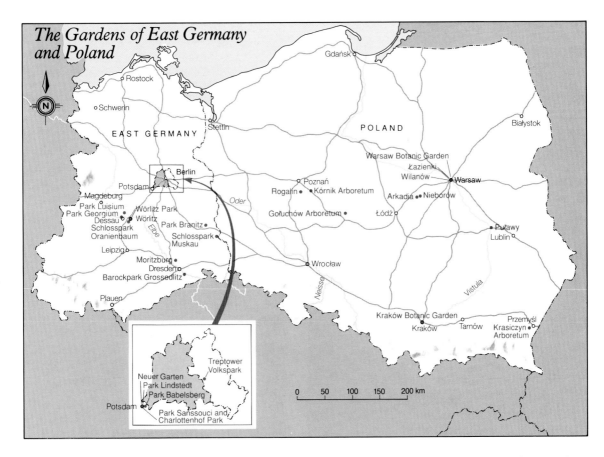

The Gardens of East Germany and Poland

is set on an island in an immense lake surrounded by a wooded hunting park of the 16th and 18th centuries. On the shore to the north is a parterre garden with garden rooms and a green theatre. A canal, lighthouse, grottoes and a pheasantry also date from the 18th century.

Schlosspark Muskau ★
Bad Muskau, 30km SE of Cottbus on Route 115
Owner: Bad Muskau Town Council

After 1816 Prince Hermann Pückler-Muskau designed and laid out his extensive landscape garden in the valley of the River Neisse. Unfortunately, it had to be sold in 1845. Prince Pückler-Muskau, famous travel writer as well as one of Germany's most important and sensitive garden designers, had travelled in England and was an admirer of Repton. The layout at Muskau, which made use of old forest trees and had

paths designed to accommodate changes of level and to provide views to the river and Hermannsneisse (a small artificial stream), is an artistic masterpiece, and became an important influence on the development of romantic parkland in Europe and America. The Prince published his *Andeutungen über Landschafts-gärtnerei (Hints on Landscape Gardening)* in 1834.

Schlosspark Oranienbaum
Oranienbaum, 10km SE of Dessau at junction with Route 107
Owner: Staatliche Schlösser und Gärten Wörlitz, Oranienbaum, Luisium

The park at Oranienbaum was laid out in the baroque Dutch style by Cornelius Ryckwaert towards the end of the 17th century. It included a kitchen garden, a deer park, a maze, and an island garden formed by diverting a stream. In about 1795 the island garden was redesigned by Prince Franz von Anhalt-Dessau as a Chinese garden, with a five-storey pagoda modelled on the one at Kew in England (q.v.), several small Chinese bridges, and a tea-house. In the 1920s and 1930s the Chinese garden and the large (2.6ha) parterre were reconstructed and the woodland areas of the park replanted. The star-shaped road system of the *bosquets* is still in existence.

Potsdam: Park Lindstedt

30km SW of Berlin, NW of Sanssouci
Owner: Staatliche Schlösser und Gärten Potsdam-Sanssouci
Opening times: By appointment, Schloss Lindstedt

The manor house of Lindstedt extends the park of Sanssouci (q.v.) beyond the Teufelsbrücke (the Devil's Bridge) to the north-west. The park was redesigned by Peter Josef Lenné after 1859. Today, in front of the south facade of the house, with its remarkable stairway and portico, a regularly-shaped lawn has cross paths planted as avenues with Japanese cherries. These frame vistas into the surrounding landscape and to the cupola of the Neues Palais. Behind a delicately structured colonnade, the northern garden has an axis leading from an *exedra* to a hill.

Potsdam: Neuer Garten

30km SW of Berlin
Owner: Staatliche Schlösser und Gärten Potsdam-Sanssouci

Former vineyards and little gardens along the Heiligen See and stretching north to the River Havel were developed by Johann August Eyserbeck in 1787 into the Neuer Garten, one of the earliest romantic gardens in Prussia. Extensive alterations were made by Peter Josef Lenné after 1816, all part of his overall plan for Potsdam (*see* Introduction). An oak avenue adorned with Dutch buildings leads from the park entrance to Carl Gontard's late 18th-century Marmorpalais on the lake, and the park is scattered with Egyptian, classical, Moorish and gothic buildings and features. A rectangular flower parterre by Lenné lies on the garden side of the Marmorpalais and another flower garden, enriched by rare plants, sets off the nearby orangery. In the northern part of the park is Schloss Cecilienhof, built 1913–17 in the style of an English manor house. It has four charming separate gardens. The many rare plants, the Fountain of Narcissus and the yew topiary create a world of their own.

Potsdam: Park Sanssouci and Charlottenhof Park ★

30km SW of Berlin
Owner: Staatliche Schlösser und Gärten, Potsdam-Sanssouci

In 1715 Frederick I of Prussia laid out a kitchen garden on a site at Potsdam. In 1744 his son, Frederick II, bought an adjacent hillside, built six

The colonnade in the park at Sanssouci. Engraving from Dohme's *Baroque and Rococo Architecture*.

Salzmann's plan shows the formal layout and the landscape park at Sanssouci.

The gardens at Wörlitz were laid out after 1765 as one of the earliest romantic landscapes in Germany. Temples, bridges and other ornamental buildings decorate the park.

vast terraced vineyards (recently restored), each with glazing for peaches and vines and adorned with yew pyramids, and began work on the palace of Sanssouci. A little later the terraces were extended to the south by a parterre, to which a fountain and a pond were subsequently added. During the rest of the 18th century various further additions were made to the park, most of them lying along the avenue to the Neues Palais 2km away. The orangery, later rebuilt as guest rooms, the Neptune grotto, the Chinese teahouse with its own garden, and the Dutch garden are all of this period. Sanssouci is also interesting for its rare specimen trees.

The *Charlottenhof Park* to the south was added in 1826. Its elaborate landscape garden, and that of the Hofgarten to the north of the Neues Palais, were laid out by P. J. Lenné and include Italianate buildings, a charming court gardener's house, small formal flower gardens, statuary, a lake and canals.

Wörlitz Park ★

Wörlitz, 15km E of Dessau at junction with Route 107
Owner: Staatliche Schlösser und Gärten Wörlitz, Oranienbaum, Luisium

These 'sentimental' landscape gardens were among the earliest on the Continent to adopt a naturalistic style and were laid out between 1765 and 1817 by Prince Franz von Anhalt-Dessau and his gardeners J. F. Eyserbeck, J. G. Schoch and Neumark. English influences are strong, but there are also echoes of Sicily in the imitation of the theatre at Taormina in the New Garden, and of France in the Rousseau Island built in 1782 after the original at Ermenonville (q.v.).

The five sections of the 40ha park extend into a further 80ha of meadowland and lakes, linked visually by distant buildings on the banks of the Elbe, and by canals. The Schlossgarten, laid out along the lake and around an earlier hunting lodge in 1765, shows the influence of Stourhead in England (q.v.). A canal makes the Neumarkgarten, with its labyrinth, pavilions and huge tulip trees, seem like an island. It connects with the poplar-planted Rousseau Island and was formerly used as a nursery for plants and

At Sanssouci, the six terraced vineyards designed in 1744 were equipped with protective glazing for fruit trees and adorned with pyramids of yew.

trees. The Schochgarten has a gothic house, a chain bridge, temples, romantic rocks and grottoes and a Roman column – all of which can be seen from other parts of the garden through narrow vistas cut in the trees. Statues adjoin the Weidenhegergarten, which was laid out in the 1780s on the north-east shore of the lake. A few years later J. G. Schoch created the romantic Neuer Garten, dominated by the Stein – a huge feature resembling a natural rock – and with

many canals, a pantheon and a grotto, and small gardens surrounding other buildings. Wörlitz was the culmination of a scheme to landscape an area of 25km along the Elbe between Dessau and Wörlitz, which includes Georgium (q.v.) and Luisium (q.v.).

A pastoral scene at Wörlitz, where the park is extended by meadowland and lakes.

Greece

Greece lies at the south-east extremity of Europe, forming the most southerly portion of the Balkan peninsula. Bounded on the north by Albania, Yugoslavia, Bulgaria and European Turkey, and on all other sides by the sea, it consists of interlacing mountain chains pierced by narrow valleys, small plains, islands and, above all, coastline. Local climates vary markedly over short distances. The fierce heat of early summer is tempered by dry winds from the north, then exacerbated in late summer by the humid sirocco. Winters on the coast and in the valleys and plains are mild apart from icy north winds, but snow lies in the mountains from the end of October to June. Land in the plains and valleys is rich, and, provided there is water, productive; cereals, vegetables, fruit, olives, vines and raisins are grown. Much is employed for pasturing goats and sheep and there are huge areas of state-owned forest.

The vegetation of Greece is similar to that of southern Italy and Asia Minor, and its flora is both Mediterranean and Central European. At lower altitudes there are figs, oranges, olives, almonds, pomegranates, aromatics, laurel, myrtle, oleander, plane trees, white poplar and cypress; at higher altitudes oak, chestnut, *Abies cephalonica* and *Pinus pinea*; and finally an exceptional range of alpine plants.

Greece is difficult gardening country and the rich native flora can best be seen in the marvellous national parks (a list is available from the Greek national tourist board). Most flowers bloom in the spring and autumn and lie dormant through the hottest months and it is easy to see why early gardening was strictly utilitarian, with a practical emphasis on the sustaining fruits of the earth such as the vine, leaving floral delights mainly to be eulogized in poetry. This was the kind of garden described by Homer in the 8th century BC in the 5th book of the *Odyssey*: 'Pears and pomegranates and apples full of fruit, also figs and bounteous olives . . . here too a fertile vineyard.' The palace courtyard gardens of the Minoans at Knossos in Crete, where shrubs and flowers were watered with the aid of a sophisticated system of irrigation canals, do not seem to have had parallels elsewhere. (Developed before 1400 BC, these are known to us from the remains of large flower-pots.) Trees have always been important for protection against the fierce midday sun. By tradition, Hippocrates taught the art of healing under the shade of an oriental plane tree on his native island of Cos, and planes as well as tall cypresses and

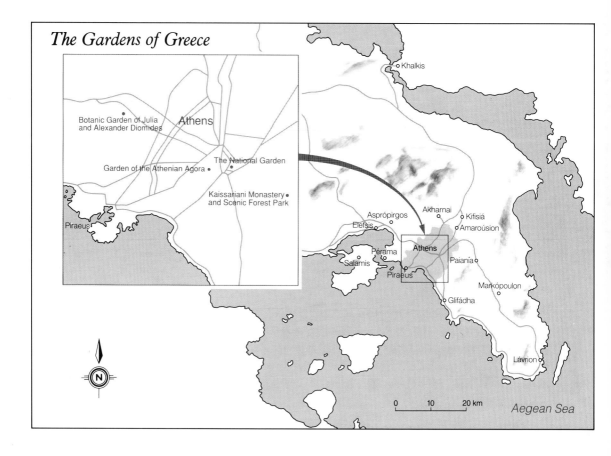

The Gardens of Greece

Botanic Garden of Julia
and Alexander Diomídes

Athens

Garden of the Athenian Agora •

The National Garden

Kaissaríani Monastery
and Scenic Forest Park

Piraeus

Khalkis

Asprópirgos
Elefsís

Akharnai
Kifisiá
Amaroúsion

Athens

Pérama
Salamís

Paianía

Piraeus

Markópoulon

Glifádha

Lávrion

Aegean Sea

0   10   20 km

N

bays were planted to give essential shade to the 'peripatetic' school of Greek philosophers.

The ancient Greeks, although not ornamental gardeners, nevertheless had an eye for the beauty of landscape, placing their temples and theatres among groves of trees (essential for shade) on sites which enjoyed awe-inspiring panoramas. The Agora (q.v.) was first planted with plane trees in the 5th century BC by Cimon of Athens, who also turned the wasteland of the Academy outside the city walls into a well-watered grove, later described by Aristophanes as 'all fragrant with woodbine and peaceful content and the leaf which the lime blossoms fling, when the plane whispers love to the elm in the grove in the beautiful season of spring.' Classical Greek architectural detail and vase decoration are firm evidence of an appreciation of flowers, many of

Vikos Gorge is one of the Greek national parks which provide habitats for an immensely wide range of plants.

which had mythological significance. As early as the 4th century BC Theophrastus (370–285 BC) wrote botanical treatises and described favourite trees and shrubs, including fruit and nut trees, bay, myrtle and twining ivy and grapevines. Flowers to be appreciated were the wild crocus, dianthus, hyacinth, iris, lily, narcissus, rose (*Rosa canina* and *R. centifolia*, probably introduced from Macedonia), violet, and all the usual aromatic herbs such as basil, marjoram, mint, rosemary and sage.

It is said that the first Roman 'peristyle' gardens (*see* Pompeii) were inspired by a Greek layout found on the island of Delos in the 2nd century BC. Although Hellenic aristocrats were planting pleasure gardens modelled on Persian *paradeisoi* soon after Alexander the Great's victorious march to India in the 4th century BC, with tree-lined paths bordered by flowerbeds, and the tyrant Dionysius (430–367 BC) is said to have created a pleasure park in Persian style in the Greek colony of Sicily, it is hardly possible to maintain that the mainland Greeks were responsible for developing gardening as an art form. But the Greek civilization nevertheless influenced that of the Romans as it developed to high levels of sophistication.

In succeeding centuries in Greece, at first as part of the Byzantine empire and later under Turkish rule, there was virtually no ornamental gardening. Monasteries had enclosed courtyards where culinary and medicinal plants were grown; vines, olives, fruit trees and vegetables grew on adjacent terraces. Greece had no land-owning class to foster the gentle art of gardening, and after the liberation from the Turks in 1829, towns and cities were laid out by the modern Greek state. The style was formal: small parks and shady squares, broad tree-lined walks and streets with geometric parterres were designed to match a neo-classical style of architecture (*see* the National Garden of Athens). The French landscape architect F. Barauld worked in Athens in the middle of the 19th century. After that the most notable landscape designer was the Englishman Thomas Mawson, who advised in the 1920s on planting round the Acropolis, the Philopappos, and on Mount Lycabettus, although his plans for the royal gardens and for park layouts in Athens, Salonica and Corfu were not adopted.

Since 1945 modern gardens of any scale have been designed to incorporate natural features, including stone and native plants, which link the garden with the landscape. Recent excavations have revealed planting schemes for ancient sites in the capital, and some of these have been reconstructed with charming effect (*see* the Agora). But it is the wild flowers, growing in many of the great archaeological sites, in the National Parks and in the unspoilt landscape, which remain of the greatest interest to visitors to Greece.

Athens: Garden of the Athenian Agora

In the archaeological site on the NW side of the Acropolis hill

Opening times: Daily 8.30–15, except Sun, Mon
Admission charge: Yes

The Agora, the market-place of Athens, was once the centre of public life. This 10ha garden includes the restored Stoa of Attalos (a closed colonnade) and has been landscaped under the supervision of the American School of Classical Studies at Athens, who were also responsible for the excavation and erection of the Stoa.

Using the evidence for contemporary planting provided by the excavations, the area has been given much of its original aspect, with trees and shrubs known in antiquity and mainly indigenous to Attica. In 1954 King Paul and Queen Frederika planted an evergreen oak (revered by the Greeks for its sturdiness, long life and great height) and a bay tree on either side of the great marble Altar of Zeus, which 'stood as the focal point of civic life in the ancient square'. A white poplar, of which the dark side of the leaf symbolized the Underworld and the paler surface the Upper, grows in the south-west corner of the Agora, where the old drains from the Areopagus, the hill of Ares, provided water. Round the Temple of Hephaistos myrtle and pomegranate (with its plentiful seeds, symbolizing fertility) have been planted. Figs, cultivated for fruit – 'the god-given inheritance of our mother country, the darling of my heart, the dried fig' – again flourish on the slopes above the Agora with the cypress (both *Cupressus sempervirens* 'Horizontalis' and *C. sempervirens* 'Stricta'), the tree for long associated with death and planted in burial grounds.

Athens: The National Garden (formerly the Royal Garden) ★

Centre of Athens; access through seven gates, from Queen Sofia Avenue, Queen Amalia's Avenue, the Zappio Gardens and Herod Atticus Street
Opening times: Sunrise–sunset

In 1834 Athens became the capital of a Greece only recently liberated from Turkish occupation. King Otho and his young queen Amalia moved from Nauplion to the new capital, but the palace designed for them in the south-eastern part of the city was not completed until 1843. The ground to the south and east of the palace was to be the Royal Garden – a site almost identical to that of the Lyceum, the sacred grove and recreation area of ancient Athens where, as early as the second half of the 5th century BC, Socrates used to discuss philosophy and ethics with his friends and pupils. Less than a century later, Aristotle had his school of 'Peripatetics' here, and his successor as head of the school was Theophrastus, the father of botany.

The garden was designed by the French landscape architect F. Barauld. But the work was personally supervised by Queen Amalia and in accordance with her wishes most of the trees and shrubs are indigenous examples of Greek flora – some planting still dates from her time. On a high rock in the garden, still called Amalia's Rock, is the original iron bench on which the queen used to rest.

The garden was laid out partly as an English park and partly in the French style, though both were adapted to local conditions. From the windows at the back of the palace (today the Parliament House) the queen could look right through her garden over a series of beautiful lawns to the Acropolis and the sea.

After the king and queen left the country in 1862 the garden became sadly neglected, though the young Danish prince who succeeded paid great attention to the upkeep and improvement of the park. He also introduced the first greenhouse to Greece. Since the beginning of this century the garden has been open to the public and in 1927 its name was changed to the National Garden. Today, there are 519 different species and varieties of trees, shrubs and climbers, of which 102 are of Greek origin. Most are evergreens (conifers, broad-leaved plants and palms). The conservation of such rich vegetation in such a dry climate would not be possible without abundant irrigation: remarkably, most of the water for the garden comes from an aqueduct built from the foothills of Mount Hymettus in the 6th century to supply the fountain of Callirrhoe, although this supply is now topped up by the Athens Water Company.

Botanic Garden of Julia and Alexander Diomides

14km W of Athens city centre, at no. 405 on the Sacred Road (Iera Odos)
Owner: Private foundation, affiliated to the University of Athens under Government supervision
Opening times: Mon to Sat 8.30–14; Sun 9.30–16.30
Admission charge: No

This beautiful wooded garden on the slopes of Mount Aegaleo has been created since 1946 and is named after the banker Alexander Diomides who endowed it. The collection of plants, laid out over 150 hectares, is still far from being complete; it includes species from other parts of the world as well as trees and shrubs indigenous to the Mediterranean.

Kaissariani Monastery and Scenic Forest Park

6km SE of centre of Athens, on Mount Hymettus
Owner: Friends of the Trees Society
Opening times: *Park* sunrise–sunset; *precincts of monastery* 9–15
Admission charge: No

The Friends of the Trees Society, founded in 1904 by Crown Princess Sofia, was re-established after World War II. It has been responsible for the reafforestation and upkeep of 600ha round the Byzantine monastery of Kaissariani on Mount Hymettus. The forest is densely planted with indigenous and foreign trees, shrubs and flowers, with a nursery for young plants, and a botanical garden for native Greek flora. The latter is fenced and is accessible only with permission. A further small garden contains medicinal and aromatic herbs.

Hungary

For map, see p.282.

The republic of Hungary lies within the drainage basin of the Danube and consists chiefly of plains (the Great Hungarian Plain covers more than half the country); mountains and hills are found only in the north and west. The climate is continental, with long, hard winters and hot summers. Most of the generally sparse rainfall – under 620mm per annum – falls in summer.

The development and survival of gardens has inevitably been affected by Hungary's troubled history. Since the unification of Hungary by Stephen I (997–1038), no other country has suffered so much under its different rulers and invaders: the Tatars, Angevin kings, the Turks, and the Habsburgs (through whom it was linked with Austria from the 16th century onwards). The country became a republic in 1918.

Early gardens were made by monks from western Europe but were essentially utilitarian, with a few flowers for altar decorations. After the Tatar invasion of 1242, both the king, Bela IV, and the aristocracy built castles, laid out pleasure gardens and extended the range of trees and flowers. No trace of these gardens remains. In the late 15th century King Matthias Corvinus, influenced by early Italian renaissance garden architecture, laid out the grounds of his palace at Buda with parterres decorated with fountains and aviaries. At his country home, Visegrad, garden terraces overlooking the Danube provided more sites for plants he brought from Italy. Both gardens, described by 16th- and 17th-century scholars and illustrated by contemporary engravings, contained elaborate labyrinths, probably inspired by the 15th-century *Hypnerotomachia Poliphili* published in 1499 and famous for its woodcut illustrations and detailed descriptions of gardens. All traces of these and other renaissance gardens vanished during the Turkish occupation of 1526–1699, but many new plants came from the orient. Citrus fruits, pomegranates, scented herbs and tulips were introduced. A garden at Hodkovice, an estate owned by the Counts Csáky from 1636, may have been laid out in the French baroque style during the Turkish occupation; later it developed into a *jardin anglo-chinois* with a proliferation of buildings. A painting by Johann Rombauer, now in the Hungarian National Museum, portrays these buildings in a *capriccio* of the garden, and they were described by F. Kazinszy, who visited Hodkovice in 1806. After 1699 French-style layouts, of which Eszterháza (now Fertőd, q.v.) was the grandest and most famous, became fashionable and many gardens were designed with radiating avenues and symmetrical parterres punctuated with clipped trees and shrubs, although, because of shortage of water, few were embellished with the canals typical of late 17th-century gardens in France.

By the end of the 18th century many landowners were pursuing their interpretation of the more naturalistic English landscape style, introducing picturesque features such as garden buildings (including wooden cottages and tea-houses) and theatrical structures. All through the 19th century new gardens and public city parks were laid out in the English style, considerable trouble being taken to effect satisfactory drainage and provide shelter belts of woodland in order to grow exotic trees in the difficult continental climate. Several hundred private gardens of this type existed; amongst pioneers were Count Sandor Erdody, owner of the park at Vep, and Count István Ambrózy-Migazzi, who introduced exotic conifers to his estate at Malonya (now in Czechoslovakia) at the end of the 19th century. There was no tradition of public access to these parks. Since 1945 many garden restoration projects have been, or are being, carried out, and visiting is encouraged. Most gardens belong to the Hungarian State and admission is free.

Alcsútdoboz (formerly Alcsút)

8km S of Bicske, 35km W of Budapest via M1
Owner: Hungarian State
Opening times: Sat, Sun 9–18; tel. Vesprém 080 13 754

Mihály Pollack, the Hungarian neo-classical architect who built a mansion for Duke Joseph of Habsburg here (1818–25) probably also had a hand in the English-style landscape garden laid out from 1825. The first gardeners were the brothers Tost, gardeners to the the court, who also worked on Margaret Island (q.v.) in Budapest. Hillocks and rocky outcrops were created artificially on the flat site, and two small rivulets, the Acsa and the Val, were used to form a large pond. Lawns alternated with dense groups of trees, winding paths leading from one to the other and crossing the streams on wooden and stone bridges. Ravaged during World War II, when all but the front facade of the mansion and the former chapel – now a small museum – were destroyed, the garden is currently being restored. Fortunately, a number of the specimen trees planted by the duke, who loved his garden and continually enriched it, still survive. Apart from the famous cedar of Lebanon, planted in 1820, there are also Austrian pines,

ironwoods (*Ostrya virginiana*), white and black maples, purple-leaved beeches, Turkish hazels (*Corylus colurna*), Japanese acacias (*Sophora japonica*), as well as tulip trees, elms and poplars.

Budapest: City Park (formerly Városliget)

Off Heroes' Square, NE of city centre
Owner: Hungarian State
Opening times: At all times

The 100ha park, situated to the north-east of the city, is partly on sandy and partly on marshy ground, close to the edge of the Great Hungarian Plain. The municipal engineer Charles Degen and the gardener Rudolf Witsch helped to turn the area into a public park in the late 18th century. The sandy soil was enriched for planting, and the marshy areas drained to form a large lake with two islands. In addition, a long avenue leading to the city was planted.

Many parts of the garden were based on designs by C. H. Nebbien, the German architect who worked in Czechoslovakia as well as in Austria and Hungary. In 1817 he won a competition for laying out this city park at Pest; his plans included a neo-classical triumphal arch at the garden entrance. He also made detailed lists of trees he recommended for planting and wrote on environmental problems for urban parks. Lithographs of the 1840s by Rudolf Alt show a romantic design with sinuous paths winding round the contours of a lake under weeping willows. After 1863 Armin Petz, the head gardener, introduced many more trees and shrubs. Modern developments have produced wide roads, a zoological garden, a swimming-pool and other features which have reduced the area of the park, but it still remains a very attractive English-style garden.

Budapest: Margaret Island

N of city centre, enclosed by two arms of the Danube
Owner: Hungarian State
Opening times: At all times

Hugged by two arms of the Danube, the 66ha Margaret Island has been a favoured spot since medieval times. In the 13th century Dominican nuns built a church and a convent of which some ruins are still visible. In the last years of the 18th century the island was acquired by the Habsburgs, who began planting with the help of the gardener Rudolf Witsch. In about 1810 the English-style garden was laid out by the court gardener Charles Tost and his brother (*see* Alcsútdoboz). Tradition maintains that the first London plane trees in Hungary were planted here. Now a great number of these can be seen, together with old beech trees, hornbeams and chestnuts. On the west side of the island a large rose garden, with beds in an expanse of lawn, contains more than 1,400 kinds of roses, blooming at different times throughout the summer. Some modern buildings are flanked by flowerbeds for annuals.

Dég

50km S of Székesfehérvár via M7 and Route 64
Owner: Hungarian State
Opening times: At all times

Formerly owned by the Counts Festetich, these picturesque gardens, watered by meandering streams, surround an impressive manor house built 1812–22. The architect was Mihàly Pollack. Large open lawns are flanked by limes, maples, poplars and other trees. Weeping willows hang over the streams and margins of a lake. The so-called Dutch House on the island was built of stone and brick in 1870. The estate was enlarged in 1983 to include the Bozót river valley; the whole area is now part of the Hungarian Agricultural Museum, and the house is a boarding-school.

Fertőd (formerly Esterháza) ★

Fertőd, 30km SE of Sopron on the Austrian border; Route 85 to Fertőszentmiklós, then left
Owner: Department of Woods and Forests
Opening times: Daily 8–17

The sumptuous palace of Prince Nicholas Esterházy ('the magnificent') was built 1766–84, and its garden was designed to rival Versailles (q.v.). The names of the architect and garden designers are not known, but the garden shows all the characteristics of French style.

There were parterres beside the palace and three long avenues, flanked by box hedges, led to the wilderness and hunting-ground beyond the garden. Cross axes led past water basins where fountains played. The end of the garden was raised and had a cascade built by Franz Gruss 1782–4. Behind it there were more garden features: a rose garden, a pheasantry and a zoo led into dense forest where pine trees were interplanted with deciduous trees such as horse chestnuts, oaks and limes.

Sculptures, fountains and garden buildings were scattered throughout, the largest building being a Chinese tea-house called the Bagatelle. Smaller features included an opera house where Haydn performed frequently in his capacity as *Kapellmeister* to the prince; he composed and produced two operas there in honour of the Empress Maria Theresa when she visited in 1773.

After Prince Nicholas's death in 1790, the garden began to decay, and buildings and garden were almost obliterated during World War II. Reconstruction based on Prince Esterházy's own published plans and descriptions of 1784 is going forward. So far the Bagatelle has been rebuilt as a tea-room and some of the fountains have been repaired. Box once more flanks the avenues, while to the north and south of the palace *parterres de broderie* have been reinstated. The park bordering the formal garden has a large variety of trees, including limes, sweet chestnuts, beeches, sycamores, poplars, giant redwoods and over forty kinds of pines.

Jeli

Near Kám, 9km E of Vasvár via Route 8
Owner: Department of Woods and Forests
Opening times: Daily, May to Jun 8–16; Jul to Oct, Apr, Sat, Sun 8–16; or tel. Vasvár 094 70 063

Founded by the landowner Count István Ambrózy-Migazzi in about 1929, the 80ha garden at Jeli has a very special character. Its main purpose was to provide an experimental ground for the acclimatization of southern species in this sub-alpine region. There are many Chinese and other exotic trees, as well as a number of evergreens, including the finest collection of rhododendrons in Hungary. The small River Koponyas flows through the garden between fern-covered banks.

RIGHT **At Martonvásár, a late 18th-century land-scape garden provides an arcadian setting for the gothic house.**

BELOW **A modern reconstruction of a French *parterre de broderie* recalls the spirit of the now vanished elaborate baroque garden laid out in the early 18th century at Nagycenk.**

Kámon ❀

NW Szombathely
Owner: Department of Woods and Forests
Opening times: Daily, Apr to Oct 9–18; or by
permission, H-9707 Szombathely, Voros Zászló U. 162,
tel. 094 11 352

Kámon is one of the most elaborate botanic gardens
in Hungary. Situated in the low foothills of the
eastern Alps, it was founded in 1860 by Mihàly
Saaghy, whose main intention was to acclimatize
unusual species in these alpine surroundings. A small
stream, the Gyongyos, adds to the character of the
informal English-style layout. There are now more
than 3,000 botanical specimens, including a large
rhododendron plantation, some purple-leaved
beech, Italian poplars, maples, ginkgos and thuyas.

Keszthely˙

On N shore at W end of Lake Balaton
Owner: Hungarian State
Opening times: Daily sunrise–sunset

Once the estate of the Counts Festetich, this garden
was laid out in a formal French pattern at the end of
the 18th century; there are anonymous contemporary
records of the designs. From 1793 onwards, in
imitation of Versailles (q.v.), great festivities and
pageants took place. The Georgikon, the first
agronomical academy in Europe, was founded here.

In 1886 the English landscape architect Henry
Ernest Milner was engaged to restore the neglected
garden to frame a new castle designed for Count
Tassilo Festetich by Rumpelmeyer. Milner concealed a neighbouring roadway by lowering it, moved
mature trees to hide unsightly buildings, and created
interesting undulations in flat areas north of the
castle. To the south, a formal sunken garden was
planted with dwarf conifers. The rest of Milner's
design was in the English style, opening views over
the lake and to distant hills. The 73ha garden has
since suffered badly from neglect but is being restored. The main feature is the collection of mature
trees, which includes pines, old yews, ginkgos, oaks
and purple-leaved beeches. The parterre in front of
the castle (now a museum) is planted with annuals.

Martonvásár

30km SW of Budapest via M 7
Owner: Hungarian State
Opening times: Daily, Apr to Sept 10–18; Oct to Mar
10–16
Admission charge: Yes

The surviving 50ha of Martonvásár lie in a valley
surrounded by hills. The estate was acquired by the
Brunswick family in 1758 when the marshy land was
successfully drained to allow planting of rare trees
and shrubs. Nothing is known of the French garden
which originally framed the baroque country house,
but we do know that trees were imported at this time
from North America.

The English-style garden was begun at the end of
the 18th century with a layout probably contributed
by C. H. Nebbien, the German designer who also
worked for the Brunswicks at Alsókorompa (now
Dolná Krupa in Czechoslovakia). The banks of the
Szent Laszlo stream and the shores of a lake were
planted in the picturesque style, a romantic layout
that was admired by Beethoven when he visited the
family here in 1809 and 1811 (there is a Beethoven
Memorial Museum). Liriodendrons, purple-leaved
beeches and plane trees planted beside indigenous
trees date from this period; the branches of a large oak
tree in front of the main building form a tent-like
structure. The garden does not appear to have been
altered when the house was reconstructed in the
gothic style in 1870.

Nagycenk

10km SE of Sopron near the border with Austria
Owner: Hungarian State
Opening times: Daily, tel. 099 12 080

Formerly the estate of the Counts Széchenyi, today
the garden at Nagycenk covers only a small area. In
the second half of the 18th century there was still an
elaborate 9ha French garden, several plans of which
have recently been discovered. Some of the stone
ornaments are still extant. Towards the end of the
century the garden was gradually transformed in the
fashionable English style, although a famous 3km
avenue of lime trees was planted at about this time,
some of which has survived. An unusual feature was

an artificial hill with a cave inside, said to be for coolness in summer. From 1814 Count Stephen Széchenyi, a leading politician, and his English wife were the devoted owners. Availing himself of new technical facilities, the count drained the marshland to enlarge the garden, built glasshouses and planted many exotics – pines, limes, ironwoods (*Ostrya virginiana*) and tulip trees. Subsequent owners further enriched the garden with many new species. Severe damage occurred during World War II, but the mansion has been rebuilt as a museum, and a *parterre de broderie* has been laid out in the French manner.

Seregélyes

15km SE of Székesfehérvár
Owner: Hungarian State
Opening times: Tel. Veszprém 080 13 754

This 19th-century landscape park is surrounded by hills, and the many small streams and wells were used to form a large lake for swimming and rowing. Formerly a Zichy-Hadik estate, the property is now run by the Taurus tyre factory. The neo-classical house was built in about 1820 by an unknown architect, whose style suggests that of Mihàly Pollack. The main features of interest today are trees and shrubs, some of which are more than 200 years old. Among them are sycamores, silver maples, hazels, a paulownia with a trunk 355cm in diameter and a fine Turkish hazel (*Corylus colurna*).

Szarvas

80km E of Kecskemét via Route 44
Owner: Hungarian State
Opening times: Daily, mid Mar to early Nov 8–18; early Nov to mid Mar 8–16; tel. Budapest 01 850 666
Admission charge: No

In spite of its position in the middle of the Great Hungarian Plain, the advantageously damp river site of Szarvas made it possible to create a botanic garden here. In 1770 the soil was improved by Samuel Tessedik, a pastor who was also a well-trained agronomist. Ten years later the Counts Bolza bought a large tract of land here and built a house on the bank of the River Kőrös in imitation of the royal palace of

Schönbrunn in Vienna (q.v.). In the middle of the 19th century the garden was enlarged to 10ha and the so-called 'Anne Garden' added. By degrees a substantial arboretum was created, covering 17ha, with a large number of trees and shrubs formerly unknown in Hungary introduced from the American northwest and later from Asia.

Tata

Surrounds Lake Cseke-Tó, 60km W of Budapest via M1
Opening times: At all times

This huge, informal, English-style garden, now a public park and sports training centre, originally covered about 240ha – including the artificial lake, the Cseke-Tó. The marsh was drained by J. Mikoviny in the second half of the 18th century and the garden was possibly designed by Charles de Moreau, architect to the court and to the Esterházy family. A number of early 19th-century architectural features give character to the garden. The Chinese tea-house and Turkish pavilion have gone, but Charles de Moreau's 'ruined' church of 1801 still exists. There are lovely views of the garden from the lakeside, its most important feature today being the many fine trees: weeping willows, poplars, catalpas, beeches, ironwoods, and many kinds of pine.

Vácrátót ❀

10km SE of Vác, 35km N of Budapest via Route 2
Owner: Hungarian State
Opening times: Weekdays 7–18; Sundays 8–18

Vácrátót, the richest botanical garden in Hungary, was founded in 1872 by Count Sándor Vigyazó and laid out in the informal English style by the garden architect Vilmos Jámbor. It lies in a hilly area, and a small stream, the Sződrákos, made it possible to form various rock gardens as well as a huge lake with a rich selection of water plants. The plants in the garden have been collected from all parts of Europe, and many rare species have been acclimatized here. Hothouses even grow oranges and bananas, and many kinds of pine, other conifers, tulip trees, a collection of rhododendrons, a rose garden, and greenhouses add to the attractions of the garden.

Poland

For map, see p.303.

Apart from local variations along the Baltic coast and on the northern slopes of the Carpathians, which form the country's southern boundary, the climate reflects Poland's proximity to the continental mass of the USSR. Winters are cold, with average temperatures below freezing-point for two or three months; summers are hot, with average temperatures just below 20°C, and maxima of 35°C and above. There is a marked difference between the warmer south-western region and the cold north-east and spring flowers are usually one to two weeks earlier in Kraków than they are in Warsaw. The annual rainfall is a little above 500mm over much of the country, but is higher in the mountains, and the snow cover lasts from one to three months according to latitude and situation. The conditions are not favourable for the cultivation of good turf and lawn mowers are a rarity.

More than half the country is covered by light morainic soils on which the natural vegetation was open mixed woodland; conifers now predominate in the large tracts which are still forested. Botanically the most interesting areas are the Tatra National Park in the Carpathians, with its alpine flora, and the Pieniny and Ojców National Parks in the south, where the underlying rock is limestone.

The history of garden design in Poland is both long and rich, but fifty years of neglect and limited budgets mean that much of the evidence is now to be found in old maps and views. Of the 5,000 parks, botanical gardens and arboreta whose sites are known, probably less than a tenth are recognizable today and only a small proportion of those are maintained. One of the pleasures of visiting Poland lies in exploring fine formal gardens which have been abandoned since 1939. Three such gardens spring to mind: Ksiaz Wielki, at Miechów 40km north of Kraków, is an early renaissance and neo-gothic house, now occupied by a secondary school and still surrounded by the embankments, terracing and pavilions of formal gardens of the late 16th and 18th centuries. At Kruszyna, 6km north-east of Czestochowa, the tangled undergrowth of the former gardens to a disused house hides a chapel-like grotto and a collapsing hermitage; while at Koscielec, close to Koło and about 130km east of Poznán, the self-seeded trees in a neglected park

The 'Roman' aqueduct in the park at Arkadia was
built at the turn of the 18th century.

322

belonging to a school of agriculture conceal a Moorish minaret and mosque. The best time to visit Polish gardens is the early summer – late May and early June. After that parching and poor maintenance usually take their toll.

The oldest preserved examples of gardens in Poland are cloister and castle gardens. 16th- and early 17th-century renaissance gardens followed western European styles: symmetrical and axial layouts were linked to the house, and designers were conscious of views to the surrounding landscape. Baroque gardens developed with local innovations, many of them designed to link fortified houses, bastions and gardens in a homogeneous whole. Later in the 17th century French layouts became popular, with elaborate axial gardens behind the house (including, by the 18th century, *parterres de broderie*, sculpture, *bassins*, fountains and clipped trees) and often very large sanded courts in front. A few great dynastic families lived like princes at this time, possessing enormous wealth and thousands of retainers. Families such as the Czartoryskis (*see* Puławy), the Radziwills (*see* Arkadia and Nieborów) and the Raczynskis (*see* Rogalin) made their palatial homes the centres of political and social life, and the later partitions of Poland failed to eliminate much of their influence and power. Some fled abroad, but many put their energies into remodelling their houses and gardens and most of the great houses were still occupied by the same families until 1939.

The 'natural' style arrived late in the 18th century, influenced by contacts with England and led by the Polish garden designer S. B. Zug (sadly all his gardens except Arkadia have now vanished). An even more romantic style followed, and from the middle of the 19th century public interest in botany was reflected in the planting of parks and some valuable arboreta.

Flower gardening in Poland is seen at its best in the colourful allotments, which are intensively cultivated by city flat-dwellers. In the evenings and at weekends they become popular resorts for promenaders. One of the finest allotment enclosures in Warsaw lies about 2km to the south of the centre, close to the junction of Niepodległosci and Odyńca Streets. The giving of flowers is an everyday, and expected, compliment in Poland, and those who do not grow them will buy them. Extensive market gardens are a feature of the outskirts of all the major cities.

Polish parks and woodlands were devastated during World War II and the areas that survived were often those reserved for sport. The dominating figure in the post-war period of reconstruction was Gerard Ciołek (1909–66), who was both a garden historian and garden designer. He was involved in most of the major renovation schemes, such as Wilanów, Nieborów and Rogalin (q.v.), and wrote a magisterial illustrated history of Polish gardens, *Ogrody Polskie* (not, unfortunately, translated). For an earlier record of the appearance of the gardens there are the 18th-century paintings of Warsaw by Bernardo Bellotto, which include Łazienki and Wilanów, and the most important of the many later topographical artists who depicted park landscapes is Zygmunt Vogel, active in the late 18th and early 19th century.

The latest available opening times have been given, but they should not be relied upon. Gardens, like shops, are often closed without warning and a visit that involves travelling any distance should be preceded by a letter or telephone call. At most gardens a small charge is made for admission.

Arkadia ★

5km SE of Łowicz, 80km W of Warsaw via E8/12
Owner: The National Museum in Warsaw
Opening times: Summer only; openings erratic. Check with the National Museum, Aleje Jerozalimskie 3, 00–495 Warsaw, tel. 022 21 31 10

Once one of the most famous gardens in Europe, and a fine example of the romantic style, Arkadia was laid out 1778–1821 for Helena Radziwill as a second garden for the nearby Nieborów (q.v.). Szymon Bogumił Zug was the original designer. The site, which was otherwise flat and featureless, had a small stream running through it and that was used to feed a lake. An island with poplars and a tombstone with the inscription *Et in Arcadia Ego* was reminiscent of Ermenonville in France (q.v.), but little of it remains. Features also included a Temple of Diana, which doubled as a picnic house, and other monuments and 'ruins', classical and gothic. The original plan was partly recreated *c*.1950 and after some neglect and storm damage the garden is awaiting further restoration.

Gołuchów Arboretum

Gołuchów, 20km N of Kalisz, SE of Poznań
Owner: Academy of Agriculture, Poznań
Opening times: Daily, May to Oct 8–sunset

This 'English' landscape park of 170ha was laid out in the last quarter of the 19th century as an adjunct to a French renaissance-style castle. It lies along both sides of a valley in ancient woodland and there are many old oak, beech and ash trees as well as several hundred varieties of exotics.

Kórnik Arboretum

Kórnik, 20km SE of Poznań
Owner: Institute of Dendrology of the Polish Academy of Sciences
Opening times: Daily, May to Oct 8–17

An 18th-century formal garden was enlarged to about 60ha in the mid 19th century when the house was being remodelled in neo-gothic style by the German Karl Friedrich Schinkel. The wide-ranging collection of trees and shrubs, now totalling about 3,500 species and varieties, was formed by a succession of private owners, the last being Count Władysław Zamoyski, who left it to the nation in 1924. It is rich in birches, poplars and conifers, as well as in ornamental shrubs, including lilacs and honeysuckles.

Kraków: Botanic Garden of Jagellonian University

27 Kopernika Street
Owner: Institute of Botany, Jagellonian University, Kraków
Opening times: May to Oct, daily 9–sunset; winter, Sun 10–14

The garden, which was established in 1783, covered less than 2.5ha, but later additions, particularly since 1930, have brought it up to about 10ha, all on a fairly level site with light soils. The original garden had a

rectangular layout of paths and beds which can still be recognized today. The first addition, of 1825, was an 'English garden' – a lawn surrounded by trees; more recent additions have followed this informal style. There are extensive areas of glass, including a palm house, and collections of medicinal plants, lilies and orchids, as well as an alpine garden. Air pollution, especially from the steel works at Nowa Huta to the east of Kraków, has affected many species, such as the tall conifers.

Krasiczyn Arboretum

Zamek Krasiczyn, W of Przemyśl, 53km SE of Rzeszów via E22
Owner: Supervised by Kraków Botanic Garden

Most of the planting in this 20ha park surrounding a moated castle of the early 17th century dates from the 19th and early 20th centuries. In spite of many fine specimen trees, the arboretum now has a romantic atmosphere of gentle decay.

Nieborów ★

4km SE of Łowicz, about 80km W of Warsaw via E8/12
Owner: The National Museum in Warsaw
Opening times: Closed in winter. Check with the National Museum, Aleje Jerozalimskie 3, 00–495 Warsaw, tel. 022 21 31 10

The park surrounds a late 17th-century country house of the Radziwill family (*see also* Arkadia), which is now a museum. The house is approached from the north by a broad gravel drive which, with the palace and outbuildings, forms the main axis. The original small formal garden lay under the south front of the house. It was enlarged, in similar style, in the early 18th century; later in the century a small romantic park was added to the west and a kitchen garden backed by a neo-classical orangery was formed along the east side. Today the garden retains its formal atmosphere. Geometrical parterres front the house and beyond them a short avenue is flanked by enclosures formed by hornbeam hedges, trellising and espaliered limes. Most of the planting dates from

Lime trees flank an axial grass walk leading to the facade of the late 17th-century house at Nieborów.

a restoration of *c*.1950, but two giant planes survive from the late 18th century. The boundary between the garden and the park is marked by a formal canal which is of 18th-century origin, but whose present form dates from the restoration.

Puławy ★

47km NW of Lublin, W of E81
Owner: Institute of Soil Cultivation of the Ministry of Agriculture
Opening times: Usually daily sunrise–sunset, tel. Puławy 34 21

The late 17th-century house sits on the edge of a cliff overlooking the valley of the Vistula. Like the house, the park has been remodelled and enlarged several times and little remains of the formal gardens of the 18th century. The present landscaped layout, with its ornamental park buildings and groups of trees, stretches for about a kilometre along the slope of the cliff and the adjoining plateau. It derives from that created 1798–1806 for Princess Izabela Czartoryska (*see* Introduction) who, having travelled in France and England, brought in foreign specialists, including the Irish designer Denis MacClair (called by the Poles Mikler Dionizy). The Englishman James Savage was appointed head gardener. The princess also introduced many species to Poland, including the Lombardy poplar, and in the 19th century the park was said to have included 250 varieties of trees, half of them foreign. The planting, mostly since 1945, is now less varied but the setting is a dramatic one.

Rogalin

13km S of Poznań, W of Kórnik
Owner: The National Museum in Poznań
Opening times: Check with Rogalin (tel. 061 13 27 94) or the museum in Poznań (tel. 061 20 07 67)

This small formal garden below the east front of a country house of the Raczynski family (*see* Introduction) was laid out in the later 18th century and has a striking similarity to the garden of New College, Oxford, in England, as recorded in early 18th-century engravings. The ground slopes across the axis but has been remodelled to provide a high terrace walk along the south and east sides. Much of the eastern part of the garden is taken up by an earth ziggurat and in the trench between it and the surrounding terraces there are regular compartments formed by clipped hedges. Nearer to the house there are parterres flanked by espaliers. After being restored, not very accurately, in *c*.1950, the garden became rather overgrown and a new restoration programme was started in 1985. Beyond the garden enclosure there is a park in which some oaks survive from an area of ancient woodland.

Warsaw: Botanic Garden of Warsaw University ❀

Łazienki Park, between the Belvedere Palace and Agrykola Street, about 2km S of the Old Town of Warsaw

Owner: Warsaw University

Opening times: May to Oct, weekdays 8–19, Sun and public hols 10–18; Sept, daily 10–18; Oct, daily 10–16

Founded in a corner of the Łazienki royal park (q.v.) in 1818, the garden originally covered an area of almost 16ha. However, in 1834, following the failure of the November Insurrection and the closure of the university, much of the area was restored to the park and the garden now covers just over 5ha. It was almost entirely destroyed during World War II but has been carefully restored since, and some trees date from the original planting. Including those under glass, the number of species totals about 4,500, of which about 1,000 are trees and shrubs. The garden specializes in succulents, cycads and dahlias, but there are also medicinal plants, culinary herbs, protected plants and plots illustrating the lowland and mountain flora of Poland. There are systematic beds on the level ground near the entrance and the arboretum is on a slope next to the park.

Warsaw: Łazienki

About 2km S of the old town of Warsaw

Owner: The National Museum in Warsaw

Opening times: Daily sunrise–sunset

The park was laid out 1766–95 around the royal bath house for King Stanislas Augustus. It occupies about 72ha on the western flood plain of the Vistula and the adjacent escarpment, and is close to the northern end

of a row of great houses and parks which in the 18th and 19th centuries extended southwards for about 7km from close to the centre of Warsaw. The palace is romantically placed across the centre of a long irregular lake. Most of the park is lightly wooded, and although much of the planting is informal and dates from the post-1944 restoration, the layout of paths and watercourses reveals the underlying formality of the 18th-century plan. Pavilions, a lakeside theatre and an orangery are also dotted around the park and on the escarpment, and it was here that J. C. Loudon, who visited Warsaw in 1813, recorded that, on special occasions, living figures dressed in character were placed on pedestals 'and taught to maintain certain attitudes after the manner of the representations called *tableaux*'.

Warsaw: Wilanów

S suburbs, 7km from city centre

Owner: The National Museum in Warsaw

Opening times: Daily 10–sunset. Both palace and garden may be closed for state visits or banquets; tel. Warsaw 022 42 07 95

A small park surrounds the late 17th-century baroque palace of King John III Sobieski and extends along the bank of a lake formed from an old course of the Vistula river. The present plan is largely the result of restoration 1955–65, when an attempt was made to recreate 17th-, 18th-, and 19th-century elements from the complex and well-documented history of the gardens. Immediately around the house everything is formal: a loose grid of gravel and tarmac paths with a magnificent *parterre de broderie*, fountains and occasional statuary. To the east a broad terrace drops down to more bedding and then a tall clipped hedge along the edge of the lake. To the north the formal garden is bordered by a neo-classical orangery; to the south it ends in a balustrade beyond which there is an area of grass and trees (the English park) leading down to a small stream, where boulders have been arranged to simulate a cascade. The romantic theme is continued along the bank of the lake to the north of the terrace. There are winding paths, a 'Roman' bridge and a Chinese temple, but much of the planting is new and immature.

Romania

For map, see p.282.

Almost bisected by the horseshoe curve of the Carpathians, which rise to over 2,500m, and with the River Danube marking most of its southern border, Romania divides into three geographic and climatic regions. Over most of the country the climate is continental, although the regime in the hills and lowlands of Transylvania, a continuation of the Great Hungarian Plain, is less extreme than in Moldavia to the east of the mountains, where hot, dry summers are followed by severe winters with devastatingly cold east winds. In the Danube basin (Wallachia) to the south, Mediterranean conditions prevail in sheltered areas in a narrow coastal strip along the Black Sea, allowing lusher vegetation and plants typical of the Balkan peninsula and Asia Minor to thrive. Rainfall on the coast is about 400mm, increasing to 700mm in the mountains, which support coniferous forest. The Danube, which breaks through the Carpathians at the Iron Gates, has been an important east–west route for centuries.

Gardens in Romania will have been laid out round monasteries of the Metropolitan Church; early 17th-century chronicles describe groves of chestnuts, fruit trees and a garden of roses near the church of Tîrgoviște in Wallachia. Later in the century gardens on great estates such as Mogoșoaia (q.v.) were Italian Renaissance in style, but by the early 18th century German garden architects were implementing more baroque concepts, as at Avrig (q.v.) and Bontida. By the end of the 18th century many of these formal gardens were redesigned in the so-called English style and other landscape parks were newly laid out on estates throughout Romania. During the 19th century and more recently, many city parks – some adaptations from private estates – were designed for public use by architects such as F. von Rebhun (*see* Bucharest), who also re-landscaped the park surrounding the 19th-century royal summer residence at Peleș in the forest at Sinaia in the Carpathians. A garden 'folly' at Peleș was visited by most of the crowned heads of Europe in the years before World War I and King Carol's nephew's English bride, Crown Princess Marie, also constructed an eccentric three-roomed tree house in the grounds. Designed by M. H. Baillie Scott in 1897–8, it was called Le Nid and built high up in a group of pines; it could only be reached by rope ladder, but provided an afternoon's entertainment for the king's guests and a welcome relief from court etiquette.

Whereas foreign landscape architects, including Carl F. W. Meyer, E.

Redont, Pinard and F. von Rebhun, played a major role in developing Romanian parks in the past, today Romanian specialists continue the work of 'greening' and embellishing the country's cities. The range of plants which will thrive in each region has been greatly extended by successful experimentation with exotic species.

Avrig Park ★

Centre of Avrig, behind the station; 20km SE of Sibiu, on DN1 to Braşov
Owner: People's Council of Avrig and Sibiu towns
Opening times: At all times

The 5ha garden was laid out from 1768 by Baron Samuel Brukenthal, a former governor of Transylvania, round a castle built five years earlier. It was described in 1826 by Constandin Golescu, whose own estate was on the outskirts of Bucharest. This account indicates Italian/French-style architectural features from the 1760s – terraces connected with wide staircases cut into the hill and basins with rococo fountains throwing up jets of water, as well as later, English-style features – 'natural' winding rivulets which united to fall in a romantic cascade. Plantations of fruit trees included 95 sorts of pears, 40 sorts of peaches, 17 sorts of apples and other fruits besides ornamental shrubs. An orangery contained 1,000 lemon trees, oranges, palm trees and many other exotics, including species of *Opuntia*. There was a pheasantry and a garden of medicinal herbs. Ruins were modelled on the 1778 sham Roman ruins at Schönbrunn (q.v.). Golescu describes 'alleys of tall trees and shorter ones, and some shorn to look like walls', but says that the garden is much 'degraded' from its condition when he first visited in 1802.

By the mid 19th century carnations, narcissi, primulas, verbenas, violets, pelargoniums and roses were growing at Avrig. In 1873 the Brukenthals exchanged the estate for a property in Vienna; in 1912 it came into the possession of the Evangelical Church of Sibiu, which used the castle as a sanatorium (it is still one today, although now owned by the Romanian State). The park is in good condition, retaining many of its original features. Avenues of spruce, chestnut, juniper, lime, hornbeam and oak as well as alleys of box and lilac are well kept. There are some fine individual trees, such as a tulip tree (with a diameter of 130cm), magnolias, catalpas and yews. The ornamental garden has shrubs, perennials and a good display of sun-loving annuals in summer. Cool fountains and clear streams remain an important and refreshing feature.

Bucharest: Botanic Garden of Bucharest University

Şoseaua Cotroceni
Owner: Ministry of Education and Bucharest University
Opening times: Daily, summer 8–20; winter 8–17; *greenhouses* 7.30–14
Admission charge: Yes

Founded in 1860, the gardens were moved here in 1874; landscaping was completed by the Belgian L. Fuchs in 1891. Although severely damaged in World Wars I and II, the 17.5ha gardens, with greenhouses, botanical museum and herbarium, provide important teaching facilities. A bowling green with box in geometric patterns and wide lawns with scattered groups of ornamental trees and shrubs are features of general interest.

Bucharest: City Parks

Cişmigiu Gardens (16ha), Herăstrău (198ha), Cotroceni (17ha), Kiseleff (14ha) and the Park of Liberty (49ha) are all public parks in Bucharest originating in the late 19th or early 20th century. *Cişmigiu*, in the centre of the city, was developed in the 1830s by the German landscape architect Carl F. W. Meyer, who created it round an existing grove and reed-fringed lake. 30,000 trees and shrubs were planted. Since then the garden has been redesigned several times, most recently in 1910 by another German, F. von

Rebhun, and is in a mixture of geometric and romantic styles. Clipped lime trees, yews and box-edged beds for seasonal bedding provide a formal structure. A round lawn decorated with busts of Romanian writers, boating on the lake and a rose garden are further attractions. *Herăstrău*, on the shores of Lake Herăstrău in the northern part of the city, was first laid out with the help of Pinard and Rebhun during the 1920s. The natural landscape of water and islands planted with willows and poplars provides an attractive recreation area (there are also restaurants). A village museum with collections of traditional houses and crafts is of interest and there are annual exhibitions of ornamental flowers – the Expoflora. *Cotroceni* (Str Gh. Marinescu near the botanic garden) was designed by Rebhun towards the end of the 19th century. Flowerbeds with colourful seasonal planting lie below a steep terraced slope, where balustrades are covered with climbing vines, ivy and wisteria. *Kiseleff* lies on either side of the Şoseaua Kiseleff in the northern suburbs, and the *Park of Liberty* is in the southern part of the city, bordered by the Calea Serban Vodă.

Cluj-Napoca: Botanic Garden of Cluj-Napoca University

Republicii Street; 480km NW of Bucharest via Route 1
Owner: Ministry of Education and Cluj-Napoca University
Opening times: Daily, summer 8–20; winter 8–17
Admission charge: Yes

The present botanic garden, including a collection of ornamentals and an area for Romanian flora, was laid out in the 1920s by Professor Borza, who remained director until 1947. The herbarium, seed bank and laboratories are used for research and teaching and the garden plays an important conservation role in Romania. Garden areas in the style of classical Rome and of Japan add to the interest of the garden.

The botanic garden at Cluj-Napoca includes an area designed after World War II as a Japanese garden.

Craiova: The People's Park (Ghika Park)

230km W of Bucharest on E70
Owner: People's Council of Craiova
Opening times: At all times
Admission charge: No

Originally laid out in the English style early in the 19th century around the summer residence of the Bibescu family, the park with its gazebo and other pavilions was described in 1846 as 'of exceeding beauty'. In 1853, after five years of neglect following the 1848 revolution, Chancellor Iancu Bibescu sold the 80ha of land to the town of Craiova. In 1898 the French landscape architect E. Redont was asked to recreate a much enlarged park with lakes and a network of roads and walks for the city's inhabitants. Redont's romantic landscape with waterfalls (and an elaborate irrigation system), rockeries and ruins surrounded by lush green vegetation made the park one of the most impressive in Europe. A rose garden, an arboretum (fine groves of swamp cypress grow by the lake), a botanic garden and a zoo were later additions.

Gornești Park (formerly Parcul Teleki)

30km NE of Tîrgu-Mureș via DN15
Owner: People's Council of the Gornești Commune
Opening times: At all times
Admission charge: No

The garden surrounding Count Joseph Teleki's mansion was laid out in the French style in 1797 on the left bank of the Mureș river. Interlocking canals and pools and elaborate scrolled parterres on the slopes near the house date from the 1790s. In a landscaped area willows, oaks, maples, birch, pine trees and firs are mixed with ornamental shrubs. Gornești Park is now a children's nursing home.

Jassy (Iași): Botanic Garden of Al. I. Cuza University

Dumbrava Rosie Street
Owner: Ministry of Education and University of Al. I. Cuza of Jassy
Opening times: Daily, summer 8–20; winter 8–17
Admission charge: Yes

The 100ha garden was founded in 1856 by the naturalist Dr Anastasie Fatu on his own land. It was moved to Copou Hill in 1963. Although young, its scientific section and glasshouses are extensive. The decorative area includes geometric parterres and a rose collection.

Jibou: Botanic Garden

Jibou, on the River Someș
Owner: Ministry of Education and the School-Inspectorate of Salaj County
Opening times: Daily, summer 8–20; winter 8–17
Admission charge: Yes

Founded in 1968 on the initiative of Professor Vasile Fati as a teaching centre, the 20ha garden on the banks of the River Someș grows a wide range of plants from many parts of the world.

Mogoșoaia Park ★

Mogoșoaia, 15km NW of Bucharest on the DN1A to Tirgoviște
Owner: Bucharest Municipal Council
Opening times: At all times
Admission charge: No

The park surrounding the palace (1702) belonging to Constantin Brîncoveanu, Prince of Wallachia (beheaded in Constantinople by the Turks in 1714), was originally almost square and formal in design; it was replanned in the landscape style after 1780. Its present layout only dates from the years after 1870. A double avenue of chestnuts marks the approach from the road to Tirgoviște. Inside ancient walls a formal terraced garden descends below the palace to the shores of a lake formed by the River Colentina, while the rest of the park is landscaped in romantic style. Geometric box-edged walks, in some cases patterned in pink brick, meet at right-angles, with pyramid-shaped junipers accentuating the corners, to give simple and charming effects. The palace, reached through a courtyard, is framed by green lawns; parterres, planted with purple-flowering iris, are visible from the balconies above. Laburnum walks open out to reveal groves of lilac. In a secret walled garden periwinkle, violets, lilies-of-the-valley and sweet jasmine scent the air. Walks lead to the lake below and to romantic parkland where, amongst

The box parterre at Mogoşoaia in winter.

chestnuts, willows, plane trees and pines, hidden vistas are revealed. An avenue of old elms links the palace with handsome wrought-iron gates framing the southern entrance.

Simeria Arboretum ✤
12km E of Deva, N of Simeria
Owner: Ministry of Forestry and Research Institute of Forestry
Admission charge: No

Originally an 18th-century park and still in private hands until 1948, today the 70ha arboretum contains the richest collection of trees in Romania. In the meadows on the banks of the River Mureş are fine examples of exotics, most of which were planted in the second half of the 19th century – magnolias, cypresses, cedars of Lebanon and giant redwoods as well as venerable oaks 200–300 years old, and a beautiful rose garden.

Snagov Park
30km NW of Bucharest on DN1; bus from Scinteia Place, Bucharest; 4.5km walk from Snagov Brasserie
Owner: People's Council of Bucharest and Ministry of Forestry
Opening times: At all times
Admission charge: No

A woodland collection of indigenous and exotic trees arranged in systematic and environmental order for research and teaching rather than for pleasure. Part of a 250ha pleasure park.

Timişoara: Botanic Garden
60km E of the Yugoslav border at junction of Routes 59, 69 and D6
Owner: People's Council of Timişoara
Opening times: At all times
Admission charge: No

Designed on the site of a 9.8ha city park, demonstration areas include ornamental plants from many different regions of the world as well as from Romania and the Balkans. More public parks are laid out along the banks of the Bega canal.

European Russia

The USSR in Europe lies west of the Urals, extending from the Barents Sea beyond the Arctic Circle in the north, to the Black Sea and the Caucasus in the south. In general the interior consists of huge areas of gently swelling plateau lying between 150 and 300m above sea-level and deeply intersected by river valleys. The only mountainous areas are at its borders: the Urals to the east; the Carpathians in the south-west and the high Caucasus separating it from Turkey in the south. Great rivers such as the Volga, the Dnieper and the Don link places thousands of kilometres apart. These major arteries are navigable in the spring floods but freeze during the winter and may be too low for river traffic in the summer.

The USSR has many climates and this is true to a lesser extent of European Russia. In the broad central belt, winters are very cold and summers warm, a Continental regime that becomes more polar towards the north. Sea ice covers the Baltic and Barents Seas in winter, bringing sub-polar conditions far south from November to March or April. The ground is snow-covered and there are piercing winds from the intensely cold Siberian landmass to the east. Precipitation is generally low.

In the south, the climate of the Ukraine and Black Sea coasts is milder and damper, with an almost Mediterranean climate in the southern Crimea and heavy rain in the Caucasus. An average January temperature of 6°C at Batumi, on the Black Sea, compares with $-6.9°$ at Riga on the Baltic, $-9.9°$ at Moscow, and $-16°$ at Archangel. At the height of summer, average temperatures on the Black Sea reach 22°C and above, compared with 19° in Moscow, 16.5° at Riga and 15°C at Archangel.

Some of the USSR's most fertile farmland lies in European Russia, in a broad belt rich with dark *chernozem* soils, which stretches west from the Urals. But vast areas are unsuitable for cultivation, covered by marsh, forest or tundra. The flora is surprisingly uniform. In the north, coniferous forests predominate, with aspen, alder, birch, poplar and mountain ash. In the south there are oaks, birch, ash, Scots pine rather than *Pinus abies* on the sandy plains, and apples, pears and cherries. In the southern Crimea, in a narrow strip along the Black Sea, there is a rich flora very similar to that of the valley of the Arno in Italy. Soviet botanic gardens reflect this range of climate: Kirovsk (q.v.) demonstrates polar-alpine vegetation, while Batumi and Sukhumi (q.v.) on the Black Sea have subtropical planting.

The Gardens of European Russia

0   250   500 km

N

Leningrad and Environs (inset)
- Leningrad Botanic Garden
- Lomonosov (Oranienbaum)
- Summer Garden
- Elagin Island
- Peterhof (Petrodvorets)
- Pushkin (Tsarskoe Selo)
- Pavlovsk
- Gatchina

Moscow and Environs (inset)
- Arkhangelskoe
- Moscow Botanic Garden
- Kuskovo
- Tsaritsno
- Gorki Leninskie

Murmansk

Polar-Alpine Botanic Garden of Kirovsk

Archangel

Leningrad
Leningrad and Environs

Kadriorg (Ekaterintal)
Tallinn

Riga • Riga Botanic Garden
The Baltic States and North-West

Palanga

Baltic Sea

Kaliningrad
Vilnius

Moscow
Moscow and Environs

Minsk • Minsk Botanic Garden

Volga

Kiev Botanic Garden
Kiev

Kharkov

Volgograd

Volga

Lvov • Lvov Botanic Garden

Dnepropetrovsk

Don

Astrakhan

The Ukraine,
Black Sea
and Georgia

Rostov

Odessa Botanic Garden
Odessa

Caspian Sea

The Gardens of European Russia (Crimea inset)
- Nikitsky Botanic Garden of Yalta
- Sevastopol
- Massandra
- Livadia
- Alupka
- Yalta

Black Sea

Sochi Arboretum
Sukhumi Botanic Garden
Tbilisi Botanic Garden
Tbilisi
Batumi Botanic Garden
Baku

ABOVE **The Hermitage at Pushkin, designed by Rastrelli in 1759, from an engraving by A. A. Grakov.**

BELOW **The cascade and upper garden at Peterhof, from an engraving by Suboff (1909).**

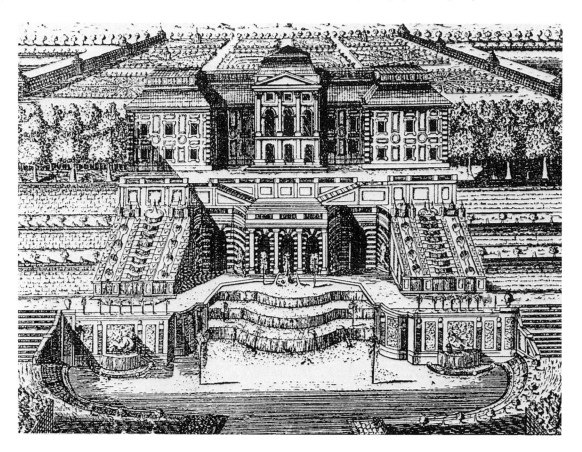

There were gardens in Russia in the 11th century and probably earlier, but the greatest Russian parks and gardens – Peterhof, Pushkin, Pavlovsk (q.v.) – were created in the 18th century and rank with the best in the world. Peter the Great's visits to gardens in western Europe in the 1690s inspired a number of gardens in and around his new capital city, St Petersburg (now Leningrad), with Peterhof pre-eminent among them. In the second half of the 18th century Catherine the Great's enthusiasm for the English landscape park led to the refashioning of Pushkin. Pavlovsk, which is more sentimental in character but no less impressive, owed much to the Empress Maria Fedorovna.

Legislation in the 1760s and 1780s, which freed the nobility from compulsory state service and encouraged them to live on their country estates, led to the making of many new parks around St Petersburg, Moscow and in the provinces. The gardens near the house were usually formal with a landscaped park beyond. In the 19th century a number of notable parks were laid out by the Black Sea for the imperial family and the very rich. A much greater variety of plants will be found in these Crimean parks than in those around Leningrad and Moscow, where the choice is restricted by the severe winters.

Since the Revolution no parks have been privately owned in the Soviet Union. While the most outstanding parks and some of those associated with famous owners have been admirably restored (particularly after wartime destruction), most estates have been put to other uses, and, in general, little attempt has been made to maintain the designed landscapes of once private estates. Most Soviet citizens live in flats, but many also have *dachas* in the country with gardens which combine fruit trees, fruit bushes, vegetables, herbs and flowers. In many towns and cities much has been achieved by Soviet landscape architects in providing green open spaces.

Leningrad and Environs

Gatchina

48km S of Leningrad on Route 20/E
Opening times: Summer months
Admission charge: No

Antonio Rinaldi's rather severe palace for Catherine the Great's favourite, Count Gregory Orlov, was extended by Vincenzo Brenna in the 1790s for the Grand Duke Paul, later Paul I, and was further altered in the 1850s. The park was created in the 1770s and 1780s by John Bush (*see* Pushkin) around a group of picturesque lakes and pools. Walks by the lakes, linked by bridges to some of the islands, offer the visitor changing views of this remarkable waterscape whose mirror surfaces reflect the patterns of the sky, the dark green of conifers and the silver grey of willows. Some features in the park – an area of woodland walks called the Old Sylvia and the Temple of Love on the Island of Love – were inspired by the visit of Paul and his wife to Chantilly in France. After the French Revolution, the Prince de Condé, the owner of Chantilly, spent some time in Russia. He was Prior of the Knights of Malta, and Paul, who was Grand Master of the order, had the Priory Palace built for him by the Black Lake. It was designed by the architect and polymath N.A.Lvov. The most curious building in the park is the small Birch House, which was made to look like a pile of logs while the interior was luxuriously decorated and furnished.

Leningrad: Botanic Garden of the Komarov Botanical Institute

2 Professor Popov Street, N of the Karpovka
Owner: USSR Academy of Sciences
Opening times: Daily, except Fri, summer 11–17; winter 11–16

Founded by Peter the Great for the cultivation of medicinal herbs in 1714, the Leningrad Botanic Garden, now covering 16ha, has a long-established international reputation. The formally laid out earlier part of the garden has been conserved, and there are also attractive landscaped areas. There are plants from the Soviet Union, Europe, North America and Asia in the open, and impressive collections of subtropical plants in the hothouses, with sections devoted to the Soviet Union, the Mediterranean, South Africa, the Americas, Australia, New Zealand and the Far East.

Leningrad: Elagin Island

In the estuary of the Neva; approached by footbridge
Admission charge: No

The palace built on Elagin Island in the Neva estuary in the late 18th century was an occasional summer residence of the Dowager Empress Maria Fedorovna, widow of Paul I. The island was landscaped in the 1820s by Joseph Bush (son of John Bush, *see* Pushkin), when a chain of nine interconnected picturesque pools was formed and many thousands of trees were planted, mainly oak, lime, ash, birch and sycamore. The pools solved a drainage problem and

at the same time enhanced the beauty of the island. A large formal garden in front of the palace became the vast meadow we see today. Carlo Rossi, who remodelled the palace in 1818–22, also designed the stables, orangery, music pavilion, guard-house and the remarkable kitchen building in the park. In 1933 Elagin became part of the Central Park of Culture and Rest, and a grid of concrete paths, a big wheel and other apparatus were installed, but in recent years much sensitive restoration has taken place.

Leningrad: Summer Garden

On the Kutuzov Embankment near the Kirovskii bridge
Admission charge: No

Peter the Great's first garden in his new capital city of St Petersburg (founded in 1703) was inspired by the gardens he had seen in Holland, and was laid out early in the 18th century with straight walks, formally clipped trees and hedges, and many fountains and statues. The trees are now allowed to grow naturally and no fountains remain, but there is still a fine collection of early 18th-century Italian garden statues. Peter's small palace is in one corner of the garden. The park railings and gates are by the architect Yuri Velten and are particularly fine examples of 18th-century wrought-iron. The Summer Garden has been a favourite meeting-place for more than two centuries.

Lomonosov (Oranienbaum)

41km W of Leningrad, between Peterhof and Kronstadt
Opening times: Daily sunrise–sunset
Admission charge: No

Oranienbaum was one of the most splendid palaces built during the reign of Peter the Great. As at Peterhof (q.v.), the palace (under restoration) was built on the natural terrace that overlooks the Gulf of Finland. Artificial terraces and stairways connect it to the lower park which, although partially restored, lacks its original statues and fountains.

Antonio Rinaldi designed Catherine the Great's

The Sliding Hill pavilion at Lomonosov was designed by Rinaldi in the second half of the 18th century.

much smaller Chinese palace of 1762–8 in the upper park, so called because some of the rooms have Chinese decoration. This has been well restored and is surrounded by lawns with statues and flowerbeds; it looks out over a large basin, which is now less formal than it was originally. Peter III's small palace has also been restored and the flowerbeds nearby have been recreated from contemporary engravings. Much of the upper park was landscaped in the second half of the 18th century.

The most striking building in the park is Rinaldi's blue and white Sliding Hill Pavilion. This once gave access to the sliding hill, a kind of early roller-coaster built in the 1760s, which extended for more than 500m. There is a model inside the pavilion, as well as a remarkable collection of Meissen figures.

Pavlovsk ★

25km S of Leningrad, off Route 20, 3km beyond Pushkin

Charles Cameron's classical palace, built in the 1780s for the Grand Duke Paul (later Paul I) and his wife Maria Fedorovna, stands on high ground looking over the very large 600ha park surrounding it. Cameron also designed the rather formal gardens near the palace, including the triple lime avenue, and began the landscaping of the park in the English style along the valley of the Slavianka.

Maria Fedorovna, a princess from Württemberg and a keen plantswoman, directed the development of the garden and park over a period of forty years.

The former private apartments of the imperial family look out into their private garden where there is still a good collection of flowering shrubs and where the flowerbeds are planted with a succession of bulbs and flowering plants. The many bereavements suffered by Maria Fedorovna are commemorated in the park by monuments to her parents, her husband and to the children who predeceased her. Her taste for simple pastoral buildings is reflected in the thatched dairy, but the charcoal-burner's hut no longer survives. More imposing are Cameron's domed rotunda – the Temple of Friendship – and the Apollo Colonnade, which collapsed during a storm and was not restored since it was seen to be more picturesque as a ruin. The Peel Tower, thatched and painted to look like a ruin taken over by peasants but with an elegantly appointed interior, still stands by the river.

The large area known as the White Birches was landscaped in the 1820s by the Italian stage designer Pietro Gonzaga and was an idealization of the meadow and forest landscape of northern Russia.

OPPOSITE PAGE **The turreted Turkish cascade lies among wild-flower meadows at Pushkin.**

BELOW **Wild flowers have seeded round the base of the picturesque ruin of the Apollo Colonnade built by Charles Cameron at Pavlovsk.**

Peterhof (Petrodvorets) ★

34km W of Leningrad. Best approached by hydrofoil from the embankment near the Hermitage
Admission charge: Yes

Peterhof (Petrodvorets) is one of the world's greatest water gardens. Peter the Great's palace, begun in 1714, is imposingly situated at the edge of a natural terrace and looks across the lower park to the Gulf of Finland. Water flows out from grottoes under the terrace and cascades down flights of marble steps to a basin with a fountain of Samson and the lion. Samson, symbolizing Russia's victory over Sweden in the Great Northern War (1700–21), has overpowered the lion and has prised open its jaws, from which a jet of water shoots high into the air. The many other gilded fountains and statues by the basin and the cascade seem to applaud the lion's defeat. From the basin the water flows along the Samson canal, flanked by fountains and trees, to the sea.

The lower park on either side of the canal is laid out with avenues, *bosquets* and fountains. There are also three small early 18th-century palaces here: Marly, surrounded by fishponds; the Hermitage, surrounded by a moat with a drawbridge; and Monplaisir, inspired by Dutch domestic architecture, with a garden of box-edged flowerbeds – now usually planted with tulips or begonias – and gilded fountains, surrounded by hostas. There are 173 fountains at Peterhof; among the most remarkable are the Neptune fountain, the Roman fountain, the Adam and Eve fountains, the Great fountains and the Triton fountain. Of particular interest are the joke fountains, among them the Tulip fountains, the Umbrella fountain and the Bench fountain, all waiting to drench the unwary.

It is difficult for the visitor to Peterhof to grasp that what is seen today has been almost entirely recreated since 1945, for the palace and the park suffered almost total destruction during World War II.

Pushkin (Tsarskoe Selo) ★

Pushkin, 22km S of Leningrad off Route 20
Opening times: Daily 6–22
Admission charge: No; *Ekaterininsky park* yes

Nothing remains of the small palace built for Catherine I, wife of Peter the Great, here, but there are two later palaces, both with their own gardens and parks. The Italian B. F. Rastrelli's great baroque palace for Elizabeth I dates from the middle of the 18th century and looks out across formal gardens which have been carefully restored. Immediately in front of the palace – called Ekaterininsky ('Catherine's') – there is an impressive parterre of arabesques formed from turf, red ash and anthracite.

OVERLEAF, LEFT **The Komarov Botanic Garden has a landscaped 'wild' area in addition to the formal botanic beds.**

OVERLEAD, ABOVE RIGHT **Charles Cameron's domed Temple of Friendship at Pavlovsk.**

OVERLEAF, BELOW RIGHT **The central parterre below the main facade of the Palace of Kuskovo.**

Beyond are straight avenues, embellished with statues, and a canal. The older trees have long been allowed to grow naturally, but the many recently planted limes are clipped as they were in the 18th century, to form green walls.

To the south and west of the palace lies the *Ekaterininsky Park*. This is one of the earliest examples in Russia of landscaping in the English style, and was carried out towards the end of the 18th century for Catherine the Great by the English Nurseryman John Bush or Busch and the Russian architect Vasily Neyelov. They made the large lake with its promontories and inlets from what had been a formal basin, formed other stretches of water, reshaped the contours of the land and planted many trees. Neyelov's fine Palladian bridge was inspired by the one at Wilton House in England.

A number of structures in the park, including an obelisk, a tower-ruin and a Turkish bath in the form of a mosque with a minaret, were built to celebrate victories in the wars against Turkey in the 18th and early 19th centuries. One of the most striking buildings is B.F.Rastrelli's grotto by the lake, lined with sea-shells and decorated with tritons, dolphins, sea-horses and masks of Neptune. The most original building is the Cameron Gallery, designed by the Scottish architect Charles Cameron (*see* Pavlosk) as a covered promenade for Catherine, from which she could view the formal garden on one side and the landscape park on the other. Cameron also designed the small pyramid in the park as the last resting-place for Catherine's greyhounds. A popular feature is P.P.Sokolov's fountain-statue of a milkmaid with a broken pitcher, based on a fable of La Fontaine, which stands by the lake.

There are a number of Chinese buildings, among them Yuri Velten's creaking pavilion (the weather-vane creaked), a Chinese theatre (not yet restored) and an entire Chinese village. Since Giacomo Quarenghi designed the Aleksandrovsky Palace for Catherine the Great's grandson Alexander I in the 1790s, the Chinese theatre and village have been in the *Aleksandrovsky Park*, which is formally laid out near the palace with avenues and canals. Beyond this formal layout the Scottish architect Adam Menelaws created a romantic landscape park in the early 19th century.

In 1918 the town of Tsarskoe Selo ('Tsar's Village') was renamed Detskoe Selo ('Children's Village'). Then, in 1937, a hundred years after the death of Russia's greatest poet, it was changed again to Pushkin. The young poet spent his schooldays at the lycée next to the Ekaterininsky palace. The parks were a great influence on his life, and this is widely reflected in his poetry. No other European parks are so rich in literary associations as those at Pushkin, and many important Russian writers lived and worked here.

Moscow and Environs

Arkhangelskoe
16km W of Moscow

The former house of the Yusupovs, one of the richest families in Russia, stands at the top of a slope looking out over the River Moskva and a fine landscape of meadow and woodland. There is a terrace in front of the house, with many statues and vases, and a second terrace below it. Between the lower terrace and the river there is a vast lawn or meadow with, until recently, avenues of limes on either side. These have now been felled to restore the earlier tunnels of pleached lime. This is unfortunate, since the two large sanitorium buildings by the river, which replaced conservatories in the 1930s, are now exposed to view. Architectural features in the attractive park include a tea-house, a monument to Pushkin and a mausoleum built for Prince Yusopov in 1916 but never used. The house and much of the layout of the park date from the late 18th century, when the estate was owned by the Golitsyns.

Gorki Leninskie

34km S of Moscow
Opening times: Daily 10–18, except Tues

The estate dates from around 1800. Like the house, it was reconstructed in the early years of the 20th century, when garden temples, bridges and a grotto were built. The immediate setting of the house is formal with woodland beyond, planted mainly with larch, Crimean pine (*Pinus nigra caramanica*), oaks, maples and limes. V. A. Lenin lived here towards the end of his life and died here in January 1924. The house and estate are now a Lenin museum.

Kuskovo

In E suburbs, 10km from Moscow city centre; 2km N of Rianzanskoe Highway

The wooden palace, once the home of one of the most prominent Russian families, the Sheremetevs, was built in the 1770s. It looks out to the south across a large basin and along a canal. To the north, the view across a large central parterre, embellished with statues, is closed by an orangery which is almost as imposing as the palace; it is now a museum of ceramics with a fine collection of Russian, Chinese, German, French and English porcelain. From the central parterre, paths lead through *bosquets* to various notable garden buildings, including a fine grotto, a menagerie, a small Italian villa and a Dutch house which was once surrounded by a Dutch garden.

Moscow: Botanic Garden ✳

W Botanicheskaya Street, near Ostankino, N outskirts of city
Owner: USSR Academy of Sciences
Opening times: Daily, May to Sept 10–20; *greenhouses* Jun to Sept 10–18, except Mon

The principal botanic garden of the Soviet Union, established in the northern outskirts of Moscow in 1945, covers 360ha and consists largely of woodland, with more than 1,800 species of trees. Collections representing all the continents include 3,000 species native to the Soviet Union and the country's largest collection of roses, with more than 2,000 cultivars. There are also impressive collections of dahlias, hyacinths, irises, lilies, narcissus, peonies and phlox.

The first botanical garden in Moscow was the Apothecary's Garden near the wall of the Kremlin. It was moved by Peter the Great in 1706 to its present site at 28 Prospekt Mira, where it may still be visited.

Tsaritsno

20km S of Moscow

The gothic palace, built for Catherine the Great in the 1780s but never completed, is now being restored and will become a museum of ceramics. It is set in a large wooded landscape park with lakes, pools and some fine park buildings – particularly the Temple of Ceres, the Milovida belvedere, the tower-ruin and the bridge at the entrance to the park.

The Baltic States and North-West

Kadriorg (Ekaterintal)

On the Gulf of Finland, on the E outskirts of Tallinn

The attractive small baroque palace and formal park on sloping ground near the sea were designed by an Italian, Niccolò Michetti, for Peter the Great's wife Catherine I in the 1720s. (Ekaterintal means Catherine's valley.) Although many of the early features of the park have gone, some of the avenues and trees – mainly chestnut, oak and larch – have survived. The large pool (Swan Lake) is also part of the original layout. The site of the upper garden behind the palace is now occupied by an exhibition of modern sculpture.

Polar-Alpine Botanic Garden of Kirovsk

8km from Kirovsk in the Khibini mountains S of
Murmansk
Opening times: Daily 9–16

The garden was established in 1931 and occupies
570ha in the Khibini mountains by the River
Budiavriok and on the slopes of Mount Budiavr-
chorr. Taiga gives way to birch forest at about 360m,
which is succeeded by tundra at about 420m. Rocky
desert is reached at about 1,000m. There is also a
small collection of tropical and subtropical plants
under glass and an underground nursery in a disused
mine.

Minsk: Botanic Garden

2a Surganova St
Owner: Belorussian Academy of Sciences
Opening times: Wed–Sun 10–20

Founded in 1932 and re-established in 1945 after
total destruction in World War II, the garden covers
106ha. From the central parterre, avenues of birch,
lime, walnut, ash, bird-cherry, maple, apple and oak
lead in all directions through the garden. There are
outstanding collections of rhododendrons and lilacs.

Palanga

Palanga, 25km N of Klaipeda
Owner: Communal Enterprise Unification of Palanga
Opening times: At all times, except two weeks in early
spring
Admission charge: No

Edouard André designed the palace (now housing a
museum of amber) and the 70ha wooded park in the
late 19th century for the Polish Count Tyszkiewicz.
Separated from the Baltic Sea by pines and sand-
dunes, the park is romantic in character, with winding paths, streams, pools, open glades and a wide
variety of trees.

Riga: Botanic Garden

2 L. Kaudavas St, Riga, on Route 21
Owner: Latvian Academy of Sciences
Opening times: Daily, Jun to Sept 10–20; Oct to May
8–15, except Sat, Mon
Admission charge: Yes

The garden, founded in 1922, is strong in ornamental
plants, particularly rhododendrons, and there are
good collections of tropical and subtropical plants
under glass.

LEFT **The Italian courtyard at Livadia, based on the
cloister of San Marco in Florence.**

RIGHT **The romantic park at Alupka on the Black Sea
is seen against the steep rock face of Ai Petri.**

The Ukraine, Black Sea and Georgia

Alupka ★
On the Black Sea, 6km W of Yalta

The setting of the palace at Alupka, lying between the Black Sea and the steep rock face of Ai Petri, is unrivalled. The palace was designed 1828–37 for Count M. S. Vorontsov by the English architect Edward Blore (who never visited Russia), in a surprising mixture of English gothic and oriental styles. The main terrace in front of the palace is remarkable for its marble fountains, clipped box, vases with agaves, three pairs of marble lions from the studio of Francesco Bonanni in Italy and the view. Below the main terrace a series of terraces descends to the sea.

The romantic park on the other side of the palace was laid out in the 1820s to 1840s by Karl Kebach with winding paths, streams, pools, waterfalls, rocks, grottoes and, above all, magnificent trees around open glades seen against the mountain background – cedars, cypresses, various pines, sequoias and yews, chestnuts, magnolias, oriental planes, and many others. Many of the plants came from the Nikitsky Botanic Garden (q.v.), among them two roses introduced in 1829, 'Alupka' and 'Countess Elizabeth Vorontsova', which gained international recognition.

Sir Winston Churchill stayed at Alupka in 1945 during the Yalta Conference.

Batumi: Botanic Garden ❀
Zelenyi Mys, a suburb of Batumi at the E end of the Black Sea, on Route 19
Owner: The Georgian Academy of Sciences
Opening times: All year
Admission charge: Yes

Established in 1811, the garden covers 120ha and has a rich collection of plants from warm climates. There are 60 species of eucalyptus, 94 of roses and 17 of magnolias. There is also a Japanese garden, a bamboo grove and a citrus plantation.

Kiev: Botanic Garden
Timiryazevskaya St, on the bank of the River Dnieper S of the Monastery of Caves, S of city centre
Owner: Ukrainian Academy of Sciences
Opening times: Daily 8–19, except Mon
Admission charge: Yes

The garden covers 130ha on hills by the Dnieper. Ornamental plants are well represented, particularly magnolias and lilacs, and there is an interesting formal fruit garden.

Livadia
On the Black Sea, 2km W of Yalta

The White Palace, built as a summer residence for Nicholas II by the architect N. P. Krasnov, and replacing an earlier palace on a wide terrace above the Black Sea, was completed in 1911. Designed in the style of the early Italian Renaissance, it has one Moorish courtyard and another based on the cloisters of San Marco in Florence. The large park dates from the 1830s. The layout near the palace is formal, with terrace walks, flower parterres, clipped evergreen shrubs and hedges, rose borders, fountains and vases. The park is landscaped, with winding paths down to the sea. There are many fine trees, among them cedars, pines, redwoods and magnolias.

The Yalta Conference was held here in 1945, and there is an exhibition on the conference in the palace.

Lvov: Botanic Garden
14 Marc Cheremshina St, Lvov, on Routes 12/14
Opening times: Daily 9–17

The garden is on two separate sites. The older part, of 2.5ha, was established in 1851 and has an arboretum, a collection of ornamental flowering plants and hothouses, but is not normally open. The later site, of 4.5ha, was added in 1911; it was previously a private park. The varied terrain has been exploited to provide a wide range of habitats for an extensive collection of plants indigenous to the area.

Massandra

Near the Yalta hotel, 2km E of Yalta

The park at Massandra on the eastern outskirts of Yalta slopes steeply down to the Black Sea. It is divided into two separate parts, Upper and Lower Massandra. In the first half of the 19th century it belonged to Count M. S. Vorontsov and was laid out for him by the German Karl Kebach (*see* Alupka), who introduced many exotic trees and shrubs. It became the property of the Tsar in 1889. There are some particularly fine cypresses and indigenous oaks in the lower park, while other notable trees include cedars, junipers, pines, sequoias, yews, magnolias and an avenue of palms. A small palace in the upper park, built in 1911 in the style of Louis XIV, is set off by a formal composition of parterres, lawns, a basin and fountains. Count Vorontsov's hunting lodge survives in the lower park.

Nikitsky Botanic Garden of Yalta ❀

On the Black Sea, 6km E of Yalta
Owner: V. I. Lenin All-Union Academy of Agricultural Sciences
Opening times: Sat–Wed, May to Sept 8–20; Oct to Apr 9–17
Admission charge: Yes

A large garden – 272ha – of great beauty by the Black Sea, the Nikitsky botanic garden was founded in 1811 and was responsible for introducing many plants to the Crimea. There are impressive collections of trees and shrubs from all the subtropical regions of the world, and a very large collection of roses. Attractive architectural features include a water staircase and belvederes.

Odessa: Botanic Garden

At the Novorossiisk University, Odessa, on Routes 20/26
Opening times: Wed, Fri 8–16

The garden was established in the 19th century and covers 16ha. The older part of the garden is by the sea, a later addition on the site of two former private parks with many old trees. There is a wide range of plants in the open and under glass, with good collections of citrus plants, peaches and flowering annuals.

Sochi Arboretum

74 Kurortny Avenue, Sochi, on the Caucasian coast road, Route 19
Owner: Caucasian Research Institute of Silviculture and Forestry Mechanism
Opening times: 10–18

A collection of exotic trees was established here in the late 19th century. There are many species of pine and oak, as well as acacias, bamboos, magnolias, palms and a rose garden. Cascades, pools, fountains, statues and garden temples add to the 16ha park's attractions.

Sukhumi: Botanic Garden

Sukhumi, at the E end of the Black Sea, Route 19
Owner: Georgian Academy of Sciences

The 25ha Sukhumi Botanic Garden originated in the garden of the medical officer of the local garrison in the early 19th century. The 5,000 species represented here include 1,300 trees and shrubs, 2,800 herbaceous plants and 500 plants grown under glass. Fourteen species of palms grow in the open, and the impressive collection of aquatic plants includes the giant South American water-lily *Victoria amazonica*.

Tbilisi: Botanic Garden

In a valley on the edge of Tbilisi, on Routes 17/16
Owner: Georgian Academy of Sciences
Opening times: Daily 9–20

There has been a garden here for more than three centuries, situated in a beautiful and sheltered valley near Tbilisi and once attached to a palace. It has been a botanic garden since 1845 and now covers 128ha. It is particularly strong in Mediterranean, North American, Japanese and Sino-Himalayan plants, and there are 925 rose cultivars.

Turkey:
Istanbul and the Bosporus

Exposed in winter to cold snow-bearing winds from the Black Sea and in summer to the warm humid winds from the Sea of Marmara and the eastern Mediterranean, the natural forests round the Bosporus are predominantly of oak and Spanish chestnut. The *korus* or woodlands owned by the Istanbul Municipality and open to the public on the Asian shore also have field maples, Cornelian cherry, Atlas cedar, *Phillyrea latifolia*, tree of heaven, *Robinia pseudacacia*, silver lime and pines. On the hottest south-facing slopes dropping to the Bosporus, shallow soils grow a pseudo-*maquis* vegetation: pines, cypresses, Judas trees and aromatic shrubs and herbs are typically Mediterranean. To these have been added tender exotics which give essential shade and flower in the hot summers.

Turks tend to admire nature in its virgin state, and although the Seljuk dynasty (at its height in the late 11th century) must have had palace gardens in Anatolia, it was not until the arrival of the Ottomans at the end of the 13th century and the Turks' conversion to Islam that the lovely courtyard gardens began to appear – reflections on earth of Muhammed's Garden of Paradise. In the 15th century, Sultan Muhammed II destroyed the old Turkish families, after which all Turkish subjects and their land had to remain at the sultan's disposal. Deprived of hereditary estates, few apart from the rulers had the means (in an often difficult climate) to create beautiful gardens.

To the Ottoman Sultans (later 13th century to 1922) gardens were for luxuriant repose and enjoyment. Walled enclosures were planted with trees, particularly cypresses, the symbol of continuing life; roses were emblems and scented flowers had their own precise language, continually hinted at in calligraphy, carpets, embroideries and tiles. Patterns of Iznik tiles which decorate the Topkapí Palace (q.v.) unite the cool interiors with flower-festooned pavilions and kiosks (round, open-sided pavilions often containing a pool or fountain) in the outer courts. A 17th-century traveller, Robert Withers, describes gardens which 'contained fountains in such abundance that almost every walk had two or three of them'; and square and rectangular pools were for contemplation and sometimes swimming. Flowerbeds each contained a single genus, regardless of colour.

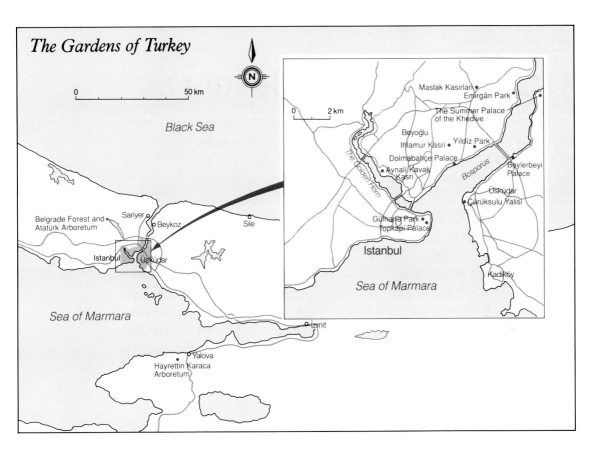

The Gardens of Turkey

Black Sea

Sea of Marmara

Belgrade Forest and
Atatürk Arboretum
Sariyer
Beykoz
Sile
Istanbul
Üsküdar
İzmit
Yalova
Hayrettin Karaca
Arboretum

Maslak Kasirlari
Emirgân Park
The Summer Palace
of the Khedive
Beyoğlu
Ihlamur Kasri
Yildiz Park
Dolmabahçe Palace
Aynali Kavak
Kasri
Beylerbeyi
Palace
Üsküdar
Çüruksulu Yalisi
The Golden Horn
Bosporus
Gülhane Park
Topkapi Palace
Istanbul
Sea of Marmara
Kadiköy

For the humbler Turks orchards of almond, fig, apricot, plum and mulberry, sometimes on steep terraced hillsides, adjoined the small shady courtyards where plane trees and vines provided essential shade for summer living. Roses, jasmine, orange and lemon trees, pomegranates, tuberoses and carnations grew beside more useful crops of tomatoes and leeks. It is a measure of the Turkish love of flowers that the Grand Vizier Kara Mustafa Pasha laid out a garden in front of his tent during the second siege of Vienna in 1683; potted plants were common baggage for Turkish armies.

Lady Mary Wortley Montagu, friend of Addison and Pope and wife to the British Ambassador to Turkey, lived in the Belgrade Forest (q.v.) from 1716–18. She described the gardens of the Topkapí Palace of Ahmed III during the so-called Tulip Period, when the Sultan's envoy to the French court sent back rare tulip bulbs, bred in western Europe and descended from Ogier Ghiselin de Busbecq's first introductions to Vienna from Turkey in the late 16th century (see Vienna: Botanic Garden). Her references to 'parterres enamelled with flowers' and 'walls encrusted with emeralds and sapphires' may seem far-fetched, but the luxuriance of the palace is legendary. At night flowerbeds were illuminated by candles and mirror-reflected oil-lamps while Ahmed entertained his guests to April 'tulip picnics'. Sadly, by the end of the century other sober and reliable reports describe the courtyards as drab and ill-kept.

In 1723 Ahmed had laid out a French-style garden at Sa'dabad Kasri above the Golden Horn. No traces remain, but drawings by an Austrian officer, Gudenus, show classical wooden architecture and the wide eaves typical of all the sultan's garden buildings; a long canal is bordered with weeping willows. During the 17th and 18th centuries Turkish pavilions and tents became features in picturesque gardens all over Europe (*see* Haga Royal Park in Stockholm), while European garden designers came to Constantinople to build formal terraced gardens and parterres for palaces and houses (often for foreign embassies) all along the Bosporus shore. Cemeteries, too, were an important part of travellers' lore at this time, though the tradition has long since died. From the cemetery on a steep slope below the battlements of Rumeli Hisari on the west shore of the Bosporus it is still possible to imagine the strait before the arrival of concrete. Yahya Efendi Dergahi does not always welcome strangers but views from the tiny cemetery and *dergâh* (dervish sanctuary) are breathtaking. The British Crimean War Cemetery on the Asian side comes as a contrast. Immaculately tidy, it overlooks the port of Haydarpasa, not far from the barracks in which Florence Nightingale worked.

During the 19th century the gardens along the Bosporus, Byron's 'ocean stream', were influenced by the romantic movement, each garden becoming a secret paradise with tangled wisteria and vines, groves of lilac and luxuriant rose bushes occasionally glimpsed through latticed window frames. All this has gone, and although cypresses still frame Istanbul's skyline of domes and minarets, and tulips are again planted in the parks, much of the Bosporus shoreline has become a concrete jungle where orchards and flower-symbolism have no place.

Istanbul and the European Shore of the Bosporus

Aynalíkavak Kasri

N of the Golden Horn, on Kasimpasi-Sütlüce road
Owner: Directorate of Royal Palaces
Opening times: Daily 9–17, except Mon, Thurs

Only the 19th-century pavilion now survives from the large complex that once looked across the Golden Horn to the Mosque of Yavuz Salim and the Greek Patriarchate on the southern shore, and even this is today hidden by a shipyard. The pavilion and the sloping garden are given privacy from the industrialized surroundings by high walls and many fine trees. Besides the exotic magnolias, these include old specimens of trees indigenous to the eastern Mediterranean, such as a fine *Pinus brutia*, and the nettle tree (*Celtis australis*). Central lawns and traditional paths of fine reddish dust fringe box-edged parterres, decked out in spring with tulips and later with ubiquitous salvias. Roses, lagerstroemias and hydrangeas add charm and informality. Concerts of Turkish classical music are performed in the garden during the Istanbul Festival in July.

The Belgrade Forest and Atatürk Arboretum

In the N of the Istanbul peninsula, *c*.5km W of Büyükdere on the Bosporus, 20km from Istanbul
Owner: University of Istanbul: Faculty of Forestry
Opening times: *Forest* daily 8–20; *arboretum* 9–17.30, except weekends
Admission charge: Yes

The 400ha *Belgrade Forest* takes its name from the village founded by Sultan Suleiman the Magnificent after his conquest of Belgrade in 1521. The forest is a natural woodland of native oak, birch, beech, ash, hornbeam and Spanish chestnut undercarpeted with native flora. There are welcoming kiosks, arbours and fountains, and picnic sites. Lady Mary Wortley Montagu (*see* Introduction) lived here in the early 18th century and grew carnations, roses and jonquils in her garden. Historically an important source of drinking water for the city of Istanbul, there are seven *bends*, or reservoirs, with impressive dams and aqueducts dating from the 16th–19th centuries.

The *Atatürk Arboretum* has been developed during the last thirty years on a 50–60ha site within the forest. Slopes with different aspects provide conditions for experimenting with a wide variety of plants, including exotics.

Dolmabahçe Palace ★

On the Bosporus, 4km N of the Golden Horn
Owner: Directorate of National Palaces
Opening times: Daily 9.30–17, except Mon, Thurs
Admission charge: Yes

This impressive building in neo-rococo style was completed in 1853 by the Turkish Armenian architect Nikoğos Karabet Balyan and his father. On the edge of the Bosporus, and on the site of an older palace, Dolmabahçe became the dwelling of the sultan as well as the administrative centre of the empire, taking the place of the Topkapí Palace in the old city. The formal gardens, laid out in a series of courtyards to frame the vast buildings, were punctuated with ornamental *bassins* and fountains and had typical 19th-century planting, where box-edged beds were dominated by specimen cypresses and vast clipped yews. Today the garden is in good condition after a sensitive restoration programme. The pattern of flowerbeds is simplified, with planting of tulips and violets for spring, and red salvias in summer. In both sun and shade *Ophiopogon japonicus* (only introduced to Europe in the late 19th century) makes an effective substitute for grass, which cannot withstand the hot summers. There is an impressive number of specimen trees, including the Chinese fir (*Cunninghamia lanceolata*), a monkey puzzle, and a number of tall *Magnolia grandiflora*, the latter a feature of all these shoreside gardens. Behind the palace a vast *Magnolia stellata* is glorious in spring. In one garden a pool surrounded by a circle of lime trees contains a grotto constructed of concrete 'woodwork'. On the hillside, above an avenue of plane trees, cedars are being cut down to make space for a Turkish-Japanese-Swiss hotel venture.

Emirgân Park

On the Bosporus, about 15km N of the Golden Horn
Owner: Municipality of Istanbul
Opening times: Daily 8–18
Admission charge: *Pedestrians* no; *cars and buses* yes

The woodland site of what is now the Emirgân Park was presented during the 19th century to Ismail Pasha, the Khedive (Viceroy) of Egypt. The Khedive built a wooden palace and three pavilions and had the park landscaped in the currently fashionable English style. The pavilions, which have been restored by the Turkish Touring and Automobile Club, are open to the public as restaurants and a concert hall. A wide variety of specimen trees and shrubs has been planted in the park. Conifers include umbrella pines, Aleppo pines, *Pinus brutia*, incense cedars and maidenhair trees. Deciduous trees include oak, lime, tulip trees, *Koelreuteria paniculata* and albizias. Evergreens, like the camphor tree, *Magnolia grandiflora*, and tender shrubs such as feijoas flourish.

Ihlamur Kasri

Near Beşiktaş, on W shore of Bosporus
Owner: Directorate of Royal Palaces
Opening times: Daily, except Mon, Thurs, summer 9.30–17; winter 9.30–16
Admission charge: Yes

Surrounded by tall modern buildings, the Ihlamur Kasri Palace, built in 1865, is an oasis as unexpected as it is attractive. The white marble and creamy stone facade is so richly sculptured that it almost serves as a grotto to the small but lovingly-kept garden. The white lamp-posts and pool, often depicted by the 19th-century naïve landscape painters patronized by the later sultans, are softened by roses, lagerstroemia, pampas grass and the usual annuals. Fine trees include ginkgos, *Magnolia grandiflora*, limes and plane trees in the bed of an old stream.

Looking over the Bosporus from Dolmabahçe Palace.

Istanbul: Gülhane Park

Part of the outer garden of Topkapí Palace; main entrance
on Alemdar Caddesi beside the Alay Kiosk
Owner: Directorate of the Parks and Gardens of Istanbul
Opening times: Daily 8–18

An avenue shaded by giant oriental plane trees runs
through the centre of the Gülhane Park, an extensive
woodland which was originally the hunting park of
the sultans and surrounds the Topkapí Palace. Further planting took place in the 18th century, when
elm, ash, ilex, oak, wild pear, planes and terebinth
were brought from the forests of the Gulf of İzmit. It
became a public park towards the end of the Ottoman
era, when the sultans left Topkapí to reside at the
Palace of Dolmabahçe and at Yíldíz.

Istanbul: Topkapí Palace ★

Old town, overlooking the Golden Horn
Owner: Directorate of the Topkapí Palace Museum
Opening times: Daily 9–17
Admission charge: Yes

The Topkapí Palace, one of the oldest surviving
palaces in the world, was begun in the 15th century
after the capture of Constantinople by the Turks in
1453. On a peninsula overlooking the Golden Horn,
the Bosporus and the Sea of Marmara, the whole
palace and garden complex, including the outer
Gülhane Park (q.v.), is surrounded by 5km of walls.
Fires and additions led to alterations over the centuries, but the inner gardens remain much as they
were in the 15th and 16th centuries. In 1593 50,000
white roses were ordered for the series of open
courtyards, but although the gardens were arranged
for pleasure and delight, Ogier Ghiselin de Busbecq
(see Vienna: Botanic Garden) reported at this time
that the Pasha was selling superfluous roses, violets
and vegetables for profit.

   The main entrance to the Inner Palace (the Gate of
Salutations) leads to the second court, where today
there are roses and flowerbeds, and cypresses and
plane trees give shade. Through the Gate of Felicity
is the square third court where there are more fine
trees, including oriental planes, nettle trees, an Atlas
cedar, magnolias, *Lagerstroemia indica* and box; there
are scented flowers in summer. The fourth courtyard

is on several levels and has pavilions surrounded with
trees, shrubs and flowers; yew trees shade banks of
hydrangeas. In the 18th century this was the site of
tulip festivals.

Maslak Kasirlari ★

Next to the Fatih Forest, 10km N of Istanbul between
Levint and Büyükdere
Owner: Directorate of National Palaces
Opening times: Daily, except Mon, Thurs, summer
9.30–17.00; winter 9.30–16.00
Admission charge: Yes

This small 19th-century summer palace and its
annexes were built at the edge of thick woods and
were first used by the imperial family as a country
retreat. Today the main building is open to the public
as a museum, and there is a café in the conservatory,
among *Cycas revoluta*, *Coffea arabica* and camellias
planted at the end of the 19th and beginning of the
20th century. The park surrounding these buildings
is planted with various evergreen and deciduous trees
and shrubs, including yew, *Magnolia grandiflora*,
rhododendrons and roses. A giant yew is one of the
most conspicuous landmarks in the park. On the
north-eastern slope behind the palace complex a
natural woodland has been preserved, although some
exotics have been introduced. Among the oldest trees
are oaks, limes, sycamores, field maples, nettle trees,
horse chestnuts, hornbeam, alder, and Austrian pine.

Yíldíz Park ★

Between the suburbs of Beşiktaş and Ortaköy, N of the
Golden Horn
Owner: Municipality of Istanbul
Opening times: Daily, except Mon, Tues, summer
9.30–17; winter 9.30–16
Admission charge: *Pedestrians* no; *cars and buses* yes

Yíldíz Park, the garden of the 19th-century former
royal palace of Abdul Hamid II (who preferred it to
Dolmabahçe), occupies a sloping site on the shores of
the Bosporus. The garden is divided into two parts:
the outer garden, known in Ottoman times as the
Grand Park, and the inner or 'harem' garden immediately surrounding the palace behind high walls.
Both gardens were redesigned in the 19th century in

the English landscape style and are now being restored by the Turkish Touring and Automobile Club. The outer garden, open to the public, contains several buildings, including the Cadir and Malta pavilions, now cafés, and the Yíldíz porcelain factory. There are two attractive artificial lakes.

The garden is richly wooded, with ancient stands of oak, ash, pine, cypress, cedar and yew, and there are many flowering trees and shrubs, including Judas trees, *Magnolia grandiflora*, *Robinia pseudacacia*, bay, silver limes, and red- and white-flowered varieties of horse chestnuts.

The Asian Shore of the Bosporus

Beylerbeyi Palace ★

At the foot of the northern slope of Mt Bulgulru, just above the new bridge across the Bosporus; 14km from the centre of Istanbul
Owner: Directorate of Royal Palaces
Opening times: Daily 9–17, except Mon, Thurs

This seaside palace, built in 1865 in much the same style as Dolmabahçe (q.v.), was intended principally as a residence for visiting royalty and heads of state. It has an immaculately kept terraced garden with spacious pools and pavilions. Cedars and yews, lime trees and magnolias, bamboos and box give the garden an air of relaxed formality.

Cürüksulu Yalisi

Salacak near Usküdar
Owner: Mr Selaaddin Beyazit
Opening times: By permission, Salacak Toprakli Sok. 11, Usküdar, Istanbul

Once described as the most beautiful house in Asia, the *yali* (the name given to an Ottoman mansion on the Bosporus) is situated on the edge of a steep escarpment covered with bay and fig trees. The garden is surrounded by a high wall and has a breathtaking view across the Bosporus towards Topkapí Palace (q.v.) and the Golden Horn. Between clouds of ancient wisteria, roses of many varieties, a magnificent paulownia and box-edged borders that impart to the garden the complexity of a Turkish carpet, there are glimpses of distant domes, minarets and water.

Hayrettin Karaca Arboretum ✹

On the Asiatic shore S of İzmit, on the Yalova road to the hot springs of Termal
Owner: Mr Hayrettin Karaca
Opening times: By permission, Samanlı Köyü, Yalova

The Hayrettin Karaca Arboretum is far and away the finest plantsman's garden in or near Istanbul. It boasts marvellous collections of irises, maples and conifers, set against a backcloth of open, unspoilt countryside.

The Summer Palace of the Khedive

400m walk above the village of Çubuklu between Kanlica and Paşabahçe
Owner: Municipality of Istanbul

The Khedive was the hereditary Viceroy of Egypt under Ottoman rule. This palace, built in 1900, belonged to Abbas Hilmi Pasha, the last Khedive, and its distinctive tower is one of the most conspicuous landmarks on the Asiatic side of the Bosporus. An avenue lined with silver lime and horse chestnuts runs from the main gate. In front of the palace lies a rose garden, bordered on either side by a terrace with colourful groups of hydrangeas shaded by giant umbrella pines and yews. The palace has now been converted into a hotel.

Yugoslavia

For map, see p.282.

The Federal Socialist Republic of Yugoslavia, made up today of Croatia (Hrvatska), Slovenia (Slovenija), Serbia (Srbija), Bosnia and Herzegovina, Montenegro (Crna Gora) and Macedonia (Makedonia), borders the Adriatic on the west side of the Balkan peninsula. Three-quarters of the country is mountainous, with many peaks over 2,000m. The climate ranges between a true continental regime in the north and north-east, and Mediterranean conditions in the south, with southern Serbia and Macedonia having a moderate version of the continental extremes. Throughout the country these basic divisions are modified by altitude, the peaks over 2,500m being covered with snow for much of the year.

The richness of Yugoslavia's native and endemic flora on the alpine and sub-alpine slopes, and on high plateaus round lakes formed during the recession of the last Ice Age, is still being explored. For any garden enthusiast Yugoslavia, even without garden art, provides an exciting range of plants. There are twenty national parks where the native and sometimes endemic flora can be enjoyed and studied, species confined to Yugoslavia including the Serbian spruce, *Picea omorika*, which grows among limestone rocks on the slopes above the River Drina and in some other locations. Some of the parks are readily accessible to visitors, but others, which contain regions of scientific importance growing the most interesting flora in Europe, are less easily explored.

Lying on the Danube, a major route from the East to Western Europe, Yugoslavia has benefited since Roman times from plants introduced from Asia and the Middle East. Some plants, such as the grape vine, were brought by invading armies (it is thought the Turks brought onions and garlic to the Balkans), or by Crusaders or pilgrims returning from the Holy Land; other new plants, bulbs and seeds travelled from village to village during the five centuries of Turkish occupation, giving cultivated gardens a strongly oriental flavour. In all parts of Yugoslavia humble gardening has always reflected a love of flowers, evidenced by vegetable plots decorated with roses,

The national parks of Yugoslavia contain a vast variety of indigenous plants (some endemic) in natural settings – as at Plitvice National Park in Croatia.

lilacs and dianthus; in the northern Croatian valleys pollarded willows (*Salix alba* 'Chermesina'), with brilliant orange bark in winter, grow by each cottage, their supple stems used for binding vines in spring; southern gardens will have a vine pergola and climbing gourds, and the obligatory basil, pot marigolds and amaranths, as well as more perennial favourites such as roses, lilacs, violets, primroses and German iris. In autumn houses are garlanded with drying scarlet peppers; tomatoes, melons and pomegranates are all cultivated for food.

Slovenia contains high altitude alpine areas where the flora reaches a peak for two weeks in July. There are woods of Spanish chestnut, beech and oak on the lower slopes and open meadowland where wild poet's narcissus, summer snowflake and fritillaries spread; vines and orchards of walnuts and other fruit are grown for profit. In Vojvodina, north of the Danube towards the Hungarian plain (and itself once Hungarian), collective farms have replaced the great estates, but native poplars, willow, ash, mulberries and nettle trees grow with exotic robinias, maples, American walnuts and kolreuterias planted as city shade trees. The western parts of Slovenia and Croatia touch the Adriatic and a Mediterranean climate, with greater gardening opportunities, prevails. In Serbia, with a mainly Orthodox population, and in the Muslim republic of Bosnia and Hercegovina and the more southern Macedonia, Turkish influences after the 15th century encouraged a love of flowers (often expressed in poetry and embroidery) and the countryside. Intimate Muslim back courtyards had flowerbeds surrounded by white pebbles and were shaded by oaks, lime trees and walnuts. Sarajevo was described by the 17th-century Turkish traveller Čelebija as a 'town with 2,000 heavenly gardens with clear running waters, delightful summer houses of all kinds'. (These *čardaks* shaded by vine pergolas are still built in Turkey.) Flowers brought by the Turks from Asia Minor included tulips, lilies, hyacinths, roses, ranunculus and pomegranate.

Mountainous Macedonia, with lakes and valleys open to the south, is rich in native flora but has no tradition of classical European gardening, although the Romans gardened at Heraclea Lynkestis in the 3rd century AD. Even today, houses are situated to take advantage of the natural scenery; town planning ensures that only one third of any settlement is occupied by buildings, leaving the rest of the land for green vegetation provided by small courtyard gardens and shade trees.

On the Dalmatian coast, the Roman gardens at Split have vanished, but the 15th- and 16th-century renaissance gardens round Dubrovnik in Croatia still retain sufficient evidence of their layout to interest the gardener as well as the historian. Further north the outlines of terraced gardens adjacent to defensive medieval castles such as Ptuj, Negova, Sevnica and Borl can still be traced; these will have been mainly for culinary and medicinal plants and not devoted to decorative horticulture. By the 18th century, with Turkish penetration contained, more spacious country houses were built in the northern plains. This region was closely linked with Central European culture until 1918, and for two centuries the few grand garden layouts reflected western European and especially Austrian trends; early formal gardens were mainly of a simplified French baroque style, with an avenue approach and a box-edged parterre in a courtyard, although orchards and vegetable areas continued to be cultivated. These gardens were converted into naturalistic romantic parks in the 19th century and still contain many interesting trees from that period, which have proved suitable for the continental climate. Today most formal elements have vanished, and wild flowers spread in the open meadows near the old houses.

Dornava Castle

Just E of Ptuj on the River Pesnica

In the early 18th century the family of Count Attems converted a 14th-century manor house into a palace with a formal garden. The axis of a long avenue centred on the forecourt of the building was continued at the back of the palace by a 90m parterre, with central water basin and Neptune sculpture, and ended in a symmetrically laid-out orchard. Fountains, orangeries and statuary made this the most important garden in Slovenia. In the 19th century an English-style park was developed on the west side of the palace. Statues still remain, but Dornava, now a children's hospital, has been badly neglected since World War II. Plans exist for restoration.

Dubrovnik: Franciscan and Dominican Monasteries

Opening times: *Franciscan* daily 9–dusk; *Dominican* daily 9–12, 15–18

Two monasteries in Dubrovnik, one Franciscan and the other Dominican, still retain their cloister gar-dens. Mihoje Brajkov built the Franciscan cloister with its exquisite double columns and decorated capitals in 1317. It is divided by a central path and a double row of stone benches, terminated by a fountain. The Dominican cloister is 16th-century, a blend of gothic and renaissance; today its central court is paved.

Dubrovnik: Environs

Many palace and seaside gardens from Dubrovnik's Renaissance in the 16th century still have important and recognizable outlines for the garden historian. Terraces, pergolas and rectangular subdivisions of regular plots were typical of these gardens, and plants were grown for both pleasure and use. Owing to the shortage of water, small fountains and irrigation channels took the place of their more spectacular counterparts in western Europe. The sites outside the city walls are often of great beauty.

At nearby Rijeka-Dubrovačka, the Sorkočević family built seaside villas, both on the bay and at Lapad to the west of the old town; the gardens were laid out in the second half of the 16th century. At *Rijeka Dubrovačka*, the geometric four-part parterre and stone pergolas are still visible (open in summer, no charge). At *Lapad* (where the palace and gardens are visitable by appointment only), a loggia fronting the gothic-renaissance villa opens on to a terrace where there is a view to a formal *bassin* and the sea. On an upper terrace there are parterres and a stone pergola. Of many other 16th-century palaces built in Rijeka-Dubrovačka, the remains of Sorgo, which became Marnia, are still impressive, with a monumental staircase decorated with stone baskets.

Two other important gardens of the same period belonged to the Skočibuha family on the island of *Šipan*; these are now rather derelict, but the outlines of terraces and unique stone-carved pergolas are still recognizable (visitable by appointment only).

At *Trsteno*, 30km NW of Dubrovnik, a garden was built in 1502 for the Gučetić family. The geometric renaissance layout is now disguised by luxuriant plant growth, but old plane trees date from the original garden. A baroque fountain was an addition of 1736. (Open daily, no charge.)

In the old town of *Hvar*, on the island of that name north of Dubrovnik, the Croatian poet Hanibal Lučić had a summer residence. His garden, of which the early 16th-century outline still remains, is today a botanic garden. At *Starigrad*, 20km north-east of Hvar, another poet, Petar Hektorović, built a charming and eccentric renaissance garden with a central 16th-century fishpool enclosed by vaulted and arcaded terraces.

In the beautiful city of *Trogir*, 30km W of Split via Route 2, is an 18th-century garden that belonged to the Garanjin-Fanfogna family; on *Dugi Otok* there is a terraced garden, in Soli, which is at present threatened by road-widening.

Hajducica Park

E of Banat in Vojvodina, NE of Belgrade between Pančevo and Uršac, Route 1.9

The park was planted in the 1880s; a maze in box and some fishponds still exist. The house is the office of a state farm.

Lisičine Arboretum

E of Zagreb, S of Podravska Slatina

This new arboretum with a rich indigenous flora,

good soil and plentiful water has been planted according to geographical regions. There are many new cultivars from eastern Europe.

Našice Castle

Našice, 50km W of Osijek on Route 3
Opening times: Daily
Admission charge: No

The early 19th-century castle, built by Count Pejacevic, has baroque and neo-classical features. The first planting was contemporary with the building, but the park was much enlarged and a lake added in the late 19th century. The original woodland was mainly oak and whitebeam. Plans for restoration of the garden are in hand.

Nova Gorica

Just N of Gorizia and near the Italian frontier

Trees and bamboos planted in the late 19th century in this 3ha garden reflect the milder climate of the northern Adriatic. The Bhutan cypress (*Cupressus tortulosa*), cork oak, *Magnolia grandiflora*, camphor trees and camellias flourish in the overgrown park. The upper garden, surrounding a pseudo-Moorish palace, is well kept.

Castle Park – Arboretum Opeka

Vinica, 20km W of Varaždin
Admission charge: No

An entrance gate bears the inscription 1674, but the 64ha park was extended and largely planted by Count Bombelles in the 19th century. Large deciduous trees and conifers, once forming the biggest collection of trees in Croatia, are grouped round open lawns in an English landscape style, with a hilly woodland area beyond. Although neglected, the park is still botanically interesting; weeping spruce, swamp cypress, nettle trees, limes and tulip trees grow amongst groves of rhododendrons.

Castle Viltos

On left bank of the Drava valley, 11km W of Maribor on the Klagenfurt road
Opening times: Now a home for the elderly and not normally accessible, but permission may be given

This romantic but neglected park surrounds a 17th-century castle altered in the 19th century when the trees were planted. Trees suitable for the continental climate include specimens of large-leaved *Magnolia macrophylla*, the Kentucky coffee tree (*Gymnocladus dioica*), and a Japanese umbrella pine (*Sciadopitys verticillata*).

Arboretum Volcji Potok

Kamnik, 20km N of Ljubljana, N of Route 10

This well-maintained arboretum, sheltered by the mountains of the Savinjske Alps to the north, was first planted in the 17th century, but much of the best planting was done between World Wars I and II. Collections of rhododendrons, magnolias and herbaceous plants were established in a beautiful landscape setting enriched by lakes. There is a nursery and garden centre. The castle was destroyed by fire in World War II.

Zagreb: Maksimir Park

On E outskirts of city

The 195ha park was first laid out by Bishop Vrhovac in the 18th century; from 1846 G. Haulik (or Horlic), Bishop of Zagreb, expanded the park for the education, recreation and enjoyment of the people of the city. Forest was felled to allow space for open meadows, lakes and garden features such as belvederes and kiosks. A straight entrance avenue leads to a one-storey building, from where views open in four different directions over glades and water.

The 14th-century Franciscan monastery in Dubrovnik has an arcaded courtyard with formal gardens.

Biographical List of Principal Architects, Garden Designers and Gardeners

Aiton, William (1731–93) Scottish gardener who worked at the Chelsea Physic Garden (q.v.) and, from 1759, at Kew (q.v.). Author of *Hortus Kewensis* (1789).

Alberti, Leon Battista (1404–72) Florentine architect whose reinterpretation of classical Roman ideals, published in a treatise in 1452, influenced renaissance architecture in Italy and subsequently the whole of Europe.

Alessi, Caleazzo (1512–72) Italian architect who built what is now the Via Garibaldi to the west of Genoa in the 1550s, and a string of villas along it. The garden of the Villa Durazzo Pallavicini (q.v.) survives.

Alphand, Jean-Charles-Adolphe (1817–91) French landscape architect and engineer, especially associated with Paris where he laid out many parks, including the Bois de Boulogne, and modernized the Parc Monceau (q.v.).

Ammanati, Bartolomeo (1511–92) Florentine architect and sculptor who worked on the Boboli Gardens (q.v.) in Florence, and also in Padua, Rome and Venice.

André, Edouard François (1840–1911) French landscape architect who designed gardens all over Europe (*see* Weldam and Twickel in Holland, Palanga in Russia, and the Villa Borghese in Italy) and drew up recommendations for adapting English landscape gardening to public parks.

Anhalt-Dessau, Prince Franz von (1740–1817) German landowner much influenced by English ideas concerning agriculture, horticulture and forestry. He introduced the neo-gothic style to Europe, and in 1764 he and his gardeners J. G. Schoch and J. F. Eyserbeck created the 150 sq.km *Gartenreich* along the Elbe, which included Wörlitz (q.v.), Luisium (q.v.) and Oranienbaum (q.v.).

Bac, Ferdinand (1859–1930) French artist and garden designer whose best-known garden was for his own house, Les Colombières (q.v.) in Menton.

Balyan, Karabet and *Nikoğos* (father and son) 19th-century Turkish Armenian architects working in Istanbul.

Barillet-Deschamps, Jean-Pierre (1824–75) French landscape designer who worked in Paris with Alphand (q.v.) and designed a landscape park at the Borély gardens (q.v.) in Marseilles.

Barry, Sir Charles (1795–1860) English architect of the Houses of Parliament whose architectural garden designs in England and Scotland (*see* Dunrobin) popularized the fashion for the Italian garden.

Beaumont, Guillaume Shadowy figure, possibly French, who probably laid out the garden and park at Levens Hall (q.v.) in England 1689–1712.

Beckford, William (1760–1844) English author, aesthete and maker of gardens at Fonthill Abbey and at Montserrate (q.v.) in Portugal.

Benque, Wilhelm German garden designer who specialized in public parks in the late 19th century (*see* the Bürgerpark in Bremen) and worked with F. L. Olmsted in laying out Central Park in New York.

Blaikie, Thomas (1758–1838) Scottish garden designer working chiefly in France at the Parc Monceau (q.v.), Bagatelle (q.v.) and elsewhere, where he introduced the English landscape style.

Bosse, Carl Ferdinand German garden designer who worked at Lütetsburg (q.v.), Rastede (q.v.) and Dyck (q.v.) at the end of the 18th century.

Boutelou Family of gardeners of French origin who settled in Spain. Esteban (Stéphane) Boutelou (d. *c.*1741) was head gardener at the palace of Aranjuez (q.v.) in 1712. His son, also Esteban, and grandsons Pablo and Pedro continued the tradition and the family were associated with Spanish royal gardens until the exile of Queen Isabella II in 1868.

Bramante, Donato (*c.*1444–1513) Italian renaissance architect who worked mainly in Rome, where he designed the Belvedere Garden (q.v.) in the Vatican.

Bridgeman, Charles (d. 1738) Pioneer English landscape designer. His gardens include Blenheim (q.v.), Rousham (q.v.), and Wimpole Hall.

Brown, Lancelot 'Capability' (1716–83) English landscape designer, the most influential of his day, who worked at Stowe (q.v.), Blenheim (q.v.), Petworth (q.v.) and at many other great country houses.

Bruce, Sir William (1630–1710) Scottish architect influenced by renaissance styles. He designed his own garden at Kinross House and that at Balcaskie and influenced the design of Pitmedden (q.v.).

Buontalenti, Bernardo (1536–1608) Florentine architect, engineer, and manager of 'spectacles' for the Medici. He was famous for his mechanical contrivances and his surrealistic decoration of garden grottoes, etc (*see* Pratolino).

Bush (or Busch), John (*fl.*1730s–90s) English nurseryman (Hackney in London) and landscape gardener, of German origin, who worked in Russia for Catherine the Great. Bush's daughter married Charles Cameron (q.v.).

Buyssens, Jules Belgian garden designer, contractor and painter who worked in Belgium and in Eastern Europe in the early part of this century.

Cameron, Charles (*c.* 1743–1812) Architect and landscape architect of Scottish descent, who worked in Russia for Catherine the Great from *c.* 1779 (*see* Gatchina, Pushkin, Pavlosk).

Candolle, Augustin Pyramus de (1778–1841) Influential Swiss botanist who visited many European gardens and helped found the first botanic garden in Geneva in 1817.

Cane, Percy (1881–1976) English garden designer associated with informal beds in formal settings. Designed new borders at Falkland Palace (q.v.).

Caus, Isaac de (1590–1648) French architect and engineer, designer of grottoes and garden buildings at Rueil, Wilton and Stalbridge Park. Brother of Salomon de Caus (q.v.).

Caus, Salomon de (*c.* 1576–1626) French engineer and garden designer who designed gardens or garden features in Brussels, Heidelberg (the Hortus Palatinus, q.v.), and at Hatfield House (q.v.) and Richmond Palace. Brother of Isaac de Caus (q.v.).

Cerceau, Jacques Androuet du (*c.* 1515–*c.* 84) French architect and artist whose engravings are a most important source of information about French renaissance gardens.

Chambers, Sir William (1723–96) Scottish architect who introduced chinoiserie to England. He laid out Kew Gardens (q.v.) from 1757, where several of the existing garden buildings (including the Chinese pagoda) are his.

Chotek, Count Jan Rudolf Czechoslovakian. Leading minister in Austro-Hungarian Empire and *Oberstburggraf* of Bohemia in the late 18th and early 19th century. He designed the gardens at Veltrusy (q.v.) and Kacina (q.v.).

Ciołek, Gerard (1909–66) Polish garden historian and designer; the dominating figure in post World War II garden restoration in Poland.

Clerk, Sir John, of Penicuik (1676–1755) Scottish landowner and garden theorist. Laid out gardens for his own houses at Penicuik and Mavisbank.

Clusius, Carolus (Charles de l'Écluse) (1526–1609) Flemish botanist, doctor, and the first scientific horticulturist in Europe, who was responsible for the distribution in Europe of many exotic plants and especially tulips (*see* Botanic Gardens of Leiden and Vienna).

Copijn, Henri (1842–1913) Dutch garden designer (*see* Menkemaborg and Kasteel de Haar).

Desgots, Claude (d. 1732) French garden designer, one of a large family of French royal gardeners and nephew of Le Nôtre with whom he worked. Also worked in Germany and in England where he designed parterres at Cliveden (q.v.).

Dezallier d'Argenville, Joseph (1680–1765) French naturalist, engraver and author. His *La Théorie et la pratique du jardinage* (1709) popularized the style of Le Nôtre (*see* Bantry House in Ireland).

Duchêne, Achille (1866–1947) French garden designer specializing in the restoration of classical French gardens as at Vaux-le-Vicomte (q.v.) and Courances (q.v.) in France, and Schlosspark Nordkirchen (q.v.) in Germany. Made water garden at Blenheim (q.v.).

Eyserbeck, Johann August (1762–1801) German garden designer who worked at Oranienbaum (q.v.), Der Grosser Garten in Dresden, at Sanssouci (q.v.) and at Charlottenburg (q.v.). Son of J. F. Eyserbeck (q.v.).

Eyserbeck, Johann Friedrich (1734–1818) German garden designer and court gardener at Luisium (q.v.) and at Dessau (q.v.), where he worked for Prince Anhalt-Dessau (q.v.). Concerned with improvements in horticulture and to the countryside.

Finlay, Ian Hamilton (1925–) Scottish poet and garden designer.

Maker of garden at his house, Little Sparta (q.v.) in Scotland, and designer of gardens in Germany and Holland.

Fischer von Erlach, Johann Bernard (1656–1723) Austrian architect and garden designer who worked at Kleissheim (q.v.), the Mirabell Gardens (q.v.), Schönbrunn (q.v.) and also in Czechoslovakia.

Fish, Margery (1888–1969) English gardener and writer. Maker of garden at her own house East Lambrook Manor (q.v.) and author of many influential books extolling the cottage-garden style.

Foerster, Karl (1874–1970) German nurseryman, plant breeder and garden writer, especially concerned to integrate natural planting with public landscape design.

Fontana, Carlo (1634–1714) Italian architect, a pupil of Bernini who worked mainly in Rome but also on Isola Bella (q.v.), at Cetinole (q.v.), and in Vienna.

Fontana, Giovanni (1546–1614) Italian architect and hydraulic engineer who worked at Villa Aldobrandini (q.v.).

Forestier, Jean Claude Nicolas (1861–1930) French garden designer who worked on public parks in Paris (including Bagatelle, q.v.). He designed many gardens in Spain (*see* Parque Maria Luisa in Seville, Moratalla near Cordoba and the Parque Montjuïc in Barcelona) and also worked in the USA and Central and South America.

Frigimelica, Girolamo (1663–1732) Italian architect from Padua, who worked in the Veneto and in particular at the Villa Pisani (q.v.) at Strà on the Brenta canal.

Fuchs, L. 19th-century Belgian garden designer and pupil of Le Nôtre, who worked in Belgium (*see* Kasteel de Beervelde) and also in Bucharest.

Gaudi, Antonio (1852–1926) Catalan architect in the *art nouveau* style and maker of the Parque Güell (q.v.) in Barcelona.

Girard, Dominique (d. 1738) French garden designer who, influenced by working as a young man at Versailles (q.v.), designed gardens at Clemenswerth (q.v.), Nymphenburg (q.v.) and Schleissheim (q.v.) in Germany, and at the Belvedere (q.v.) in Vienna with Lukas von Hildebrandt (q.v.).

Haussman, Georges-Eugène, Baron (1809–91) Administrator of Paris under Napoleon III and subsequently Minister for Paris. Responsible for new urban layout and the creation of many public parks including the Bois de Boulogne, Buttes de Chaumont (q.v.), Parc Monceau (q.v.) etc.

Hildebrandt, Lukas von (1668–1745) Austrian exponent of the style of Le Nôtre. He remodelled the Mirabell Gardens (q.v.) in Salzburg and the Belvedere (q.v.) in Vienna with Dominique Girard (q.v.).

Japelli, Giuseppe Early 19th-century Italian neo-classical architect and 'romantic' garden designer who worked at the Villa Selvatico Emo (q.v.) in the Veneto.

Jekyll, Gertrude (1843–1932) English artist, garden designer (especially in collaboration with Edwin Lutyens) and writer. Designed many gardens including Hestercombe (q.v.). Author of several influential books including *Wood and Garden* (1899).

Jellicoe, Sir Geoffrey (1900–) English landscape architect and garden designer who worked on Pusey House (q.v.), Ditchley Park and many other gardens.

Johnston, Lawrence (1871–1948) American gardener educated in Europe and long settled in England and in France. He created two outstanding and influential gardens – at Hidcote (q.v.) in Gloucestershire and at Le Serre de la Madone (q.v.) on the French Riviera.

Jones, Inigo (1573–1652) English architect and painter who laid out gardens at Lincoln's Inn and, with Isaac de Caus (q.v.), at Wilton House.

Juvarra, Filippo (1685–1735) Sicilian architect, pupil of Carlo Fontana (q.v.), who worked in and around Turin and at the Villa Mansi and the Villa Reale in Tuscany.

Kebach, Karl German garden designer working in the Crimea (*see* Alupka and Massandra) in the 1840s.

Kent, William (1685–1748) English architect and garden designer, pioneer of the landscape park. Designer of gardens at Rousham (q.v.), Stowe (q.v.) and Claremont (q.v.).

Krieger, Johan Cornelius Early 18th-century Danish architect and garden designer especially associated with Frederiksberg Castle (q.v.) and Fredensborg Castle (q.v.).

La Quintinye, Jean-Baptiste de (1624–68) French gardener to Louis XIV, who laid out the surviving royal kitchen garden at Versailles (Parc Balbi) (q.v.).

Lenné, Peter Josef (1789–1866) German landscape gardener, an important influence as an exponent of Italian renaissance garden design and for his arrangement of the landscape round Potsdam (*see* Charlottenburg, Sanssouci, the Neuer Garten etc).

Le Nôtre, André (1613–1700) French garden designer and director of building to Louis XIV. He made gardens at Vaux-le-Vicomte (q.v.) and Versailles (q.v.) and at many other great houses in France. He influenced the development of gardens in Europe for the next hundred years.

Ligorio, Pirro (c. 1500–83) Italian architect and archaeologist who brought his imaginative understanding of the ancient world to his garden designs; he worked mainly in Rome and at the Villa d'Este in Tivoli (q.v.).

Lindsay, Norah (1866–1948) English garden designer in the Arts and Crafts tradition. Designed own garden at Sutton Courtenay which does not survive and new beds at Blickling Hall (q.v.).

Linnaeus, Carl (1707–78) Swedish naturalist who systematized the binomial system of plant nomenclature. He read medicine and became Professor of Medicine and Botany at Uppsala University. His own garden (*see* Linnaeus's Garden in Uppsala) was visited by eminent scientists from all over Europe.

Lloyd, Christopher (1921–) English gardener and writer. Custodian of the family garden at Great Dixter (q.v.) and author of influential books.

London, George (d. 1714) English garden designer and nurseryman in partnership with Henry Wise (q.v.). Amongst many other gardens, London worked at Blenheim (q.v.), Chatsworth, Castle Howard and Longleat; at Melbourne Hall his entire layout survives.

Lorimer, Sir Robert (1864–1929) Scottish architect and garden designer. Designed gardens in the Arts and Crafts tradition at Earlshall and Hill of Tarvit House and, as a child, the garden of his family's house at Kellie Castle (q.v.).

L'Orme, Philibert de (c. 1510–70) French architect who introduced Italian ideas about architecture and garden design to France. His most famous garden was at the Château d'Anet (q.v.), of which little survives.

Loudon, John Claudius (1783–1843) Scottish garden designer and writer settled in England. Author of *Encyclopaedia of Gardening* (1822), *Arboretum et Fruticetum Britannicum* (1838) and many others. Editor of and contributor to *The Gardener's Magazine*.

Lutyens, Sir Edwin (1869–1944) English architect and garden designer, especially in collaboration with Gertrude Jekyll (q.v.). Designed gardens at Hestercombe (q.v.), Folly Farm, New Delhi and many others.

McEacharn, Neil (1885–1964) A Scotsman who laid out the Villa Taranto (q.v.) in Italy.

Mackenzie, Osgood (d. 1922) Scottish gardener and plantsman and maker of the garden at Inverewe (q.v.).

Maderno, Carlo (1556–1629) Italian baroque architect. He worked on the Villa Aldobrandini and the Villa Torlonia in Frascati (q.v.).

Marot, Daniel (1661–1752) French Huguenot artist and garden designer, especially for William III in Holland (at Het Loo, q.v., and Rosendael, q.v.) and in England (at Hampton Court, q.v.).

Mattern, Hermann (1902–71) German landscape architect, especially after World War II (*see* Killesberg Park in Stuttgart). Also influential as Professor of Garden and Landscape Design at Berlin University from 1961.

Mayer, Johann Prokop 18th-century German court gardener to Prince Bishop von Seinsheim, and responsible for the garden layouts at Veitshöchheim (q.v.) and Würzburg (q.v.).

Michael, J. G. (1748–1800) Dutch garden designer (*see* Beeckestijn and Elswout).

Michelozzi, Michelozzo (1396–1472) Florentine architect and sculptor who worked for Cosimo de' Medici the Elder at Careggi and Villa Medici (q.v.) at Fiesole.

Mikler Dionizy (MacClair, Denis) (1762–1853) Irish garden designer who worked in Poland from *c.* 1790 (*see* Puławy and Arkadia).

Milner, Henry Ernest (1819–1894) English landscape gardener who also worked in Hungary.

Mollet, André (d. *c.* 1665) French garden designer and author who worked also in Holland, Sweden and England. Especially associated with ornate *parterres de broderie*. His father Claude Mollet's *Théâtre des plans et jardinages* (1652) is the main source of information for French gardening practice in the late 16th and early 17th centuries.

Moore, Jacob (1740–93) Scottish landscape designer who worked in England and also remodelled the Borghese Gardens in Rome (q.v.) at the end of the 18th century.

Morel, Jean-Marie (1728–1810) French architect who advised on the design of the landscape park at Ermenonville (q.v.).

Nebbien, Christian Heinrich (1778–1841) German garden designer and consultant who made English romantic gardens in Austria, Hungary and Czechoslovakia.

Nesfield, William Andrews (1793–1881) English artist and garden designer especially associated with revival of the 'Italianate' parterre.

Neyelov, Vasily Ivanovich (1722–82) Russian architect who worked at Pushkin (q.v.) with John Bush (q.v.) and Charles Cameron (q.v.). He visited England and was influenced by William Chambers's (q.v.) writings on Chinese architecture.

Nicolson, Sir Harold (1886–1968) English diplomat and writer. Maker, in collaboration with his wife Vita Sackville-West, of the garden at Sissinghurst Castle (q.v.).

Niven, Ninian (1799–1879) 19th-century Irish garden designer who worked on the National Botanic Garden (q.v.) at Glasnevin in Dublin.

Page, Russell (1906–85) English garden designer who practised in England, France, Italy and Spain. His influential book on garden design, *The Education of a Gardener* (1962), remains essential horticultural reading.

Palladio, Andrea (1508–80) Venetian architect and author of *Quattro libri dell'Architettura* (1570) (*see* Villa Capra and Villa Barbaro).

Paxton, Sir Joseph (1803–65) English architect and garden designer. Designed parts of Tatton Park (q.v.), Chatsworth, Lismore in Ireland (q.v.) and a landscape park at the Château de Ferrières (q.v.) in France.

Pechère, René 20th-century Belgian garden designer (*see* Parc du Roeulx).

Peruzzi, Baldassare (1481–1537) Sienese architect and painter who worked in Rome and Siena.

Peto, Harold (1854–1933) English architect and garden designer influenced by the Italian formal garden (*see* Ilnacullin in Ireland).

Petzold, Eduard Adolf (1815–91) German landscape gardener who worked with and was influenced by Prince Hermann Pückler-Muskau. His arboretum at Muskau (q.v.) and his many textbooks influenced tree nurseries and nursery management as well as landscape design (*see also* Twickel in Holland).

Pinsent, Cecil (1884–1964) English garden designer who worked in Florence from the 1920s.

Piper, Fredrik Magnus (1746–1824) Swedish artist and garden theorist who, influenced by English landscape gardens, introduced the style to Sweden at Drottningholm (q.v.) and elsewhere.

Plečnik, J. 20th-century Czechoslovakian garden designer, responsible for the restoration and alteration of many gardens in Prague, both before and after World War II.

Pliny the Younger (*c.* 61–112) Pliny's description of the layout of his gardens at Laurentum and in the valley of the Tiber north of Rome, and of their relationship to the surrounding countryside, profoundly influenced Italian renaissance garden design.

Pollack, Mihàly Leading Hungarian neo-classicist of the early 19th century (*see* Dég and Alcsútdoboz).

Poortman, Hugo A. C. Dutch landscape architect of the late 19th and early 20th century. A pupil of the French landscape architect Edouard André (q.v.), he worked at Twickel (q.v.), Kasteel Verwolde (q.v.) and Kasteel Weldam (q.v.)

Pope, Alexander (1688–1744) English poet, garden designer and theorist. Designer of a garden for his own villa at Twickenham, where he combined a formal style with elements of the new English landscape. He advised at Cirencester Park and Sherborne Castle.

Porta, Giacomo della (1540–1615) A follower of Michelangelo; designed the Villa Aldobrandini (q.v.) in 1598.

Pückler-Muskau, Prince Hermann (1785–1871) German landowner and landscape gardener, influenced by Humphry Repton (q.v.). His own gardens at Muskau (q.v.) and Branitz (q.v.), his work at Babelsberg (q.v.) and elsewhere, and the *Andeutungen über Landschaftsgärtnerei* (1834) all influenced European garden design.

Rainaldi, Girolamo (1570–1655) Roman architect who worked on the Villa Borghese (q.v.) and made grottoes at the Palazzo Farnese (q.v.).

Raphael (Raffaello Sanzio or Santi) (1483–1520) Italian artist of the Renaissance, brought to Rome by Bramante and responsible, with others, for the garden of the Villa Madama (q.v.).

Repton, Humphry (1752–1818) English landscape designer, after 'Capability' Brown (q.v.) the busiest and most influential of his day. Made designs for Sheffield Park (q.v.), Sheringham, Tatton, Woburn Abbey and very many others.

Robinson, William (1838–1935) Irish gardener and writer settled in England, where he designed his own garden at Gravetye Manor and wrote the influential *The English Flower Garden* (1883, with fifteen new editions up to 1933). Proponent of 'wild' gardening, with marked influence on the woodland and natural garden styles practised in modern times.

Roman, Jacob (1640–1716) Dutch sculptor and architect to William III; mainly responsible for Het Loo (q.v.).

Romano, Giulio (1492–1546) Italian architect and painter-decorator, pupil of Raphael. He designed the Palazzo del Té (q.v.) and probably carried out the work at the Villa Madama (q.v.).

Roper, Lanning (1912–83) American landscape and garden designer long resident in England. He worked also in Ireland.

Rothe, Rudolf (1802–77) Danish gardener and designer especially associated with the layout of woodland gardens in the romantic style. Designed park at Fredensborg (q.v.), where he was head gardener.

Ruys, Mien (1904–) Dutch designer and gardener; influential in the development of modern gardening in the Netherlands, especially through her own garden, Tuinen Mien Ruys (q.v.).

Sackville-West, Victoria (known as *Vita*) (1892–1962) English gardener, writer and journalist. Maker with her husband Harold Nicolson (q.v.) of the garden at Sissinghurst Castle (q.v.).

Sangallo, Antonio da (1455–1534) Italian architect working in Rome. He laid out part of the Vatican Gardens (q.v.).

Sangallo, Antonio da (the Younger) (1483–1546) Italian, a pupil of Bramante (q.v.), who worked in Rome and assisted at the Villa Madama (q.v.).

Sangallo, Giuliano (1445–1516) Florentine architect who worked on the Medici villas in and around Florence (q.v.)

Schinkel, Karl Friedrich (1781–1841) German architect and town planner who worked closely with P. J. Lenné (q.v.). He also worked in Poland.

Schlaun, Johann Conrad German architect and garden designer of the 18th century, who worked at Clemenswerth (q.v.) and elsewhere in Germany.

Schoch, Johann Georg (1788–1826) German landscape gardener, a member of an important family of gardeners in the Dessau-Wörlitz area, where he worked also for Prince von Anhalt-Dessau (q.v.).

Sckell, Friedrich Ludwig von (1750–1823) German landscape designer, the first to be influenced by the English landscape style. He worked at Schwetzingen (q.v.), the Englischer Garten (q.v.) in Munich, at Nymphenburg (q.v.) and at Schönbusch (q.v.), and was also much concerned with the planning of public parks.

Shenstone, William (1714–63) English writer and philosopher of garden design who made an important picturesque landscape garden at The Leasowes near Birmingham.

Tessin, Nicodemus the Elder (1615–81) and *Nicodemus the Younger* (1654–1728) Swedish architects and garden designers both associated with formal gardens at Drottningholm (q.v.). Nicodemus the Younger was deeply influenced by Le Nôtre (whom he knew), whose ideas he introduced to Sweden.

Touret, Jean Early 20th-century French designer who worked in Czechoslovakia (*see* Dobřiš) and Austria.

Tribolo, Niccolò (1485–1550) Florentine sculptor and engineer who worked for Cosimo de' Medici on the Boboli Gardens (q.v.) and at Castello (q.v.).

Vanbrugh, Sir John (1644–1726) English playwright, architect and garden designer. Designed garden buildings at Claremont, Blenheim (q.v.) and Stowe (q.v.).

Vanvitelli, Luigi (1700–73) The son of a Dutch painter who worked as an architect in Rome, Naples and Ancona and drew up the plans for the royal palace at Caserta (q.v.).

Vignola, Giacomo Barozzi da (1507–73) Italian architect involved in all the finest landscape designs in and around Rome from the 1550s. These include the Villa Lante (q.v.), the Palazzo Farnese (q.v.), and the Villa Giulia (q.v.) in Rome.

Viollet-le-Duc, Eugène (1814–79) French architect and archaeologist, known for his neo-gothic restorations and as author of a dictionary of French architecture.

Vredeman de Vries, Hans (1527–1606) Dutch painter, architect and garden designer; author of the first garden pattern book, *Hortorum viridariorumque elegantes et multi plicis formae* (1583). This and his mannerist gardens and their *parterres de pièces coupées* influenced garden design throughout Europe. He also did work in Prague for the Emperor Rudolph II.

White, Thomas the Elder (1736–1811) and *Thomas the Younger* (*c.* 1764–1811) English landscape designers who practised, in the style of 'Capability' Brown (q.v.), chiefly in Scotland.

Willmott, Ellen (1858–1934) English garden owner and patron of plant collectors. She occasionally advised on garden design.

Wise, Henry (1653–1738) English nurseryman (at Brompton Park) and, in partnership with George London (q.v.), the busiest garden designer of his time in England, at Chatsworth, Castle Howard and many other estates.

Zocher, J. D. (1791–1870) Leading Dutch landscape architect of the 19th century. His designs include those at Rosendael (q.v.).

Zug, Szymon Bogamil (1733–1807) Polish garden designer in the English picturesque style (*see* Arkadia).

Glossary

allée (French)
Literally a 'way', but in gardening used to denote a passage lined with trees, often pleached or clipped to form smooth 'walls'.

art nouveau (French)
Literally 'new art', a style of decorative and fine arts originating in the 1890s, associated with sinuous flowing lines and stylized natural forms.

Arts and Crafts
A group of artists and craftsmen – including John Ruskin and William Morris – who influenced English garden designers such as Gertrude Jekyll whose gardens are characterized by the use of local building materials and traditional plants and the rejection of the regimented artificiality of much Victorian planting.

azulejo (Spanish)
A glazed tile, usually but not invariably blue (*azul* is the Spanish for blue) very widely used in Spanish and Portuguese gardens and houses.

bassin (French)
A formal pool of a regular shape, usually lined and edged in stone.

belvedere (Italian)
An ornamental building in some commanding position from which a view may be admired. See also *mirador*.

berceau (French)
Literally 'cradle'. A shady arbour enclosed in growing plants, usually with a seat.

bosco (Italian)
A formal grove of trees. See also *bosquet*.

bosquet (French)
A formal grove, often with a decorative glade in which statues or other ornaments may be disposed. Especially associated with French gardens of the period of Le Nôtre.

buffet d'eau (French)
A fountain, found especially in 17th-century French gardens, in the form of steps down which water splashes like a waterfall.

carmen (Spanish)
A form of miniature urban estate – including both house and enclosed garden – unique to Granada.

casino (Italian)
Literally a small house. An ornamental house within a garden.

charmille (French)
From *charme* meaning hornbeam. A tree-lined walk in which the foliage has been evenly clipped back to a certain height.

clairvoyée (French)
An opening in a wall or hedge permitting a view of what lies beyond. Sometimes framed with ornamental piers supporting light railings or grillework.

cottage orné (French)
Literally, 'ornamental cottage'. A small rustic building, often thatched, used as a picturesque feature in a landscape garden.

cour d'honneur (French)
The main entrance court of a great house.

entrelac (French)
Interlacing, low, clipped hedges forming the pattern of a knot garden. May be used for the knot garden itself.

exedra (Greek)
A decorative, open garden building, usually curved and containing a bench.

Gartenschauen (German)
Garden shows started in the 19th century in Germany and now regularly held in many large German towns.

giardino inglese (Italian)
Literally 'English garden'. See *jardin anglais*.

giardino segreto (Italian)
An intimate walled garden especially associated with the Italian Renaissance.

giochi d'acqua (Italian)
Garden jokes – jets of water, first associated with gardens of the Italian Renaissance, designed to surprise unwary visitors.

glorieta (Spanish)
An arbour or pavilion, often made of clipped plants and usually set at the centre of a formal garden at a meeting-place of paths.

gloriette (French)
From the Spanish *glorieta*. An ornamental pavilion, usually at the centre of a walled garden.

herm
A bust on a four-cornered, usually tapering pillar.

isolotto (Italian)
A small decorative island within a garden.

jardin anglais or *jardin à l'anglaise* (French)
An informal arrangement of lawns, shrubs and trees loosely based on English 18th-century landscape principles.

jardin anglo-chinois (French)
Literally 'anglo-Chinese garden'. The French believed that the English landscape garden drew its inspiration from China and sought to undermine its originality with this expression.

jardin potager, see *potager*.

Jugendstil (German)
The German for *art nouveau* the name of an art journal started in 1896.

knot garden
A formal garden of elaborate design with beds of dwarf hedges forming intricate patterns.

limonaia (Italian)
A glasshouse in which lemon trees are protected in the winter.

mirador (Spanish)
An airy, open summer-house from which a view may be admired.

mosaïculture (French)
A style of planting invented in 19th-century France which combines carpet bedding with annuals in a regimented pattern.

mudejar (Spanish)
A decorative style of architecture associated with Muslim work under Christian rule in Spain (usually 15th-century and later).

nymphaeum (Latin)
A grotto or shallow cave, supposedly the home of nymphs.

parterre (French)
A formal bed with low hedges, often of box, disposed in a regular way and often incorporating topiary, urns or other decorative devices. A *parterre de broderie* is a particular form in which the hedges are arranged in clipped arabesques. In a *parterre à l'anglaise* the patterns are cut out of turf. A *parterre de pièces coupeés* was designed for the display of rare plants.

patte d'oie (French)
Literally a goose-foot. An arrangement of three (or sometimes more) alleys or avenues radiating from a semi-circle; especially associated with the gardens of André Le Nôtre.

potager (French)
Kitchen garden, usually taken to mean a formal, decorative kitchen garden.

riego a manta (Spanish)
Literally 'irrigation blanket'. A network of irrigation channels, often arranged in attractive geometric patterns, associated with Islamic gardens.

rocaille (French)
Ornamental shell- or rock-work of the kind commonly found lining the interior walls of grottoes.

sala terrena (Italian)
A garden room at ground level in the form of an open loggia.

salon de treillage (French)
An enclosed 'room' of trellis-work in a garden.

salon de verdure (French)
Literally, a sitting-room of greenery. A formal garden enclosure whose 'walls' are clipped hedges.

sterrebos
Star-shaped arrangement of avenues through woodland particularly associated with baroque gardens. See also *patte d'oie*.

Swiss cottage or chalet
After the end of the Napoleonic wars in 1815 Switzerland became a fashionable destination for tourists and Swiss buildings with steeply overhanging roofs and walls of unpeeled timber were used as ornamental buildings in picturesque gardens.

taiga (Russian)
Coniferous forest bordered by tundra to the north and steppe to the south.

théâtre de verdure (French)
Stage and backdrop formed of vegetation.

tori (Italian)
Raised beds found in Italian renaissance gardens.

treillage (French)
Trellis-work, particularly in the context of the more ornate uses in garden buildings, walls and ornament. See also *salon de treillage*.

trompe l'oeil (French)
Literally 'deceive the eye'. A painting or garden ornament made to appear to be something which it is not.

tufa
A porous, easily worked rock much used in grottoes.

viale (Italian)
An avenue or alley.

villeggiatura (Italian)
Literally 'country-residence' or 'country-life'. In the 15th century in Italy it became the custom to live in the country as well as in the town and this was associated with the great period of villa garden design.

Wasserspiele (German)
Literally 'water games', see *giochi d'aqua*.

zampillo (Italian)
A jet of water.

Bibliography

Note: In those areas where the literature is relatively sparse we have tried to be as comprehensive as possible.

Europe
Guidebooks
Guide to the Gardens of Europe, Elizabeth Drury and Harriet Bridgeman (Granada, 1979)
History
Ancient Roman Gardens, ed. Elizabeth B. MacDougall and W. Jashemski (Dumbarton Oaks, 1981)
L'Art des Jardins, Georges Gromort (Ch. Massin, no date)
Coup d'Oeil sur Beloeil et sur une grande partie des jardins de l'Europe, Prince de Ligne (trans, 1786)
Encyclopaedia of Gardening, J. C. Loudon (Longman, Hurst, Rees, Orme, Brown and Greene, 1822)
A History of Garden Art, Marie Louise Gothein (trans, 1928)
The History of Gardens, Christopher Thacker (Croom Helm, 1979)
An Illustrated History of Gardening, Anthony Huxley (Paddington Press, 1978)
Mediaeval Gardens, John Harvey (Batsford, 1981)
The Oxford Companion to Gardens, ed. Geoffrey and Susan Jellicoe, Patrick Goode and Michael Lancaster (Oxford University Press, 1986)
Theorie der Gartenkunst, C. C. L. Hirschfeld (1779–85)
Periodicals
Journal of Garden History (quarterly, Taylor & Francis)
Garden History (quarterly, Journal of the Garden History Society)

Austria
History
Baroque Gardens of Austria, G. A. Jellicoe (Ernest Benn, 1932)
Die Gärten der Wiener, Maria Aubock (Wien, 1975)
Geschichte der deutschen Gartenkunst, Dieter Hennebo and Alfred Hoffmann (Hamburg, 1963)

Belgium and Holland
Guidebooks
Castella (Eccho, 1987)
Parcs et Jardins de Belgique, René Pechère (Rossel edn, 1976)
Tuinengids, Bonica Zijlstra and Jos Ratinckx (Groei & Bloei, 1987)
History
'The Anglo-Dutch Garden in the Age of William and Mary', *Journal of Garden History*, nos 2 & 3, Apr–Sept 1988

Bulgaria
Guidebooks
Parks, Gardens and Landscape Architecture, D. T. Sougarev (in Bulgarian; Sofia, 1976)

Czechoslovakia
Guidebooks
České zámecké parky a jejich dřeviny, Karel Heike (Státní Zemědělské Nakladatelství, 1984)
Moravské zámecké parky a jejich dřeviny, Karel Heike (Statni Zemědělské Nakladatelství, 1985)
(Both these books have long bibliographies)
History
Historic Gardens in Bohemia and Moravia, Z. Dokoupil (in Czech; Prague, 1957)

Denmark
Guidebooks
Abne Haver i Danmark (leaflet, new edn each year)
Parks and Gardens in Copenhagen and Environment (Kunstakademiets Arkitektskole, 1981)
History
Europas Havekunst Fra Alhambra til Liselund, C. Th. Sørensen (G. E. C. Gad, 1959)
Havekunsten i Kulturhistorisk Belysning, Georg Boye (DSR, 1972)
De Kongelige Lysthaver, Hakon Lund (Gyldendal, 1977)

France
Guidebooks
Guide des Parcs et Jardins de France (Editions Princesse, 1979)
Guide des 300 Plus Beaux Jardins de France, Philippe Thébaud (Rivages, 1987)
The Historic Houses, Castles and Gardens of France (Newnes, 1986)
History
Description des nouveaux jardins de la France, A. L. J. de Laborde (Paris, 1808–25)
The French Garden 1500–1800, W. H. Adams (Scolar, 1979)
Gardens of Illusion, F. Hamilton Hazlehurst (University of Nebraska Press, 1980)
Parcs et Jardins sous le Premier Empire, Marie-Blanche d'Arneville (Tallandier, 1981)
Paris Jardins, Anne Soprani (M.A. Editions, 1986)
The Parks, Promenades and Gardens of Paris, William Robinson (John Murray, 1869)
The Picturesque Garden in France, Dora Wiebenson (Princeton University Press, 1978)
Princely Gardens, Kenneth Woodbridge (Thames & Hudson, 1986)
Private Gardens of France, Anita Pereire and Gabrielle van Zuylen (Weidenfeld & Nicolson, 1983)

East Germany
Guidebooks
Bauten und Plastiken in Park Sanssouci, H. Hoffmann (Potsdam-Sanssouci, 1987)
Cecilienhof und der Neuer Garten, H. Günther and H. Schonemann (Potsdam-Sanssouci, 1985)
Der Muskauer Park, K. H. Kurland (Bad Muskau, 1982)
Der Park Babelsberg, H. Hamaan (Potsdam, 1984)
Park Georgium, H. Günther (Dessau, 1983)
Der Park von Oranienbaum, H. Günther (Oranienbaum, 1973)
History
Barockgarten Grossedlitz, H. Koitzsch and W. Richter (Leipzig, 1967)
Der Branitzer Park, beiträge zur Gartendenkmalpflege, H. Rippel (Herausgeber Kulturbund der DDR, Berlin, 1985)
Dessau-Wörlitz: Aufklärung und Frühklassik, E. Hirsch (Leipzig, 1985)
Gartenkunst der Renaissance und der Barock (Cologne, 1983)
Peter Josef Lenné, H. Günther (Berlin, 1985)

West Germany
Guidebooks
Knaurs Naturführer in Farbe (Droemer Knaur, 1981)
Parks und Gärten in Berlin und Potsdam, C. A. Wimmer (Berlin, 1985)
Der Schlossgarten zu Schwetzingen, Claus Reisinger (Worms, 1987)
Die schönsten Gärten Deutschlands (Wiesbaden, 1977)
History
Bayreuther Gartenkunst, Sylvia Habermann (Worms, 1982)
Düsseldorfer Gartenlust, Katalog Ausstellung Düsseldorfer Stadtmuseum (Düsseldorf, 1987)
Erfassung historischen Gärten und Parks der Bundesrepublik Deutschland, compiled by the Deutsche Gesellschaft für Gartenkunst und Landschafts-pflege (Deutscher Heimatbund, 1988)
Gärten im alten Frankfurt, Otto Derreth (Frankfurt, 1976)
Der melancholische Garten, Ebba Drolshagen (Frankfurt, 1987)
Private Gardens of Germany, Ursula Gräfin zu Dohna (Weidenfeld & Nicolson, 1986)
Unsere historischen Gärten, Margot Lutze (Umschau, 1986)

Great Britain
Bibliography
A Bibliography of British Gardens, Ray Desmond (St Paul's Bibliographies, 1984)
Guidebooks
Gardens of England and Wales (The National Gardens Scheme; new edn each year)
Gardens of the National Trust, Graham Stuart Thomas (Jonathan Cape, 1979 and subsequent rev. edns)
Guide to Gardens in Britain (Ordnance Survey/Hamlyn; new edns periodically)
Historic Houses, Castles and Gardens Open to the Public (British Leisure Publications; new edn each year)
History
The Edwardian Garden, David Ottewill (Yale University Press, 1989)
The English Garden, Laurence Fleming and Alan Gore (Michael Joseph, 1979)
The English Garden Tour, Mavis Batey and David Lambert (John Murray, 1990)

Gardens of a Golden Afternoon, Jane Brown (Allen Lane, 1982)
Georgian Gardens, David Jacques (Batsford, 1983)
Mediaeval Gardens, John Harvey (Batsford, 1981)
Private Gardens of England, Penelope Hobhouse (Weidenfeld & Nicolson, 1986)
The Renaissance Garden in England, Roy Strong (Thames & Hudson, 1979)
Victorian Gardens, Brent Elliott (Batsford, 1986)
Periodicals
Country Life, weekly, 1897 onwards
The Journal of the Royal Horticultural Society (The Garden), monthly, 1875 onwards

Greece
History
Garden Lore of Ancient Athens, American School of Classical Studies (Princeton, 1963)

Holland
See Belgium and Holland

Hungary
History
Arboreta in Hungary, ed. G. Mészoly (Budapest, 1984)
The Art and Practice of Landscape Gardening, H. E. Milner (London, 1890)
'The English Garden in Hungary', Anna Zador, in *The Picturesque Garden and its Influence outside the British Isles*, ed. N. Pevsner (Washington, 1974)
Hungarian Gardens, Rajmund Rapaich (Budapest, 1940)
'A Hungarian Landscape Garden around 1800', Anna Zador (*New Hungarian Quarterly* no. 100, winter 1985)
Report on the Preservation of Historic Gardens in the Last Ten Years, Károly Örsi (Hungarian Preservation Work, Budapest, 1972)

Ireland
History
The Gardens of Ireland, Michael George and Patrick Bowe (Hutchinson, 1986)
In an Irish Garden, ed. Sybil Connolly and Helen Dillon (Weidenfeld & Nicolson, 1986)
Irish Gardening and Horticulture, ed.

Charles Nelson and Aidan Brady (Royal Horticultural Society of Ireland, 1979)
Irish Gardens and Demesnes from 1830, Edward Malins and Patrick Bowe (Barrie & Jenkins, 1980)
Lost Demesnes, Edward Malins and The Knight of Glin (Barrie & Jenkins, 1976)

Italy
Guidebooks
The Gardens of Pompeii, W. F. Jashemski (1979)
Guida ai Giardini d'Italia, Mario Faccini (Ottaviano, 1983)
Italian Gardens, Alex Ramsay and Helena Attlee (Robertson McCarta, 1989)
A Tour of Italian Gardens, Judith Chatfield (Ward Lock, 1988)
History
Ancient Roman Gardens, ed. Elizabeth MacDougal (Dumbarton Oaks, 1981)
Art of Garden Design in Italy, Harry Inigo Triggs (London, 1906)
Civiltà delle Ville Venete, M. Azzi Visentini (Udine, 1986)
Diary of John Evelyn, ed. E. S. de Beer (London, 1959)
I Giardini d'Italia, Bianca Marta Nobile (Calderini, 1984)
Il Giardino Veneto tra sette e ottocento e le sue Fonti, M. Azzi Visentini (Milan, 1988)
Il Giardino Veneto, storia e conservazione, ed. M. Azzi Visentini (Milan, 1988)
L'Idea della Architettura universale, V. Scamozzi (Venice, 1615)
Italian Gardens, Georgina Masson (Thames & Hudson, 1961)
Italian Gardens of the Renaissance, J. C. Shepherd and G. A. Jellicoe (1st pub. 1925; Academy Editions, 4th edn, 1986)
Italian Journey, Johann Wolfgang von Goethe
Italian Villas and their Gardens, Edith Wharton (Bodley Head, 1904)
Jardins Italiens, Günter Mader and Laila Neubert-Mader (French edn, Office du Livre, 1987)
Journal de Voyage en Italie, 1580–81, Michel de Montaigne (1st pub. 1774; English trans. Trechmann, 1929)
Lives of the Painters, Sculptors and Architects, Giorgio Vasari (trans. A. B. Hinds, London, 1963)
On the Making of Gardens, Sir George

Sitwell (Duckworth, 1909)
L'Orto botanico di Padua e il giardino del Rinascimento, M. Azzi Visentini (Edizione il Polifilo, 1984)
Palermo e il suo Verde, G. Pirrone (Palermo, 1965)
I Quattro Libri del' Architettura, A. Palladio (Venice, 1570)
Tuscan Villas, Harold Acton (Thames & Hudson, 1973)
The Villa d'Este at Tivoli, David Coffin (Princeton, 1960)
Ville del Brenta e degli Euganei, B. Brunelli and A. Callegari (Milan, 1931)
Le Ville Venete, Giuseppe Mazzotti (Libreria Editrice Canova, 3rd edn 1954)
Ville della provincia di Vicenza, R. Cevese (Milan, 1980)
Ville Venete, Antonio Canova (Edizione Canova Treviso, cat. of Exhibition, 1984)
Periodicals
Archivo Italiano dell' Arte dei Giardini, during 1970s

Norway
History
'Historic Gardens in Norway', Magne Bruun in L. Hinsche *et al*., *Monuments and Sites* (ICOMOS, 1987)
Hundre grønne å, Magne Bruun (Norwegian Horticultural Society, 1984)
Norske Haver, C. W. Schnitler (Kristiania, 1916)

Poland
Guidebooks
Łazienki, Marek Kwiatkowski (English edn, Warsaw, 1976)
Łazienki Warszawskie, Wladysław Tatarkiewicz (Warsaw, 1957)
Nieborów, Vlodzimierz Piwkowski (Warsaw/Kraków, 1983)
Nieborów Arkadia, K. Jablonski and P. Wlodzimierz (1988)
Wilanów, Jacek Cydzik and Wojciech Fijałkowski (Warsaw, 1975)
History
Architecture of Poland, Brian Knox (London, 1971)
Gardens in Poland, G. Ciolek (Polish edn, Warsaw, 1952; German edn, 1954)
Historia Ogrudu Botanicznego Uniwersytetu Jagiellónskiego w Krakówie, Alicja Piekiełko (Warsaw/Kraków, 1983)
A History of Gardens, Longin

Majdecki (in Polish; Warsaw, 1981)
The Landscape Garden in Poland, Bohemia, ed. N. Pevsner in *The Picturesque Garden outside the British Isles* (Washington, 1974)
Thoughts on the Manner of Planting Gardens, Izabela Czartoryska (in Polish; Wrocław, 1804)

Portugal
History
Gardens of Portugal, Patrick Bowe (I. B. Tauris, 1989)
Portuguese Gardens, Helder Carita and Homem Cardosa (Antique Collectors' Club, 1989)

Romania
Guidebooks
The Botanic Gardens of Bucharest
Parcuri şi Gradini in România, R. Marcus (Editura Tehnica Bucuresti, 1958)
Ville de Craïova, Florea Firan (ed. par le comité pour la culture et l'art du département de Dolj)

Russia
History
Botanical Gardens of the USSR, P. I. Lapin (Moscow, 1984)
Kuskovo, G. Baranovo (Leningrad, 1978)
Pavlovsk, A. Kuchumov (Leningrad, 1975)
'Pavlovsk' (*The Garden*, June 1982)
Peterhof, A. Raskin (1979)
'Peterhof' (*The Garden*, February 1982)
Pushkin: Palaces and Parks, F. Lemus (Leningrad, 1984)
'Pushkin' (*The Garden*, April 1982)

Spain
History
The Islamic Garden, ed. E. Macdougall and R. Ettinghausen (Dumbarton Oaks, 1976)
Los Jardines de Granada, Francisco Prieto-Moreno (Arte de Espana, 1983)
Spanish Gardens, Marquesa de Casa Valdés (Antique Collectors' Club, 1987)
Spanish Gardens, Constance Villiers-Stuart (Batsford, 1929)

Sweden
Guidebooks
Parkguiden (LT:s, forthcoming, 1991)
History
En Bok om Trädgårdar, Gunnar

Martinnson (Stockholm, 1957)
Förnya och bevara gamla trädgårdar och parker (Signum, forthcoming, 1990)
Trädgårdskonstens Historie i Europa, C. W. Schnitler (Stockholm, 1917)

Switzerland
Guidebooks
Gartenführer der Schweiz, Eva Ruoff (Office du Livre, 1980)
Unterwegs in Schweizer Parks und Gärten, H. P. Bützer and Mark Jeker (Kümmerli & Frey, 1980)
History
Bauerngärten der Schweiz, Albert Hauser (Artemis, 1976)
Historische Gärten der Schweiz, H.-R. Heyer (GSK & Benteli, 1980)

Turkey
Guidebooks
Camlica' dan Bakislar, Celik Gülersoy (Guzel Sanatlar Press, 1982)
The National Palaces (English and Turkish edns; bi-annual 1, 1987, no. 1 Tevfik Pülten for the TBMM National Trust Regional Offices)
The Pearls of the Necklace (booklet)
History
Archives of Dolmabahçe Palace, Çelik Gülersoy (Tiglat Press, Istanbul, 1984)
Eski Türk Bahçeleri ve Özellikle Eski İstanbul Bahçeleri, G. A. Evyapan (ODTU Press, Ankara, 1972)
Evliya Çelebi 'Seyahatnamesi', trans. Zuhuri Danişman (Istanbul, 1969)
A Study of the Floristic Analysis of the Vegetation of the Belgrade Forest and the Composition of the Main Stand Types, F. Yaltirik (Istanbul, 1966)
Türk Bahçeleri, Eldem Sedat Hakki (M.E. Press, 1976)

OVERLEAF **The magnificent borders at Crathes Castle are backed by yews planted in 1702.**

Index

Prospectus amœnißimi Horti
versus

7

6

5

1. *Templum S. Jacobi.* 2. *Arx Regia.* 3. *Turris Templi S. Nicolai.* 4. *Armamentarium Reg.* 5. *S.*